Rethinking Peace and Conflict Studies

Series Editor: **Oliver P. Richmond**, Professor, School of International Relations, University of St. Andrews, UK

Editorial Board: **Roland Bleiker**, University of Queensland, Australia; **Henry F. Carey**, Georgia State University, USA; **Costas Constantinou**, University of Keele, UK; **A.J.R. Groom**, University of Kent, UK; **Vivienne Jabri**, King's College London, UK; **Edward Newman**, University of Birmingham, UK; **Sorpong Peou**, Sophia University, Japan; **Caroline Kennedy-Pipe**, University of Sheffield, UK; **Michael Pugh**, University of Bradford, UK; **Chandra Sriram**, University of East London, UK; **Ian Taylor**, University of St. Andrews, UK; **Alison Watson**, University of St. Andrews, UK; **R.B.J. Walker**, University of Victoria, Canada; **Andrew Williams**, University of St. Andrews, UK.

Titles include:

Roland Bleiker
AESTHETICS AND WORLD POLITICS

Morgan Brigg
THE NEW POLITICS OF CONFLICT RESOLUTION
Responding to Difference

Susanne Buckley-Zistel
CONFLICT TRANSFORMATION AND SOCIAL CHANGE IN UGANDA
Remembering after Violence

Karina Z. Butler
A CRITICAL HUMANITARIAN INTERVENTION APPROACH

Henry F. Carey
PRIVATIZING THE DEMOCRATIC PEACE
Policy Dilemmas of NGO Peacebuilding

Jason Franks
RETHINKING THE ROOTS OF TERRORISM

Sarah Holt
AID, PEACEBUILDING AND THE RESURGENCE OF WAR
Buying Time in Sri Lanka

Vivienne Jabri
WAR AND THE TRANSFORMATION OF GLOBAL POLITICS

Daria Isachenko
THE MAKING OF INFORMAL STATES
Statebuilding in Northern Cyprus and Transdniestria

James Ker-Lindsay
EU ACCESSION AND UN PEACEMAKING IN CYPRUS

Roger Mac Ginty
INTERNATIONAL PEACEBUILDING AND LOCAL RESISTANCE
Hybrid Forms of Peace

Roger Mac Ginty
NO WAR, NO PEACE
The Rejuvenation of Stalled Peace Processes and Peace Accords

Carol McQueen
HUMANITARIAN INTERVENTION AND SAFETY ZONES
Iraq, Bosnia and Rwanda

SM Farid Mirbagheri
WAR AND PEACE IN ISLAM
A Critique of Islamic/ist Political Discourses

Audra L. Mitchell
LOST IN TRANSFORMATION
Violent Peace and Peaceful Conflict in Northern Ireland

Sorpong Peou
INTERNATIONAL DEMOCRACY ASSISTANCE FOR PEACEBUILDING
Cambodia and Beyond

Sergei Prozorov
UNDERSTANDING CONFLICT BETWEEN RUSSIA AND THE EU
The Limits of Integration

Michael Pugh
LIBERAL INTERNATIONALISM
The Interwar Movement for Peace in Britain

Oliver P. Richmond, and Audra Mitchell (editors)
HYBRID FORMS OF PEACE
From Everyday Agency to Post-Liberalism

Oliver P. Richmond
THE TRANSFORMATION OF PEACE

Bahar Rumelili
CONSTRUCTING REGIONAL COMMUNITY AND ORDER IN EUROPE AND SOUTHEAST
ASIA

Chandra Lekha Sriram
PEACE AS GOVERNANCE
Power-Sharing, Armed Groups and Contemporary Peace Negotiations

Stephan Stetter
WORLD SOCIETY AND THE MIDDLE EAST
Reconstructions in Regional Politics

Also by Michael Pugh

THE ANZUS CRISIS, NUCLEAR VISITING AND DETERRENCE

EUROPE'S BOAT PEOPLE: Maritime Cooperation in the Mediterranean

MARITIME SECURITY AND PEACEKEEPING (*with Jeremy Ginifer and Eric Grove*)

SECURITY SECTOR TRANSFORMATION IN POST-CONFLICT SOCIETIES (*with Neil Cooper*)

WAR ECONOMIES IN A REGIONAL CONTEXT: Challenges of Transformation (*with Neil Cooper and Jonathan Goodhand*)

Edited

EUROPEAN SECURITY TOWARDS 2000

REGENERATION OF WAR-TORN SOCIETIES

SUPERPOWER POLITICS: CHANGE IN THE UNITED STATES AND SOVIET UNION (*co-editor Phil Williams*)

THE UN, PEACE AND FORCE

THE UNITED NATIONS AND REGIONAL SECURITY: EUROPE AND BEYOND (*co-editor Waheguru Pal Singh Sidhu*)

WHOSE PEACE? CRITICAL PERSPECTIVES ON THE POLITICAL ECONOMY OF PEACEBUILDING (*co-editors Neil Cooper and Mandy Turner*)

Rethinking Peace and Conflict Studies
Series Standing Order ISBN 978–1–4039–9575–9 (hardback) &
978–1–4039–9576–6 (paperback)

You can receive future titles in this series as they are published by placing a standing order. Please contact your bookseller or, in case of difficulty, write to us at the address below with your name and address, the title of the series and one of the ISBNs quoted above.

Customer Services Department, Macmillan Distribution Ltd, Houndmills, Basingstoke, Hampshire RG21 6XS, England

---

Liberal Internationalism

The Interwar Movement for Peace in Britain

Michael C. Pugh
University of Bradford

palgrave
macmillan

First published 2012 by
PALGRAVE MACMILLAN

Palgrave Macmillan in the UK is an imprint of Macmillan Publishers Limited, registered in England, company number 785998, of Houndmills, Basingstoke, Hampshire RG21 6XS.

Palgrave Macmillan in the US is a division of St Martin's Press LLC, 175 Fifth Avenue, New York, NY 10010.

Palgrave Macmillan is the global academic imprint of the above companies and has companies and representatives throughout the world.

Palgrave® and Macmillan® are registered trademarks in the United States, the United Kingdom, Europe and other countries.

ISBN: 978–0–230–53763–7

This book is printed on paper suitable for recycling and made from fully managed and sustained forest sources. Logging, pulping and manufacturing processes are expected to conform to the environmental regulations of the country of origin.

A catalogue record for this book is available from the British Library.

A catalog record for this book is available from the Library of Congress.

10 9 8 7 6 5 4 3 2 1
21 20 19 18 17 16 15 14 13 12

Printed and bound in Great Britain by
CPI Antony Rowe, Chippenham and Eastbourne

In Memory of

Mabel Elsie Antill, *formerly Pugh, née McGeehan (Private), conscript, Auxiliary Territorial Service, anti-aircraft batteries.*

Charles Pugh *(Sergeant), conscript, Wiltshire Regiment, killed and buried near Cheux, Normandy.*

Leslie Antill *(Private and Lance-Corporal unpaid), volunteer, Essex Regiment, patrolled in Piraeus without a weapon to avoid firing on Greek comrades.*

Contents

Preface viii

Note on Usage and References x

Abbreviations and Acronyms xi

1 Introduction: Liberal Internationalism, a Social
  Movement for Peace 1

2 Governance: Ideological and Political Trespass 11

3 Education: Democratic Accountability and
  Paper Guarantees 26

4 Disarmament: White Robes of Peace or Jackboots
  and Spurs? 48

5 Innovation: Arming the League with Air Power 69

6 Resistance: Pacifism and the Power of Defiance 89

7 Imperialism: Economic Security and Sanctions 110

8 Revisionism: Rearmament and Peaceful Change 132

9 Conclusion: Retrenchment, Reform and Colonisation 154

Appendix I: Group Memberships 167

Appendix II: Circulation Figures 174

Notes 175

Bibliography 210

Index 229

Preface

This book is the product of many years of reflection on peace and politics. It began as a history thesis that took me into many archives. It has since been informed by critical international relations theories and the political economy of peace and conflict, topics that continue to fascinate. In particular, I became interested in the conceptualisation of liberal peace, and especially the neoliberal formulations of economic governance and politics. It seemed logical to revisit some of the foundations of liberal internationalism in the light of my subsequent critiques to help explain the *zeitgeist* of its hegemony, why the liberal peace came about, its governmentalities and resistances.

The research has been largely based on non-government archives, but I owe thanks to the staff of the National Archives (former Public Record Office) for their assistance in my researches on official documents. I recall with gratitude the late Lady Kathleen Liddell Hart's kind hospitality and permission to access the Liddell Hart Papers that were moved to King's College London. For access to other manuscript collections, I am indebted to the staffs of the British Library (Cecil and Balfour); the British Library of Political and Economic Science (Adams and Dalton, Papers); Churchill College, Cambridge (Alexander Papers); the University Library, Cambridge (Baldwin, and Templewood Papers); the University of Birmingham Library (Austen Chamberlain Papers); Nuffield College, Oxford (Cripps Papers); the Beaverbrook Library (Lloyd George Papers); the Scottish Record Office (Lothian Papers); the Bodleian Library, Oxford (Murray Papers); and the House of Lords Record Office (Samuel Papers). Acknowledgements are also due to the staffs of the Marx Memorial Library, the Gladstone Library, the National Liberal Club, the Labour Party Library, and the National Union of Conservative and Unionist Associations. For the empirical work, I also had useful discussions with Lady Liddell Hart, Lord Brockway, Frank Hardie and Professors Martin Ceadel and H. Noel Fieldhouse. Permission to reuse parts of my article, 'Policing the World: Lord Davies and the Quest for Order in the 1930s', *International Relations*, Vol.16, No.1, 2002, pp. 97–115, has kindly been granted by Sage Publications, London.

I am deeply indebted to Professor Geoffrey Searle, who guided my research, and to Professors Paul Kennedy, CBE, and Donald Cameron Watt for important suggestions. I owe thanks to the support of colleagues and the many debates on international issues with Professors Edgar Feuchtwanger, Oliver Richmond, John Groom, Mats Berdal, Christopher Cramer and Tom Woodhouse, among others; and for their insights and productive partnership, Neil Cooper and Mandy Turner. Responsibility for the work is mine. Production would not have been possible without the superb secretarial support of Kay Roberts and Michele Mozley. Finally, I owe special thanks to Margaret, Ingrid, Evan, Ella and Brannoc for humouring me.

Note on Usage and References

As was usual in the period, surnames were preceded by initials, but where there might be doubt about identification and where the person generally used their first name, this has been given. Philip Noel Baker was inconsistent about hyphenating his surname. It is given without here, as in the 1940 edition of *Who's Who*.

The complexity of primary sources has obliged me to use notes, except where the press is cited in the text with a date in parenthesis.

For parliamentary debates: 291 *HC Deb.*, 5s., 3671 (12 February 1926) refers to volume 291, fifth series, column 3671.

Abbreviations and Acronyms

AC Papers	Austen Chamberlain Papers
ACIQ	Advisory Committee on International Questions (Labour Party)
Add.	Additional Manuscript (British Library)
C/A	Council of Action (Lloyd George Papers)
CID	Committee of Imperial Defence
CIGS	Chief of Imperial General Staff
Cmd	*Command Paper*
CPGB	Communist Party of Great Britain
DBFP	*Documents on British Foreign Policy*
DRC	Defence Requirements Committee
HC Deb.	*House of Commons Debates*
HL Deb.	*House of Lords Debates*
IFTU	International Federation of Trade Unions
ILP	Independent Labour Party
IPC	International Peace Campaign
IPF	International Police Force
LNU	League of Nations Union
LSE	London School of Economics and Political Science
NCPW	National Council for the Prevention of War
NFRB	New Fabian Research Bureau
NLF	National Liberal Federation
NMWM	No More War Movement
NPC	National Peace Council
PDC	Preparatory Disarmament Commission
PPU	Peace Pledge Union
RIIA	Royal Institute of International Affairs
RUSI	Royal United Services Institute
TUC	Trades Union Congress
UDC	Union of Democratic Control
UN	United Nations

1
Introduction: Liberal Internationalism, a Social Movement for Peace

Towards the end of his life, Alfred Milner, the nineteenth-century British colonial administrator, member of Prime Minister Lloyd George's cabinet and liberal imperialist, gave a statement of his political creed. 'I am', he recorded, 'a Nationalist and not a Cosmopolitan. This seems to be becoming more and more the real dividing line of parties'. Describing himself as a 'race patriot' favouring a 'British League of Nations' (the Empire), he claimed that 'competition between nations, each seeking its maximum development, is the Divine order of the world, the law of Life and Progress'.[1] It had ceased to be a dominant view before his death in 1925. Cooperation rather than struggle between nations had become the *leitmotiv* of mainstream British discourses on security. This study contributes to the literature on peace by analysing the historical contingencies and internecine politics, the streams and flows, of the potent British socio-political movement for an interwar liberal peace that assembled a dominant orthodoxy.

With notable exceptions there has been limited research on liberal internationalism and its focus on one of the important issues of the time – collective (or 'pooled') security. This affords a contrast to the interest in public opinion by contemporaries. Kingsley Martin provided regular commentaries for *Political Quarterly*; and pronouncements on the state of 'the public mind' about international questions frequently cropped up in other journals. The contemporary fascination reflected a widespread belief among intellectuals that public opinion was, or should be, concerned about foreign policy to a far greater extent than before the Great War. Indeed, the book shows that there was a good deal of public interest in international affairs; powerful social movements such as the League of Nations Union (LNU) existed to cater for it.

Seemingly impelled to adopt a teleological perspective because the period ended with an even greater world war, commentaries have attached pejorative labels to all or parts of the period: 'lost decade' (Rab Butler), 'unforgiving years' (Leo Amery), 'locust years' (Thomas Inskip and Winston Churchill), 'fateful years' (Hugh Dalton) and the 'lost peace' (*BBC* documentary). Interwar narratives of peace were disqualified by association with appeasement, the decline of the Liberal Party and the rise of competing ideologies. However, as Richard Overy argues, intellectuals were torn between creative modernism and angst about a civilisational crisis, but they failed through 'lack of power rather than lack of faith'. [2] In exploring liberal internationalism, this book contends that internationalists exerted hegemonic power domestically (though not internationally), and operated effectively in civil society to shape people's ideas by trailing liberal tenets about peace across political boundaries.

The argument

Although, clearly, liberal internationalism had roots in previous, centuries the justification for focusing on a period that ended badly is that it was, nevertheless, a halcyon period for liberal internationalists. The core argument is that the underlying principles of liberal internationalism had both a strong ethical dimension and a pragmatic adaptation to changes in international and domestic circumstances. This enabled the movement to trespass across political borders and spaces and appeal to people who also had allegiances elsewhere. In a curious way, as the Liberal Party itself disintegrated, liberal ideas about peace dispersed into a receptive population. Moreover, liberal internationalists had an imaginative view of global order that centred on peace through international law and collective security, and that foreshadowed the efforts in the Second World War to establish this approach on a firmer footing. Although many achievements of liberal internationalism lay partly in the future – and in the twenty-first century are associated with neo-colonial models of peace – the interwar internationalists displayed innovation in spreading bourgeois internationalism in Britain. Overshadowed by the subsequent Manichaean struggles of the next war, the end of Empire and the Cold War, the movement nevertheless had a profound influence on British approaches to international politics, and subsequently influenced the UN's approach to peace and international security. And, as a movement of resistance, interwar liberal internationalism had worthy successors in campaigns for nuclear disarmament and anti-war coalitions. A complex movement that can be disaggregated into wings, factions and fluidities, the generic term 'liberal internationalism' captures the mainsprings of a movement suffused with values that were at once humane and superior, tolerant and dogmatic, universalistic and imperial.

The political imaginations of liberal internationalists were informed by a 'scientific' approach to the liberal belief in progress, H.G. Wells with his notion of a world-state perhaps representing the most innovative. At an international level, they pursued progress by developing a modern way of ordering the international system. This required a new architecture of peace based, in theory if not always in practice, on diversity, equality of sovereign states, social justice, self-determination, and a probing of received views about colonialism and the status of colonial subjects. International law, intergovernmental conferences and collective security would be the main mechanisms for transcending conflict. Liberal internationalists also elevated the idea of public opinion as a check on government, notably through the Union of Democratic Control. 'Open diplomacy' was a transparency mechanism that, in theory, would break a monopoly of privilege and the legacies of dynastic warmongering and territory swapping. It would also democratise foreign policy in ways that would avoid international misunderstandings and ensure that those most vulnerable to war would have a say about peace. One might even argue that an end to secret diplomacy was the reparation demanded by the classes whose public school and university offspring had been sacrificed. They also exuded a spirit of transnationalism, arguing that global public opinion would play a role in the system. The war had denied scientific rationalism, and so liberals aimed to develop knowledge and educate the British population in rational choices about international engagement. It was no coincidence that international relations became an academic study with the establishment of the first (Woodrow Wilson) Chair in the University of Wales in 1918, and as a policymaking tool in the foundation of the Royal Institute of International Affairs (RIIA) in 1919, financed by the John Jacob Astor family. While polemic remained much in evidence, the sophisticated quality of much analysis, on the political economy of reparations and sanctions for example, had solid empirical foundations. Finally, liberal internationalism attempted to counter *realpolitik* through a moral, ethical approach to international order, with a concern to stress international justice and provide an alternative to power politics. A significant element of religious faith permeated the movement, whether the High Church Anglicanism of Robert Cecil, president of the LNU; the Christian pacifism of the Labour Party leader, George Lansbury; or the Christian Scientism of the liberal imperialist, Philip Kerr (Lord Lothian). In the proposed revised Prayer Book of 1927, the House of Bishops gave the League of Nations its *imprimatur* with a variation on 'Jerusalem':

> He maketh wars to cease in all the world
> He breaketh the bow and knappeth the spear in sunder,
> And burneth the chariot in the fire.[3]

But not for nothing was the LNU called the Liberal Party at prayer. It can be argued that the Great War had caused a crisis of faith in liberalism as well as of international order, the Liberal Party having completely split in 1916. In Britain, Great-ness survived somewhat unhinged by the effort of 'victory'. It was also a crisis of liberalism, and, indeed, the liberal internationalist movement exposed a crisis of liberal governmentality, the techniques of control and social reproduction in the quest for liberal rights (discussed below). In this respect, liberal internationalism represents a rescue mission, signifying resistance to decay. This investigation begins with a conceptual framework deriving in part from the literature on social movements and from the characteristic of liberal internationalism as a coalition or assemblage of resistance to war through dependence on collective security.

The scope and conceptual framework

Interwar liberal internationalism has gone largely unheeded in the literature on social movements. Cecelia Lynch's *Interpreting Interwar Peace Movements in World Politics* (1999) has two chapters specifically on Britain; Andrew Williams's *Liberalism and War* (2006) has a useful chapter on ideas of war and peace in a book mainly concerned with liberalism in war settlement and reconstruction; and David Cortright's general survey of the history and philosophy, in *Peace: A History of Movements and Ideas* (2008) has valuable chapters on war resistance and disarmament campaigns in the 1930s. But the bulk of international relations focus has been on the institutional spread of liberal norms.[4] As well as Overy's research, perhaps the most erudite and enduring in historical studies has been Michael Howard's *War and the Liberal Conscience* (his Trevelyan lectures at Cambridge published in 1978). Peter Wilson's biographical studies and Martin Ceadel's work on pacifism have also paved the way for reinterpretations about peace movements in British politics.[5] The focus here, however, is on liberal internationalism as a socio-political movement that expressed both elite preferences and attracted resistances. The study derives from historical investigation but also takes into account concepts of social movements,[6] and explorations of liberal peace in international relations.[7] It disaggregates the controversies that reached beyond officials and policymakers, but generally avoids the intricacies of state policy formation by governments, in order to give some weight to non-governmental diversity. Nor have I been primarily concerned with the appeasement debate about whether public opinion influenced British foreign policy.

Social movements are often framed, however, as resistance to the exercise of authority and its privileged discourses. Indeed, there have been significant shifts in the focal points of political history and international relations towards revealing the governed, the subjects of sovereignty and, in postcolonial scholarship, 'subalterns' whose voices are frequently neglected. In establishing the kind of phenomena presented by liberal internationalism, it is helpful to associate it with concepts of civil society and the philosophical stance of cosmopolitanism. From its emergence in the mid-eighteenth century, Enlightenment figures such as Adam Ferguson had considered civil society as a natural, universal and constructive political economy of societies.[8] And while a century later, Karl Marx argued that the struggle for bourgeois civil rights had no historical leverage without change in the mode of production, Antonio Gramsci, writing in the 1930s, believed that because the ideological and cultural ramparts of oppression would not end social strife, bourgeois civil society could be mobilised through intellectual leadership and education to foster emancipation and political orders.[9] By contrast, in the twentieth century, Robert Putnam conceives civil society as a kind of health farm for citizen relations. Located apart from state and market, it comprises voluntary civic engagements that knit society together, builds trust, produces 'social capital,' and sustains democracy, public affairs and economic life.[10] In this guise, it meshes with the neoliberal dissolution of state power, giving precedence to a new technology of governance in which assemblages of citizens seek consolation, sociability and solutions to problems through self-help organisations and associations. It is unclear how this neoliberal turn to civic responsibility can deal with the structures of global dominance, of which 'global civil society' is a constituent element. But seemingly influenced by transformation in central and eastern Europe, the concept was appropriated in the 1990s for the causes of social justice and cosmopolitanism. Indeed, transnational advocacy coalitions have given rise to a prolific literature on the restructuring of international politics.[11] A vibrant civil society is regarded as the route not only to a peaceful domestic life, but to a fair and just international society free from genocide and other forms of uncivil behaviour.[12]

Resistance to war complemented a renewed interest in social resistance to power that engaged Michel Foucault, for example, in investigating the circularity and non-linearity of power, its contingent nature and fragmentation. A multitude of resistance techniques could be uncovered by bringing to the surface the 'hidden transcripts' and coded critiques of subjection of apparently powerless subalterns.[13] Similarly, from the engagements between colonial attempts at imposition and the reactions of colonised peoples (including counter-hegemonic resistances), hybrid forms of culture, politics and social life emerge, including what has been characterised as hybrid forms of peace.[14]

Whether the claims for resistance are too readily conflated with measures for coping with adversity remains an open question. A psychological reliance on hopes for peace to cope with fears of war was clearly a factor in liberal internationalism that resulted in a degree of wishful thinking. Moreover, for some critics of neoliberal globalisation, resistance based on the concept of civil society is a fiction. For example, Jean-François Bayart demolishes the apolitical, autonomy claims of non-governmental organisations (NGOs), since they are nationalised, even militarised, to reproduce global inequalities: '[t]he constitutive organisations of "civil society" are an essential part of "governance" (or "governmentality"), both national *and* global, of which they risk becoming mere cogs in the machine from the point of view of political co-option, economic accumulation, ideological legitimization or quite simply of foreign policy'.[15] Indeed, global civil society mobilised by governments in the name of rights and survival stands accused of constructing a simulacra of international peace.[16] Alternatively, in the quest to save strangers from abuse,[17] civil society provides rationales for wreaking havoc on illiberal governance and ousting dictators through regime-change wars. From the multifaceted character of the concept, it is reasonable to agree with Robert Cox in his revival of Gramsci, that '[c]ivil society is both shaper and shaped, an agent of stabilization and reproduction, and a potential agent of transformation'.[18]

Social movements obviously thrive on a sense of participation and trust, because they mobilise a collective mass of participants. But they cannot necessarily be regarded as builders of Putnam's civic virtue. They have projects and goals that seek to control a way of life and, whether or not imbued with a transforming consciousness, imply that an aspect of history is at stake. They often represent and construct resistance, promoting a policy realm against orthodoxies, and implying the need to disrupt a civic structure or regime, including a liberal regime. Thus *Via Campesina* ('the Peasants' Way'), dedicated to respecting a balance between everyday living, food production and the environment, is a transnational social movement that counters agribusiness – and, thus, a social movement can foster solidarity across frontiers and mobilise cosmopolitan attributes of universalism.

This does not mean, however, that social movements are inevitably cosmopolitan, in the sense of forging an 'impartial, universal, individualist and egalitarian' philosophy of life.[19] Social movements offer partisanship. They may not be considered emancipatory or universal, may have protection of territorial, religious or ethnic identity as their cause, and can have collectivist rather than individualist ideas. Whereas 'civil society' is a layering concept variously appropriated and whereas cosmopolitanism portrays a humanistic philosophy of identity and conduct in the world, social movements can be thought of as mobilisations not necessarily separate from governing authority, offering courses of action to affect aspects of politics and history, such as the prevention of war. They frequently manifest resistance and struggle, marking a determination to make history answerable to their interests, values, fears and politics. Particularly significant for the analysis here, social movements are by definition fluid, transgress boundaries, and often display bottom-up, anti-hegemonic attributes as well as ideological connections with the state and the world order that make them possible. As Rob Walker remarks, social movements are at odds with the politics 'associated with the modern state and its self-identical subjects' and, further, 'it must be the capacity of some social movements to speak to the poverty of the contemporary political imagination that gives them significance beyond their immediate demands, achievements and even failures'.[20] Liberal internationalism, however, was only partially at odds with state politics: rather it trespassed on conventional political spaces and was constantly in political transit. On the other hand, it did inhabit a realm of imagination, envisaging a regulated international order that would safeguard a liberal peace.

Liberal internationalism operated within civil society *and* governmental authority. It was partly top down, boasting membership from the political elite, and influential in the structure of governance. As the career of the LNU president Lord Robert Cecil demonstrates, there was often no rigid distinction between rulers and civil society on issues of collective security. In this respect, the linkage between government and non-government bodies suggests that liberal internationalism was a form of governmentality and not, contra Alejandro Colás, fully a commotion of non-state actors.[21] To paraphrase Foucault, the movement produced knowledge and discourses, and techniques and procedures for governing the population's mentalities, facilitating a political economy of social control. In the specific British interwar power system, liberal internationalism, led mainly by the middle class and liberal aristocracy, also conserved a whiggish radical tradition that might prevent chaos and revolution from right or left, as experienced in continental Europe. Liberal internationalism thus performed a disciplinary function for the governing classes, blocking any attempt to reify fascist or communist ideologies.

It was also partly bottom-up and resistant, though not so much a revolt from below as an organic educational movement that might have been approved by Gramsci. The movement exercised considerable sway in the governing elite and breached the portals of decision-making in a way that democratic politics might be expected to work. The adherents resisted an orthodox view of conflict that had taken Britain into the war, and then forged a modus operandi with political elites after it. They had a teleological sense of right, with goals that would alter the history of peace. For some, a world government was ideologically comfortable, but for the majority, national or class interests precluded such a cosmopolitan vision. On the other hand, most adherents had a determination to push international politics towards a value system based on an international collective of states of all political hues. An intergovernmental body of the powerful would provide global governance – with norms and behaviours schooled and modified by interactions within an institution, the League of Nations.

Procedure and structure

Pinning down a social movement and hearing its voices is no easy task and has exercised postcolonial scholars such as Gayatri Spivak, the philosopher–historian Michel Foucault and the anthropologist James C. Scott.[22] Likewise, gauging the strength and directions of public opinion and of influences on civil society is a hazardous undertaking, because of the fluid and abstract nature of these concepts and the difficulties of measurement. The method adopted here is historical, to identify and examine streams of opinion and discourse through the words of individuals and organisations: their public and private pronouncements, in conference minutes, literary propaganda, manifestos and actions.

Although most of these are no longer 'hidden transcripts' in Scott's phrase, but publicly available in collections scattered across various archives, a great many primary records were consulted and the analysis relies on these and the memoirs of participants.

No doubt, voices are missing and subaltern expressions are recorded as hearsay or reported as 'unrest' at public meetings, marches and protests. But the largest, most vociferous body to act as a conduit for liberal internationalism, the LNU, moved from a pressure group to a mass movement, with a million members at its peak. Its genealogy is outlined in the next chapter. It provides a litmus for the fortunes of liberal internationalism. And although one can never be sure that the interpretation of records accurately represents the meanings of the authors and speakers, or that the selection of material is safely representative, the range and depth of sources suggests a popular ideology with many strands. Knowledge existed at various levels, informed and uninformed, articulate and inarticulate, and of varying degrees of cohesion. For the most part, this study is concerned with bodies of opinion which operated through some form of organisational structure, sought to make converts through propaganda, and produced public spokespersons recognised as such by followers and opponents alike.

With this conceptualisation and method in mind, the structure of the book traces the scope of the movement's political and ideological trespassing through various campaigns. Chapter 2 provides a political sociology of liberal internationalism and traces its credentials as a movement that resisted party politics but was by no means apolitical.

Chapter 3 investigates the early campaigning trespass that opened debate about democratic control over Britain's international security policy. It also reveals a contest between the early movement and elite constructions of peace and security, as demonstrated by agonistic discourses over Germany's entry into the League of Nations, and over the various 'paper guarantees' for regulating international conduct – particularly the Optional Clause and the Kellogg–Briand Pact.

Chapter 4 plots the manner that threats were perceived as deriving from the acquisition of weaponry. Rather like post-1945 concerns about 'the military balance', interwar liberal internationalists expressed considerable angst about arms racing. In addition, as shown in Chapter 5, they assumed that the 'new weapon of mass destruction', air power, had to be controlled and preserved for peaceful purposes. Deterrence theory becomes part of the imagining, and the fear of air technology led to the notion that air power could be allocated to the League of Nations to implement collective security against aggressors.

Chapter 6 investigates a renewal of social movement resistance to war in response to crisis. The anti-war movement of the late 1920s and 1930s foreshadowed protests in the era of Kosovo and Iraq. Both collective protest and individual resistance were considered to be more effective than transpired in the specific cases of Japanese and German aggression, and the movement was fatally divided about peace, intervention and international justice. In brief, liberal internationalism encountered its strongest resistance, but it had to be acknowledged, manipulated or repressed by elites in order to reclaim control over national policy.

Chapter 7 examines the political trespassing by liberal internationalism, through the campaigns against reactionary imperialism and in favour of economic security through a 'have-not' discourse and welfarism. A growing interest in economic stress arose partly from direct experience of economic crisis, and partly from awareness of international economic interdependence. Privileged states such as Britain had an obligation to assist poorer countries that would pose a threat to peace if their needs remained unsatisfied. Interwar liberal internationalists were, as now, concerned to deny Empire and to rescue the undeveloped world from disease, famine, poverty and internal conflict. The power of economic sanctions to affect state behaviour was also a key aspect of liberal internationalism, coming to a head with the great debate over Italy's invasion of Abyssinia/Ethiopia.

Chapter 8 analyses the depreciating imagination of liberal internationalists in their efforts to ascertain whether a 'rogue state' had to be confronted by concession or by collective military power. The issue deeply affected liberal internationalists in contemplating German nationalist revisionism. Many proposed a strategy of 'peaceful change'. But ultimately most reconciled themselves to war though the preferred collective security institution, the League of Nations, had no residual clout. The Conclusion, Chapter 9, considers the solutions proposed by liberal internationalists to problems raised by the League's incapacities. Many urged reform of the League, while others sought to morph collective security into an alliance of anti-expansionist states.

Afterwards, although Britain (increasingly referred to as the United Kingdom) counted for less in world politics, and although a paternalistic liberal morality seemed to have little place in a world dominated by cold war realism, the tenets of liberal internationalism were to survive in the concepts of collective security, peacekeeping and peacebuilding. The study of contemporary state policies to explain the dynamics of conflict prevention and resolution is incomplete without understanding the historical role of the liberal internationalist movement in imaginations of peace.

2
Governance: Ideological and Political Trespass

Having examined the phenomenon of liberal internationalism as a socio-political movement, this chapter unravels its ideology and sociology. Liberal internationalism was a broad-based coalition of concepts, principles, adherents and advocacy for peace that, using Gramscian terms, had within it the seeds of revolt against the *realpolitik* that the Great War had disturbed. Its leadership had close links with the British governing class but developed an intellectual critique that had ramifications that would undermine its privileged knowledge of international affairs and control over foreign policy. As a political movement, it also trespassed across party territories, consistent with Rob Walker's argument concerning the constructive disorder of social movements, noted in the previous chapter. The analysis here turns to the movement's political and ideological position as trespasser, through a depiction of its concepts, adherents and confrontations.

An ideology of peace

While they adhered to the notion that 'world loyalty must grow out of patriot loyalty',[1] liberal internationalists also conceived of crossing frontiers through appeals to utilitarian as well as ethical sensibilities. Liberal internationalists generally distrusted supreme statist theories, as formulated by Hegel and Treitschke in Germany, and Froude, Seeley and Dilke in Britain. Those hawkers of *realpolitik* glorified states in their command of unquestioned loyalty through a mixture of honour, patriotism and fear of sanctions. Even less amendable to internationalists were doctrines that preached the ennobling activity of war. The grotesque bloodbath proved that interstate rivalry or 'international anarchy' could end in the negation of Milner's view of 'Life and Progress'.

The majority of liberal internationalists did not propose ushering in a world state. But they represented states as subjects equivalent to moral individuals that could be transformed. Thus, Robert Cecil, the *primus inter pares* of internationalists, declared:

> I am prepared to say that the State is an individual, a moral individual, and is subject as such to the moral law. I believe that through the development of a mysterious but essential capacity of our nature, human beings can join together and make themselves, for one reason or another, into a corporate whole; and having done so, they assume a new character, ceasing to be wholly and solely an aggregation of units, and becoming a new entity, subject to its own moral lives and moral duties.[2]

In addition, the impressive agency of liberal internationalism signified not only an ethic that transgressed the space of security-as-brute-force but also a political project to shake off the past. Peace was achievable through various tools and techniques of domestic and international governance. Nascent ideas of transnational advocacy could also be practised through institutions such as the Women's International League for Peace and Freedom (established in the United States in 1915) and through international conferences, where attendees were invariably called national 'delegates'. But liberal internationalism was not primarily construed as comparable to workers of the world uniting, more akin to liberalism spreading paternally from centres of highly educated and superior civilisation, where democratic liberalism had its foundations – almost a century later echoed by the Bohemian exile in England, Ernest Gellner and the American, Robert Kaplan.[3] Gilbert Murray, the LNU Executive Chair, noted the difference between 'cultivated' opinion in England and on the continent: '[n]o doubt', he argued, 'it is due to the work of the LNU. Intelligent people here [Geneva] seem to be about where the English were ten years ago'.[4] Well before the electronic communications age, too, national conversion and domestic proselytising had priority, and also greater resonance.

First, foreign policies had to be democratised because the interests of the population did not coincide with national interests as defined by governments. Moreover, secrecy in diplomatic exchanges had been identified as a factor in generating the recent conflict.

Second, peace meant conflict avoidance between what were termed 'great powers', including the defeated powers. Empires were not regarded as especially problematic, nor League mandates for nurturing subject peoples;

undeveloped territories could not yet claim equal status. Third, the movement considered that the environment, and hence the behaviour of states, would benefit from conflict prevention norms and institutional regulation of international conduct. For example, international law among states would be respected because rule of law based on arbitration and other mechanisms would discipline states and establish predictability. Law and diplomatic consensus in the open would be promoted by the society of states institutionalised in the new League of Nations. Fourth, in these, endeavours the British Empire occupied a special place because of its democratic credentials, global interests and wartime sacrifices in upholding international law. Britain could not retreat into isolation, especially from incendiary Europe, where conflict prevention was most needed. National interest also dictated that peace required arms control and 'pooled sovereignty' to obviate the need to mobilise another expeditionary force for the continent. Unsurprisingly, the foremost organisation promoting liberal internationalism, the League of Nations Union (LNU), would turn to a military advocate of 'limited liability', Basil Liddell Hart, for advice on military issues. Britain could not shoulder the burden of keeping the peace alone. The concept of 'pooled' or collective security set limits to an independent policy of pacification. Internationalists frequently argued about the extent of these limits and about the precise obligations imposed under the terms of the League's Covenant. But for the most part, they stressed the force of international law, disarmament, 'rational' and transparent diplomacy, and the weight of moral opinion, rather than military power, as a means of preserving peace.

Political positioning

Participants in the movement adjusted their political attitudes and tactics according to circumstances, without losing sight of a fundamental quest for regularised international conduct. One need hardly stress that in the period between the wars, the changes in international circumstances were momentous. Between the Armistice and the capture of Addis Ababa by Italian troops in May 1936, an atmosphere of international reconciliation and stability gave way to rising tension, conflict and, by the end of that decade, the virtual collapse of the League. This deterioration obviously posed acute intellectual and political problems for governments and all sections of society, not least for liberal internationalists.

Sections of the movement adapted their policies, split, reformed and were divided by alternative approaches to peace. In the 1920s, liberal internationalism spread throughout the 'mainstream' British opinion, and was politically constituted in the greater parts of the Labour, Liberal and Conservative parties. Variegation marked the mainstream, and liberal internationalism transgressed party boundaries and exhibited a convergence of views. It was not, therefore, an anti-establishment social movement for peace. Rather, it could inspire and meld with those in power in an interplay of transactions 'at the interface of governors and governed'.[5] And on international questions, the Labour and trade union leaderships had stronger ideological ties with liberal internationalists than with proponents of Marxism. Conservatives who supported sanctions against Italy for the invasion of Ethiopia in 1935 pursued a collective security design advocated by the Labour Party. Beyond this core, other groupings, while often commanding support and respect, had competing spheres in civil society. On one side were 'pacifists' and socialist war resisters in groups such as the 'No More War Movement'; on the other side were isolationists and nationalists who sustained the charity-cum-lobby group, the Navy League founded at the end of 1894, and the Imperial Policy Group of 1934. Further removed from the liberal hegemony on the left, and either ignored or viewed with suspicion by liberal internationalists, stood communists and members of the Independent Labour Party (ILP) after its disaffiliation from the Labour Party; proto-fascists and Oswald Mosley's 'Blackshirts' on the right. These subdivisions were permeable. Individuals such as Winston Churchill could transfer from an anti- to a pro-League stance. Absolute pacifists cooperated with liberal internationalists in promoting disarmament policies. The LNU derived prestige from its ability to trespass across rival political groups and to impose an element of cohesion on the movement. Its ability to offer an alternative politics explains the extent and impact of a social movement for peace beyond conventional party formations.

The chapter now gives a brief anatomy of the LNU as the fulcrum of the movement, revealing its composition, intellectual strength, status and, above all, its liberal credentials. The chapter then surveys the territories of other politics and ideologies on which international liberalism trespassed.

The liberal core

The LNU's pre-eminence as a foreign policy pressure group that mobilised a mass movement drew adherents from various sections of public life, and its patrons were a formidable array of establishment figures, including the heads of dominion governments and party leaders (see Appendix I). The lists of vice-presidents for 1931 and 1936, for example, contain the names of the Lords Sankey, Reading, Simon, Samuel, Londonderry, Maclean, Halifax and Baldwin – all one-time members of the 1931–35 cabinet. Military personalities, such as Vice-Admiral S.R. Drury-Lowe and Sir Frederick Maurice, sat on the Executive Committee with the journalist, author and 1933 Nobel peace laureate Norman Angell and the conscientious objector Clifford Allen (Lord Allen of Hurtwood). Throughout most of the period, Lord Queenborough (president of the National Union of Conservative and Unionist Associations in 1928–29) acted as treasurer. His Conservative colleagues, Austen Chamberlain, Lord Hartington, Duff Cooper and Walter Elliot, regularly attended executive meetings, and Mrs (Baffy) Dugdale, niece and biographer of Arthur Balfour, headed the LNU's Information Section. Speakers on LNU policies in the House of Commons included Philip Noel Baker, S. Vyvyan Adams, Geoffrey Mander, Eleanor Rathbone and Maj. Jack Hills; in the Lords, Robert Cecil, David Davies, Victor Bulwer-Lytton and Clifford Allen. The movement's City of London branch had a membership list which might have been taken from a page of the *Directory of Directors*, and church interests were equally well represented. Conforming to a Gramscian concept of bourgeois governance, there was no rigid, binary distinction between this sector of society and political authority.

And support outside the political elites burgeoned. Between 1933 and 1935, total nominal membership of the LNU exceeded a million, though actual subscribers, including affiliated bodies, represented about a third of that number. The movement ran more than 3,000 branches and youth groups, and published pamphlets and a monthly journal, *Headway*, which in 1928 had a circulation of 94,500.[6] The LNU's expenditure frequently topped £30,000 a year (£1 million at 2012 values). Embodying mainstream attitudes in favour of collective security, the LNU marshalled support through disarmament rallies, deputations and petitions, and played a leading role in the Peace Ballot campaign of 1934–35. The LNU could muster a wide section of the political class and exercise pressure on governments. Establishment figures patronised the LNU; it sported a Royal Charter; and the official imprimatur reached a climax when the LNU dined delegates to the 1930 Imperial Conference (with the Prince of Wales as guest speaker).

Its strength and impetus owed much to post-war disillusion with the organic state: its militarism, nationalism and 'secret diplomacy'. No movement of comparable stature and influence emerged in France or in other continental countries affected by the war. As Michael Howard shows, the British 'liberal conscience' is traceable to absorption of the teachings of Thomas Aquinas, Erasmus and Hugo de Groot, among others, who lamented the barbarity of war and its disruptions to commerce.[7] And there are intellectual continuities with nineteenth-century thought about peace.[8] In Woodrow Wilson, they also had a champion at the top table in Versailles, albeit perverted by compromise and 'betrayals'. Wilson corresponded with Cecil during the war, and his role as mediator and publicist for a 'just peace' and a League of Nations had endeared him to British liberals. Theodore Marburg of the American League to Enforce Peace, who visited Britain in late 1916, also elicited support for a post-war League, from among others, Asquith and Grey. The impact of Wilsonian principles led the historian E.H. Carr to conclude that popular internationalism in post-war Britain represented nineteenth-century liberal thought reflected in a US mirror.[9]

But as a distinctively British phenomenon, albeit influenced by the US 'progressives', liberal internationalism invoked recent memory of nineteenth-century Radical and Gladstonian traditions of applying rationalism and justice to international affairs. In fact, it was the Bryce Group, chaired by the lawyer James Bryce at the beginning of the war, that influenced not only various proposals of H.N. Brailsford, H.G. Wells, J.A. Hobson, Cecil, the Fabians and a League of Nations Society founded in 1915, but also Marburg's movement in the United States.[10]

The crisis in liberal governmentality arose not only from the war but from economic and political pressures, including Irish Home Rule and Women's Suffrage. George Dangerfield suggested that these pressure had caused the Liberal Party's death by 1913. But further stressed by the war, liberals summoned formidable resistance to disintegration.[11] The LNU attracted many supporters of the Liberal Party, a large proportion of them high-minded supporters of Lords Asquith and Grey, disenchanted with David Lloyd George and concerned about their own and their party's political future. The joint activities of the LNU and the Liberal Party will be discussed in future chapters, but between the wars, the LNU virtually acted in a realm of surrogate politics. The list of patrons drawn from the establishment disguises the fact that many who sat on the executive were being 'dis-established' by the Liberal Party's decline. In 1927 Cecil, himself a Tory, estimated that the executive comprised 20 Liberals, 14 Conservatives and 9 Labour adherents.[12] The minority representation reflected the labour movement's distrust of the League of Nations as a 'League of Victors' in the early post-war years. By contrast, the 1931–2 LNU Committee included the following prominent Liberals (and ex-Liberals): Lord Grey (joint president of the LNU), Gilbert Murray (Chair – an Asquith supporter), Viscountess

Gladstone, Lord W.H. Dickinson (a Liberal until he joined the Labour Party in 1930), Lady Layton, Sir John Harris (MP 1923–24 and secretary of the Anti-Slavery and Aborigine Protection Society), Sir Percy Harris (MP and Liberal Chief Whip after 1935), David Davies (a former PPS to Lloyd George), Sir Arthur Haworth (MP 1906–12), Lord Rhayader (MP 1923–24;1929–31), Mrs Walter Runciman (MP 1928–29), Lt. Commander J.M. Kenworthy (MP 1919–26 and then Labour MP 1926–31), Col. David Carnegie (Liberal candidate 1924, 1927, 1929), Geoffrey Mander (MP from 1929), L.J. Cadbury (chairman of the pro-Liberal *Daily News*) and P.J. Noel Baker (son of a Radical MP, and a Labour MP from 1924 onwards). Other Liberals who joined the executive at various times included Dame Elizabeth Cadbury, J.A. Spender, and Philip Kerr. A former leader-writer on the *Daily News*, H. Wilson Harris, became editor of *Headway*. Financial support came from the Cadbury family, which provided £2,000 a year, and from Lord Cowdray, a Liberal newspaper proprietor who gave £50,000 in 1927.[13] The Hon. Reginald McKenna (Liberal Minister 1905–16) was a joint trustee for the LNU, along with David Davies.

The intellectual lustre which liberals brought to the LNU is also beyond dispute. It included the historians G.P. Gooch and C.K. Webster and the philosophers C. Delisle Burns and Goldsworthy Lowes Dickinson. Professor Gilbert Murray of Oxford University, the foremost Greek scholar in Britain, associated the 'Hellenic genius and the modern Western genius with the liberal spirit'.[14] Two other classical scholars, Professor A.J. Toynbee (who married Murray's daughter) and Alfred E. Zimmern (author of *The Greek Commonwealth*, 1911) likewise seem to regard collective security as the civilised weapon of both ancient and modern society against the forces of 'international anarchy'. Clearly, though, it was in William Gladstone (the Grand Old Man or GOM), rather than the Greeks, that liberals sought a model of public morality and responsibility. Murray had grown up a fervent Gladstonian, but had also penned a 1915 pamphlet in defence of Sir Edward Grey's foreign policy. Grey, though implicated in pre-war diplomacy, had cultivated a reputation for moral propriety, and was described by the Liberal Party chair, Sir Donald Maclean, as a new man, 'heart and soul in favour of the League of Nations'.[15] It is not too fanciful to see parallels between the public indignation (in which the LNU participated) over Italy's invasion of Ethiopia and the popular agitations over the Bulgarian atrocities in 1876 and the Armenian massacres in 1894. The GOM's crusading spirit seems to have passed to his daughter-in-law, the Viscountess Gladstone, who launched an appeal to provide a Red Cross aeroplane for the harassed Ethiopians.[16] 'At a League of Nations Union meeting recently', wrote one subscriber, 'I said we needed a Gladstone to deal with the Bully Mussolini as he did with the Sultan of Turkey when the Armenians were massacred ... To me we seem to have degenerated terribly since the days of Gladstone, Cobden and Bright'.[17]

The dominant figure in the LNU and 1937 Nobel Peace Prize holder, Cecil, son of Prime Minister Lord Salisbury was nominally a Conservative, but he also exuded the kind of moral tone with which Liberals could identify. Like the nineteenth-century Radicals, he had questioned the wisdom of the South African War, though he was not opposed to war as such, having served as Minister of Blockade from 1916 to 1918. He had long been attracted to Grey's Olympian rectitude. As two French commentators remarked: '*Conservateur, disciple pieux autant qu'influent de la Haute Église, Lord Cecil était un symbole remarquable de ce mélange de traditionalisme et idéalisme tourné vers l'avenir qui est au fond de chaque Anglais par delà les divisions des parties politiques.*'[18] But Cecil was not so much above politics as a political operator dissatisfied with post-war politics. After the war he instigated a conspiracy against the Lloyd George Coalition, hoping to establish a new party led by Grey and including Lord Lansdowne and the right-wing trade unionist and Labour politician J.R. Clynes – an anti-socialist force with overtones of gentry paternalism. However, in August 1921, Maclean had persuaded him not to sacrifice the traditions and organisation of the Liberal Party.[19] Cecil's scheming was noted by a German observer, who described his:

> pale, intellectual face which, seen in full, might have been that of a Salvationist, in profile that of a vulture, and in half-profile that of a Roman, but which commands many other expressions, reflects a dozen and hides a dozen opinions – the face of a man who, like the State he represents, can effect compromises with equal ease between others, with others, and with himself.[20]

To liberal internationalists, however, he had leadership qualities and, even when partly responsible for unpopular policies, he usually managed to evade public criticism. Cecil continued to cavil at the rigidity of the party system,[21] with the LNU perhaps providing an outlet for his frustrations. As a leader, he proved adept at keeping intramural controversy to a minimum, whilst promoting potentially divisive policies on collective security. In conventional politics, 'he has a peculiar position in our public life', commented a Liberal editor, 'no other Conservative is trusted by so many Liberals'.[22]

Cecil personified *par excellence* the transactional interface between governors and governed – in Foucauldian terms the 'governmental technology we call liberalism'.[23] He strove to remain above party politics, belonged fractiously to the Conservative–Unionist Party, sat on the crossbenches in the Lords, felt most comfortable in a Labour government, and at one stage contemplated joining the Liberal Party – a servant to all parties and master in none. But with a large following in the country and an unrivalled knowledge of League affairs, he was useful to governments as a figurehead of democratic opinion. The same can be said for Alfred Cripps QC (Lord Parmoor), a vice-president. Parmoor had held a Fellowship at Oxford, and became a Conservative MP but crossed the floor to join Labour. He disapproved of the treatment of conscientious objectors and founded a famine relief NGO during the war. Like Cecil a High Churchman, but unlike Cecil, Parmoor had stronger relations with Prime Minister Ramsay MacDonald, who appointed him to the cabinet and as the Labour Government's representative at the League of Nations.

Radical dissent

In addition to Gladstonian liberalism, LNU members reflected on ideas tangential to support for the League. In its demand for accountability and transparency in foreign policy the LNU was affected by the campaigns of the Union of Democratic Control (UDC). In turn, the members of the UDC came a long way towards accepting the League of Nations by the mid-1920s. Radical 'dissenters' such as H.N. Brailsford and J.A. Hobson continued to criticise the 'Club of Victors', following Lenin's branding it the 'Thieves' Kitchen', but after Germany's admission to the League in 1926 hostility diminished and lines between the UDC's dissent and the LNU's high-mindedness were increasingly breached. Several activists hovered between the two. The Cambridge scholar Goldsworthy Lowes Dickinson, for example, co-founder of the Bryce Group, mentioned above, maintained contact with the UDC. Norman Angell, W. Arnold-Forster and Hugh Dalton were members of the UDC who became converted to the necessity for League sanctions. In 1926, these three sat on both the General Council of the UDC *and* the Executive of the LNU. The pacifist Helena Swanwick, editor of the UDC's *Foreign Affairs*, also officiated in both organisations – though she remained hostile to economic sanctions. Indeed, in 1928 the UDC would split on the issue of sanctions, and it entered a decline, its philosophy of 'open diplomacy' captured by liberal internationalism.

Further, as long as concepts of 'pooled security' and 'disarmament' lacked precise definition, the LNU could count on the assistance of a 'pacifist' group. Among those associated in the 1920s with the National Council for the Prevention of War (NCPW) were Earl Beauchamp, Philip Noel Baker, J.A. Hobson, Helena Swanwick, William Arnold-Forster, Gaetano Salvemini, Charles K. Webster, Ellen Wilkinson MP, Wedgwood Benn MP, Lady Parmoor, the Dean of Canterbury, Hewlett Johnson, and historian G.P. Gooch (president). Such was the fluidity of liberal pressure group politics that several of them also held posts in the LNU. They were 'believers in peace' rather than pacifists and it was not inconsistent for them to support collective security. Absolute pacifists and unilateral disarmers occupied another space. While respected and sometimes admired for their sincerity, Dick Sheppard and George Lansbury of the Peace Pledge Union were looked upon as naïve and misguided, whereas, in theory at least, the collective security advocates did not rule out the use of force in certain circumstances. In 1926 the membership of the NCPW's affiliated organisations (excluding the LNU and the Society of Friends) was about 26,000, and the small but dedicated nature of the peace movement in the 1920s is graphically conveyed by the Council's single sheet, cyclostyled annual reports.[24] Nevertheless, the small peace societies chipped away at the foundations of militarism long before the children's novelist A.A. Milne and social commentators Aldous Huxley and Beverley Nichols made 'pacifism' fashionable. By 1931, the NCPW cooperated closely with the LNU in a disarmament campaign.

Imperialism

Further cross-fertilisation occurred between the LNU and the imperial strand of liberalism as represented by the Round Table group: John Dove, Lionel Curtis, and Philip Kerr. Less stridently nationalist than their mentors Joseph Chamberlain and Milner, and, following the example of General Smuts (an architect of the League Covenant), they welcomed the League as a contribution to the peace essential for development of the Commonwealth. Curtis (a personal friend of Murray), had joined the LNU Research Committee in 1918. Kerr joined the Executive in 1929. Whether urging a British lead in disarmament or promoting the spread of 'Anglo-Saxon' civilisation, the LNU and Round Table group shared a paternalistic sense of responsibility to the rest of the world. In the Round Table group, Curtis announced that ['r]esponsibility for backward races is one of the main reasons why the British Empire should be held together'.[25] However, the common liberal hubris masked vital differences which caused endless controversies between the two groups. Milner's 'kindergarten' graduates worked towards closer association with the Dominions and the United States, and only supported the League as a means of keeping Europe quiet. Their views ranged from Lothian's dic-tum: 'we have to make up our minds between the ideal of Geneva and the ideal of Rhodes', to the notion that the Commonwealth might embark on a kind of takeover bid for the League. Like many Conservatives, they regarded the League as a praiseworthy clearinghouse for ideas and a fac-tor for peace.[26] However, such divergence did not detract from the status of the LNU and its liberal support as the key movement for collective security in British opinion. Cecil thought the League put the Dominions on an equal footing in Assembly debates, arguing that because most of the Dominions would no longer have their foreign policy dictated from London, '[i]t is not too much to say that the system of the League is an almost ideal machinery for the preservation of the British Empire'.[27]

Conservatism

It tried to hold a middle ground between various wings of interna-tionalism. This was demonstrated by Sir Austen Chamberlain's rather turbulent period as an LNU adherent. Conservative Party officials persuaded him to join the Executive in February 1932 to improve the party's image among League supporters. But the one-time foreign min-ister felt compromised in associating with 'cranks', and had written to Cecil the previous month, declining to join because he disagreed with the LNU's disarmament tactics.[28] Once involved, he conducted a run-ning battle with members of the Executive, and Murray was frequently forced to intercede to restore peace. On one occasion, with the aid of Viscount Cranborne (Cecil's nephew) and documents provided by the foreign secretary, Sir John Simon, Chamberlain successfully forced the Executive to shelve proposals for a League Police Force.[29] A more serious split developed in July 1934 when, in Chamberlain's absence, the Executive decided to participate in the national Peace Ballot. Chamberlain objected to the reduction of complex questions to 'Yes' or 'No' answers and warned Cecil: 'My sleeping partnership in the Union has become a shirt of Nessus which I do not think I can longer endure'.[30] He was slightly mollified by the Executive's willingness to publish Conservative reservations about the ballot. But, complaining to Murray of Cecil's domineering methods, he wrote: 'I differ from Bob [Cecil] as to the true policy for the League itself. I differ still more from his conception of the proper task of the Union ... [and] though I recog-nise that the majority of the Executive do try to harmonise their views with mine, I find myself constantly committed to something I dislike as the price of preventing something I dislike more'.[31] In December 1935, he protested bitterly at the public endorsement by Cecil and Murray of the Labour candidate (Noel Baker) in a by-election.[32] Finally, after opposing continued sanctions against Italy, he decided in May 1936 to resign and announced his severance from the LNU the following month.

'Sleeping partnership' aptly describes the curious arrangement. As a former foreign secretary, Chamberlain lent prestige to the movement and provided a channel through which Cabinet members could be informed about what the LNU was up to. But, as incumbent upon someone 'planted' by his party, Chamberlain also sought to influence the LNU in directions compatible with the National Government's policies. As he indicated to Lord Tyrrell, he had 'tried to put a little water into their wine.'[33] To some extent, he had succeeded; Cecil and Murray considered that shelving the police force issue was a price worth paying for the retention of Chamberlain's name on LNU notepaper.

The majority of Tories had less enthusiastic attitudes towards liberal internationalism. In objecting to 'unlimited Covenant commitments' and 'militant' disarmament campaigns, they held to a nationalist security policy. Thinly disguised as Sir Orpheus Midlander in a play by George Bernard Shaw, Chamberlain is made to say: 'I am intensely reluctant to lose my grip of the realities of the moment and sit down to think. It is dangerous. It is unEnglish. It leads to theories, to speculative policies'.[34] In reality, Chamberlain did complain about internationalists turning the League into a 'meddlesome mother' and, like most Conservatives, regarded Geneva as a forum for debate, as a sounding board and an opportunity to continue 'hotel diplomacy'. But there was often little distance between this stance and the LNU's utilitarian internationalism that took national interests into account. Lord Balfour's liberalism, for example, included a desire to have wars classified into public and private conflicts, the latter equated with imperial policing of the undeveloped world.[35] On the other hand, in 1934 Austen's half-brother, the Tory leader Neville Chamberlain, proposed an international police force for western Europe.

Imperialist nationalism

A greater distinction lay between the Chamberlains and nationalists who followed Sir John Seeley's theories of imperialism.[36] The latter urged a free hand in foreign policy and defence, deprecating the League's threat to sovereignty, and believing in the inevitable violence of interstate competition. In an address at the University of Aberdeen in 1931, the anthropologist of evolution Sir Arthur Keith observed that racial conflict was inevitable: '[t]his antipathy or race prejudice Nature has implanted within you for her own ends – the improvement of mankind through racial differentiation ... Nature keeps the human orchard healthy by pruning; war is her pruning hook'.[37] The speech raised a storm of indignation. The war had scythed the young, and relatively fit and healthy. George Bernard Shaw retaliated by hoping to see octogenarians shuffling off to battle.[38]

This did not necessarily mean that nationalists were also isolationist; imperialism was an important element in Conservative attitudes. The *Morning Post* (12 September 1927) put forward a typical argument: '[a] powerful Continental Power which lies at the centre of Europe, like Germany, could always mobilise, if she were so minded, the majority of ... [the League's] members against us. This is one danger – the danger of isolation. There is another, the danger of encroachment by the League upon the sovereign national rights now centred at Westminster.' In the post-war internationalist hegemony, such anxieties were generally confined to the pages of the *Morning Post*, *Daily Mail* and military circles.[39] Not that all military veterans had a common view. Parliament was packed with returned soldiers, many of whom upheld an internationalist idea of peace. But it was not until after the failure of the Disarmament Conference of 1932 that imperialists, including Churchill, made any discernible progress in defence debates. Sir Maurice Hankey, the Milnerite cabinet secretary who seemed to wield more power than many a cabinet minister, argued that '[u]nder an international system and in a long era of peace the military spirit is exposed to exceptional dangers ... The symptoms of degeneracy manifest themselves so gradually that at any given moment they are not easy to discern'.[40] Ironically, Hankey had once been favoured as a secretary-general of the League of Nations.

Socialism

The shape of left-wing politics was also moulded by forces outside the liberal internationalist movement. Communist influence was small in the 1920s, and after the General Strike, the Communist Party of Great Britain lost ground, its membership falling from 10,730 to 1,376 between 1926 and 1930.[41] It had marginal support and failed to command the respect often accorded to pacifists, its conspiratorial style matched only by Conservatives who took it seriously. Also in the 1920s, radical dissenters were listened to, but not voted for. In March 1926, Lansbury failed to collect more than nineteen votes for a House of Commons motion to virtually abolish the navy.[42] There was pressure, as well, from the Independent Labour Party (ILP) which wanted: 'to meet any threat of War, so-called defensive or offensive, by organising general resistance, including the refusal to bear arms, to produce armaments, or to render any material assistance'.[43] But whilst the Marxists Fenner Brockway and James Maxton continued to demand unilateralism and to caricature the League of Nations as a capitalist enterprise, the Labour Party as a whole had veered in favour of the League, under the influence of Arthur Henderson and Hugh Dalton, who rejected the war resistance attitude as inconsistent with League obligations. Dalton argued that an aggressor would not be halted by pacifist speeches: '[s]ome residue of armaments may still be needed for a time in order to guarantee "pooled security" and constitute, in effect, an international police force'.[44] The Labour Party responded to left-wing criticism of the League on the grounds that it could not be blamed for the policies of reactionary governments, and that the party should work to get a socialist government represented at Geneva.[45] In general terms, however, the party's foreign policy, as opposed to its rhetoric, was not especially socialist.[46]

Conclusion

These, then, were the main borders transgressed by liberal internationalism (in causing reactions, if not adherence). From its position of resistance to liberal stress and decline, the internationalist movement could undertake remarkable transgressions: a preferred and privileged mentality that affected the outlooks of, for example, foreign secretaries from Austen Chamberlain to Anthony Eden.

Controversies arose because the League of Nations itself had been a compromise, seeking a third way between a superstate and anarchy: 'working not by force but by the operation of the public opinion of the world as the requisite sanction'.[47] The response of the liberal internationalists to the failure of this sanction invites explanation. It will be shown, for example, that, confronted with the impossibility and undesirability of imposing physical sanctions against Japan in 1931, Cecil (as head of the British Delegation to Geneva) 'had either to painfully revise a deeply-held belief, or to find "proof" of conspiracy and betrayal'.[48] But liberal internationalists responded to setbacks not merely by slumping into conspiracy-mindedness. Writing in 1935, Liddell Hart commented: 'The strength of British policy is its adaptability to circumstances as they arise; its weakness, that the circumstances (which are usually difficulties) could have been forestalled through forethought'.[49] Inter-group conflicts and the controversies which surrounded the LNU were as much the result of tactical manoeuvring as of fundamental differences in the concept of international engagement. Dealing with each crisis, often with delaying tactics and usually with an eye to the internal harmony and other allegiances, liberal internationalists only gradually changed their conception of peace through collective security. They maintained a deep commitment to conflict prevention.

In its anti-war ideology, internationalism drew upon an enlightenment rationalism and the 'liberal conscience', a distinctively British bourgeois liberalism that mixed human, civic and political rights, and economic justice, with cultural superiority, privilege and paternal imperialism. Democracy, rule of law and demilitarisation are common conceptions in contemporary peace and peacebuilding enterprises. But in the Great War and its aftermath, these gained mass adherence, harnessing a widespread sense that history had to change, was changing. Armed with liberal principles rather than guns, history could be ridden to skewer the nature of war, like the hunts that some of the internationalists rode at weekends. The movement represents a form of governmentality that enabled the governing class to avoid the revolutions affecting the Continent. It also represented a quiet, intellectual revolt, if not revolution, that shifted ideas of war and peace. The following chapters explore debates on questions of international engagement and the often utilitarian course taken by the movement as it transited the interwar years, beginning with its disruption to conventional ideas about the making of security policy.

3
Education: Democratic Accountability and Paper Guarantees

Liberal internationalism transited the 1920s with a series of peace campaigns that tested its autonomy and ability to work within an increasingly disturbed politics. This chapter first examines the campaign for transparency and accountability in international policy that obliged governments to manage debates on foreign policy. It reveals disputes about constructions of peace and security, as demonstrated by furious reactions in the movement over the government's failure to get Germany into the League of Nations in 1926. The remainder of the chapter analyses the movement's campaign for regulating international conduct through arbitration, and its responses to outlawing war by declaration – the so-called 'paper guarantees'. The chapter demonstrates how collective security became an influential issue in party politics by drawing on debates over the 'Optional Clause' for arbitration and the Kellogg–Briand Pact for outlawing war. Peace-as-collective-security developed in elite circles, both government and non-government, through an exchange of privileged information about relatively esoteric legalistic debates. The parties had to operate in an environment of distrust of diplomacy. The liberal internationalists also had to manoeuvre in an abrasive political context, marked by the Zinoviev Letter of 1924[1] and the General Strike of 1926. The Conservative Party's exercise of power seemed assured with a landslide victory after the collapse of a minority Labour Government in 1924 formed with Liberal support to counter economic protectionism. However, Labour replaced the Liberals in Opposition and took office again after the 1929 General Election. Collective security surfaced as an issue in party politics, though at some distance behind domestic concerns. Nevertheless, in the fractious political context, splits affecting the liberal internationalist movement camouflaged common positions on the exceptionalism claimed by Britain.

Internationalists expressed a degree of consensus that Britain had to safeguard its imperialism and maintain a balancing act between keeping Continental Europe quiescent and the United States engaged in a cooperative approach to international security.

Accountability and education

Due partly to the work of the Union of Democratic Control (UDC), noted in the previous chapter, few assumptions were more widely held in the liberal internationalist movement than that impersonal factors caused war – alliances, secret diplomacy and armaments competition. Politicians had succumbed to these entanglements because foreign policy and diplomacy were unaccountable to public opinion. Referring to the presumed Foreign Office grip over Sir Edward Grey, one back-bench MP concluded:

> Not to be affected by these persistent anti-German views, held by the highest officials, would have required in a statesman of unusual calibre, a first-hand knowledge of Europe, and something of an international mind. Unfortunately Sir Edward Grey had none of these qualifications. His particular outlook would render him readily susceptible to the imperialistic views of his advisers.[2]

Often at the cost of imprisonment, UDC members represented radical resistance to state secrecy and discipline during the war and early 1920s. E.D. Morel, veteran campaigner, pacifist and former Liberal who became a Labour MP from 1922, had founded the UDC with Norman Angell, Charles Trevelyan and Ramsay MacDonald in 1914. The UDC and Morel, also editor of *Foreign Affairs*, led criticism of the German humiliation at Versailles for laying the basis for another war. A new 'open diplomacy' would make war less likely because the procedures in foreign policy would be transparent and accountable. The war-averse public would safeguard peace and the global opinion would deter aggression. Cecil told the House of Commons in July 1919 that: 'what we rely upon is public opinion ... and if we are wrong about it, then the whole thing is wrong'.[3] In fact, in 1921, the League experimented with an international epistemic community. Supposedly acting in their private capacity and independent of governments, members of a Temporary Mixed Commission on Armaments comprising notable public figures, including Cecil, investigated disarmament questions and made proposals. In Parliament, UDC supporters pressed for democratic

control over foreign policy, international regulation for conflict prevention and post-war peace terms that would preserve stability. Morel
demanded, unsuccessfully, that no diplomatic agreement should occur
without parliamentary consent. But with MacDonald and several other
UDC members running the government in 1924, the UDC's independence in civil society diminished, though Morel did begin the process by
which (selective) official documents on pre-war diplomacy were later
published.[4]

In 1923–25, an economic consequence of Versailles became critical
with the Franco-Belgian occupation of the Ruhr. The League of Nations
had no impact on the crisis because, after several German defaults on
reparation payments, extracting German resources by force was allowed
under the Versailles Treaty (which France was desperate to uphold). So
again, the UDC, suspicious of the League as a product of Versailles and
vindicated by Keynes's critique of the economic consequences of the
peace, took the lead in castigating the occupation and sympathising
with the civil unrest in Germany that followed.[5] A drastic reduction
of reparations under the 1924 Dawes Plan failed to mollify the liberal
internationalist critics, many of whom increasingly despised French
policy and agitated for Germany's rehabilitation.[6] And since the Ruhr
crisis had continued the war by other means, the need for transparent
diplomacy increased.

Liberal internationalists, supported by many Oxbridge academics,
thus claimed an educative role to foster interest in international relations
that would encourage a well-informed public to monitor diplomacy and
keep foreign offices and the League itself honest. The education campaign included attempts to engage the country's youth. The LNU joined
socialists and the UDC in calling for less patriotic bias in schoolbooks –
to the irritation of reactionaries, who accused the LNU of infiltrating
schools 'to falsify history in the interests of peace'.[7] But generally, the
LNU's activities were unimpeachably respectable and unobjectionable
in the system of British governance. The movement's most successful
events were quasi-religious mass rallies. The LNU's magazine, *Headway*
(August 1926), reported a ceremony at York Minster where 3,000 congregated to commemorate the signing of the League Covenant. Gilbert
Murray told the throng that the League Covenant represented a 'great
charter of repentance on the part of the diplomatists of Europe'.

Notwithstanding the Ruhr crisis and social unrest in Europe, the international situation seemed to stabilise in the mid-1920s. Reliance on the
'charter of repentance' and civil society monitoring seemed feasible; sanctions and collective security were rarely mentioned. A breakthrough had

come with security agreements at Locarno, negotiated in 1925–26. They were designed to stabilise the western territories of Europe and pave the way for German entry to the League, while leaving the eastern borders of Germany open for revision. Arranged by the new government's foreign secretary, Austen Chamberlain, a new German Chancellor, Gustav Stresemann, and Aristide Briand, it modified but did not replace the pre-war mechanism of alliances.[8] The key element, the Rhineland Pact, involved mutual guarantees: Germany, France and Belgian pledged not to attack each other (with Britain and Italy as guarantors), and if one of them did, then the other parties – including Britain and Italy – would assist the victim. It had a mixed reception among liberal internationalists. For the LNU, it weakened the League's authority but was welcomed as a contribution to making the French feel more secure.[9] The UDC and the left were hostile to guaranteeing French security, but welcomed the opportunity to modify Versailles and give Germany equal international status. But having anticipated a League triumph in acquiring German membership, liberal internationalists of all stripes joined in condemning a revival of old diplomacy when the Weimar Republic's admission collapsed in 1926. The process got bogged down by the claims of Spain, Poland and Brazil to seats on the League Council (rumoured to have been encouraged by Chamberlain and Briand).

Although the League's technical procedures aroused little concern outside Parliament and the Foreign Office, a general sense had prevailed that 'open diplomacy' would lead to a 'fair deal' for Germany. The LNU leaders rejected reconstitution of the League's Council: 'the Germans will feel that they have been tricked – the balance altered against them after they have committed themselves and before they have a right to make themselves heard'.[10] The League of Nations Parliamentary Committee (under its Conservative chair, Sir Ellis Hume-Williams) agreed that Germany would be antagonised, and that further enlargement of the League Council would hinder crisis management.[11] Conservative, Labour and Liberal press editors alike attacked the 'unsavoury tactics' and 'undignified haste' of states to stake claims that Chamberlain had apparently failed to discourage. The *Daily Telegraph* momentarily put fairness to Germany above loyalty to the government, and *The Times* complained 'whispering behind closed doors'.[12] The radical UDC and imperialist Beaverbrook press, though strange bedfellows, both hinted at a French conspiracy to pack the League Council.[13]

Chamberlain hit back in speeches which the *Manchester Guardian* (25 February 1926) described as 'the most pernicious … that any British politician has delivered since the League was formed'. In a direct challenge to open diplomacy, he said that governments should discuss the problem without 'listeners in'.[14] But he appeared to have the support only of Germanophobes such as Sir Alfred Mond Conservative MP and Lord Rothermere (who accused the LNU of 'rapidly degenerating into a pro-German society').[15] The consensus cut across party lines. The Conservative MPs Robert Boothby, Harold Macmillan and Edward Cavendish (Marquess of Hartington) joined a parliamentary deputation to the Prime Minister.[16] *The Times* (26 February 1926) contended that Chamberlain could not fail to ignore 'the remarkably determined and unanimous expression of British opinion, which far outweighs the personal views, or it may be even the preliminary commitments, of any member of the British Government'.

Under this kind of pressure, and with Cecil, now in the Baldwin Cabinet, leading opposition on the inside, the government's usual majority on major issues was halved in a parliamentary division in March.[17] The controversy fizzled out, and Tory criticism abated when the German government refused to join a League Council devalued by the admission of 'lesser powers'. In part, the prolonged wrangling in Geneva had blunted the indignation; in part, too, there was a realisation that whatever Chamberlain had done to poison the atmosphere with his 'old style' diplomacy, he had not encouraged Brazil, which eventually blocked Germany's entry. Consequently, in a second Commons debate, following the collapse of the negotiations, the government secured a comfortable majority.[18]

However, the episode indicates the extent to which cross-party agreement had been possible on a principle of foreign policy conduct. Liberal internationalists were to be found in all parties, and what might otherwise have been a minor setback to Germany's rehabilitation had become an issue of international justice as well as security. The impasse had particularly angered League supporters because they expected German membership not only to herald an era of peace, but also to make the League more acceptable to critics. These factors, plus an element of Francophobia, played a part in the controversy, though without wholesale conversion of Conservatives to the UDC's creed of democratic control and open diplomacy. Nevertheless, even Conservative news editors had employed the discourse of open diplomacy, a testimony to the sway of the internationalist movement for an ethical foreign policy. For the liberal internationalist movement, the débâcle had vindicated the need for open diplomacy. Trapped by his part in the governmentality of liberal internationalism, Cecil complained to Baldwin about the 'secret meetings of Locarnoites' (to which he had been invited as part of the British delegation to Geneva), and threatened to resign from the cabinet.[19]

For the movement, failure to secure Germany's admission was 'due at every stage to the lack of publicity and to the neglect of the proper constitutional machinery that was at hand'.[20] Behind the rhetoric, however, LNU leaders understood the practical limitations of open diplomacy and popular control, and themselves engaged in the exercise of paternalistic governmentality. Few would have disagreed with Bernard Shaw, who argued that 'Geneva is not the place for the man in the street. The street is full of persons with parochial minds'.[21] For all Cecil's complaints about secrecy, both he and Grey had stressed throughout the crisis that Britain, France and Germany should sort out the muddle. They were especially anxious that the League Council, which Cecil had always regarded as an instrument of the powerful, should not be swamped.[22] Public opinion was something to be educated and mobilised to keep the authorities in check. But the LNU itself had limitations in its own procedures. The list of nominees to the Executive remained almost unchanged every year (until Conservatives defected in 1936). Notables were occasionally ushered on to the governing body by backdoor invitations – including Clifford Allen and Austen Chamberlain. And, as shown in later chapters of this book, Cecil sometimes rode roughshod over colleagues on matters of policy.

Nevertheless, the volume of criticism during the crisis had plainly stirred policymakers. Sir William Tyrrell (permanent undersecretary at the Foreign Office) complained to Chamberlain about the LNU's agitation: '[i]t has been one of the most ill-informed and mischievous ramps that I have ever seen in the domain of foreign affairs'.[23] The Royal Institute of International Affairs claimed that acceptance of the principle of parliamentary control over foreign policy had 'introduced a dynamic and imponderable factor into the conduct of foreign relations'. And officials and former diplomats frequently argued that public influence on foreign policy worked through 'mass suggestion', undermining the authority of accredited and trained experts.[24]

Public opinion has been a commonly cited 'cause' of the inability of statesmen to manoeuvre and to rearm and confront the interwar dictatorships. The generalised support for the League and transparent diplomacy undoubtedly influenced the policy environment. The Foreign Office (and foreign secretaries, generally), also shared the Eurocentric interests of many liberal internationalists. In 1933, Sir Robert Vansittart at the Foreign Office showed an interest in the movement when he was looking for sources of anti-German opinion. But foreign policy

remained mostly a preserve of upper-class privilege, perhaps less con-
strained by public opinion than by finance, imperial overstretch and
the views of Dominion governments.[25] Except on rare occasions when
an upsurge of public disapproval affected the government's own political support (as in the case of the League Council crisis of 1926 and the
Hoare–Laval Pact of 1935), there is no substantial evidence that public
opinion directly swayed governments to adopt or reject specific policies. Although the galaxy of landed, legal and educated gentry associated with the LNU could not fail to wield some influence, there were
always internal controversies on particular issues, which became more
acute as the Locarno spirit faded. Policymakers would have been hard
put to discern *the* voice of public opinion on detailed questions. The
movement's main contribution was to condition the environment to
promote peace through collective security under the League and to foster norms of conflict prevention. In the twenty-first century, this would
be called 'norm entrepreneurship'.

In Cecil, the movement had a representative who held government
posts until 1932. But Cecil's power varied according to his relationship with the ruling party and according to the balance of conflicting
interest within government. As Chancellor of the Duchy of Lancaster
in the second Baldwin Government (with responsibility for League
affairs), he had formed a close relationship with Austen Chamberlain –
despite Chamberlain's refusal to allow him a room in the Foreign Office
and despite the League Council crisis. Both shared a commitment to
European security.[26] On the other hand, Cecil suspected the military
and Churchill, who he said 'likes to kill foreigners'.[27] Early in 1926, following an interdepartmental meeting on disarmament, he remarked to
Baldwin that '[t]he Admiralty and the War Office almost frankly regard
[disarmament] as nonsense, and dangerous nonsense at that'. As a principal delegate to the Geneva Naval Conference of 1927 (see Chapter
4), Cecil bemoaned the rigidity of his instructions and the Admiralty's
obduracy in negotiations.[28] He failed to persuade the crucial cabinet
meeting of 26 July 1927 to accept the US terms for mathematical parity in cruisers. Although he returned to Geneva to represent a policy
with which he disagreed, he resigned five days after the talks collapsed,
despite appeals by Lord Salisbury and Chamberlain to stay. He had been
betrayed, he said, by the 'Blue Water School' of Churchill, F.E. Smith,
Amery, Worthington-Evans and Walter Guinness.[29]

If he hoped to precipitate a government crisis, he overestimated his significance. *The Times* political correspondent (31 August 1927) noted that
the resignation caused remarkably little comment; Cecil himself thought

that Baldwin was glad to be rid of him; and Tyrrell at the Foreign Office told a colleague that Cecil's resignation was not worth a shilling.[30] The LNU could exercise no direct political influence when its advocate in the government was so dispensable. Cecil never held ministerial office again. Yet his influence in the successor Labour Government of 1929–31, as British Representative at the League with a room in the Foreign Office, was probably greater than at any other time. Two other LNU activists – Will Arnold-Forster (Cecil's private secretary) and Philip Noel Baker (parliamentary private secretary to the foreign secretary, Arthur Henderson) – also enjoyed footholds in the government. As state agents, they enjoyed privileged access to decision-making while conducting orchestras of civil society activism. Cecil also owed his standing mainly to the fact that Arthur Henderson and a junior minister, Hugh Dalton, regarded him as a useful makeweight against the armed services. Cecil's relations with MacDonald never recovered from a squabble in 1924 on account of a supposed slight which the LNU had dealt the Labour 'pacifists' of the war. Dalton doubted whether MacDonald wanted Cecil in the government at all, and thought that because Cecil would not join the Labour Party, he hardly qualified for a cabinet seat; the position was 'ambiguous and unsatisfactory'.[31] Cecil's presence probably made little difference to a government predisposed to internationalism rather than isolationism, but he knew how to control a social movement to exclude extremism and transgress political boundaries.

After the collapse of the Labour Government, Cecil engaged with the new foreign secretary, Sir John Simon, but refused invitations to represent Britain as a delegate at the Disarmament Conference due to open in February 1932. He knew his influence would be limited: 'my opinion ought to be officially accepted by the Foreign Office subject to the control of the Secretary of State ... and I am certain that will never happen unless I am put in such a position as will give me the necessary official authority in that regard'. He complained that the government's policy contained no constructive disarmament proposals comparable to an LNU scheme based on 25 per cent reduction in world arms expenditure over five years. As the president of a social movement, he could not satisfactorily represent a government at Geneva (though he later regretted that he had weakened his authority by resigning).[32]

The LNU constantly insisted that major international transactions be conducted through the League. But this did little to prevent 'secret diplomacy', the Geneva Assembly usually serving as platform for protestations of good faith by state representatives. Self-delusion seems to have affected Murray when he wrote to Bernard Shaw in 1938: '[i]t is practically impossible for a Foreign Minister, when questioned in the Assembly, to stand up before fifty-two nations and a hundred journalists and confess that his Government has been lying or behaving like a cad'. [33]

Arbitration

Clearly, however, liberal internationalists had never relied solely on moral force to normalise international relations, but also on conflict-resolution measures, technical mechanisms and deterrence. Thus, they supported the proposal of the League's Mixed Commission on Armaments for the Draft Treaty of Mutual Assistance of 1923, which would have required League members to send military assistance to a neighbouring victim of aggression – as a precursor of disarmament. [34] But, as with UN collective security, potential commitment scenarios were too unpredictable for states to accept.

Conservatives, sensitive to imperial defence, were more hostile than others to collective security commitments, but further controversy emerged when naval arms control talks with the United States collapsed in 1927 (see Chapter 4). Taking stock of the post-conference situation, liberal internationalists developed a twin policy. First, they insisted that there should be no retaliation in British shipyards. A few more US ships would not matter, whereas naval rivalry could only lead to bankruptcy and, according to a spokesman for the ILP, even to a war with the United States. [35] Second, disarmament should be tackled by conflict-resolution procedures. Arnold-Forster declared that the collapse of the conference 'would have at least one good result, in bringing people to the view the [LNU] has long maintained, as to the connection of disarmament with arbitration and security'. [36] Arbitration machinery would not only regulate international conduct per se, it would 'guarantee' the security necessary for states to disarm. Accordingly, the innovative 1924 Geneva Protocol enjoyed a period of popularity. The Protocol for the Peaceful Settlement of Disputes called for amendment of the Covenant to commit states to using the Permanent Court of International Justice and to binding arbitration procedures for conflict resolution, failing which League and Court rulings on aggressors would be supported by economic sanctions and military support to victims. All 47 League states signed the draft, but the Baldwin Government declined to ratify it.

Noel Baker initiated the revival of interest with a letter to the *Manchester Guardian* (31 August 1927), and Lord Parmoor and the Oxford historian R.B. Mowat urged Murray to promote it through the LNU. [37] The issue became significant as liberal internationalists tried to take advantage of the government's conference setback. For the LNU, it was partly a matter of expediency – as an additional lever in its campaign against the government's disarmament policies and to prevent some of its members drifting off into the Labour Party, which had taken the lead in support of the Protocol.[38] Ramsay MacDonald defended it, claiming that its sanction powers had no importance 'except in so far as their presence on paper is a harmless drug to soothe the nerves'.[39] After the Locarno Treaties, the notion of arbitration as a prop for collective security had hardly featured in LNU campaigning, until the autumn of 1927. Even now, Cecil had doubts about the value of resurrecting the Protocol as too technical for public opinion, and he had reservations about comprehensive arbitration. But here was an opportunity to bring Liberal and Labour into some kind of accord on the League.[40]

Liberals, however, were extremely reluctant to succumb, especially on a rather esoteric issue. Since January 1927, the party had revived under Sir Herbert Samuel's leadership. He had the use of Lloyd George's money to run 500 candidates at the next general election and discounted any possibility of an electoral pact with Labour.[41] The Protocol was an unwelcome distraction from the interventionist domestic platform which the Liberal leaders were erecting based on a report published as *Britain's Industrial Future* (1928). Cecil's resignation from the government had not been treated as a signal to make party capital out of foreign policy, in spite of the temptation to do so. Besides, the Protocol was controversial. The National Liberal Federation (NLF) had accepted it in 1925 as the best scheme for securing peace to date, but with the proviso that amendments to facilitate treaty revision be incorporated. The liberal *Manchester Guardian* (10 September 1927) praised Chamberlain's refusal to consider further British commitments. And as the author and former journalist J.A. Spender remarked, the Protocol would petrify the existing territorial arrangement of Europe to the advantage of France. It could only operate in an environment that rendered the guarantees unnecessary:

> it is obviously a different matter to shoulder these obligations in a heavily armed world exposed – in one part of it at all events – to the possibility of conflicts in which one or other of the disputants would be unlikely to accept arbitration, and in which all might be faced with the incursions of a Great Power not bound by any Protocol.[42]

LNU leaders found it difficult to generate support, and an extraordinary situation arose in which the Labour Party, whose attachment to the Protocol was at best ambiguous, had forced the LNU leaders, who liked it even less, to take it up and propose it to a wary Liberal Party. Few people on the left were committed to the Protocol – either because it would perpetuate French 'domination' in Europe or (in Cecil's case) because it would involve surrendering a free hand on matters of vital national interest, especially at sea. There is no clearer evidence that the movement had limits to its transgressions than in responses to the Protocol. Although the coalition of forces fostered basic conceptions of peace, unravelling these conceptions fostered political antagonisms that weakened its ability to trespass.

The LNU leadership had always made strenuous efforts to maintain a non-party image and to suppress contention within the movement. In contrast to the UDC's liberal–socialist partisanship, the LNU's discourse stressed the: 'honourable tradition that the main lines of foreign policy should be above party. Under the new circumstances of international life, the League of Nations Union is the custodian of that tradition'.[43] Cecil himself could hardly claim to be a good party man, but 1927 was a crucial year for the LNU. Taking a lead from Cecil's resignation letter, in which he catalogued the government's misdemeanours – refusal to accept the Protocol, unwillingness to sign the Optional Clause and failure to disarm – the LNU's tone grew more abrasive. It employed party organisation methods and attempted to distance itself from authority. It stretched its role as a mechanism of governmentality beyond supplying information and educating the public, into gingering the government. With half a million members, it strove to become a 'fourth estate' on foreign policy without breaking away from the elite club of governance. Rapport with the Conservatives suffered. From the end of 1927, J.C.C. Davidson (Conservative Party Chairman), Chamberlain and Lord Cushendun (who took Cecil's place in the government) charged the LNU with bias and attempting to dictate government policy. Cecil and Murray responded that the LNU was entitled to pass opinions on policy:

> [t]he reason why in many of the local Branches the lead has fallen into the hands of non-Conservatives is simply that the Conservatives are not, in point of fact, as keen for the League as other people. When you get down to the working classes I do not think that it is true, but...I am constantly appalled by the bloodthirsty and reactionary conversation of Belgravian tea-parties.[44]

Perhaps Cecil was up to his old tricks and angling for a centre coalition with moderate Labour and the Liberals, to enhance his status as the country's spokesman on League affairs. His approaches to the Liberal Party did bear fruit in mid-September 1927. Grey, Samuel and Lloyd George agreed to confer with the LNU on disarmament and arbitration. Cecil proposed that as a first step, disarmament should be achieved through adherence to the Optional Clause of the Permanent Court of International Justice. Less far-reaching and less controversial, unlike the Protocol, the Optional Clause provided only for *legal* disputes to go to arbitration. Even so, Grey and Lloyd George continued to protest at the League becoming a party issue, for such a strategy, as Lloyd George put it, would be 'childish and undignified'.[45] But pressure from rank-and-file Liberals removed any doubts about the popularity of doing otherwise. A joint manifesto produced by the NLF, the Women's Federation, and the Young Liberals in October urged four immediate peace measures: reference to The Hague of all legal disputes, the signing of arbitration treaties, the reduction of arms beyond 'the needs of the present situation', and a specific repudiation of naval competition with the United States. The Liberal Council Executive passed a similar resolution on arbitration but noted the desirability of a reservation on maritime law to protect the right of blockade. Despite his own misgivings, Lloyd George added a barb against Chamberlain for failing to see beyond Locarno:

> It is no use standing on the shores of Lake Maggiore, like a stork on one leg, looking preternaturally wise, and looking very satisfied because he has swallowed one trout ... Guaranteeing an eastern frontier of France may lead to war. Arbitration can lead to nothing but peace. Arbitration is the only base for disarmament.[46]

Divisions sharpened appreciably. Peace through collective security now became a contention about the limits of British obligations – with the majority of the movement firmly ranged against the government, which announced in Parliament that there was no possibility of Britain signing the Optional Clause. Chamberlain took a firm stance at the League's Geneva Assembly, not only rejecting the Optional Clause, but also, in what the *Daily Herald* (12 September 1927) called a sneering tone, talked of the League being a last resort after conventional diplomacy had failed. The entire Conservative press praised him: so-called gaps in the Covenant were 'spaces deliberately left to ease the strains' on the League structure. 'We cannot and will not', remarked *The Times* (3 December 1927), 'undertake obligations which we feel that we might not have the power to fulfil'. Britain would never surrender sovereignty on imperial issues. Other arguments betrayed isolationism. The Beaverbrook press consistently told its readers that Geneva was no more than an adjunct to the Quai d'Orsay. Rothermere's nostalgia for the Austro-Hungarian Empire led the *Daily Mail* (14 September 1927) to argue that it was the Little Entente of Czechoslovakia, Romania and Yugsolavia against Austro-Hungarian claims that had wanted military insurance from Britain 'against any revision of the treaties which gave them large accessions of territory to which they are not entitled'. Chamberlain had given reactionaries every encouragement.

He had also attracted renewed criticism by the liberal press for using the Empire as a cloak for base motives, which suggested that government feared arbitration 'might appear remotely to endanger our irregular position in Egypt'.[47] This conjecture resonated with critics. The Admiralty was anxious to safeguard the Suez Canal; but Grey quashed his declaration of 1895 that Britain's interests covered the whole Nile waterway, and now thought that Britain had no business in Egypt and that the canal ought to be under League control.[48] As to the government's sophistry about Dominion objections to the Optional Clause, Canada and the Irish Free State were willing to sign; New Zealand generally left foreign policy to Britain; only Australia was hostile. In any case, the Empire had not prevented Chamberlain from signing the Locarno Treaties.

On the other hand, proponents of the Optional Clause argued, arbitration promised to help with the age-old problem of defining aggression. An aggressor could be determined as a state 'which commits an act of war while refusing arbitration', though, as Noel Baker pointed out, a state which refused arbitration might not start a subsequent war even if it were forced to join in.[49] Adherence to the Optional Clause also promised to curb British indecision by having decisions thrust on it by arbitrators.[50] More generally, liberal internationalists envisaged an extension of the rule of law (of particular importance to Britain, so they argued, because of its global interests). Sir John Simon, for example, said that as far as disputes susceptible to judicial treatment were concerned, the Permanent Court would build up a body of international case law.[51] Above all, the Optional Clause would close the 'gap' in the Covenant which 'allowed' a state to go to war if a dispute remained unresolved by the League Council.

Such ideas about commitment and security figured prominently in debate. But were the coalition factions as diametrically opposed as the discourses indicate? Clearly, differences surfaced on the place of the League in imperial policy. Conservatives preferred to meet Dominion representatives in London rather than in Geneva. But the LNU's Special General Council in October 1927 took into account the national and imperial interests that Tories wanted to protect. It supported adherence to the Optional Clause 'with any reservations that may be necessary to provide for the special position of this country'.[52] Many of the government's leading critics were not unalterably opposed to this. During the drafting of the Covenant, Cecil had objected to arbitration, on the grounds that Britain should be free to fight for what was right, and even now in the late 1920s he frequently hinted at exceptionalism: 'I should be quite willing to see our acceptance of the optional clause accompanied by a reservation as to any particular class of dispute as to which we might be in a disadvantageous position'. Fresh from his experience early in 1927 as chair of a Committee of Imperial Defence (CID) charged with supervising a blockade against Chinese nationalists, this was hardly surprising. And when Chamberlain told an LNU deputation in June 1928 that there would have to be a proviso to cover the Britain's exceptional status, Murray agreed. On the whole, the LNU held that two reservations might be justified – where the parties agreed to accept some other 'arbitral method', say through the Privy Council, and in disputes relating to naval matters (because British prize law differed from that of other countries).[53]

Ironically, in view of his assurances about prize law and the Empire, Cecil found himself in the 1929 Labour Government working with two men who were reluctant to admit any reservations at all. Henderson and Dalton advocated ratification of the Optional Clause in opposition to Whitehall officials, the Australian government, and also MacDonald, who thought that 'the Liberals would pounce'. Henderson told Foreign Office staff that Labour was completely opposed to the previous administration.[54] Eventually, the Dominions agreed to sign the Clause at the forthcoming League Assembly, provided that talks on reservations were held before ratification. The Admiralty received assurances that an enemy could not take Britain to the Permanent Court of Justice in wartime and that prize law would be unaffected. The three reservations – concerning inter-Dominion disputes, matters falling exclusively within British jurisdiction and those covered by alternative machinery – did much to quell the Conservative opposition and were perhaps less far-reaching than the LNU and the Liberals would have been prepared to accept.

The most striking aspect of the whole controversy was the extent to which political manoeuvres had made the wings of liberal internationalist coalition appear further apart than in reality. In the last months of the previous government, Balfour (as Chair of the Belligerent Rights

Sub-Committee of the CID) had worked on a limited form of compulsory arbitration.[55] In Parliament, Chamberlain's amendment to ratification in September 1929 called for an additional reservation about laws of war at sea but acknowledged that the House was divided not in kind but in degree. Conservatives expressed general satisfaction at the reservations. Marginalised opposition came from the *Morning Post* (4 September 1929), which differed as much from Chamberlain's view as Chamberlain's did from Henderson's in railing against the surrender of liberty: '[a]n English King declined to kiss the toe of the Emperor; an English Church refused to accept its orders from the Pope. England has fought not one, but several wars rather than submit to any Continental domination'. A similar pattern of attitudes arose over the General Act (which extended arbitration procedure to non-legal disputes). The MacDonald Government adhered to it in 1931 with the support of the Dominions (bar South Africa), though ratification was made conditional on completion of a disarmament convention. Chamberlain again resorted to niggling, and opposed the Act on the grounds that it would diminish the authority of the League – a sophistry that nationalists and left-wingers alike had no difficulty deriding.[56] But the Act aroused little interest and the columns of *Headway* failed to give it much publicity.

It was not simply that the economic crisis had eclipsed questions of foreign policy. Liberal internationalists had relaxed their pressure for arbitration after Labour came to power. The party had already announced a full-blooded commitment to strengthening the League in its policy statement of 1928, *Labour and the Nation*. This differed hardly a jot from LNU policy, and prior to the 1929 General Election, Cecil advised electors to vote for those candidates who supported a strong League. Privately, he confessed to Grey: 'I could not honestly advise people to vote for the Conservatives, for I am uneasy as to their recent conduct in foreign affairs and feel that another five years of invertebrate action at Geneva might seriously endanger the League'. Subsequently, Cecil rejoiced in Labour's victory, which also gave him a role.[57] David Carlton argues that the 1929 vote for Labour may have been due partly to the Tory record in foreign affairs since the League Council crisis of 1926. He cites in particular the universally unpopular Anglo-French Naval Compromise of 1928 (see Chapter 4) as a major blunder.[58] Nevertheless, the arbitration campaign in the late summer of 1927 can be considered the beginning of the post-Locarno recrimination that turned peace into a party issue. The collapse of the Geneva Naval Conference had led internationalists to demand guarantees that would enable states to disarm. They revived the Protocol, and leading figures in the LNU begin to canvass support for arbitration and a means of cementing the various elements of centre-left internationalism in opposition to the government. Yet a fundamental consensus about interstate conduct is still discernible beneath the party divides.

The Kellogg–Briand Pact

To some extent, the US–French initiative to renounce war in the Kellogg–Briand Pact of August 1928 (eventually signed by over 50 states) also became a political issue within the movement. Initially, few apart from the Round Table group took it seriously. In view of the subsequent reification of the Pact by liberal internationalists, especially during the 1931 Manchurian crisis, reactions ranged from the patronising to the derogatory. Observers as divergent in outlook as the UDC's H.N. Brailsford and the militarist Sir Maurice Hankey expressed scepticism. To Brailsford, the proposal was so much hot air and no substitute for the Protocol; to Hankey, it was a fraud perpetrated while the United States was invading Nicaragua.[59] For Cecil, the declaration had no arbitration and conciliation machinery and tolerated war in self-defence (the justification for most wars). He simply disliked any proposal that detracted from the Covenant. Grey also thought the proposal worthless because of US isolationism: '[t]hey always reserve "the Monroe doctrine" which is not a Treaty or a doctrine at all, but a Policy: it is in fact, whatever the U.S.A. chooses to say it is'.[60] The Liberal press reflected the wariness. From November 1927 to the summer of 1928, for example, the *Manchester Guardian* maintained that the Pact had no provision for removing the underlying causes of war. It did nothing for disarmament or conflict resolution and could be likened to an abstainer taking the pledge: '[t]he pledge is a help, a reminder to his conscience and a solemn act of resolution. The pledge to renounce war is no more. Who can say which pledges will be kept and which will be dishonoured?'[61]

This appraisal accompanied shrewd suspicions about US motives; electoral considerations seemed to lurk behind the anxiety of the Republicans to appear pacific. Murray interpreted 'outlawing war' as a distraction from US naval expansion: '[t]he one way open to America without America admitting that Europe had done better than she had in the way of peace was this proposal for the complete renunciation of war'.[62] It was outrageous for the Americans to celebrate the outlawry of war whilst engaged on a cruiser-building programme.

However, scepticism gave way completely by the summer of 1928 as Kellogg's proposal caught the public imagination. Left-wing internationalists began to show greater enthusiasm as the government procrastinated. Earlier scepticism turned into anxiety and then rigorous criticism of the government's silence.[63] When Chamberlain did respond in May 1928, his reservations provoked dismay – particularly one that asserted freedom of action in 'certain regions of the world the welfare and integrity of which constitute the special and vital interest for our peace and safety'. It challenged the League Covenant, allowing Britain to indulge in a 'private' war or blockade. Reflecting the movement's pique, the *Manchester Guardian* (7 August 1928) developed a new concern for the 'pledge' it had previously dismissed:

> the case for Germany's right to invade Belgium in 1914 is complete.
>
> A treaty originally and quite sincerely intended to prohibit resort to war has been twisted into an agreement which gives its signatories the unqualified right to declare war on their own unsupported assertion that it is a war of self-defence ... No one will suppose that either M. Briand or Sir Austen Chamberlain is consciously disloyal to the Covenant. Yet they have gone out of their way to give to the Kellogg Pact an interpretation which if applied to the Covenant would destroy it.

Labour went further and saw in Chamberlain's attitude evidence that the Tories wanted a free hand in places that in the twenty-first century continued to appeal to interventionists: the Persian oilfields, in Arab states generally and in Afghanistan. Ironically, the interventions conducted a century later on behalf of an imagined 'international community' had general Labour support. The earlier critics refused to join in the popular euphoria when the Pact was signed in August 1928. The left objected to a ruse by the vanguard of modern capitalism where a red scare had been in full swing. A cartoon in the ILP's *New Leader* (24 August 1928) depicted the ghosts of Sacco and Vanzetti (the New England anarchist immigrants executed after a gross miscarriage of justice), hovering behind the figure of US Secretary of State Frank Kellogg as he signed the Pact.

By contrast, the Pact's one redeeming feature for nationalists was its acknowledgement of special interests and the right of self-defence. Rivalries and antagonisms between states would not be abated by a simple declaration on standards of international conduct; but at least Kellogg had provided the necessary loopholes. As the *Morning Post* (20 July 1928) put it, 'this treaty commits nobody to anything he would ever confess to doing, we can hardly suppose that the most ardent "non interventionist" will object to it'. Imperialists acclaimed it as a counter-vailing measure to Locarno and the Covenant.

Privately, some LNU leaders also thought it reasonable to protect the rights of self-defence and vital interests. As Murray explained to the historian and diplomat Sir Charles Webster: 'I think the vague imperial Monro[e] doctrine well grounded but exceedingly dangerous. If admitted at all as a purely national right, it ought to be very strictly limited. I really feel rather nervous about the whole situation'.[64] Vice-Admiral Drury-Lowe, similarly nervous about Chamberlain's reservations, thought he should have left unsaid the right to protect certain territories, as this would fall automatically under self-defence.[65] But the reservations issue was useful in berating the government, and when Noel Buxton forwarded £200 for the LNU's pro-Pact campaign suggesting that the movement concentrate on magnifying the Pact's value rather than on criticising the government, Cecil replied that it was possible to do both.[66]

Ultimately the liberal internationalist movement ignored the reservations in order to promote the Kellogg–Briand Pact as a moral gesture for peace. Correspondents in *Headway* hailed it as an end to private wars. Wilson Harris, its Quaker editor, wrote that 'the predominant feeling must be one of profound gratitude' to Kellogg and US President Calvin Coolidge. He even took the risk offending Cecil in claiming that it would be unfortunate if anyone created the impression that renunciation of war should be put on the less-important level of 'choosing certain particular methods of settling international disputes'. Despite the reservations, or 'explanations' as they were known, most liberal internationalists agreed that the spirit of the Pact meant more than the letter. Grey qualified his earlier opinion and hoped that the Pact would be signed: '[i]ts value is not so much in its words as in the fact that the demand for it is evidence of the set of public opinion for Peace and against War'.[67]

In contrast to their earlier distrust of US motives, commentators stressed the importance of US involvement in Europe: 'a new and glorious vista has opened up. The United States of America has come back into the peace movement'.[68] The ground had been well prepared by the *Daily News & Westminster Gazette*, a strong campaigner for an instrument 'more stringent that the League Covenant ... [that would] make war a contingency more remote than it has ever been since the Armistice', with the United States offering 'to come in and play a noble part in saving the democracy of the world from the consequences of its own follies, blunders and passionate prejudices'.[69] Since many, if not most, Americans regarded the move as a plate in the armour of isolation, to accompany the new cruisers, this was stretching things a bit far.

While a New Jerusalem remained a long way off, internationalists nevertheless anticipated a new psychological atmosphere – public opinion having 'fastened upon it as one of the great imaginative gestures of all time'.[70] A gesture, certainly, but in 1928 few could have predicted the revolution needed to end US isolation.

Critics obviously found it more difficult to make political capital out of the Kellogg Pact than out of the Optional Clause. Labour's scepticism not only went against the tide, it was also potentially divisive if, as pacifists and the NCPW hoped, support for the Kellogg–Briand Pact was the start of a more redoubtable peace politics. The party turned away and campaigned on disarmament and arbitration. Furthermore, LNU leaders and the Liberal Party shared official qualms. Many of them had suspected the idea originally, felt it expedient to support it against the government's reservations (with which they basically agreed) and finally embraced it as an imaginative moral gesture. There is little evidence to suggest that LNU leaders thought US policy had changed; they spent much of 1929 and part of 1930 investigating the compatibility of the Pact with the Covenant.

After its success in creating interest in arbitration procedures, the LNU was now distracted by the Round Table liberal imperialists, who argued that the Eurocentric security system should be made compatible with US isolationism. Throughout 1929, the LNU's leaders strived to safeguard the Covenant from those who preferred reliance on an 'unenforcible Pact'. According to internationalists, any concern that the Pact might affect the legitimate use of force to defend Locarno or the Covenant could be discounted, because any state which broke these other security schemes *ipso facto* broke a treaty renouncing war, and thereby released the other signatories to the Pact.[71] In effect, the LNU added its own reservation and resurrected the question of League sanctions. Article 16 of the Covenant – which provided for non-military sanctions and military recommendations against a member resorting to war in breach of the Covenant – was to be the crux of the problem which separated the Round Table group from the main body of the LNU leadership.

A Round Table stalwart, Philip Kerr, who joined the LNU Executive early in 1929, decided that the United States had emerged from isolation and waged a private crusade to have the Pact taken more seriously than as a mere 'international kiss'. He proposed a scheme to 'put the Pact into the Covenant' by eliminating parts of the Covenant that permitted war.[72] Otherwise, it would be difficult to encourage US cooperation. But after working on an LNU sub-committee, he concluded that it would be better to keep the two instruments distinct; the LNU Executive reported that 'from the legal standpoint [amendment] would involve far-reaching changes, difficult, if not impossible, to carry ... the signatories of the two instruments are not the same, and although the Treaties do not conflict, it seems best to keep the obligations thereby created as concurrent obligations, rather than try to make them identical'.[73] Kerr then proposed conflict resolution machinery for the Pact signatories. The LNU substituted this with a proposal to require states (including the United States) to submit questions of self-defence to the League. This was too radical for Kerr, and both he and Cecil were quite happy to let the matter drop, on the grounds that official Anglo-American negotiations on the Pact were in progress.[74]

There the matter would have rested had not the Labour Government reopened the debate by submitting amendments to the League Assembly in September 1929 (with a proposal that would have introduced the sanctions of Article 16 to the Pact). Drury-Lowe explained that because the United States had signed the Pact and a maritime conflict with Britain was ruled out, it could participate in collective security. The United States should be pinned down and made to accept Article 16.[75] This provoked sharp reactions from the internationalists, who deplored the Versailles system and the notion that the Covenant could be involved to enforce it. Delisle Burns of the UDC commented that the United States would never accept 'the French view' of security, and wanted the LNU to reject it, too.[76] Atlanticists simply dismissed sanctions. Kerr noted that if it came to a choice, 'we must go with the United States and the Empire, but I have by no means given up hope that if we stick to the proposition we shall gradually bring the two within the nucleus of a single international system'. The main obstacle was France, 'constitutionally incapable' of understanding anything but arms: '[t]he trouble is that the League fanatics, including, I am afraid, Bob Cecil, are so intoxicated with their worship of Geneva that they are always lending themselves to French propaganda'.[77]

The Kellogg–Briand Pact threatened to open up Versailles sores. Few students of international affairs denied that the Versailles system needed revision in Germany's favour. But there was a clear distinction between those such as Cecil who believed in first securing the operation of international regulations and procedures within the given conditions of Europe, and those such as Kerr who believed that the system could be changed with the United States in tow as a counterweight to France. Cecil had no patience with this. The United States would be more of a problem in the League than out, and the attempt to put the

Pact into the Covenant was mischievous, since its aim was to weaken the League's 'peacekeeping apparatus'. As for Kerr's curious 'will-o'-the-wisp' of summoning a conference of the Pact signatories to deal with a threat to peace: '[s]uch folly seems to me worthy of Alexander I of Russia'.[78] Although expectations of the League were fanciful, at least most of its British supporters read the temper of US policy correctly. The Pact added little to Kerr's meagre hopes for Commonwealth–United States unity. In the end, both groups feared Covenant revision. Cecil and Murray dismissed its dilution simply to please the United States. Those anxious to involve the United States feared that altering the Covenant might be misinterpreted as an attempt to embroil it in Europe. The LNU Executive compromised and supported the League's Sciajola Committee, which recommended that the Pact and Covenant be made 'verbally compatible' with the proviso that a disarmament convention should precede any changes. As the next chapter shows, it proved impossible to square this particular circle.

Conclusion

In the late 1920s, peace issues were not dramatic, but aroused the interest of lawyers and educators in the movement for a liberal international order. In 1926, the LNU was only half the size it was to become by 1932; the peace groups were small-scale; the main parties were immersed in domestic matters and anti-bolshevism; and except on the question of disarmament, the demands on liberal internationalism were not great. Internationalists were preoccupied with procedural restraints in foreign affairs. They contended that higher standards of conduct between states could be achieved, not by force, but through the establishment of ethical conduct in the formation and execution of foreign policy, and through 'paper guarantees' for international arbitration and the outlawry of war. If public opinion could be mobilised and the rulebook of international relations amended, governments would abide by international norms, and the prospects for disarmament would increase. A peace could result from new methods for dealing with international conduct.

Party-political factors were increasingly important in debates on peace from the end of 1927. But neither the political disputes nor disputes about the precise limitation of Britain's international commitments were seriously debilitating to an umbrella organisation such as the LNU, despite the harsh words that passed between Cecil and the Conservative Party. The differences between sections of the liberal internationalist movement were largely differences, as Chamberlain said, in degree rather than in kind. In part, this reflected the role of liberal internationalism in providing a tool of governmentality, and they were half in and half out of government. Their situation was conducive to the making of policy suggestions to the government of the day, and to indulging in post-crisis recriminations that were to increase in intensity as prospects for collective security deteriorated. To many internationalists, the real test of paper guarantees would be the willingness of governments to reduce armaments. In any case, there were limits to the value of international restraints through open diplomacy, arbitration, moral force and declarations of peaceful intent. As Dalton noted in closing his diary for 1930: 'there is a fear in Europe and Old Adam stalketh in the noonday. We go on signing new bits of paper, but who believes in the undertakings they enshrine?'[79] Disarmament would be the next key to peace.

4
Disarmament: White Robes of Peace or Jackboots and Spurs?

By the late 1920s, disarmament had become central to all liberal internationalist campaigns aimed at strengthening collective security. For the movement, it was a more tangible peace issue than the esoteric problems of paper guarantees, though the military communities claimed higher expertise. While a minority advocated unilateral disarmament, most favoured arms limitation agreements (the term 'arms control' having no currency). Organisers of parties and pressure groups had no difficulty in drumming up support for disarmament rallies. Most sections of the movement came to fix their hopes for peace on the successful conclusion of a comprehensive treaty. Consequently, the collapse of the General Disarmament Conference in 1934, though not unexpected, would be disastrous. The transit of internationalism through disarmament became a party issue. But political contention was muted, and a Three-Party Disarmament Committee reached consensus in 1931, not only on an arms convention but also on the limits for Britain. However, as preparatory negotiations between the military powers reached deadlock in 1931, the campaign grew more frenetic and leaders adapted their policies in ways that could only divide opinion. The dimensions of agreement on disarmament, the impulses and strains that moulded it, constitute the chapter's content.

The chapter begins with the ethical, economic and security discourses of disarmers. The doctrine of imperial requirements for maintaining sea power is discussed as an issue raised by the 1927 Geneva Naval Conference in the second part. With the advent of Labour to power in 1929 and consensus on weapons limitation rather than disarmament, the liberal internationalists broadly accepted a compromise in 1930 for limitations on cruisers. The final section shows how Germany's claims and the Labour Government's disintegration in the economic crisis provided conditions for serious splits in the governmentality of liberal internationalism and the rise of a resistant mass peace movement.

Ethical, economic and security rationales

Few liberal internationalists disagreed with avoiding or limiting a military commitment to continental Europe. Even among reactionaries, only a minority, such as Lt.-Gen. Archibald Montgomery-Massingberd (Chief of Imperial General Staff, 1933–36), agitated for a substantial army to avoid the kind of military neglect that had followed Waterloo.[1] But army expansion in the war had been a temporary expedient, and few objected when the regular forces were decimated and reverted to 'peacekeeping' in turbulent parts of the Empire. The core of liberal internationalists regarded the League of Nations as a substitute for a large military force. Their faith coincided with the priorities of the followers of Milner, Churchill and Baldwin's colonial secretary, Leo Amery, who wanted Britain to renounce an interest in the continent in order to maintain relations with the Empire at a time when the Dominions were wresting greater autonomy from Westminster. By contrast, these imperialists adhered rigidly to naval power to protect trade routes and communications. Nevertheless, this did not prevent the majority of conservatives accepting a limitation on the navy's cruiser strength under the terms of the 1930 London Naval Agreement. In 1932, First Lord of the Admiralty, Sir Bolton Eyres-Monsell, introduced the lowest naval estimates in 19 years. Imperialists also believed in the creation of an air deterrent as an alternative to a British Expeditionary Force. As demonstrated in Chapter 5, successive governments considered the air arm to be an exceptional case. Even the 1924 Labour Government had not taken risks with this new and relatively cheap branch of the services. All the same, the fulfilment of a 1923 air programme for 52 home defence squadrons proceeded at a snail's pace under all administrations.

Disarmers could always pose the question: weapons against what and whom? It was beyond the ability of most commentators to envisage Germany as a threat. Nor did France feature as a potential enemy, though French policy seemed to jeopardise peace in Europe. The most likely threat to the Empire, as visualised by the Committee for Imperial Defence (CID), was a Soviet threat to Afghanistan and India.[2] Nothing could have been further from Joseph Stalin's mind, but in the hands of the *Daily Mail*, strident anti-Soviet agitation functioned primarily to denigrate the left. With the German fleet scuttled, the main challenges at sea came from the United States and Japan. The former could effortlessly out-build

Britain, and, anyway, no one seriously contemplated a transatlantic war. By contrast, the service chiefs refused to discount a Japanese threat and pressed for early completion of the Singapore base in the annual review of 1926. But the CID had already accepted Austen Chamberlain's opinion that war with Japan in the next ten years 'was not a contingency to be seriously apprehended'.[3] Churchill also dismissed the possibility and, on 5 July 1928, the cabinet adopted his rolling policy assumption, subject to annual review, that Britain would not go to war for ten years except to put down rebels. The decline of Britain's armed services in the 1920s is, thus, understandable in view of the absence of a clearly identifiable threat. The main predicament confronting internationalists concerned sea power and naval requirements for imperial defence. But against this unknowable quantity, they could deploy a trinity of ethical, economic and Eurocentric security discourses.

Liberal internationalists took their ethical cue from the undertaking by the victors at Versailles to work for general disarmament, given and backed by a French private assurance to the Germans. 'We cannot get out of the fact', wrote Cecil, 'that we – the Entente Allies – have repeatedly said that a general scheme of disarmament was to follow German disarmament and that that was a condition of their accepting the disarmament clauses of the Treaty of Versailles'.[4] Although at Versailles Cecil and Lloyd George had focused almost entirely on disarming Germany, failure to honour the promise could have fateful repercussions. Noel Baker prophesied as early as 1927 that the several million men in Germany who underwent wartime training could answer a summons to secure equal military status for their country.[5] Disarmers took up the point more forcefully in the early 1930s, but the perils of dishonour were not evident to many in the 1920s, and not as dire as the dangers of prodigal public expenditure.

In a climate of economic orthodoxy, all governments in the interwar period struggled to keep total public spending to a minimum, usually below 15 per cent of GNP (as opposed to a pre-war average of about 12 per cent). Defence expenditure in the 1920s was generally less in real terms than in 1913. There was little protest. In the parliamentary debate on the Army Estimates in March 1926, speakers on all sides complimented Sir Laming Worthington-Evans (Secretary of State for War) on his achievement in reducing the budget by £2 million (£100 million at 2012 prices) – though Clydeside MPs agitated for further reductions. Even military experts supported economies. Referring to a £500,000 cut in the 1928 estimates, *Army Quarterly*'s editor remarked: 'urgent economy is necessary and the Secretary of State for War and his colleagues on the Army Council are to be congratulated upon having effected a reduction in expenditure of the Army'.[6] The respective merits of horse and armour, and the cavalry relinquishing the lance, seem to have been the main causes of dispute.[7]

Widespread agreement for austerity also applied to the naval estimates. One Liberal MP thought the saving of £2.5 million for 1926–27 insufficient and called for a further reduction, on the grounds that Britain could not keep pace with US naval expenditure, anyway.[8] Churchill, as Baldwin's Chancellor of the Exchequer, took draconian measures that brought him into sharp conflict with the Admiralty.[9] But it would be difficult to choose between interwar chancellors (Churchill, Philip Snowden and Neville Chamberlain) for parsimony. As Lt.-Cmdr Kenworthy remarked, 'if the World Disarmament Conference were attended only by Finance Ministers and Treasury officials from the various countries, reinforced by presidents of the Central Banks, its success would be assured'.[10]

Moreover, it was not simply a case of satisfying Treasury accountants: there were social benefits to be considered, and prodigal expenditure on war could be diverted to social services.[11] Tories were unsympathetic, proposing an overall decrease in taxation, whereas Liberals argued that arms expenditure adversely affected the general level of prosperity. The Liberal Party expressly linked arms expenditure to the economic slump, resolving at their conference in May 1931 that 'high expenditure upon armaments and high tariffs are among the main causes of the present world crisis, and their reduction essential to the world's peace and prosperity'.[12] Academic economists held this view, too. A.L. Bowley, F.W. Hirst and J.E. Allen stressed that war produced nothing but devastation, debt and economic waste, and Sir Josiah Stamp calculated that the abolition of arms expenditure would increase the standard of living by ten per cent.[13] This analysis gained publicity through Francis W. Hirst – editor of *The Economist* (1907–16) and survivor of the Cobden Club which had published *The Burden of Armaments* (1905). Hirst's new tract, *Armaments: The Race and the Crisis* (1937), admitted, however, that vast wartime expenditure on arms had increased employment. Indeed, A.C. Pigou recognised that spacing out government contracts had a counter-cyclical impact. Similarly, when Keynes developed his theory of government pump priming as a stimulus to aggregate demand, he could hardly avoid concluding that failing anything else, war preparations represented investment stimulus.[14] But classical economics also meshed well with liberal internationalist policy. In 1932, prominent economists, including Sir William Beveridge (director of the LSE), T.E.G. Gregory (professor of Social Economics at Manchester University),

Sir George Paish (a wartime adviser to the Chancellor of the Exchequer) and J.A. Hobson, supported Hirst in a campaign for '[t]he lightening of the crushing burden of taxation due to excessive armaments'.[15]

Opponents of large-scale disarmament frequently goaded their critics about the social consequences of cancelling arms contracts.[16] But Conservative governments had presided over the inevitable contraction of war industries. Labour MPs who represented munitions or shipbuilding constituencies faced greater dilemmas. Unemployment in some shipyards reached 60 per cent in the Depression, though not entirely due to disarmament. Yet the trade unions, also, had a commitment to arms reduction. Ben Turner (chair of the TUC in 1928) argued that: 'it is cheaper to pension all employees fully and well...than to continue this unholy system of living on making killing machinery'.[17] In view of the critical economic conditions, there was little chance of men being pensioned off 'fully and well', and given the determination of chancellors not to raise taxation or borrowing, defence cuts would have added only marginally to the revenue available for welfare purposes. Despite the political sparring, however, all parties agreed about the economic propriety of disarmament. From time to time, liberal internationalists feared that the economic argument would overshadow the ethical case. But disarmers generally found the economic justifications not only useful but intrinsically sound. Liberal economic doctrine and ethical internationalism were traditionally bound together, and to have acknowledged any economically beneficial ramifications of defence expenditure would have been tantamount to bestowing moral approval on war preparations.

Furthermore, liberal internationalists said that the true cost of armaments lay in the international unrest and insecurity they perpetuated. The pre-war arms race had increased tension between states and created a mood of fatalism in ruling elites and populations. A mechanistic theory of war, supported by G.L. Dickinson's *The International Anarchy* (1926), complemented the liberal belief that man was neither stupid nor irrational enough to seek war. Unsurprisingly, politicians who had directed foreign policy in the early twentieth century fully endorsed the 'international anarchy' thesis. Grey, for example, lifted responsibility from his own shoulders in suggesting that '[t]he enormous growth of armaments in Europe, the sense of insecurity and fear caused by them – it was these that made war inevitable'.[18] His pronouncement passed into the realm of historical truth. Noel Baker, the foremost exponent of disarmament between the wars, described Grey's 'evidence' as 'conclusive', and Dalton referred to Grey's 'respectable platitude'.[19] Possession of arms meant *ipso facto* that other powers felt insecure; this encouraged competition strained international relations and led to war. The crucial value of disarmament would also lie in its contribution to peace-as-collective security. Liberal internationalists regarded the two as coupled rather than as contradictory.

All shades of opinion in the social movement spoke confidently about attempting to reduce arms. French security fears were said to have been appeased; Germany would disarm in accordance with Versailles; continued investment in munitions would merely create unnecessary tension. Anxious to show positive results from the Locarno Treaties, Conservatives emphasised the clause which promised to hasten disarmament, as provided for in Article 8 of the League Covenant. The King's Speech in Parliament in February 1926 mentioned the prospect of *'a substantial step forward in the direction of disarmament'* [original emphasis], though no specific proposals were announced. Liberal internationalists commonly regarded disarmament by France and Britain as the true test of Locarno's acceptability. Lloyd George remarked: 'The Treaty of Locarno, without disarmament, is simply a steel trap with very tricky springs which may one day snap with crushing teeth'.[20] Sir Samuel Hoare (Minister for Air) introduced the 1926 air estimates as a deceleration of expansion justified by Locarno.[21] Chamberlain's diplomacy, then, had improved the international environment sufficiently to make disarmament possible.

Imperial requirements: the Geneva Naval Conference

Clearly, however, Conservatives listened to the advice of the Admiralty on issues of imperial security. Its advice dominated the Government's approach to the Geneva Naval Conference in July 1927, and stirred dispute among naval and political commentators. The Admiralty fixed its minimum cruiser requirements at 55 small and 15 large cruisers (existing numbers were 43 and 11, respectively). It resisted parity with the United States in large cruisers with 8-inch guns, unless it could gain superiority in the smaller vessels mounted with 6-inch guns. US superiority in large cruisers might also encourage Japan to augment its fleet with larger ships.[22] Under Churchill's baton, with the Navy League and much of the press singing loudly, the Conservative Party Conference in October unanimously approved a motion praising the Baldwin Government's refusal to limit potential naval strength.[23] The pro-Japanese *Morning Post* (5 August 1927) criticised Cecil's effort to 'tamper' with British security merely to get an agreement with the United States. Likewise, the *Daily Mail* (30 July 1927), pausing in its crusade against the enfranchisement of 'socialist flappers', joined the Beaverbrook press in arguing that Britain should pursue a naval policy suited to its own requirements.

To some extent, non-Tory internationalists agreed, though they later held the Admiralty responsible for the collapse of the talks. The *Daily Chronicle* (5 August 1927) admitted that Britain's case for 70 cruisers was wholly reasonable, generally supported the government's line and featured the former First Lord Reginald McKenna's contention that whilst armies could be improvised rapidly, it took years to train sailors. Grey hedged. He acknowledged that Britain should have a navy sufficient to protect its interests, but he provided no answer to the crucial questions – what kind of navy and of what size?[24] Nor did Cecil, who, as noted in the previous chapter, resigned from the government over the cabinet's subservience to imperial requirements doctrine. Yet he had warned Noel Baker not to underestimate Britain's needs and did not think that European peace would be safer with the fleet eliminated.[25] He still baulked at the Admiralty's conditions for granting parity to the United States, but his own position was ambiguous. His resignation, which he delayed for a month after the conference, surprised Austen Chamberlain.[26] Cecil may have been primarily anxious to avoid being associated with the failure of the negotiations. No doubt he was sensitive to taunts that the power and prestige of the League of Nations partly depended on the efficiency of the Royal Navy. But the explanation lies in his attempted compromise. He wanted to secure universal, general disarmament under British leadership, though not by yielding British power too cheaply. Before the Naval Conference met he had expressed doubt about the value of a limited agreement in one particular kind of armament. He favoured a general convention and told MacDonald that 'a relatively weak British Army must be balanced by a relatively strong Royal Navy, lest an undue share of international authority should pass into the hands of the Continental powers'. Before Britain reduced its naval strength, other states should agree to reduce their land and air forces.[27] The president of the LNU was, therefore, less out of sympathy with his Conservative colleagues on disarmament than he sometimes claimed. His reasoning tried to make the best of both worlds: retention of British naval strength as a bargaining counter, and the prospect of a treaty for wholesale disarmament. On the basis of a limited commitment, Britain would, nevertheless, remain an independent power in the international system.

By contrast, Noel Baker led a full-blown assault on imperial requirements doctrine. Seventy cruisers would not provide adequate security at all and, after deducting a number required for battle duties and those undergoing refits, some 33 would have to patrol 80,000 miles of trade routes – or one per 2,500 miles. It would be more sensible to agitate for a decrease in potentially hostile raiders, since cutting other navies would give British 'armed merchantmen' greater superiority. Against Cecil he also argued that if Britain failed to take a lead and reduce its navy, others would justify holding on to their comparative advantages. In addition, requirements doctrine simply discounted collective security; other countries would help protect Britain's trade routes in any crisis.[28] Confident about the prospect for naval coalitions, Noel Baker did not indicate how many cruisers Britain should possess for League obligations – which were even less susceptible to doctrine than imperial defence.

The movement's disarmament campaign

Such difficulties were brushed aside and, like arbitration, disarmament became a centrepiece of internationalist campaigning, a social movement agitation that culminated in the emotive Albert Hall rallies of the early 1930s. Despite Cecil's ambiguity on the question of British naval power, the LNU advised a 'drastic' reduction in the number of warships, and formulated proposals for an 'Ocean Locarno' between Britain, Japan and the United States. Between October 1927 and January 1928, the LNU held well over a thousand public meetings on disarmament, and the dull if informative *Headway* became more polemical in tone. The disarmament campaign was not yet sensational or enlivened by tracts denouncing the private profiteering in weapons, but the mileage to be gained from publicising the government's failings seemed increasingly attractive. The Liberal Party participated with a spate of pamphleteering, with the Liberal MP Geoffrey Mander predicting that the League would increasingly figure as a party issue because Britain's record at Geneva was so bad.[29] Rank-and-file Liberals grew impatient. At the NLF Conference in 1928, they baulked at a resolution calling for 'the reduction of our own armaments to the lowest limit compatible with national safety' and amended it with a demand for an 'immediate and substantial reduction of our own armaments in accordance with the spirit of our undertaking in the Covenant of the League of Nations, the Locarno Treaty, and the Kellogg Pact'.[30] Moreover, the Round Table group joined in the disapproval of what J.L. Garvin in *The Observer* (13 May 1928) called the Admiralty's 'pig-tailed pedantry', and insisted on concessions to cement the Anglo-American bond.

Labour pressed home the charge in Parliament with what amounted to a vote of no-confidence in the government's handling of talks with the

United States, MacDonald arguing that 70 cruisers would be inadequate protection against submarine raiders, anyway.[31] In its 1929 election manifesto *Labour and the Nation*, the party prescribed arms reductions 'to the minimum required for maintaining national and international order'. It dissatisfied those who demanded a definite pledge that within a year of coming to power a Labour Government would urge a League plan for complete and universal disarmament. But with the General Election imminent, the party concentrated mainly on condemning Tory foreign policy. Sir Oswald Mosley, Labour MP, delivered a powerful speech which, in view of his subsequent politics, is worth citing. Conservative warmongers, he claimed, were 'dressing up in the white robes of peace', but 'lift the corner of the robe and [socialists] would see the jackboots and spurs'.[32] The government hedged. Labour placed unspecified limits on Britain's disarmament. Liberals made no attempt to specify the number of cruisers in each class 'required' by Britain's international role, albeit complaining that the Admiralty's figure of 70 was too high. Factions of liberal internationalism may have differed on naval disarmament, but it was patently impossible for anyone to distinguish between imperial defence and collective security requirements.

Four months after the Geneva Naval Conference, Maxim Litvinov, the Soviet representative on the Preparatory Disarmament Commission (PDC), tested liberal internationalist ambiguities with a proposal for the complete abolition of armaments. The most favourable reaction, in the *Daily Chronicle* (1 December 1927), merely admitted the desirability of the USSR's involvement in disarmament talks. The *Manchester Guardian* called it 'a piece of chicanery', and Sir Herbert Samuel remarked that its result would be 'that some Chinese war lord would march triumphantly across a disarmed and unprotected Europe and occupy each capital in turn'.[33] Such dismissals infuriated war resisters. Speaking at a disarmament meeting in Manchester, Cecil was heckled with shouts of 'No!' by members of the audience when he referred to the Soviet plan as impractical and likely to retard negotiations.[34] Nor did the Labour Party offer anything more than lip service to abolition. George Lansbury, president of the 1928 Party Conference, welcomed 'with deep gratitude' the demand for it, but the National Joint Council of Labour had already ruled it out unless accompanied by arbitration and collective security.[35] Certainly, Labour failed to match the enthusiasm of peace societies and sectarian groups increasingly vociferous in the borderlands of liberal internationalism.

Disarmament had been an important focus for peace groups. Their coordinating body, the National Council for the Prevention of War (NCPW), noted in 1927 that the campaign for disarmament would continue to engage its energies for the year and probably until the Disarmament Conference met. Contrasted with the Litvinov proposals, the NCPW's programme seemed moderate: disarmament in all countries down to the German level (the '1919 standard'), the elimination of militarism in schools, and the cessation of compulsory military training in the British Empire.[36] Nevertheless, the NCPW seized on the Soviet proposals, and at a National Peace Congress it organised in 1927, delegates enthused about them. The Rev. F.W. Norwood, Minister of the City Temple, described the Soviet initiative as a 'pivot of destiny', and Lucy Cox, representing the No More War Movement, argued that there was no half-way house and the Soviet government should be taken at its word.[37] The peace movement grew more radical as the PDC failed to progress in Geneva. Accordingly, from 1928, the NCPW agitated for unilateral reductions of some munitions and drastic reductions of others by international agreement, to the bare minimum needed to suppress piracy. This represented the minimum level of agreement in the peace movement. Many groups and individuals wanted to go further – the UDC's London Regional Council uncompromisingly demanded Britain's unilateral disarmament as an example to others.[38]

Predictably, Marxist resisters also supported the Litvinov proposal, explaining away the Red Army as 'a powerful educational institution closely bound up with the life of the workers, trade unions, and peasants'. Only the Soviet Union could make a total disarmament proposal with honesty. Armaments in the rest of the world existed to enable capitalist powers to hold down the workers, to subjugate millions of colonial peoples, and to fight one another over the division of markets, raw materials and sources of cheap labour.[39] But the vast majority of liberal internationalists on the left dismissed the total abolition of armaments as impractical; it was better to work for gradual, negotiated reductions in conjunction with improvements to the League's peace machinery. Further, liberal internationalists believed in a certain level of effectiveness to contribute to a pooled military force for use against states evading an arms convention. The LNU and the Labour Party were under pressure only momentarily from their pro-Soviet adherents. Besides, by the summer of 1928, the government's policy had again roused indignation, pushing unilateralism into the background. The next (Labour) government would curtail such alternatives and continue framing policies in the framework of liberal internationalist governmentality.

Arms control with France

Government policy seemed to undergo an aberration in 1928 when the cabinet sought a naval compromise with France that ignored US sensibilities and risked antagonising Germany. Chamberlain, who inspired the negotiations, attempted to take imperial requirements doctrine to a logical conclusion. He figured that by accommodating French military needs, France would drop objections to limiting navies by class of vessel. France had required limitation by 'global tonnage' because it would allow submarine construction, a category appropriate to French defence, but which Britain wanted to control. Cabinet members expressed unease. Churchill advocated a completely free hand and avoidance of any agreement. Cushendun argued that an exclusive Anglo-French arrangement would antagonise other naval powers, such as the United States and Italy. However, Chamberlain accepted the exclusion from any disarmament convention of French conscripts held as trained reservists, accepted parity with France in 8-inch gun cruisers, conceded a limitation on large submarines (rather than pressing for abolition) and conceded no limitation on small cruisers (which the United States wanted to limit). In return, the French consented to the limitation of ships by category. Britain officially accepted the formula on 28 July 1928, but Chamberlain announced only the existence of an agreement two days later, without cabinet consent and without mentioning the concession on trained reserves. Rumours about the contents circulated in the press on both sides of the Atlantic before the Hearst chain leaked the plan in mid-September. The United States condemned it, and the Baldwin Government abandoned it in November.[40]

A wide range of liberal internationalists denounced this 'capitulation to French militarism'. Lloyd George described it as the most sinister event for years. At the very least, Britain would be contributing to an 'implacable French supremacy' that had ringed Germany since the war, and which a true collective security, based on disarmament, would replace.[41] In the absence of a clear official announcement, the movement suspected the worst – an Anglo-French alliance. For secret diplomacy, the affair resembled the League Council crisis. The *Daily Telegraph*'s editorial (26 September 1928) accused the government of ignominious secrecy and complained at the prospect of bolstering French security – an attitude that encompassed opinion from the Round Table group to the UDC.[42] Disarmers were particularly horrified at conceding the capacity of France to build up a trained army of reserves. As a resolution at the 1928 Labour Party Conference put it, the Tories had reached

> an Agreement with France that certain classes of cruisers, destroyers, and submarines should not be limited by international treaty. This constituted an agreement *not* to limit armaments. It was designed

to give Great Britain the cruiser programme which our Government knew to be unacceptable to the United States. The Agreement has had a disastrous effect upon American public opinion.[43]

The Anglo-French compromise did nothing to counteract divisions between sections of liberal internationalist opinion, though cross-currents of agreement continued to exist. Murray, for example, thought that the agreement could result in a worthwhile measure of arms limitation, and counselled a moderate LNU statement, arguing that Chamberlain 'may have made serious errors in diplomacy, but there is nothing whatever sinister in trying to agree with the French about naval reduction'.[44] Otherwise, support for the government came only from *The Times* because France gave way on global tonnage, and the *Army Quarterly*, which had no objection to France retaining conscription because of its need for a large army.[45]

To the majority of liberal internationalists, as well as Marxists and pacifists, Chamberlain seemed bent on dispelling the Locarno spirit. He had already bungled the admission of Germany to the League and presided over the deterioration of Anglo-American relations. Now, he had been outmanoeuvred by the French. Discord had become significant in the quest for disarmament and arbitration in the period after Locarno, and as noted in Chapter 3, it is possible that these issues played some part in the government's defeat in 1929. At least it can be said that whatever the government's shortcomings on the home front, these were not compensated by foreign policy. Liberals raged that in international relations the Baldwin Government was 'not merely a check on progress but a public nuisance and a public danger'.[46] Critical voices amplified strains in the internationalist movement, though not as seriously as in the next decade.

Multilateral naval arms control

Acrimony faded with the advent of the Labour Government of 1929, for Henderson gave every indication of pursuing a strong pro-League policy. Even when relations between the Liberal Party and the government reached a crisis point in 1931, Grey specifically excluded foreign policy from the bones of contention.[47] The disciplinary function of liberal internationalism worked well. The conservative press admitted that the international environment at the end of 1929 seemed propitious for further disarmament initiatives. A new spirit had revitalised the PDC. The United States was compromising on the French need for trained reserves; the League Assembly agreed to allied troop evacuations from the Rhineland, the occupation of which had been a running sore in European relations; and the Hague Reparations Conference had reached a conclusion. In these circumstances, *The Times* editorial commented: 'Imperfect as the present machinery for security may be, it is a great advance on anything the modern world has hitherto enjoyed, and the confidence it has inspired in the preservation of peace is surely sufficient to justify both the limitation and progressive reduction in naval armaments'.[48] Labour's Advisory Committee on International Questions (ACIQ) reminded the cabinet that progress on disarmament was imperative, not only to fulfil election promises but also to forestall a costly replacement programme on the expiry in 1931 of the 'battleship holiday' prescribed at the 1921–22 Washington Conference.[49] There was no reason why a 50 per cent cut in the naval tonnage of the five main powers should not be achieved.[50] Rapprochement with the United States was a logical first step, especially as the Hoover Administration appeared far more amenable towards compromise than its predecessor in 1927.

Liberal internationalists, including Prime Minister MacDonald, also thought about reconsidering policy on belligerent rights at sea as a gesture to the United States. Nothing came of it, but the issue highlights the problem the liberal internationalist movement faced with US isolationism. Internationalists believed that Britain's continued denial of the principle of the freedom of the seas hindered naval limitation. After Britain's wartime blockade, the United States would not yield to a convention until this was settled.[51] But to renounce belligerent rights would complicate the functioning of collective security because in a 'League war' the United States could insist on its neutrality and freedom of the seas. However, Comdr Kenworthy of the LNU offered a solution that appealed to the movement: a distinction between public and private wars. Belligerent rights would only apply in 'lawful public wars', sanctioned by or under the auspices of the League of Nations. For its part, the United States would have to adopt legislation empowering the president to prohibit dealings with an aggressor.[52] But the scheme raised as many difficulties as it purported to solve: how to define 'aggressor', could the distinction between public and private wars hold, and would other maritime powers cooperate? As critics pointed out, the loudest US complaints about belligerent rights occurred on occasions when Britain engaged in 'public wars', such as the last one. And as Grey and others argued, the Americans had consistently violated the freedom of the seas when it suited them.[53] In fact, the United States would supply fascist Italy with raw materials despite League sanctions during the Abyssinian/Ethiopian crisis in the mid-1930s. Nevertheless, when MacDonald visited Herbert Hoover in October 1929 for talks, the president offered concessions on battleship building and the total tonnages of other categories of warships subject to satisfactory submarine limits by third parties. And although the United States wanted freedom of the seas settled before accepting ship limits, Hoover (a Quaker and Wilson's Food Administrator during the war) floated the idea that ships exclusively carrying food supplies should be treated like hospital ships (which the League was unlikely to ban and from which Britain at war would benefit).

The liberal internationalist movement also welcomed the Labour Government's willingness to limit battleships and cruisers. Relinquishing expensive capital ships proved popular. Cecil spoke for most when he suggested putting a number of battleships out of commission and banning replacements before 1936, citing a commonly accepted rationale that aircraft could immobilise battle fleets.[54] The prediction had support from the journal *Naval Review* and from Admirals Richmond, Webb, Kerr, Allen and Drury-Lowe (the last three being members of the LNU). Richmond, in particular, proved a useful ally for the disarmers, as he had forthright views about the 35,000 tonnage limits for battleships agreed at Washington. 'I can find', he wrote, 'neither strategical nor tactical reason for any fighting ship of any Power being larger than 6,500 tons'.[55] Despite being *persona non grata* with the Admiralty, or perhaps because of it, Richmond influenced MacDonald, who was also under pressure from cabinet members as well as backbenchers. Confronting resignation threats by the Sea Lords, the government agreed to scrap five battleships and to the principle of a five-year building holiday.[56] It also overruled the Admiralty on cruisers, and in the light of the Kellogg–Briand Pact, assessed Britain's cruiser needs at 50 rather than 70. Remarkably little fuss greeted this decision. Conservatives who had stuck rigidly to 70 acquiesced in the reduction. *The Times* (8 February 1930) considered it worth the sacrifice to secure an international agreement. Indeed, liberal internationalists acclaimed the London Naval Agreement signed on 21 April 1930, though limited to Britain, the United States and Japan. It extended the provisions of the Washington Treaty to cover cruisers, destroyers and submarines, with the promise of economic benefits and a control on naval competition. Although regretting that France and Italy had not signed up, *The Times* concluded that 'many millions which would otherwise have been spent on instruments of destruction will now remain in the pockets of the taxpayer or be available for other purposes'. The *Daily Mail* and the *Daily Telegraph* supported MacDonald against parliamentary critics – Admirals Jellicoe and Beatty in the Lords, and Churchill in the Commons.[57] Even the *Naval Review* and *Morning Post* (23 April 1930) acknowledged the economic and diplomatic success of the conference.[58] Some internationalists tempered their praise with thoughts of what might have been. The LNU, for example, argued that the number of battleships scrapped (five by Britain, three by the United States and one by Japan) should have been higher, and that, for the most part, the agreement had merely placed limits on expansion.[59]

Critics on left and right margins of the internationalist movement were less forgiving. The UDC had advocated the total abolition of battleships and submarines. At the Labour Party Conference in October 1930, Fenner Brockway opened the foreign affairs debate with an ILP resolution calling on the government to embark on unilateral disarmament in the shortest possible time. But most delegates approved of Henderson's gradualism.[60] His foreign policy made him the most popular figure at the conference. Nor did the nationalist camp upset the consensus. The Navy League pointed to the prospect of Britain open to attack and starvation, and in a lively discussion at the Royal Institute for International Affairs, MacDonald and Alexander faced a group of irate 'sea dogs', one of whom (Admiral Fremantle) called the prime minister a traitor.[61] However, the 70 cruiser requirement sank below the horizon. Although some 80 MPs declared against the treaty on the grounds that it jeopardised imperial interests, Churchill received little sympathy when he spoke in the Commons in May and there was no division.[62] About £70 million would be saved in not building up to the 70 limit, Japan was denied parity in cruisers with either the United States or Britain, and MacDonald had improved Anglo-American relations.

Clearly, too, liberal internationalists approved the government's rejection of French security demands as the price for achieving a five-power agreement. When, in December 1929, France had hinted at a possible 'Naval Locarno' for the Mediterranean, the press universally reported that the British public would never consent to aid France against Italy or vice versa. A Mediterranean pact would be a snare leading straight to war.[63] In April 1930, another French proposal, for a joint Anglo-French declaration on an interpretation of 'prompt action' in Article 16 of the League Covenant, encountered a similar reception. Reactions to Chamberlain's policies demonstrated the degree of revulsion among internationalists against bolstering French security. The *New Statesman* (15 March 1930) remarked that the French were gluttons for national security, which had to be achieved through disarmament and, in this, France was a major obstacle by denying naval parity with Italy. Early in 1930, Cecil indicated that the LNU would back a Mediterranean

Locarno if it meant disarmament by France.[64] But such an idea may well have split the movement, so unpopular was the French quest for security. MacDonald's refusal to entertain French proposals resonated favourably with liberal internationalism.

Paradoxically, while the Baldwin Government (which generally considered foreign policy to be above party) had bequeathed faction and unrest, Labour (whose supporters had regularly cavilled at the notion of continuity) had achieved a degree of consensus. If Chamberlain had lost his touch, Henderson and MacDonald had taken a lead on peace – though without relinquishing any sovereignty or armed strength. There was no shift to a 'socialist foreign policy' in 1929, merely a more active liberal internationalist approach. The government had signed the Optional Clause, but with reservations. It had lowered the notional limit of cruiser requirements without affecting existing naval strength. Labour gained kudos by appearing to be more effective in maintaining the governmentality of liberal internationalism in good shape, partly by rejecting French 'militarism'.

General disarmament

Until 1931, pressure for general disarmament was relatively modest, reflected in proposals by students of disarmament. The common reference point for internationalists was the disarmament scheme imposed on Germany at Versailles. It held pride of place in discourses, but no liberal internationalist formulated a scheme for disarmament to the German level. In a comprehensive survey of disarmament, Noel Baker favoured interstate negotiations rather than concocting universal formulae. Flexibility within agreed budgetary limits appealed to him.[65] In similar vein, the LNU advised that:

> It is not for the average speaker at a public meeting to prescribe what precise reduction of the national armaments the Government of the day should accept. That is, in the last resort, a matter for the Government itself, and it can only formulate its final policy after discussion with the Governments of other States, for the size of a nation's army or navy depends, in some measure at any rate, on the size of the armies with which it may conceivably some day find itself in conflict.[66]

This was not just an effort to rebut accusations of partisanship. While prospects for disarmament seemed fair, the movement produced only vague statements and advocated a moderate approach, emphasising budgetary limitation and the creation of arms-monitoring machinery. Advocates remained largely uninformative about how to define and achieve 'reduction of national forces to a minimum necessary to preserve international order, plus a small margin which could be used as a contribution to the League'.[67] Moreover, at the 1930 Geneva Assembly, Cecil cautioned against undue haste in calling a General Disarmament Conference without agreement on procedural issues. This accorded closely with Conservative demands for avoiding prescriptions. Nor, in the 1920s did the Labour Party contemplate blueprints. The ACIQ did not study a formula until February 1931, and even then exempted states with small budgets from a 25 per cent cut.[68] Subsequently, the LNU defended the PDC's draft of 9 December 1930 outlining the principles for a disarmament framework, including budgetary limitations, but without proposing concrete levels for categories of weapons.

The draft exposed differences between France and Germany – with the German delegate Count von Bernstorff warning that unless France genuinely disarmed, Germany could not be bound by Versailles. But the LNU leadership criticised Bernstorff's impatience and stressed that the most critical phase in the negotiations, the trading over definite figures, still had to take place.[69] From the end of 1930, however, liberal internationalists began to lose patience with 'continental obduracy', and put more faith in formulae. Internationalists even began to look upon Germany rather than France as the chief intransigent, and from 1931 to 1933 grew increasingly critical of German nationalism, while remaining critical of Germany's treatment at Versailles. *The Times* (16 December 1930), for example, concurred with the Cecil–Henderson view that the PDC draft convention had merit and that German objections were unreasonable. Nor did the German government improve its standing in Britain by announcing on 21 March 1931 a projected customs union with Austria. In a series of editorials in the last week of March *The Times* criticised this move for wrecking the conciliatory atmosphere necessary for successful disarmament. *The New Statesman* (28 March 1931) agreed that although the proposed *zollverein* was legitimate, it amounted to a distracting irritant with a disarmament conference in the offing. Accordingly, when Henderson referred the *zollverein* plan to the League Council (for investigation as to its compatibility with the peace treaties), liberal internationalists applauded.[70] Hints in June 1931 by Chancellor Heinrich Brüning and Foreign Minister Julius Curtius, intent on abrogating Versailles, that Germany might cancel its reparations under the Young Plan of 1929 (which had reduced the burden and extended it to 1988) also aroused consternation.

Editorials argued that financial relief for Germany would be conditional on demonstrating its good faith. Labour's *Daily Herald* (6 June 1931) pointed out that Germany's pocket battleships (10,000-ton vessels with six 11-inch guns), outdid Britain's 10,000-ton cruisers with eight 8-inch guns, and asked whether the launching of the *Deutschland* pocket battleship in May revealed wicked intentions and whether it was compatible with the threat of imminent financial collapse. In June 1931, the Hoover Moratorium eased the reparations and debt issues, but German policy had soured preparations for the conference and, as shown in the next chapter, led the liberal internationalist movement to look more favourably on French security schemes.

The hardening of attitudes in Europe and the temper of German nationalism explains the consensus reached by a Three-Party Sub-Committee of the CID sitting from March to June 1931 to examine disarmament policy. In addition to Labour Government ministers it included Austen Chamberlain, Anthony Eden, Thomas Inskip and Samuel Hoare for the Tories, Lloyd George, Philip Kerr (now Lord Lothian) and Lord Samuel for the Liberals – and the arch-trespasser Cecil representing liberal internationalist governance. The sub-committee agreed that Britain would only pursue further disarmament in the event of comparable reductions by others, and the prime minister announced in Parliament that Britain had gone as far as possible unilaterally. MacDonald also showed appreciation of France's 'military needs' and was echoed by Liberals and Conservatives and by much of the press.[71]

In the long run, a vital question facing the internationalist movement was to decide where threats to European stability might arise and how to deal with them through the League. Some internationalists began to suspect that Germany rather than France was a potential threat to peace and that it might be advisable to take, as yet undefined, measures to offset Chancellor Brüning's policies. Arthur Henderson was kept well informed about Germany's evasion of the military provisions of Versailles and, as Cecil wrote to Angell, if reactionary tendencies persisted in Germany 'progressive countries will inevitably counteract'.[72] Britain plunged into a financial and political crisis that distracted liberal internationalist attention. But Franco-German deadlock led to more forthright discourses. Reinforced in his distaste for 'continental entanglement', Lothian advised Lloyd George that Britain should withdraw from collective security obligations in the event of the Disarmament Conference failing.[73] Beaverbrook took an equally hard line, and in May 1931 the *Daily Express* commenced a campaign against the League of Nations and its supporters. It provoked the *News Chronicle* to launch a 'peace crusade' culminating in a petition with half a million signatures and a mass rally in London in July addressed by party leaders. The crusade gave vent to the pacific elements of internationalism, prompted by frustration over stalemate even before the Geneva Conference opened. A livelier, crusading spirit also affected the NCPW, which in May 1931 began publishing a monthly bulletin, *Towards Disarmament*. Later in the year, the NCPW streamlined its title to the National Peace Council (NPC) – symbolic of the quickening pace of debate on the disarmament issue.

In addition, sections of liberal internationalism turned to strategies and programmes that were bound to lead to contention. The LNU, for example, promoted its first concrete formula, known as the 'Budapest Programme'. Drawn up by the International Federation of League of Nations Societies in May 1931, it proposed controls on certain 'offensive weapons' such as bombers, a universal 25 per cent cut in military budgets (except for states disarmed by the peace treaties) and equal military rights for Germany. The programme failed to indicate what equal military status would mean in practice. Furthermore, states claiming to have already disarmed would resist the 25 per cent budget cut. Proponents increasingly centred their hopes on the abolition or control of offensive weapons, acquiring an advocate in Capt. Basil Liddell Hart, the *Daily Telegraph's* special correspondent at the conference. His theory of 'qualitative disarmament' included a ban on heavy tanks and artillery to raise the balance of firepower to the advantage of defensive strategies. Consequently, new French defences would become impregnable. With similar provisions for controlling military aircraft, Britain would be less vulnerable to air attack. These ideas contradicted Liddell Hart's own concept of an 'expanding torrent' of mechanised force as a solution to stalemates that had developed in Flanders. Having advised military chiefs to invest in tanks, he now recommended that tanks be limited to less than 10-ton weight. He explained this *volte face* to his friend Gilbert Murray: 'I find that the degree of understanding which enables one to see the true nature of war leads one to see its essential stupidity, and so inspires one with a desire to help in checking it'.[74] His distinction between aggressive and defensive weapons soon became pivotal in liberal internationalism and influenced government policy. Naturally, it also led to semantic disputes. To the National Liberal Federation, qualitative disarmament meant the abolition of warships over 10,000 tons, tanks, gas, naval and military aviation, the international control of civil aviation, and budgetary limits.[75] To the government, it meant the limitation of weapons for which Britain had little use – but not tanks under 16 tons or bombers for use against rebel tribes in the Empire.

Detractors also pointed out that even if qualitative arms control worked, it would not abolish warfare. Aggression was as much a political as a military impulse, and potential aggressors would be deterred not merely by their own incapacities in attack, but also by fear of retaliation if they did attack. As Gen. Sir Hugh Jeudwine remarked to Murray, 'My belief is that the more expensive, terrible and all-pervading the process of war becomes the less likely is any individual or any nation to assent, or to allow a Government to assent, to its effects, either personal or national'.[76] Paradoxically, drawing the teeth of national military forces would have ensured a replication of trench warfare, with armies reliant on manpower and machine-gun.

Conclusion

The financial and political crisis of the late summer of 1931 brought confusion, though it made economy in defence expenditure all the more pressing.[77] Political distrust and disaffection grew more acute with the traumatic fall of the Labour Government, and the bitterness of the 1931 General Election affected the disarmament consensus. For the Labour Party, bipartisanship in foreign policy could hardly survive. At its conference in October, left-wingers received a sympathetic hearing for the view that the quest for multilateral disarmament had proved futile. And, although the conference as a whole overwhelmingly endorsed a liberal internationalist position, delegates challenged the National Government to produce a plan for 'drastic', if not unilateral, disarmament.[78] With the shift to the right at Westminster and the elevation of the guarded Sir John Simon as foreign secretary, the government would be increasingly censured for failing to 'give a lead'. Its policy conformed to the decision of the Three-Party CID Sub-Committee that Britain should not disarm further without an international agreement. The lead would have to come from others and they would have to offer concessions before Britain could respond.

The period after Locarno has seen a remarkable degree of consensus, both among the political elites and among rank-and-file supporters of the internationalist movement. Disarmament served moral, economic and security purposes. Nevertheless, part of the consensus involved recognising, at least on the part of liberal internationalist leaders, that unilateralism in reducing sea power and imperial defence was no substitute for multilateral weapons control in the form of qualitative limitations on expansion. By the new decade, the consensus entered a crisis, soured by Francophobia and German intransigence, and marked by a shift from general principles to treaty blueprints.

In the aftermath of political upheaval at home and in despair of progress in Geneva, resistance to official policy grew more exacting. By the end of 1931, Cecil again found himself at odds with authority. He condemned the advice being given to the cabinet, which involved little reduction in British armaments, and included retention of medium-sized tanks, which he wanted abolished or severely limited. Also by 1931, the deterioration in international relations had forced leading internationalists to seek new directions. Cecil, Angell, Henderson, Dalton and Allen, for example, recognised that the ultimate requirement for peace-as-collective security was military force. Hitherto, they had stressed the less-contentious mechanisms of diplomatic sanctions, arbitration and disarmament. Now they considered internationalising force to cut through the impasse, thereby arousing controversies that had earlier been avoided. From a modest social movement focusing on open diplomacy, arbitration and paper guarantees for peace, a more intensive process of politicisation ensured a mass following in the early 1930s as the General Disarmament Conference loomed ahead, but it disturbed the governmental technique by which elites had managed liberal internationalism.

5
Innovation: Arming the League with Air Power

At the turn of the decade, the editor of the LNU's *Headway* (November 1930) lamented that:

> the pace of the peace movement has slackened. The novelty of a great adventure no longer illumines the debates in the League's Assembly. An acute economic crisis, together with the rapid growth of extreme nationalism in certain countries, makes public opinion in too many of its States Members far behind the standard of progress which their delegates and experts at Geneva agree upon.

However, the depressing outlook opened up liberal internationalism to radical, innovative solutions. These may not have been realised in the interwar years, but sowed seeds for Second World War germination. While some internationalists turned to isolationism, others developed an interest in international policing and can be said to have anticipated UN peacekeeping. All but neglected in the literature, the concept of an International Police Force (IPF) is the subject of this chapter. Britain's vulnerability to, and horror of, air attack exercised internationalists long before the Spanish Civil War demonstrated the devastating physical and psychological impacts of air power. Internationalists campaigned from the early 1930s to establish some kind of collective aerial protection with an International Air Police Force (IAPF). An air police also promised to circumvent the disarmament deadlock – first, by enabling states to abolish national air forces as a prelude to more general disarmament, and second, by providing France with a military guarantee, which some internationalists began to regard sympathetically. The notion preceded serious consideration of non-military sanctions, promotion trespassed all over conventional politics.

Although there were international police advocates of long-standing,[1] the early thirties saw a remarkable upsurge of interest. During the

Disarmament Conference an IPF proposal formed the basic policy of a new liberal internationalist group – the New Commonwealth Society – led by David Davies, G.N. Barnes and Baron Henry Gladstone of Hawarden. Its vice-presidents included Cecil and the future Labour prime minister, Clement Attlee, who took it seriously enough to write a pamphlet.[2] In 1933, the Labour Party endorsed Attlee's concept; the following year the chancellor of the Exchequer, Neville Chamberlain, canvassed an IPF scheme in the cabinet; and in 1935 the Liberal Party endorsed peace-as-military-security. Organisations as diverse as the British Legion and the New Fabian Research Bureau accepted the need for an international police.[3] The idea became the subject of prize-winning essays,[4] led to an LNU conference attended by an air minister and a galaxy of experts,[5] prompted Chatham House to launch a study of sanctions,[6] and the Leverhulme Research Council to subsidise an investigation by Liddell Hart.[7]

This evolution contributed to trespassing, creating a new consensus out of the old disarmament consensus. It also stimulated factionalism because, as previously observed about the UDC, many internationalists were not prepared for the League to possess or command instruments of war. Marxists labelled it a 'capitalist force'. Nationalists thought it would drag Britain into war, though some, including Churchill, came to regard an IPF as a possible weapon against Germany – as indeed the Communist Party was to do after the Soviet Union joined the League in 1934. But in the first instance, the prospect of aerial warfare was the midwife of policing, for liberal internationalists sought to turn air power to the advantage of peace by making it a League monopoly.

The chapter begins with the fear of air war in the context of disarmament to explain the growth of interest in an IPF. Part two links the debate over air power to the disputes in international liberalism over League sanctions prior to their application during Italy's war against Ethiopia. The third section links the IPF debate to the changing reactions noted in the previous chapter to French security proposals in the context of failure in the disarmament negotiations in Geneva. Analysis of the impact of these issues on liberal internationalism forms the fourth section and leads to a fifth, which focuses on the innovative proposals of David Davies and the New Commonwealth Society.

Knock-out blow theory

Well before November 1932 when Baldwin famously warned that 'the bomber would always get through', the public had reached a consensus about the seriousness of air attacks. Paradoxically, the Air Ministry and air 'experts' initiated the panic; only in the late twenties did internationalists mobilise support on the basis of the air war issue. By the end of the Great War, Sir Frederick Sykes, architect of the Royal Flying Corps, had developed the theory of the knock-out blow, which, under Lord Trenchard, became official strategic doctrine. The new technology fired the imaginations of an epistemic community of air specialists, military intellectuals and journalists. The pioneer aviators, Sir Allan Cobham, and Brig.-Gen. P.R.C. Groves (Director of Flying Operations in 1918, and a stalwart of the Air League), admitted that the first object of an air force in war would be to terrorise enemy civilians. Groves argued that London could not be defended: 'in a short time its vital points would be in ruins and the other parts rendered uninhabitable by gas'.[8] Such cheerless predictions also applied to the effects of air war on mass behaviour. J.F.C. Fuller, whose militarism and fascism stressed the relevance of both mechanical and occult power in warfare, advocated conscription for a force to keep civilians in order during air raids.[9] By 1931, the government was examining plans for the evacuation of big cities. In the 1920s, expert opinion remained well in advance of public interest. But J.L. Garvin was already under sentence of contradiction when, in *The Observer* (19 August 1928), he wrote: 'In the development of air-power, the public imagination has lagged behind scientific achievement'.

After 1927, when the problems of collective security became more critical, the public imagination needed little prompting. As with Grey's views on armaments, so Field Marshall Foch's remark at the end of the war on the potential havoc of aerial warfare was elevated to the status of fact. There seemed every reason to suppose that the aeroplane would be just as devastating over London's air space as the Maxim gun had been in Flanders. Of the 1927 air manoeuvres, for example, one editor commented laconically: 'The heart of London was bombed yesterday, and it does not seem too much to say that the attackers did very much as they liked'.[10] In reality, the air manoeuvres of the late twenties actually contradicted the alarmism. Air Ministry analysis in 1928 revealed that only nine of the 57 mock daylight raids had managed to evade the defences. But it was assumed that even one raid would wreak untold havoc.

By the mid-thirties, people imagined the worst and were encouraged to do so by science fiction.[11] H.G. Wells renewed his former interest in air power in *The Shape of Things to Come* (1935). Official precautions grew more realistic. An Air Raid Precautions Department, set up in 1935, played safe by ordering masses of coffins and burial forms, but also took serious (though inadequate) steps to implement civil defence measures.

In addition, fighter aircraft were given greater priority in the rearmament programme. A discrepancy between expert and public opinion was also shown by the popular reaction to a collection of studies published by Gollancz: *What Would Be the Character of a New War?* (1933). The majority of the articles were not particularly alarmist, but a depiction of chemical and bacteriological warfare by a Swiss chemist had a far greater impact on liberal internationalists in Britain than did the book's more sober predictions.[12] In the event, gas was not used, the number of deaths much lower and the psychological stamina of people greater than predicted, and homelessness became the main social problem.

While all shades of opinion agreed on the seriousness of the air threat, responses differed markedly. The knock-out blow experts argued that the only hope in a conflict was to get in first and bomb the enemy's airfields. With luck, the mere existence of a strong Royal Air Force would deter potential aggressors. The deterrent argument appealed to Conservatives, who distinguished between the air force as a deterrent and the desire for disarmament in other services, on the grounds that a weak air force would constitute 'a deliberate inducement to some other nation to come here and conquer this country with all its wealth and possession'.[13] Air power was relatively untried and did not encourage defence ministers to take risks. They could also argue that, partly as a consequence of air power, land and sea forces had declined in importance. Conservatives thus resolved to deter aggressors equipped with a technology which could, according to the aviation correspondent of the *Daily Telegraph* (20 November 1933), shatter civilisation within a few hours. By 1927, the building programme for 23 squadrons (mainly bomber strength) was only half complete, four years after its initiation. But the air power was regarded as a special case and not liable for swingeing economies. The Labour Government of 1929 to 1931 continued to abide by deterrent doctrine, Air Minister Lord Thomson privately expressing support for bombing reprisals and the need for a high quality, if small, air force.[14] It is certain, however, that rank-and-file members of the Labour Party and the majority of its leaders did not subscribe to the deterrence–retaliation concept. In general, the Conservative Party, more overtly statist and nationalist than others, gave more consistent support to the air force as a special case – except for the first quarter of 1935, when the Conservative-dominated National Government groped for an air pact to curb German air power.

For liberal internationalists, retaliation not only symbolised a despair of ever removing armaments as a prime cause of war but also represented a counsel of gloom that contradicted liberal optimism about social progress. Yet they accepted that man was helpless against air attacks. This, however, made reaching an international air convention all the more crucial. Deterrence was futile; it would mean that Britain 'must embark on preparations which can never be adequate.'[15] Britain would benefit more than most from a pact, argued internationalists, because the country was extremely vulnerable and had fallen to fifth in air strength by 1933. That this decline had happened in the space of four years might have indicated to the disarmers that other countries had no intention of yielding a newly found source of strength. But the rapidly expanding air technology and absence of any existing controls on a par with the Washington Treaties for naval power, imbued agitation for an air pact with a sense of urgency. League enthusiasts went further and advocated the use of air forces as a collective deterrent.

Thus air power became a special case for the collective enforcement of international arbitration with pride of place in the scheme of sanctions. Equipped with it, the League of Nations could come to the swift aid of victims of aggression. Because air forces were relatively novel, pooling them under League authority would challenge less well-entrenched traditions, and crews would supposedly have renounced state allegiances. As a Labour MP argued: 'The air service differs from the land services and from the naval service in that it must of necessity pass over all the countries in the world, and, from the technical point of view, in a service which is in its infancy there is everything to be said for deliberate international regulations from the very beginning.'[16] But the practical difficulties of a League air force, or even international regulation of national forces, tended to multiply with each debate. Civil aviation posed insuperable problems. In Britain, its development fostered imperial communication and, in the view of the airship designer, Cdr C.D. Burney, could provide an Empire air reserve.[17] Concern about civil conversions to military use led pundits to imagine that Germany could do this 'within an hour or two'.[18] To liberal internationalists, the logical solution was for the League to control civil aviation.

This was anathema to strategists of the knock-out blow. Sykes, Fuller, Groves and Burney all denounced internationalism. J.M. Spaight, an Air Ministry official, argued that League action would simply fail to save victims of aggression in time. General guarantees were unreliable, and a League force would never replace the deterrent value of national defence because it would lack 'the healthy pressure of hate behind it.'[19] On the other hand, some naval experts, including Richmond, Drury-Lowe and R.N. Lawson, favoured an IPF, partly, perhaps, because it required internationalisation of air forces. Whether they would have put the Royal Navy at the League's disposal is another matter.

By contrast, Labour's Henderson, Dalton, Attlee, Noel Baker and Arnold-Forster regarded collective security partly as the precondition for world order, and partly as insurance against risky Tory policies. Urging the international control of aviation, they began educating the Labour Party towards accepting a powerful League. Attlee, for example, suggested that civil aircraft should be 'staffed by men drawn from all the nations of the world, in which they would get to feel that they were an international body'.[20] But domestic issues took precedence and Labour did not fully discuss an IPF until confronted by the imminent collapse of the Disarmament Conference.

Military sanctions

Cecil, an early advocate of an international *posse comitatus*, had reason to avoid splitting the LNU with a debate on sanctions, given it had already split the UDC.[21] The UDC's experience was indeed salutary. By the late 1920s, this once-powerful group (with over half a million adherents including affiliates), influential in educating the public about secret diplomacy, as shown in Chapter 2, had entered a decline. The founder, E.D. Morel, had died in 1924 and the group was eclipsed by the LNU and Labour's new pro-League stance. The UDC had served its purpose and had seen many of its radical principles become widespread assumptions. It still boasted the support of intellectuals of the calibre of Bertrand Russell, J.A. Hobson, H.J. Laski, H.N. Brailsford, C.P. Trevelyan and Leonard Woolf. But decline quickened after 1927, when they confronted the implications of collective security. Like the Labour Party, the UDC had harboured strong hostility towards the League as 'a cabal of victors', yet came to defend its normative value against Austen Chamberlain's policies. But the majority of members clung to a faith in the power of democratic opinion, and distrusted the concept of militarising the League. In the wake of the naval dispute between Britain and the United States, the UDC General Council carried a resolution, moved by the pacifist Labour MP Arthur Ponsonby, noting that:

> no effective progress can be made towards the abolition of war so long as the sanction of force is preserved in the Covenant of the League of Nations; it therefore proposes that Great Britain should take the initiative in a declaration in favour of the final abandonment of the war weapon in any circumstances whatever, thus bringing to the forefront the proposal for the amendment of the sanctions clauses of the Covenant and inviting by example the other nations to outlaw war.[22]

This decision provoked those who, like Norman Angell, favoured a stronger collective security. In March 1928 this wing forced a reconsideration of policy, and the original resolution was barely confirmed by a margin of 12 votes to 11.[23] Controversy continued in an open debate between the pacifist Helena Swanwick, who claimed that sanctions would lead to alliances, and W. Arnold-Forster, who argued that without them, aggressors would have a free hand.[24] Trevelyan resigned as treasurer, and Swanwick retired from the Executive Council, handing over editorship of the UDC's journal, *Foreign Affairs*, to Angell. By the autumn of 1928, it had been reduced in price and quality and eventually merged with another periodical. Thus divided, UDC's members paid greater attention to their interests in the pacifist societies, the Labour Party or the LNU.

Other internationalists attempted to maintain discipline, particularly in the LNU. Old disparities (prior to 1918) between the League of Nations Society, which had emphasised moral force, and the League of Free Nations Association, which had contemplated military sanctions, had lapsed on merging as the LNU. Debates occasionally flared up during the twenties; as noted earlier, the Kellogg–Briand Pact had prompted Philip Kerr to agitate against the use of force by the League. But since the Geneva Protocol and the Draft Treaty of Mutual Assistance (see Chapter 3), discussion of sanctions had been exceptional. Cecil and Murray worked effectively to avoid alienating supporters. A similar reticence affected the Liberal Party. Following the failure of the Geneva Naval Conference, a subdued debate on military guarantees in the liberal press promised future trouble.[25] But Liberals had internal politics to sort out. Nor can it be said that the Labour Party had thoroughly attended to the issue. The internationalist movement shied away from sanctions as though the mere mention of Article 16 would bring them into effect. Some interest in sanctions was generated by a government initiative to make the Kellogg–Briand Pact and the Covenant compatible, taxing Foreign Office lawyers. But the LNU's Executive avoided any notion of tampering with the Covenant and *Headway's* editor (March 1929) suggested that '[a] sudden and unheralded attack by another State is almost inconceivable to-day'. Such confidence did not survive more than a few months. Lack of progress in disarmament weighed rather more in impelling a transit to League force than the pitfalls of merging Pact and Covenant.

French militarism or a militarised league?

From 1930, internationalists increasingly discussed sanctions in general and the military variant in particular. Internationalists did not abandon disarmament; the two were often linked. For example, in its 1931 disarmament campaign the LNU suggested that all-round arms reduction would leave potential aggressors bereft as well, and the League would not need to raise a massive force or require large contributions from loyal states.[26] In a commentary that might have predicted UN peacekeeping, *Headway* (May 1930) claimed that '[a]rmed action organised by the League is not war in the normal sense of the term'. This was still an argument for disarmament rather than for military guarantees. But on the Labour Party's Advisory Committee on International Questions (ACIQ) Leonard Woolf argued that although security measures should ultimately depend for effectiveness on a disarmament convention, it would be unreasonable not to examine security proposals on their merits without one.[27] Symbolising the growing concern, the LNU held a seminar on security in March 1931, at which Gen. Sir George Macdonagh (a prominent figure in the International Law Association) seemingly anticipated the UN's Military Staff Committee. 'It will be the duty of the world's General Staff', he said, 'to draw up strategic plans so that there will be a certainty that timely help will be forthcoming, and to earmark a portion of their forces, for immediate action in response to a call from the League'.[28] This went much further than the vast majority of LNU members had contemplated, but the speech indicated changing attitudes on what was usually regarded as 'the French view' of collective security.

France angled for immediate and effective military support in the event of an attack – an idea that few in Britain thought desirable before 1931. Indeed, Briand's radical plan for a political–economic bloc – the United States of Europe (USE) – floated in July 1929 and again in May 1930, met a similar response to his idea for a Mediterranean Naval Pact. It was unclear, perhaps even to Briand, what kind of organisation he had in mind, but it had been interpreted by British liberal internationalists as another attempt to buttress French security. Some proponents of distributive or welfare internationalism regarded the plan's economic aspects as wholly inadequate,[29] while others, including Bertrand Russell, were impressed by the potential for breaking down national sovereignty.[30] H.G. Wells called it 'a gleam of sanity',[31] and Liberals professed interest in the plan's provisions for free trade. The *Manchester Guardian* (19 January 1931) suspected Briand of ulterior motives – of trying to guarantee French security, and the *New Statesman* (24 May 1930) argued: '[a] really cohesive European Federation will see we keep that we keep our weapons bright for maintenance of the everlasting principles of 1919'. Although Cecil thought the plan could go before the League Assembly, he argued that a USE might stimulate intercontinental rivalry, antagonise the Empire and, above all, challenge the League's authority.[32] LNU policy differed hardly a jot from the government's negative response or Henderson's speech to the 1930 League Assembly, which emphasised disarmament rather than collective guarantees.[33] This consensus reflected suspicion of France as the militaristic obstacle to Versailles revision, concern about rivalling the League with a USE and annoyance at attention diverted from disarmament. Over on the political right, Lady Nancy Astor regarded all Latins as 'unprincipled, bibulous and immoral' – and unforgivably Roman Catholic.[34] She shared with Lothian (her Christian Science spiritual adviser) and the editors of *The Times* and *The Observer* the idea that French policies were encouraging Germany to rearm. The Round Table group also fancied that the crucial choice in international affairs was whether Britain kow-towed to France or wooed the United States.[35] But Francophiles, such as Austen Chamberlain and Duff Cooper, were equally opposed to extending Britain's guarantees beyond the Locarno Treaties. Interestingly, Chamberlain was less willing to consummate the affair with France than were her more reluctant admirers (including the Labour Party), who were eventually more sympathetic to an International Police Force. For most Conservatives, though, the Beaverbrook crusade for imperial trade preference took more attention.

As the disarmament outlook worsened, military security and an armed League gained more traction with internationalists. French blueprints (such as the Tardieu plan of 5 February 1932) gained more support, though they were just as futuristic as the USE and more explicitly concerned with collective security. Some Francophiles, including David Davies, Brig.-Gen. E.L. Spears and Wickham Steed, approved French policy partly because they believed in armed security per se and mocked disarmament as a blind alley. Other internationalists had come round to the concept of a League force, in the air at least, because of the special awe in which they held the air menace. An IPF had attractions in promising additional security and the disarmament of national forces. Although the Sino-Japanese dispute of 1931 strengthened demands for security, Davies, Cecil and Attlee, among others, had already developed their support for an IPF long before Japan invaded Manchuria (see Chapter 6). And liberal internationalists linked the question of a League force almost entirely with the air menace and disarmament, making little connection between these and events outside Europe. The war in Asia threw a shadow over the Disarmament Conference but, except during the Shanghai crisis, a Eurocentric view dominated discussions. Besides, IPF promoters nearly always assumed that the policy would only operate in Europe.

Whilst many prominent internationalists favoured the creation of an IPF, the broader socio-political movement remained generally suspicious of French initiatives and a militarised League. A significant effect of the IPF debate on liberal internationalist politics was to cause more fluidity in much the same way as sanctions had divided the UDC. In disaggregating liberal internationalism, it is notable that backing for a League force had less appeal than did the international supervision of civil aircraft. An IPF under permanent League control, or earmarking of national contingents for League use, seemed to foreshadow the formation of a superstate and would give an unwelcome precision to Britain's international obligations. On the other hand, even the Tory-dominated National Government proposed internationalisation of civil aviation to complement its wish to control so-called 'offensive' weapons. Baldwin's only positive suggestion in the 'horrors of bombing' speech was the internationalisation of civil airlines.[36] In mid-1932, the League's Air Commission had concluded that civil planes were convertible into bombers and therefore potentially offensive. The British delegation to the Disarmament Conference informed the French that Britain ruled out a League force, but would support the abolition of bombing (except in 'outlying parts of the world'), the limitation of military aircraft, and the internationalisation of civil aviation.[37] Far from regarding this as a contribution to collective security, the cabinet rejected French schemes and continued refusing to define existing obligations under Article 16 of the Covenant.[38] For much of the liberal internationalist movement control over civil aviation was merely an extension of qualitative disarmament, blaming French military ascendancy for the growth of para-militarism in Germany.

Nor did the security-conscious internationalists deviate from the principle behind Germany's case. Cecil, Attlee and Henderson, for example, supported equality of status on the basis of general disarmament to the German level. But ominous developments in Germany – marked by the Nazi electoral successes in September 1930 and a pointed speech on the 'lost lands' by Germany's Minister of Occupied Territories – prompted a reappraisal of France and led to some ambiguity about German demands. Cecil reported critically on German 'clumsiness' at Geneva, making 'more or less dishonest, demagogic speeches explaining how badly they are being treated'.[39] The attempt to float an Austro-German *zollverein* heightened this concern as noted in Chapter 4. The Three-Party Committee on Disarmament of March 1931 unanimously agreed that France should be given confidence in view of the trend in German policy.[40] In fact, throughout the first phase of the Disarmament

Conference (February to July 1932) the British and French cooperated (though without undertaking additional obligations), and complained about the German delegation raising the question of equal status at an inappropriate time.[41] LNU leaders took an increasingly pro-French line without denying the justice of the German case.

French plans seemed worth pursuing. The LNU's *Headway* (March 1932) welcomed a proposal by the French Prime Minister André Tardieu to place French units at the disposal of the League in the event of aggression. And, with members of the LNU increasingly agitated about the likely collapse of the disarmament negotiations, Cecil concluded that the French claim for security would have to be met, either by strengthening Article 16 or by establishing an IPF. He saw no other solution to the deadlock, arguing that 'it would unquestionably appeal to the French love of something concrete and definite going beyond what they regard as the Anglo-Saxon passion for high-sounding phrases'.[42] Among others, Professor Alfred Zimmern and W. Horsfall Carter, two Oxford international relations experts, commended Tardieu's efforts.[43] Favourable comment came from such unlikely sources as the *News Chronicle* (6 February 1932), which, despite reservations about the plan's practicability, remarked that it might prove a 'first step forward to a saner, a safer, and happier world'.

A feverish atmosphere conducive to innovative panaceas such as the IPF developed; 1931 had been a particularly good year for disarmament demonstrations, poster competitions, world peace days, children's movements for peace, and a Women's International League for Peace and Freedom petition that gathered two million signatures by the end of the year. MacDonald and Foreign Secretary Simon continued to experience ordeal by deputation during the Disarmament Conference – as the *Peace Year Book* (1933) proudly recalled. Commentators detected that qualitative disarmament served as a pretext for procrastination; conference delegates engaged in special pleading to hang on to their prized weaponry. British military advisers, for example, were determined to retain large battleships, 'police bombing' in frontier areas, and the new 16-ton tank. The hypocrisy outraged Liddell Hart and the qualitative disarmers – not least because it undermined widely acclaimed proposals by Hoover in April and June 1932, which combined qualitative disarmament with a one-third reduction in armaments.[44] The movement's concern reached a climax in October 1932 with the presentation of a memorial to MacDonald, in which 400 prominent figures called for the abolition of bombing, the international control of civil aviation and the 'Hoover third'. Yet, when MacDonald announced the British Draft Convention in March 1933 with its cautious proposals on naval and air disarmament, many disarmers accepted it. So desperate had the outlook become, that Noel Baker even argued that MacDonald had 'revolutionised the situation'.[45]

New divisions

Of course, MacDonald had done nothing of the sort, and dismay at lack of progress in Geneva caused many instances of conversion to an IPF. None is more illuminating than Liddell Hart's. His credentials as a military intellectual were widely respected. Pursuing his argument that collective force complemented the abolition of aggressive weapons, he advised the LNU that aggression could be stopped by supplying a victim with forces superior in defensive weapons – notably machine-gun detachments. Towards the end of 1932, Liddell Hart explored the IPF idea for the Royal Institute of International Affairs, and then served on an LNU sub-committee investigating the same subject. He decided that air attack should be met by air reprisals. Initially, the international police would fly over the aggressor's territory 'in such force as to defy attack, dropping tons of warning manifestos instead of tons of bombs'. He would become an associate member of the New Commonwealth (discussed below), having accepted the political case for supra-nationalism after reading the monumental work by David Davies, *The Problem of the Twentieth Century* (1932) arguing for an international air police.[46] In fact, in common with the majority of converts, Liddell Hart had arrived at this conclusion via an extended detour around the disarmament impasse.

But discussion of force threatened to wreck the liberal internationalist consensus on disarmament. The IPF issue symbolised a crisis of governmentality in failing to discipline the liberal internationalist movement, though the framework of assumptions about Britain's role in collective security was weakened rather than destroyed. Opinion in civil society continued to be dominated by fear of war, distrust of Versailles and continental commitment, and attachment to Empire. But the crisis resulted in even greater fluidity of attraction and repulsion, not by dividing faction further from faction, but by causing schisms *within* factions. Proposals for military security polarised opinion inside organisations and created the conditions for new flirtations – bringing together individuals as divorced in political outlook as the internationalist Sir Arthur Salter and the imperialist Winston Churchill.

Obviously, organisations dependent on an internationalist platform, such as the LNU, experienced notable dissension over the IPF controversy. In May 1932, the Welsh Council of the LNU, with Davies as chair, expressed support for an IPF as a contribution to security and not merely as a prelude to disarmament. But Davies argued against holding a debate on the Tardieu plan, instead deciding to form a separate, complementary organisation to further his ideas. Murray responded by indicating that it would be foolish to refuse a concession to France in the form of an international force, but reported that the LNU was 'violently divided'.[47] Whereas Murray, Cecil, Davies, Maxwell Garnett (the General Secretary) and Sir Frederick Maurice (professor of military studies) accepted an IPF, Austen Chamberlain with support from Parmoor and G.L. Dickinson, opposed any trend away from sovereign control over defence. At the LNU General Council meeting in May 1932, Chamberlain and paci-fist members got the IPF proposal shelved. This odd alliance recurred at subsequent meetings, thus preventing a takeover by the Davies fac-tion. While Murray could regret that the LNU had not grasped the secu-rity nettle earlier,[48] the consequences of doing so alienated those who deprecated force, irrespective of the merits of the agency employing it. Resolute pacifists were also piqued by their failure to commit the Executive to support conscientious objection in any war declared *ultra vires* (illegitimate) by the League.[49] The LNU appeared to split from top to bottom, reviving the old antagonism between the 1918 pre-merged League of Nations Society and the League of Free Nations Association, Murray and Davies having led the Association. Still, the IPF issue was less damaging than it might have been. The LNU did not collapse but continually postponed a commitment on the grounds that the IPF had not been adequately discussed.[50] Nevertheless, the constant need for mediation absorbed the energies of Murray and Cecil, and taxed even Cecil's powers of ambiguity. Assailed by a pacifist–Conservative alli-ance on one side and IPF advocates on the other, it is not surprising that the LNU's policies were often nebulous.

Strangely, the peace groups also spoke with many voices. A Peace Conference held in June 1934 produced plenty of unrest. The Cambridge theologian Herbert George Wood remarked: 'If I mention the words "sanctions", or "international police force" I divide this conference at once.'[51] Among the conversions to an IPF, Clifford Allen, who had been imprisoned three times for conscientious objection in the war, acknowledged that force continued to rule international life. He was joined by some of the Quakers, who thought internationalising force would be the route to disarmament.[52] A more startling reversal of traditional attitudes to force would be difficult to find; it symbolised desperation, as frantic negotiations in the spring of 1934 failed to get Germany back in the Disarmament Conference. Remarkably, the Church of England, though traditionally less embarrassed by militarism than was the Quaker movement, witnessed a clash at the Anglican Assembly of February 1932 between the radical Archbishop of York, William Temple, who called for the consecration of force in the League, and the Rev. Gathorne Crabtree, who deplored Britain's weak defences. Like the LNU, the Church averted its gaze from international force and prayed for 'concurrent disarmament' by all states.[53] Concerned primarily with ecclesiastical matters, the Church could tolerate a certain amount of dispute over international affairs.

Other sections of organised opinion replicated the fluid pattern of deconstruction. After the 1933 Labour Party Conference, the political wing of the labour movement officially supported an IPF as the corollary to disarmament. It offended pacifists such as Lansbury and revolutionaries such as Brailsford, who warned fellow socialists that '[a] League army to-day would be the picked police force of allied capitalism.'[54] It would be wrong, of course, to imagine that the IPF proposal was specifically responsible for spotlighting divisions in the Labour Party over foreign policy. Brailsford's anti-militarism must be seen in the context of increasing dissent from the liberal internationalist position as a whole. After the political traumas of 1931, left-wing condemnation of capitalism (in all its manifestations) received a sympathetic hearing. At the 1933 conference, the deep and widespread distrust of government foreign policy offered a favourable environment for the newborn Socialist League to question the Party's faith in collective security. The League of Nations' failure to curb Japanese aggression played a significant role, leading C.P. Trevelyan to say that the feeble body at Geneva should be ditched. The notion that an IPF would solve both the problems of disarmament and security antagonised both pacifists and socialists. Sanctions and international force would be weapons of capitalism leading to imperialist war. Others linked security (now highlighted by the Manchurian crisis) with disarmament and an IPF – as Attlee continued to do in his denunciation of government policy. Already weakened by the political crisis, Labour supported both an IPF and organised working-class resistance to imperialist wars. The development of distinctive pacifist and Marxist attitudes to collective security is examined in the next chapter, but clearly by 1933 Labour's foreign policy consensus (as expressed in the drive for disarmament) was replaced by an ambiguity, which made reappraisal of peace through collective security doubly difficult after Hitler came to power.

Conservatives were no less at odds. Echoing Austen Chamberlain, the *Daily Telegraph* (26 May 1933) distrusted French plans, 'cast iron definitions and automatic sanctions', but from time to time readers aired the idea of international force in its pages – notably Brig.-Gen. E.L. Spears.

Much of this interest no doubt arose from anxiety about German policy rather than hopes for disarmament. This was certainly true of the *Telegraph's* rival, the *Morning Post*, which expressed no faith in the League or in internationalism generally. But by November 1932, as the British and French governments worked to get Germany back in the Disarmament Conference, the editor, H.A. Gwynne, was describing a new and conciliatory French security scheme as a valuable starting point for discussions.[55] Threat-specific collective security could be usefully directed against Germany, and after Hitler's accession, the *Post* began agitating for an Anglo-French alliance. Rank-and-file Conservatives were perturbed, both about the situation in Germany, and about the state of Britain's defences. From the spring of 1933, the Party's Central Office was nagged by local branches urging rearmament. This reaction against further disarmament negotiations continued at the Annual Conference (5–6 October) when Lord Lloyd, supported by Sir William Davison, Amery and Churchill, announced that he was 'sick and tired of seeing the Conservative Party pledged to pacifist international doctrines'.[56] But such was the confusion that having refused to pass a resolution congratulating the government on its Draft Disarmament Convention, a few hours later, delegates gave Baldwin overwhelming support for an intensified effort at Geneva.

As if to compound the confusion, Neville Chamberlain canvassed the cabinet for a so-called 'pacifist international doctrine', namely an IPF, early in 1934. He visualised a system of mutual guarantees by the principal European states, in which the liability of each partner would be limited – a plan which, he hoped, 'would gather up in support a number of currents of opinion, at present somewhat vague in direction'. The Chiefs of Staff pulled it to pieces. Nevertheless, the fact that the concept reached cabinet level indicates the extent to which collective force had become reputable. Even Churchill switched over to 'international doctrine', and in 1936 became a president of the New Commonwealth. Some liberal imperialists also displayed an interest. Edward Grigg, a former colonial administrator, split the Round Table group by proposing a guarantee of support to France.[57] He, John Buchan, and J.L. Garvin joined the New Commonwealth Society, while Lothian, Curtis, John Dove and H.V. Hodson (an editor of *Round Table*) maintained their isolationist stance towards Europe.

A new commonwealth

These splits in liberal internationalism challenged the disarmament consensus, and offered new opportunities for political transgression.

This is not to say that the IPF acted as a watershed. Organisations held on to members because of interests wider than collective security; new loyalties did not generally substitute for old. But the debate encouraged protagonists to develop additional interests in subsidiary organisations – the burgeoning peace groups or the New Commonwealth. A remarkable demonstration of cooperation among IPF advocates occurred in December 1933 when the Liberal MP Geoffrey Mander introduced a private member's bill in the Commons asking the government to consider approving an international force. Mander was seconded by a Conservative, Spears, and supported by Attlee for the Labour Party (or rather, some of it).[58] Advocates presented a mix of justifications: Mander thought an IPF would safeguard against the conversion of civil aircraft to military use, whereas Attlee regarded it as an essential step towards a world state. They disagreed about the kind of force envisaged, merely expressing a common desire to strengthen collective security to prevent further deterioration in the international system. The absence of a coherent philosophy or programme precluded military sanctions from gaining sufficient independent impetus necessary to influence mass opinion. For the most part, existing parties and pressure groups held the allegiance of their sanctionist or pacifist members, though few organisations walked such a tightrope of compromise as the LNU.

Founded in October 1932, the New Commonwealth Society captured the enthusiasts, a small and elitist focal point for taking peace through collective security to a logical conclusion. It gathered publicists and intellectuals who spread the message by means of after-dinner speeches and articles in monthly journals. Organisation was minimal, and after four years in existence, membership had reached only 1,772, including 70 MPs.[59] It owed its inspiration and exclusive character to Lord David Davies, wealthy landowner in Montgomeryshire and president of the LNU in Wales. During the war, he had commanded the 14th Battalion of the Royal Welsh Fusiliers in France, though by 1916 he had withdrawn to become a parliamentary secretary to Lloyd George, who had a keen nose for sources of wealth. As Liberal MP for Montgomeryshire between 1906 and 1929, Davies did not trouble the Commons unduly; his main interests were Welsh education and sport. He espoused international force after talking to French delegates at a Federation of League of Nations Societies meeting in 1923. He remained a staunch defender of the French thesis – on political and philosophical grounds rather than on grounds of sentiment. Indeed, sentimental Francophiles, including Austen Chamberlain and Maj. Jack Hills MP, did not go as far in validating French concerns.

Davies devoted himself to the study of collective security and the New Commonwealth, his zeal partly attributable to anxiety about developments at the Disarmament Conference. To Gilbert Murray, he wrote: 'There is nothing so dreadful as the feeling one has in the back of one's mind all the time that the Germans are playing a deep game and that their only object is simply to manoeuvre a better position for themselves out of proceedings at Geneva, with no thought whatever of peace or justice'. In contrast, French security schemes demonstrated moral courage in seeing German rearmament as the likely and dire alternative to 'effective provision for collective safety from war'.[60] Increasingly, Davies grew impatient with peace through disarmament, and claimed that it failed to grapple with fundamental causes of war. This remained central to his field of vision and his Society made full use of the Manchurian crisis as an object lesson in the need for international force. But Davies and others had advocated an IPF before digesting the implications of Japan's aggression in 1931. Davies published his theory in *The Problem of the Twentieth Century* (1930), which for length and consistency of thesis, if not in elegance of style, deserves an honourable place in the literature of the 1930s, though neglected as a liberal internationalist text. It ran to two editions, and was perhaps the most substantial and erudite philosophy of international relations to appear in the interwar period. Davies produced other books: *Suicide or Sanity?* (1932), *Force* (1934) and *Nearing the Abyss* (1936), that were variations on his *magnum opus*, and founded the first UK chair in International Relations at Aberystwyth, University of Wales.

He justified internationalism in historical terms, seeing himself as a descendent of the Acheans, Dante (in his *De Monarchia*), the Duc de Sully, Saint-Pierre, Rousseau and Kant. He contrasted the theorists of international government with the ethical, free-trade internationalists, such as Bentham and Cobden, and with the Hegelians. Davies rejected competitive nationalism and imperialism, and thought the Empire incapable of fulfilling its security needs. Given that democratic stability and justice were now threatened by nationalist revival, a federal approach to international relations should appeal to the instinct of self-preservation.[61] Of the Cobdenite stress on moral force, Davies rejected the 'mobilisation of shame' as a safeguard against war.[62] As might be expected, he had no truck with US isolationism, which he blamed for strangling the League of Nations at birth. The League suffered from the same weaknesses as the Hague Tribunal, the proceedings of which afforded 'an illustration of the futility of a loose and casual association of nations and emphasise[d] the fact that the main difficulty was the lack of an international sanction to enforce the awards of the arbitrator and the decisions of the judge'.[63]

Davies admired Tardieu's perspicacity, and proposed a federation of states that would surrender their sovereignty on questions of international law and its enforcement. The organisation would comprise an Assembly of states, an International Equity Tribunal comparable to the later International Court of Justice (composed of impartial elder statesmen who could recommend treaty revisions to an Assembly) and an IPF (to operate against states which ignored the ruling of a majority of the Assembly). There would be no hierarchy of security decision-making of the kind later established in the UN Security Council. The New Commonwealth Society advocated an IPF that could react rapidly and possess superior weaponry to aggressors. The Society offered imaginative structures. A General Staff would comprise a High Constable and Air and Naval Constables, with headquarters in Palestine (conveniently close to Britain's strategic interests in the eastern Mediterranean). Here the staff 'animated by the same purpose' would draw up tactical plans for deploying the pre-arranged state quotas of personnel and equipment.[64] Davies also outlined a code of police ethics and emphasised deterrence – but did not rule out bombing of cities and the inevitable killing of innocent civilians. Unlike the seventeenth-century Quakers William Penn and John Bellers, who believed that an international force would act as such an effective deterrent that it would never be summoned, the New Commonwealth expected the IPF to be used and Davies even drew up contingency war plans as appendices to his first book.

Despite his belief that Britain's dithering in 1914 contributed to the outbreak of war, Davies conceded that ultimate decisions about participating in enforcement in particular cases should remain with national governments.[65] But he anticipated that loyalty to states would diminish and '[i]f a new mentality can be produced by intensive propaganda and education, political parties may arise which are prepared to emblazon "I.P.F." on their banners'.[66]

The New Commonwealth Society provided a forum for participants with varied political backgrounds. The list of vice-presidents in 1934 included Attlee, Duff Cooper, Ethel Snowden, Sir Robert Horne and Lord Mottistone. Nevertheless, the two largest groups consisted of LNU converts (Cecil, Angell, Noel Baker, Sir Frederick Maurice and Margery Corbett-Ashby, for example). A Welsh multitude dominated the first subscription list, including 42 by the name of Davies, many also members of the Welsh Council of the LNU. Indeed, the New Commonwealth spent much energy attempting to convert the LNU to an IPF policy;

LNU branches organised about half the meetings addressed by the Society in its first year, and in 1934 the Welsh Council carried a pro-IPF resolution by 86 votes to eight.[67]

It is difficult to imagine how Cecil could have tolerated such activities in his organisation were it not for his own sympathies and the conversion of many of his followers. However, the debate exacerbated divisions. IPF enthusiasts, such as the former pacifist Clifford Allen, now Lord Allen (who joined the LNU Executive in June 1933, probably to infiltrate New Commonwealth ideas), and the Conservative MPs, Major Entwistle and Vyvyan Adams, caused Murray to note that 'our minute quarrels about pacifism and International Force ... [t]end now to occupy the whole horizon'.[68] Largely at the bidding of Allen, the LNU Council passed a series of resolutions on international force in 1934. However, they were strenuously opposed by Austen Chamberlain, Lord Percy and Maj. Hills. Percy simply argued against 'handing over to a world parliamentary body that most solemn of all the rights of sovereignty – the right to kill'. For the sake of harmony, Allen continued to back off for the next four years. In June 1938, after a show-down with the New Commonwealth the previous December, the LNU finally agreed to an IPF policy.[69] By then, practically speaking, it was subordinated to military alliance formation.

Conclusion

Apart from the LNU converts, the New Commonwealth's members had in common a belief in the need to preserve peace by desperate measures. Some were Germanophobes and hostile to appeasement. The presence of the anti-patriot Beverley Nichols and the imperialist Winston Churchill, on the same platform, testifies to the trespassing that Society engaged in. It is not evident that the New Commonwealth represented the first step towards a broadening anti-German consensus in liberal internationalism. The membership was too heterogeneous for that, and besides the membership fell slightly between 1934 and 1936. Nevertheless, the Society furnished space for realists. Following the death of Baron Henry Gladstone, Churchill accepted a share of the presidency with the ageing trade unionist G.N. Barnes in June 1936. A high-profile catch, Churchill's worst enemy had never accused him of being a federalist. There is little to suggest that he regarded the position as anything more than a rostrum on which to espouse war preparations. In a speech in November 1936, he warned of an ominous 'conjunction of the new air power with the rise of dictatorships'. The New

Commonwealth, he said, aimed to give democracy as soon as possible a 'strong foundation of physical and moral force', with which to speak to adversaries.[70] Churchill's late adoption of collective security, as with the Duchess of Atholl, had the ring of expediency. For others, the impetus to engage with the concept had been a combination of authoritative predictions about aerial warfare and the prospect of arms racing. Davies provided the ethical and historical justifications for a policy that also promised to guarantee France security and mitigate the threat of aerial obliteration.

Innovative thinking about international politics had ensued but with costs for the consensus on the ill-defined question of collective security. Defining it more closely redivided liberal internationalism. The IPF concept introduced an element of choice and foreshadowed UN peacekeeping. The New Commonwealth Society could trespass across political lines but established only loose cross-group agreement. The Labour Party was reluctant to abandon disarmament and enjoyed electoral success exploiting pacifism: its acceptance of the IPF plan accompanied commitment to war resistance. Despite Neville Chamberlain's engagement and Churchill's late conversion, Conservatives generally preferred national rearmament to militarised internationalism. The LNU equivocated and delayed accepting the IPF proposal till 1938. Those with privileged knowledge about collective security had the greatest difficulty agreeing on the implications. Thus, the IPF issue tested the range of factions congregated in the LNU. Perhaps the controversy sapped this institution's strength, undermining its ability to direct liberal internationalism in the Manchurian and Ethiopian crises. The leadership generally took refuge in less-contentious policies involving non-military sanctions. Such a crisis in elite governmentality quickened in the aftermath of the Manchurian crisis as resistance to liberal internationalism mounted through doctrines labelled 'pacifist' by contemporaries, the subject of the next chapter.

6
Resistance: Pacifism and the Power of Defiance

As well as fostering interest in an IPF, the air menace and the disarmament deadlock generated renewed resistance to involvement in war and antipathy to core liberal internationalist expectations of collective security. 'My belief in absolute pacifism', wrote Bertrand Russell, 'is limited to the present time, and depends upon the destructiveness of air warfare'.[1] But the growth of war rejection from the concern of small peace societies into a mass phenomenon was also attributable to the failure of collective security in Asia.

This chapter begins with the change in the scale of 'pacifist' operations in relation to the impact of Japanese aggression. Initially, contemporary critics of British policy seemed as uncertain as the policymakers themselves,[2] and the analysis indicates the main lines of dissent that heightened recriminations and resistance. The following section explains the role of what was loosely called 'pacifism' in the years bordered by the 1931 Manchurian and 1935 Ethiopian crises, and to see how the crisis in elitist liberal governmentality increased resistance to liberal internationalism, producing further shifts, disturbances and trespassing. Schisms arising from the mobilisation of peace sentiment disturbed existing boundaries of opinion and organisation. Consequentialists such as Norman Angell emphasised that there could be no winners in war; Marxist–Leninists promoted war resistance to maintain the class struggle, whereas deontologist, moral, Christian and humanist pacifism stressed individual conscientious objection.[3] The distinctions were not always clear. George Lansbury combined Christian and socialist pacifism; and in 1940 Russell adopted a just war stance, conditional on the existence of virtue among those resisting aggression. But the renaissance of these two types of war rejection – Marxist resistance to a capitalist war and individual moral resistance

89

to state power – both disrupted liberal internationalism, generating a widespread scepticism of the League's ability to preserve peace. They are examined in sections three and four, with a brief section on nationalism following. The chapter ends with analysis of the Oxford Union Debate and the Peace Ballot as signifiers of pacifism.

Manchuria

Liberal internationalism in civil society hardly reacted to the early stages of the Asian crisis. A financial slump, a change of government, the approach of the Disarmament Conference and the remoteness of Manchuria conspired to keep Japan's aggression under-reported. Labour's *Daily Herald*, for example, waited until four months after Japanese and Chinese troops clashed at Mukden in September 1931 before putting it on the front page. LNU branch secretaries wanting guidance had to fare on a diet of soothing platitudes from the leadership. 'The truth is', wrote Cecil, 'that we must be content to move rather slowly because owing to the complex condition of affairs just now we cannot threaten'. He even confided to the Foreign Secretary Sir John Simon that the abandonment of China was inevitable.[4] Cecil could not acknowledge this publicly, or admit that collective security was not working. For a Eurocentric, the Sino-Japanese dispute was an exceptional case that should not be allowed to affect the League's viability in Europe. Despite his record of friction with members of the National Government, Cecil kept in step with Simon and set the tone of the LNU's attitude to the conflict – a policy of restraint and, where possible, of praising the League for its mediation. As late as May 1933, the editor of *Headway* was exhorting his readers to 'possess their souls in patience' because the League was breaking new ground.

Airy rhetoric and dithering in Geneva was mirrored by inertia at the LNU's headquarters in London's Belgravia. LNU leaders seemed reluctant to contemplate even mild non-military measures against Japan until a League Commission led by Victor Bulwer-Lytton (2nd Earl of Lytton) had reported on the causes of the Mukden incident.[5] Other factions of liberal internationalism called for diplomatic sanctions, the non-recognition of territorial gains, an embargo on arms sales to Japan and economic sanctions.[6] More than most internationalists, the Labour Party condemned Japan at an early stage. But the parliamentary leaders, Lansbury and Ponsonby, would not demand economic sanctions for fear they could lead to war, and in a Commons debate in February 1933 Lansbury declared Labour's support for no more than an arms embargo on both sides. Exceptionally, H.N. Brailsford of the ILP advocated economic measures against Japan in the *New Leader* (13 November 1931), albeit conditional on US cooperation. He reflected the widespread respect for economic power. Together with Stafford Cripps and Harold Laski, he reacted vigorously against collective security when the League failed to check Japan. Labour's leadership presented the crisis as a test case for the League with implications for the future of disarmament and security in Europe.[7] But the fact that neither Labour nor other parties suggested sanctions against Japan without US participation was a confession that the League was hamstrung. Thus, the LNU attempted to protect the League's reputation by reasoning that '[i]f its writ does not run at the other end of Asia that is no proof that its writ does not run in Europe'.[8] While this Eurocentrism reflected a realist approach, core liberal internationalists also stressed the power of moral sanctions, to justify less-forceful action. Escalation of the war to engulf Shanghai made little difference to the notion that world opinion would halt Japan, though Lytton himself believed that an economic boycott by China would do the trick.[9]

The crisis galvanised pacifists with an approach that combined disgust at the League's failure to organise world opinion against the war and fear that sanctions would cause the war to spread. Wilfred Wellock (chair of the No More War Movement) expressed the blend of impatience and apprehension in a letter typical of those in the liberal press when he announced that vast numbers were losing faith in the existing peace machinery. Wellock called for an international 'army' of men and women to state 'that under no circumstances will they bear arms or render any form of military service'. Others wanted Article 16 pruned from the Covenant because the League was paralysed by obligations that no-one intended keeping.[10] Significantly, Cecil's main antagonists at an emergency session of the LNU in February were pacifists resisting economic pressure by the League that could lead to war.[11] The religious pacifists A. Herbert Grey, Maude Royden and R. H. (Dick) Sheppard offered a more dramatic response: 'men and women who believe it to be their duty should volunteer to place themselves unarmed between the combatants'. The 'Peace Army' symbolised a new spirit among moral pacifists, foreshadowing the formation of Peace Brigades International in 1981. The *Manchester Guardian* (27 February 1932) thought the scheme intelligent, apt, and no more fantastic than war itself, and some 320 people, including Brig.-Gen. Frank Crozier (of whom more later), signed up. However, the League's secretary-general, Eric Drummond, would only entertain proposals from governments.[12]

Apart from stimulating pacifist opinion, the Manchurian crisis exacerbated differences in the liberal internationalist movement. While the left blamed Japan, the right drew analogies between Japan's action and Britain's in Egypt and on the North–West Frontier of India. Japan was a trusted friend and had brought stability to China and foiled Soviet designs. In an editorial, J.L. Garvin judged that, since Japan's invasions, Manchuria had become 'a happy land'.[13] From a geopolitical perspective, China's relatively weak irredentism was displaced by an efficient imperialism admired by reactionaries who were both anxious to safeguard the Empire against Japan (with US help) and unctuous about Japan's newfound strength. At state level, Neville Chamberlain, Baldwin, Sir Warren Fisher and Simon thought Asia indefensible, but were realistic about US isolationism favoured amity with Japan to put the region on ice. This did not amount to complete rejection of collective security. Concerned about German rearmament, Chamberlain, Fisher and Vansittart agreed with Churchill that '[t]he League had a great work to do in Europe'.[14] But the effort to avoid provoking Japan (as illustrated by Simon's failure to condemn it at Geneva in December 1932) and the announcement of an arms embargo against China as well as Japan in February 1933, aroused considerable hostility outside Parliament.[15]

It was only a short step to blaming the government for the League's inadequacy, claiming that the United States was keen to take a leading part against Japan (though there is no evidence that it would have gone further than refusal to recognise Manchukuo). In retrieving the League's reputation, and the LNU's, Murray concluded that: '[t]he trouble is not that the sanctions are not severe enough but that the Governments will not use them at all. It is good faith and not physical force that is the key to the whole question'.[16] Other critics argued that moral pressure could have stopped the war by strengthening the 'civilian element' in Japan. However, as J.A. Spender later recognised, 'The reasonable inference from the facts was, not that the British Government had betrayed the League and the cause of world peace, but that there was something wrong with an institution that placed her in a position in which refusal to do the impossible exposed her to this charge'.[17]

Pacifism as resistance

The movement for collective security could not disguise the League's impotence. As a decline in LNU membership indicated, the Sino-Japanese war weakened support for liberal internationalism through collective security. To many right-wing observers, the episode had demonstrated the danger and futility of faith in an international security system. Further, the threats to British interests posed by both Japan and Germany involved crucial strategic and political decisions which also influenced conservative opinion about the League. An equally serious drift occurred on the left, and theories of conscientious objection – to capitalist war, national war or all war – increasingly attracted adherents.

Various factors contributed to these developments. The public were reminded of the features of modern warfare by a flood of memoirs and novels about the trenches. Most of them actually appeared between 1928 and 1930 at a time of relative international calm, and do not seem to have had any galvanising political effect at that time. Moreover, their realism often emphasised individual heroics and overlooked the mass conditioning to appalling circumstances. R.C. Sherriff's play *Journey's End* (1929) was more homage to heroism than a guide to war resistance. A more polemical literature, represented by the works of Aldous Huxley, Beverley Nichols and A.A. Milne, emerged after 1933 and was as much a symptom of pacifism as an incitement. The deteriorating international situation and lack of progress in disarmament were more potent determinants in the growth of socialist and Christian resistance. And when Brailsford announced the League's death in early 1932, he typified a response by no means confined to members of the ILP.[18]

Pacifist resistance to liberal internationalism captured various concerns. At best, the League was more involved in casuistry than giving a moral lead in international politics; at worst, it was a capitalist instrument designed to involve the working classes in war. This is not to say that all pacifists advocated ditching the League. Most took a similar attitude to conservatives, who regarded it as a useful forum for diplomacy. But pacifists also expressed scepticism about the League system. In this discourse, pacifist resistance to liberal internationalism had a more populist appeal than did the elitist-style agitation for an IPF. Peace groups became heir to the UDC's faith in the virtue of civil society's influence on foreign affairs.

Until the later test presented by the Ethiopian crisis, umbrella organisations such as the LNU tolerated disruption. Cooperation with pacifists flourished in campaigns for disarmament, in agitation for treaty revision and in a crusade against the private manufacture of armaments. The 'bloody traffic', for example, provided liberal internationalists with an explanation for the League's inadequacy, and acted as a target for pacifist war rejection. On sanctions, however, militant pacifists disturbed harmony in the Labour Party, the LNU and the National Peace

Council. The peace groups trespassed across boundaries in a similar way to the LNU in the 1920s, and the New Commonwealth Society was achieving concurrently.

The power of pacifist and socialist war resisters is illustrated by changes in the organisation and tactics of peace groups. In the 1920s, such groups had been coteries of dedicated socialists, Christian pacifists, conscientious objectors and rationalists such as Ponsonby and Russell. The combined membership could have been no more than 100,000. One such group, the No More War Movement, was founded by absolutists in 1921 in succession to the wartime No Conscription Fellowship. It founded War Resisters International but had only 3,000 members in Britain. Its leading lights in the late twenties were the war resisters of 1914–18: Fenner Brockway, Wellock, A. Barratt Brown, Rev. Leyton Richards, W.J. Chamberlain and Walter H. Ayles.[19] By 1931, such foundational groups gave way to populist methods of agitating for disarmament, the main activity of peace groups. But the Shanghai Peace Army proposal had reflected a new 'militancy', also exemplified by the establishment of the Marxist British Anti-War Movement in March 1932 and the Peace Pledge Union (PPU) in 1934. By contrast, the old No More War Movement increased its membership between 1933 and 1936 by a mere 500 and in 1937 amalgamated with the PPU.[20]

The National Peace Council (NPC) played a coordinating role, its *Peace Year Book* appeared regularly after 1931, and its monthly paper, *Peace*, after April 1933. In the summer of 1933, the NPC also sponsored the first annual Peace Congress. The Asian crisis had not killed off internationalism and the NPC could still count on the cooperation of non-pacifists. Some of these, particularly Angell, Noel Baker and Arnold-Forster, were permanent activists who strayed from one group to another with apparent tolerance of ideological variegation. For example, Arnold-Forster, an advocate of League force, served as Geneva representative of the pacifist-dominated NPC.[21] These freelance intellectuals had a degree of autonomy that enabled them to contravene political conventions. And as shown in Angell's quest for the Nobel Peace Prize, they projected Olympian knowledge of international relations.[22] In former times, their spiritual home might well have been in a vigorous Liberal Party. In lieu, their expertise contributed to the vibrant civil society debates on foreign policy. Genuinely committed to forceful collective security, they were, however, oddly out of tune with pacifist trends.

Heroes of wartime victimisation and peers of liberal conscience were still in evidence after 1931, but being joined by authors and actresses, army officers and students. The PPU, for example, was sponsored by

Aldous Huxley, Rose Macaulay, Margaret Storm Jameson, Vera Brittain, Max Plowman, Siegfried Sassoon, John Middleton Murray, Dick Sheppard and Brig.-Gen. Crozier. Opinion leaders with little political experience, they resisted at a time when orthodox views about economics, democracy and foreign policy had to be interrogated. Most of them had contributed to the war effort. Plowman and Sassoon had seen military service before making a stand against war; Sheppard had been a padre; Vera Brittain had served in a Voluntary Aid Detachment; J.M. Murray had been a censor. The much-decorated Crozier, fanatical Orangeman and former commander of the Black and Tans in the Irish civil war, who resigned in 1921 apparently in self-disgust, now displayed the same enthusiasm for peace as he had done for war. In Flanders, he had directed the execution of a man for desertion and had killed a surrendering German. But he came to believe that a future war would break up the moral fibre of civilisation.[23] As befitted a convert, his involvement in the war made his war rejection all the more zealous. The moral case made inroads in the NPC. Sheppard, Vera Brittain, E.W. Barnes (the bishop of Birmingham) and the 'Red Dean' of Canterbury, Hewlett Johnson, became members of the Executive, which by 1936 had cast off most of its sanctions enthusiasts. During and after the Ethiopian crisis, antagonism would become pervasive between security advocates and pacifists. Pacifists denounced League euphemisms: 'collective security' meant alliances, an IPF merely a force of allied powers, and 'military sanctions' simply meant war.[24]

Christian pacifists extended their reach beyond the issue of individual conscience to the prospect of converting civil society. Not content simply to justify and protect the dissenting conscience, they set out to win converts through lobbying. Liddell Hart commented that 'contact with many of my pacifist friends, with whose outlook I am naturally in sympathy, too often has the effect of making me almost despair of the elimination of war, because in their very pacifism the element of pugnacity is so perceptible.'[25] Religious validation remained salient, Sheppard paying much attention to the Christian justification for conscientious objection. But to encourage conversions, consequentialist and pragmatic reasoning affected anti-war discourses.

While many liberal internationalists idealised a system that relied on states cooperating to organise peace, pacifists confidently believed that war could be prevented, or neutralised, by conversions to war resistance. Sufficient numbers of conscientious objectors would deprive the state of manpower and cause it to sue for peace. Even aggressive dictators could be deterred from aggression by the pressure of domestic public opinion–opinion which, it was further assumed, would prefer peace to war. In addition, the deterrent effect of world opinion would persuade potentially aggressive states to 'do the decent thing'.[26] Failing this, the moral conscience of an aggressor would be impressed by non-resistance. 'I am certain', Donald Soper remarked, 'that pacifism contains a spiritual force strong enough to repel any invader'.[27] Pacifism was a practical stance because love and goodness were infectious. Inverting the metaphor, Huxley declared that: 'Pacifism is to war what clean water and clean milk are to typhoid; it makes the outbreak of war impossible'.[28] Given the condition of Europe in the thirties, this was a dubious assertion, but one intended to overcome the objections of League advocates.

Once pacifists had begun to construct an ethical international theory of peace – thereby providing the objecting conscience with a political platform – they had to address the point that, by definition, an aggressor state was not one that would be impressed by pacifist postures. To this, Russell countered that being as insecure as Denmark would be less terrible than war.[29] In the Second World War, however, Russell and the overwhelming majority of his fellow citizens opted to resist Germany and gamble on victory. On the eve of the war, the PPU alone claimed 130,000 members; after September 1939, fewer than 60,000 people claimed conscientious objection. Nevertheless, pacifism attempted to create an alternative framework to core beliefs of liberal internationalism. In a revealing comment the PPU contended that '[t]o test the truth of pacifist theory we must divorce ourselves from the meshes of immediate difficulties which owe their existence to the age-long application of wrong principles.'[30]

Socialist resistance

War resistance deriving from a Marxist interpretation of events also sought to trespass across boundaries. International working-class unity had been given a new twist by the spread of fascism. The theory recognised no contradiction in the policy of resistance to both fascism and war; it taught both as products of capitalism, initially discounting the possibility of war between fascist and capitalist states. Accordingly, the left relied on the power of domestic working-class action to foil the plans of capitalist governments. The experience of German social democracy in 1933 might have dented such hopes, but events in Germany merely heightened fears about a fascist takeover in Britain, and led John Strachey in *The Menace of Fascism* (1933) to discern fascist tendencies in British capitalism.

Under continental influence, war resisters grasped the importance of 'united front' activities. Following a peace conference in Amsterdam in the autumn of 1932 (run by the indefatigable German organiser and propagandist working with the Comintern, Willi Münzenburg, and the French communists Romain Rolland and Henri Barbusse), a British Anti-War Movement was established. The 1,500 delegates to its first public meeting in March 1933 (in Bermondsey), included the communists Emile Burns and Shapurji Saklatvala, the Labour Party stalwarts, Woolf, G.D.H. Cole, and Huxley and logicians C.E.M. Joad and Russell among the pacifists. It functioned as a popular front for most varieties – rationalist, revolutionary and religious – but its chief officers, W.J. Brown, Percy Collick, Dorothy Woodman and Lytton Strachey, were more inspired by Marx than God. This movement was primarily concerned with the growth of fascism and the apparent connivance of the Disarmament Conference in rearming Germany. But Strachey also expressed the group's disillusion with collective security:

> We assert that the methods pursued by the League of Nations Unions and other similar societies have disastrously failed. We do not believe that war can be prevented by seeking the co-operation of the very men, the foreign secretaries and the Cabinet Ministers, who are to-day making war inevitable by their policies. We do not believe that it is any more use to appeal to the present Governments of the world when they are assembled together at Geneva and call themselves 'The League of Nations', than it is to appeal to them separately at home.[31]

The working classes, argued Strachey, would ensure peace by organising mass resistance to the war policies of the ruling élite. The Anti-War Movement was not truly pacifist but entertained the possibility of a socialist war against fascism, though its assumption seems to have been that fascism would be dealt with on the home fronts.

The Anti-War Movement lasted only a year. It was banned as a communist satellite by the Labour Party at the end of 1932, and eclipsed by the Communist Party's united front activities. But its appearance indicates the extent to which the liberal internationalist movement had cracked. Marxists had never harboured admiration for the League, but their criticisms had been muted by the mainstream disarmament consensus. Now, however, the Manchurian crisis had exposed the inability of capitalist states to halt the imperialist ventures of one of their own kind. The communist-dominated Anti-War Movement acted briefly as a focus for dissent from Labour's spineless resistance to the menaces of war and fascism.

Traditional religious and socialist pacifism in the Labour Party, bolstered by radical pacifists after the war, had proved a strong combination at the 1926 Conference. An ILP-sponsored resolution calling for general resistance 'to any threat of war' passed unopposed. At that time, however, Germany had just entered the League and the prospect of war had diminished. In 1933, the outlook was much gloomier than it had been seven years earlier. Moreover, since 1926, Henderson and Dalton had pushed the party further in the direction of liberal internationalist governmentality, adopting tactics, discourses and a knowledge framework that favoured state security as a key to international security. These factors rendered the war resistance issue more critical and divisive. A labour movement already weakened by the 1931 electoral disaster was now assailed by pacifist resistance. Had this pressure arisen solely, or even primarily, as a result of the disarmament deadlock, the challenge might have been managed more deftly. Despite a resurgence of opinion in favour of unilateralism, some pacifists counselled caution. Ponsonby, for example, argued:

> The principle of Anti-War in all circumstances has grown very strongly even to the extent of Disarmament by Example. But the Party as a whole does not accept this, and some would even agree to a League war.... The best and simplest stand for us to make is to go out for disarmament down to the level imposed on Germany by the Treaty of Versailles while condemning Hitlerism within Germany.[32]

But the idealists who controlled the Socialist League wanted to commit Labour to organised war resistance. Formed on the eve of the 1932 Conference, the Socialist League claimed about 2,000 members – comprising ILPers who had stayed in the Labour Party and members of the Society for Socialist Inquiry and Propaganda.[33] The Socialist League predicted an imminent constitutional and economic collapse, and its attitude to foreign affairs largely projected its analysis of the domestic situation. Following MacDonald's 'betrayal' of 1931 by joining the National Government, left-wing politics had embraced cataclysm. The intellectuals Cripps, Strachey, Cole and Laski presented a stark choice between full-blooded socialism and outworn capitalism, supplying intellectual justification for the bitterness that gripped the left. The willingness to adopt resistance discourse on domestic issues spilt over into foreign policy. Cripps, who had advocated economic sanctions against Japan, became convinced that the Tories would find fascism at home and abroad a natural ally in times of trouble.[34] His fellow critic, Trevelyan, also reacted to the prospect of a combined crisis. Introducing a general strike resolution at the 1933 Labour Party conference, Trevelyan argued that '[t]he League of Nations is worked by feeble and sceptical Governments like our own, or by Governments that openly deride world peace, like Italy and Germany'.[35] In a twilight reddened by economic and political events, the Socialist League commanded popular support and the anti-war resolution again passed unopposed.

However, the only absolutist on the National Executive Committee was Lansbury, and 12 of the 25 places were filled by trade unionists who opposed attempts by intellectuals to saddle unions with the responsibility of calling a general strike in the event of war. But the union leaders Ernest Bevin and Walter Citrine were temporarily subdued by nazism. In fact the International Federation of Trade Unions had adopted a war resistance resolution in April 1933, and at the TUC in September delegates required the leadership to report on union action against war. Further, many of Labour's outstanding liberal internationalists (including Dalton) had lost parliamentary status in the General Election, and Henderson, as chair of the Disarmament Conference, had become a 'prisoner of Geneva'.

Convictions wavered among liberal internationalists. The conscientious objector Frederick Pethick-Lawrence, for example, retained his support for the League at the cost of much heart-searching: 'I was under no illusion that a war waged on behalf of the League would materially differ from any other war, either in its conduct or in its results'.[36] And Leonard Woolf typified the dilemma. Whilst deploring the League's failure in Asia, he reasserted his belief in collective security – mainly by eliminating the alternatives. Isolation was a policy of despair:

isolation as a policy in the mouth of people like Lord Beaverbrook or of the Nationalist Government would mean not a standing out of all wars and all commitments leading to war, but merely freedom from obligations under the Covenant of the League and freedom to commit this country to war afterwards in the interest of nationalism, imperialism, or reactionary capitalism.

He conceded, however, that the Labour Party should resort to direct action to prevent an imperial crusade by Britain, warning that Labour 'cannot ignore the dangerous possibility of such a misuse of the machinery of the League with the present Government in power'.[37]

Some proponents of collective security thus kept faith at the cost of heavy qualification. Indeed, Labour's subsequent opposition to rearmament derived in part from the rationalisations of 1933 and the government's 'betrayal' of the League system. Opposing the rearmament programme in July 1934, Attlee argued that a government which 'had left China in the lurch' and had paid mere lip service to collective security could not be trusted to use weapons purely for maintaining international law.[38] War resistance reflected disaffection from the League and foreign policy; it did not mark the party's conversion to pacifism. Labour became a party of divided counsels – the conference had also assented to an IPF policy (largely to secure disarmament). Henderson appealed to a sense of responsibility incumbent on an alternative government.[39] But in absorbing war resistance pressures, the party Executive expected that non-military sanctions would suffice to stem aggression. War resistance and League sanctions could be rendered compatible. The Socialist Leaguers could not provide an alternative international structure, and two months after the conference, Trevelyan also reverted to the Covenant, urging progressive implementation of non-military sanctions in the event of aggression.[40] By 1935, he advocated sanctions, including force, against Italy.

Paradoxically, this ambiguity made little difference to the party's standing with the electorate. Irresolution had blurred the lines of dissent within the party. In so far as the process of appealing for votes demands oversimplification, the party could turn vagueness into a virtue. In a series of by-elections at the end of 1933 (in which the average swing against the government was nearly 23 per cent), Labour posed as the party of peace and disarmament and branded government candidates as warmongers. Whatever the domestic factors in the government's poor showing, Labour acquired popularity by playing its foreign policy cards.[41] Admittedly, discursive gaps had widened and rhetoric grew more acerbic on all sides and, as will be shown, many Tories moved further away, ideologically, from the liberal internationalist movement.

Disruption occurred at Labour's 1934 conference with factions more sharply divided than the year before. Trade unionists and pro-League members had used their dominance of the National Joint Council to redefine collective security and eliminate the more obvious contradictions in policy. Nazi entrenchment confirmed their worries about the impotence of the German labour movement – hitherto Europe's strongest. Bevin had also been deeply affected by Engelbert Dolfuss's suppression of Austrian workers in February 1934, and realised the futility of war resistance under a dictatorship. He also postulated that German 'fascism' might lead to a war against capitalist states and, consequently, that fascism might have to be resisted from without.[42] The National Joint Council's programme *War and Peace*, published in June 1934, reflected these fears. Labour would support collective armed force under the Covenant, but recognised that patriotism had limits. The movement would refuse to support a government resorting to war in defiance of the League of Nations. The Council reaffirmed that under the TUC's existing standing orders, the movement would convene an emergency conference to consider the general strike weapon.[43] But the Joint Council had effectively undercut the advanced commitment to war resistance agreed at the 1933 conference. Bevin appealed to Labour conference delegates not to judge the League on its 'temporary lapse'; and the combination of trade union votes and the influence of Henderson, Dalton, Attlee, J.C. Wilmot and Noel Baker ensured the endorsement of 'War and Peace', by 1,519,000 votes to 673,000. Divisions persisted. Socialist Leaguers clung to working-class action against war. They had already aroused the ire of Labour leaders by combining with communists for a united front against fascism, an issue which marginalised the Socialist League in 1937. Cripps had also irritated colleagues with speeches on domestic issues (notably his reference to Buckingham Palace as a target for socialist attention). At the same time, the Socialist Leaguers openly admitted what had always been implied, that their war resistance was not strictly pacifist. Their basic aim was an alliance with the USSR to promote world socialism, using the League as a space for haranguing capitalist governments. A Labour Government would also 'negotiate pacts of mutual assistance and non-aggression with any countries which seriously sought to follow a pacific policy' – in other words, those countries with socialist governments.[44] This notion of an alternative world order recognised the need for an alliance against fascism, but conflicted with the gradualism promoted by Bevin and Dalton. An attempt to silence Cripps by hobbling him with the responsibility of a place on the party Executive lasted only until the Ethiopian crisis.

The debate between the Cripps and Bevin wings overshadowed Lansbury's Christian absolutism. Caught between Marxism and liberal internationalism, Lansbury elected not to speak on sanctions at the 1934 conference.[45] The party's liberal internationalists followed the LNU's practice of emphasising the power of non-military sanctions. But a substantial minority continued to harbour suspicions of League security, and youth branches continued to pass war resistance resolutions.[46] Moreover, for all its affinity with the LNU's standpoint, official policy was strongly hedged with reservations as a bulwark against illegitimate use of force by the government, a position open to wide interpretation. On the other hand, confronted by government protestations of loyalty to the Covenant (as in the Ethiopian crisis), the Labour Party had little choice but to wait until events indicated compliance or default.

No discussion of war resistance would be complete without survey-ing Communist Party of Great Britain (CPGB) and ILP commitment to a united front against fascism and war. However, the 'united' front proved as divisive on the far left as it did in the labour movement gener-ally. Adrift from the Labour Party, the ILP was free to enter into negotia-tions with the communists in March 1933. Although opposed by the official leadership, a Revolutionary Policy Committee in the ILP initi-ated negotiations. However, the CPGB ridiculed the ILP leader, James Maxton, as a reformist in Marxist clothing. For their part, the ILP dep-recated the CPGB's uncritical acceptance of Soviet policy, particularly when the USSR joined the League of Nations in September 1934. On this point, the ILP remained unyielding about the theory of collective secu-rity as a worthless illusion *'so long as the League of Nations is largely, or mainly, composed of capitalist governments'* (original emphasis).[47] Despite this hard line, the Ethiopian crisis would throw the ILP into confu-sion, it proving difficult to distinguish between working-class sanctions and bourgeois collective security. Factionalism flourished and, in the midst of the crisis, the 'revolutionary' section of the ILP defected to the Communist Party.[48]

Communists followed other deviations. As a Comintern satellite oper-ating in an overwhelmingly hostile environment, the CPGB faced uncom-mon hazards – mainly on account of the Comintern. Paradoxically, the local environment became more amenable, though the great period of expansion did not occur until the Spanish Civil War. Economic crisis, fascism and factionalism in the Labour movement contrived to favour united front resistance. Sales of *Labour Monthly*, edited by Ranji Palme Dutt, increased by 11 per cent to about 5,000 between 1933 and 1934.[49] But of all the 79 replies to a *Labour Monthly* survey, 35 per cent approved of deontological pacifism – as opposed to 51 per cent who favoured revo-lutionary war resistance, 8 per cent who backed collective security and an eccentric handful who supported outright imperialism.[50] Despite the small sample, Dutt expressed dismay that his readership harboured ethical pacifists. He overlooked the possibility that respondents may have seen no practical distinction between war resistance and 'bour-geois' pacifism. After years of anticipating a League war against the USSR, Dutt may also have been perplexed by its entry into the 'thieves' kitchen' in September 1934. He did not record it in *Labour Monthly* until

November, when it lurked in an article on 'The Labour Party Prepares For War'. The CPGB explained Stalin's switch as an attempt to spread working-class objectives in the citadel of imperialism.[51] Quite coincidentally, it occurred at the same time as the public was voting for collective security in the LNU-sponsored Peace Ballot. Instead of declaring a simple hostility towards the League, the communists now regarded it as a tool of Soviet policy and accepted military action against fascism only in defence of a 'Worker's Britain'.[52]

Nationalist resistance

For rather different reasons, opinion at the other end of the political spectrum also found association with the League uncomfortable. War resistance and pacifist offensives hardly troubled Conservative Party unity – though Baldwin included an electioneering talk to the vintage Peace Society in October 1935. But in their desire to emasculate the League, nationalists resembled pacifists, while remaining utterly opposed to pacifist philosophies. They certainly did not see each other as potential allies against a militarised League. Right-wing critics rarely discriminated between moral pacifists and sanctionists, often accusing the former of attempting to involve Britain in a 'League war'. Many Tories, too, would have agreed with Douglas Hogg (Viscount Hailsham) that foreign states would interpret 'the silly chattering of some of our boys at the universities' (a reference to the notorious King and Country debate in Oxford) as an invitation to dismantle the Empire.[53] For them, the League's failure in Asia had strengthened the case for limiting the functions of Geneva in accordance with the dictates of *realpolitik*.

Isolationists condemned international obligations with renewed vigour and increasingly regarded Geneva as little more than a debating forum. The denigrations gathered momentum from about May 1933 – when the collapse of the Disarmament Conference appeared inevitable and the prospect of a rearmed Germany added to the problems raised by Japan's imperialism. Despite the collectivist 'middle opinion' of some young Tory MPs such as Macmillan and Boothby, and of Labour MPs supporting the government, others distrusted collective security completely. Beaverbrook even urged withdrawal from the Locarno commitment. This attracted rank-and-file Conservative support and pleased the Round Table movement, but it offended Eurocentrics, including Austen Chamberlain, who viewed Locarno as the fulcrum of security policy.[54] By autumn 1934, deference towards the United States prevailed in official policy, and the prospect of Britain's participation in collective sanctions under the League or Locarno diminished appreciably. A speech by Smuts in November received widespread acclaim because he said the loose war talk was the product of pacifist scaremongering. In a fatuous dismissal of Europe's troubles, he proclaimed that '[o]nce Europeans admit to themselves that they are perhaps a little mad, the cure would come of itself'.[55] Baldwin himself took up the theme of US susceptibilities in speeches to Conservative organisations November 1934 and May 1935. In turning towards the Atlantic, Conservative opinion devalued the League at the same time that Cecil promoted its virtues through the Peace Ballot. Further, by demanding rearmament, government supporters had all but signalled an end to their acceptance of a vital international ideal. Liberal internationalism had shed lukewarm support.

Signifiers of pacifism? The Oxford debate and the Peace Ballot

In the context civil society movements, however, the 'silly chattering' that Hogg remarked on reflected a radicalisation of opinion. Moreover, the Oxford Union's resolution of 9 February 1933 (that 'this House will in no circumstance fight for its King and country') contributed to the pressure building up on all sides of the LNU. Liberal internationalists argued that the vote did not rule out fighting for international law and justice. Cecil claimed that the motion merely expressed general disgust against war and could not be taken literally.[56] Yet, if the resolution meant anything, it meant in theory that the students would not follow King and Country, even in a League war. The notion that the result signified, by implication, a vote for the League was a myth created a few days after the event by a non-participant.[57] The evidence points the other way. Frank Hardie, president of the Union, regarded the vote as symptomatic of left-wing influence in the university.[58] A communist October Club with between 200 and 300 members had been formed in January 1932, and an earlier debate in the Union resolved that 'in Socialism lies the only solution to the problems facing the country'. Michael Foot, president of the Liberal Club and Hardie's successor as Union president, also believed that the government's handling of the Manchurian crisis had 'driven student opinion into the consideration of an uncompromising attitude towards war'.[59] The students undoubtedly interpreted 'pacifism' in various ways, but this would have included suspicion of peace as collective security.

Echoes of the undergraduate vote troubled the LNU's leadership. An oblique probe by pacifists enlivened a meeting of the LNU General

Council on 22 June 1933. A delegate cited the Oxford debate and moved that the LNU legitimise refusals to participate in wars contravening the Covenant or Kellogg Pact. Cecil realised that, if accepted, this apparently harmless proposal might stigmatise the LNU as unpatriotic, saw no useful purpose in it and refused to believe that Britain would engage in a war in contravention of the Covenant.[60] His cold *douche* angered those who had less faith in the government, including Laski, and risked the loss of pacifist support.[61] But it avoided exposure of the LNU to misinterpretation and adverse publicity.

Once again, the LNU had adapted deftly to a change in civil society. It is only in this context that the LNU's involvement in the Peace Ballot makes sense. It would not simply exert influence on government policy, it could also relieve pressure on the LNU itself. The organisation's fortunes tended to fluctuate with those of the League system. Cecil had predicted that if the disarmament conference failed, 'there will be a strong movement in the country for unilateral disarmament, which I should regret and my Conservative friends even more'.[62] When the conference collapsed, he moved to forestall unilateralism as well as rearmament. The League's letdown over Manchuria added to the LNU's woes. By early 1934, Arnold-Forster reported that defections had reached a stampede – mainly in the direction of pacifism.[63] Between 1931 and 1933, LNU subscriptions fell from 410,000 to 377,824. In the London region, membership fell from 72,000 to 66,000 between 1932 and 1933.[64] Secretarial staff at Head Office criticised the Executive's feebleness during the Asian crisis and cited a lack of public confidence in the LNU.[65] The leadership preferred to blame pacifists for attempting to destroy collective security by removing sanctions from the Covenant.[66] A dramatic stroke was needed to stem the disaffection. Cecil decided, therefore, to harness pacifism by proposing a national referendum on the League and disarmament, and somehow transform the critique into support for collective security.

The project bristled with difficulties. Cecil's colleagues voiced doubts. The LNU secretary, Garnett, thought the idea impractical; Murray queried the reduction of complex questions to yes or no answers; and a wary Executive insisted on cost-sharing by a coalition of organisations operating through an independent committee.[67] Without seeking the approval of LNU branches, Cecil established a National Declaration Committee in March 1934. Confronted by this *fait accompli*, several delegates to the June Council resisted an immediate commitment, but it went ahead amid a fresh crop of disputes and resignations.[68] Disruption arose partly because Cecil had to manage the Ballot questionnaire to preclude an adverse result. A pilot survey by the editor of the *Ilford Recorder* in January 1934 had asked: 'Do you agree with that part of the Locarno Treaty which binds Great Britain to go to the help of France or Germany if the one is attacked by the other?' Only 5,898 answered 'YES'; 18,498 answered 'NO'. Decisive rejection of military commitment indicated a need for careful wording in the national ballot. The questions eventually agreed upon were:

1. Should Great Britain remain a Member of the League of Nations?
2. Are you in favour of an all-round reduction of armaments by international agreement?
3. Are you in favour of the all-round abolition of national military and naval aircraft by international agreement?
4. Should the manufacture and sale of armaments for private profit be prohibited by international agreement?
5. Do you consider that, if a nation insists on attacking another, the other nations should combine to compel it to stop by
   (a) economic and non-military measures?
   (b) If necessary, military measures?

Anti-sanctionists had a say in the drafting and it was no doubt to accommodate them that in addition to Yes, No, Doubtful and Abstain, the 'Christian Pacifist Position' was included as an optional answer to question 5. To guard against nuance and rebuff the Committee's instruction leaflet announced: 'In this Ballot you are asked to vote only on peace or war – whether you approve of the League of Nations, or not; whether you are in favour of international disarmament or not'.[69]

Naturally, the project raised Tory hackles. Austen Chamberlain had been absent from the decisive LNU meetings and organised an opposition to the ballot – accusing its promoters of fraud and 'terminological inexactitude'. The Conservative Party refused to participate in the Declaration Committee on the grounds that the questions simplified complex issues, question 5 giving the false impression that aggression could be stopped by economic measures alone. Amery attacked it as a plot concocted by 'astute political gangsters'. Lord Percy threatened that the 'loathsome' ballot would drive Tories out of the LNU and into isolation.[70] Unable to get the scheme abandoned, and conscious of the fact that some Conservatives were participating, Percy and Chamberlain obliged the Declaration Committee to issue a leaflet explaining their objections. But Cecil was able to complain that the Tories had allowed party spirit to poison a non-party enterprise.[71]

And, once Conservatives had shown their displeasure, the National Council of Labour overcame its initial wariness and openly supported the ballot. In her Putney by-election campaign in November 1934, the Labour candidate, Edith Summerskill, found it a useful campaigning issue;[72] the National–Conservative majority fell from 21,146 to 2,663.

As a public relations exercise, the ballot must have exceeded Cecil's wildest hopes. At one extreme the anti-League press was virtually cowed into silence by results made available from the beginning of 1935. An intervention against the 'Blood Ballot' by Beaverbrook had merely contributed free publicity. Pacifists had also counter-attacked in October 1934 – with Sheppard's appeal for war resistance pledges. But no permanent organisation emerged from this until the PPU's first meeting, in May 1936, after the Italo-Ethiopian War. Indeed, Sheppard paid tribute to the Declaration Committee's efficiency, though Christian pacifism came out badly.[73] A mere 14,000 gave the Christian Pacifist alternative to question 5a and 17,482 to 5b, fewer even than either 'doubtfuls' or abstentions. By contrast, 87 per cent of the responses to 5a and 58 per cent to 5b were positive.

On the surface, this was a massive vote for collective security principles, but based on assumptions about international cooperation. Certainly, a French verdict – *une évolution de la pensée Britannique vers la thèse française qui demande que la sécurité précède le désarmement* – was misleading (a move in British opinion towards the French argument for security to precede disarmament).[74] An interesting feature of the ballot was a marked fall in the proportion of 'Yes' answers to 5b as late results were reported for December 1934 and January 1935. This relapse perhaps reflected a concern that the Saar plebiscite of 13 January might present respondents with an opportunity to put principles into practice. Certainly the Labour movement was initially reluctant to allow the use of British troops in the Saar plebiscite.[75] On the other hand, the ballot had not been a vote for outright pacifism.

For liberal internationalists, it had special significance in their struggle to maintain governmental legitimacy. Cecil commented afterwards: 'I hope very much ... that one of the results of the Ballot may be a large increase in the membership of the League of Nations Union'.[76] By the end of 1934, paid-up membership had improved on the previous year by 20,000 – probably reflecting the LNU's new exertions. It was certainly an accomplished piece of social movement manoeuvring. Cecil had overcome the opposition of LNU colleagues, overshadowed the pacifists, outmanoeuvred the Conservatives, all but silenced the anti-League press, earned the *New Statesman*'s admiration and successfully veiled the LNU's policy on Manchuria – all financed by donations.

But success had its price. Isolationists were confirmed in their view that all 'pacifists' were bellicose; Conservatives suspected the ballot was an attempt to besmirch government foreign policy; and pacifism had been overshadowed but not eliminated as an element in politics. It nevertheless represented a milestone in civil society activism, temporarily addressing the crisis in liberal governmentality. Should the ideals miscarry again, desertion would be all the more swift. In 1938, Noel Baker proposed another ballot to halt a renewed flagging in LNU membership. Cecil had no hesitation in refusing: he could not have pulled it off twice.[77] It had crowned the work of the liberal international social movement for peace, even though various elements could not agree on a line of approach.

One spin-off called the Liberty and Democratic Leadership Group had emerged from the NPC's Peace Congress of 1933, deriving its initial impetus from a faith in democracy and economic planning. Its first manifesto in February 1934 denounced shirt-wearing extremists. A second manifesto in May reflected the views of Allen in advocating collective armed force against aggression as a last resort. Two pacifists, Lansbury and Siegfried Sassoon refused to sign, as did Sir Basil Blackett and John Buchan.[78] When it transformed into The Next Five Years Group, many issues commanded agreement – economic planning, vague support for the League of Nations, treaty revision and free trade. In assenting to the bulk of the proposals, the Christian pacifists Sydney Bailey, Sassoon, A. Barratt Brown and the Bishop of Birmingham undoubtedly had reservations about the statement that in cases of determined aggression 'violence is not likely to be stopped by purely economic means, but the economic sanctions will have to be supplemented by the sanctions of armed force'.[79]

Conclusion

Although reactions to the Asian crisis had been mooted in liberal internationalist and pacifist groups in British civil society, the combination of that test for the League with the disarmament impasse and disputes over military sanctions provided incentives for a pacifist renewal. Manchuria had been read by many, especially the LNU leadership, as an exceptional case that made little difference to the League's writ in Europe. But war resisters used the crisis to expand, on both the Marxist and ethical fronts. For the liberal internationalists, new pressures gathered for rejecting sanctions, rejecting the League, rejecting capitalist wars, and rejecting all species of war. In what can be seen as a brilliant tactic of liberal internationalist governmentality, the Peace Ballot kept the movement alive, though resistances had broken through the LNU's near monopoly of control over civil society debates about international relations.

On the eve of the Italo-Ethiopian War, cooperation between sanctionists and moral pacifists continued in the National Peace Council, in spite of resistance to League force in the Labour Party and the LNU. The Peace Ballot masked hardening attitudes and disagreements and new peace groups testified to dissatisfaction with the other vehicles of opinion. By 1936, the LNU and PPU were at loggerheads, and the NPC was virtually paralysed on the issue of sanctions. The New Commonwealth Society was to describe the PPU's activities as 'irresponsible and little short of subversive'.[80] In the meantime, the world depression had caused all shades of opinion to elevate the significance of economic forces in international life. Faith in economic solutions and the 'have versus have-not' debate were to dominate the approach to collective security in the African crisis confronting the League of Nations.

7
Imperialism: Economic Security and Sanctions

A growing fixation with economic issues in British liberal internationalism emerged partly from direct experience of economic vulnerability, and partly from a growing awareness of global economic interdependence. In addition, privileged states such as Britain had an obligation to assist poorer countries to sustain themselves peacefully without the need for imperial policing. Many interwar liberal internationalists aimed, as post-Second World War, to rescue the undeveloped world from disease, famine, poverty and internal conflict, and to develop it for capital accumulation. The power of economic sanctions to affect state behaviour also figured prominently, coming to a head with the great confrontations over Italy's invasion of Abyssinia/Ethiopia.

Disturbances in liberal internationalist governmentality caused by the IPF debate and the challenge of pacifism were all but suppressed by an enormous outpouring of moral outrage during the Ethiopian crisis. The conflict attracted copious newsreel and press coverage. According to Evelyn Waugh, correspondent for the *Daily Mail*, 'Everyone with any claims to African experience was cashing in...Files were being searched for photographs of any inhospitable-looking people – Patagonian Indians, Borneo head-hunters, Australian aborigines – which could be reproduced to illustrate Abyssinian culture'.[1] An attempt by the British and French cabinets to buy off the aggressor in December 1935 occasioned the greatest moral outburst on a foreign policy question apart from the world war since the Bulgarian atrocities agitation of 1876. Its intensity contrasted starkly with the level of attention devoted to the Asian crisis. The collapse of disarmament, Germany's open pursuit of rearmament and a war zone nearer home involving a European state generated mass protest. For the internationalist movement, all factions could agree that the war would either make or break the League.

Here was a chance for the League to prove itself and for the concepts supposedly embodied in the Peace Ballot to be put into practice. Furthermore, the splits in liberal internationalism were temporarily repaired by expectations of economic power as an instrument of global order.

This chapter is in four sections. The first surveys ideological, sentimental and strategic factors that affected attitudes to Italy's war. Sections two and three examine economic dimensions of the liberal internationalist response – the 'have-not' theory of imperialism in the second section and the issue of economic sanctions. The imperialism debate shows that Italy was imagined as a 'have-not' state, whose economic difficulties could be alleviated by adjusting the world economic order. Global depression had already elevated the issue of economic nationalism. More specifically, colonial mandates had been discussed during a visit to Berlin by Simon and Eden in March 1935. But 'have-not' theory, as distinct from revision of the Peace Treaties, gained prominence mainly because of the Italo-Ethiopian war. Many British commentators viewed autarky as a species of retaliation, that a trend to protectionism in general and imperial preference in particular had prompted Italy to seek compensation. When Gilbert Murray complained that 'economic anarchy' had increased world tension, his solution was fairness in international trade – a measure advocated by 'welfarists' who urged international planning on socialist lines.[2] On sanctions, liberal internationalists placed a corresponding faith in the effectiveness of economic penalties. The slump had exposed the vulnerability of even advanced economies. Sanctions would be fatal for a second-rate power such as Italy, and Italy would draw back at the threat of a boycott.[3] The fourth section shows, however, that the African war eventually shattered the internationalist movement, fragmentation beginning after Italy's invasion on 2 October 1935. Economic appeasement became more urgent to some Conservatives, but less acceptable to left and liberal opinion (as reactions to the Hoare–Laval Pact demonstrated). Furthermore, disillusion with the impact of economic sanctions brought about controversy over supplementary League action such as a blockade of the Suez Canal. From then on, peace by collective security lost ground rapidly in favour of rearmament, appeasement or popular front and grand alliance strategies.

Ideology and strategy

There are several points of interest about divisions in liberal internationalism over the war, aside from economic issues. Certain attitudes taken in the crisis had predictable ideological foundations. The left, for example, had little reason to support the Mussolini regime, and in 1932, Sylvia Pankhurst formed a Women's International Matteotti Committee (to agitate for the release from house arrest of Matteotti's widow). With the exiled Italian socialist Silvio Cario, she extended her propaganda campaign against fascism by founding the *New Times & Ethiopian News* in May 1936. The opportunity to strike at fascism provided Labour Party leaders with justification for supporting collective security.

At the other extreme, Italophile sentiment, sometimes tinged with racism, accounted for several individual standpoints which are less renowned but equally intriguing. Chief among Italophiles, Lord Mottistone, grandson of the man who had invited Garibaldi to Britain, remarked that an Italian defeat 'would be the end of every white man in Africa'.[4] Known for his court appearances after giving an engaged woman career advice in Hyde Park at night (acquitted) and grabbing another young woman in a railway carriage (fined), Sir Leo(ne) Chiozza Money, born in Genoa and a racial supremacist free-trade economist, moved from Liberal to Labour after the war but lost faith in party politics. 'Let me say', wrote Money to his friend and former boss, Lloyd George, 'how glad I am that you are enlightening people about Fascism in Germany. I wish you would do the same for the Fascist State which Germany has copied'. Money had no wish to see the British masses 'offered up as a cheap sacrifice to the fine fellows they are training in Fascist lands'.[5] The British–Italian League and the British Union of Fascists (BUF) took up the Italian cause with a vengeance. Having identified Italian fascism in alliance with Britain as the greatest threat to peace in the 1920s, Oswald Mosley now advocated a Fascist Power Bloc of Italy, Germany, France and Britain to replace the 'Russian-directed League of Nations', and in September the BUF began a 'peace' campaign to prevent an Anglo-Italian war. According to the propaganda officer, William Joyce, the real conflict involved the powers of 'Jewish-controlled Bolshevism' and 'the regenerated Fascist nations of Europe, cherishing their national patriotism and prepared to fight to the last ditch for the principles of white civilization'. Haile Selassie was reviled as a 'Negro-Jew', and Benito Mussolini praised by the BUF recruit Maj.-Gen. J.F.C Fuller as 'Napoleon compounded with Benvenuto Cellini'.[6]

But attitudes to the crisis were not always predictable. Some Catholics sympathised with Italy – Cardinal Hinsley, Archbishop of Westminster, extolled the virtues of fascism, and the convert Evelyn Waugh argued that the Italians were engaged in 'a minor colonial operation'.[7] But the virulently anti-Catholic Lady Astor agreed with them. The reactionary Henry Page Croft MP supported Italy's flattering imitation of British imperialism; he also heaped praise on Lansbury – an event as extraordinary as the acclamation of the Tory Leo Amery by the ILPer John McGovern – all of them opposing collective security. It was perhaps understandable that Italophile historians Sir John Marriott and Sir Charles Petrie should write eulogies of fascism,[8] but another friend of Italy, Austen Chamberlain, supported sanctions. And why did Lothian and Sir Edward Grigg oppose each other across the Round Table?

For many in the internationalist coalition, Germany was the primary concern, rather than Italy. In the matrix of reactions to the African war, Christian pacifists such as Sheppard and Lansbury rejected sanctions against Italy and took a sympathetic view of German revisionist claims. In the LNU, Allen, Lothian and Lord Lugard, who had been on the League's Mandates Commission, also pursued revision of the Versailles settlement, but condemned Italy.[9] The New Commonwealth Society demanded sanctions against Italy and an encirclement strategy to curb Germany. Within the fluidity of internationalism, strategies for dealing with Germany helped determine responses towards Italian expansion. Defending the appeasement of Italy, Foreign Secretary Sir Samuel Hoare explained to Baldwin that 'the future revolves round one question and one question alone – the position of Germany'.[10] Relative to Germany's ambitions, Italy's infraction of Ethiopian integrity had peripheral significance – a point also understood in Whitehall.[11] In their imagination, Mussolini had a 'natural wish' to pursue an Anglo-French alliance against Germany, on account of the latter's growing potential support for Austrian claims in the Tyrol.[12] As for the argument that action against Italy would deter German aggression, Amery gave it short shrift in a speech in October 1935, pledging that no Birmingham lad would die for Haile Selassie. The lesson ambitious powers would draw from a League war against Italy would be 'that they had better make hay while the sun shines'.[13] Reactionaries such as Amery, Croft, Lloyd and the *Morning Post* editor Gwynne, had an unfashionable view of international politics as relentless power struggles and the League as a talking shop, and they took account of Britain's military situation. Lord Lloyd, for example, fretted Italy could so weaken the Royal Navy that it would be powerless against Germany in the North Sea. And while some sailors flexed their war muscles – Chatfield, the First Sea Lord, felt confident of sinking the Italian fleet if Mussolini launched 'a mad dog act' – the Chiefs of Staff reckoned that war in the Mediterranean would impair the navy's ability to defend the Empire.[14] But to liberal internationalists, such issues took second place to peace through collective security, with economic leverage available to the League.

Have-not theory

Reviewing the events of 1935, the historian G.P. Gooch hoped that economic stability would emerge, because the crisis had forced the 'haves' to consider the claims of the 'have-nots'.[15] Sir Samuel Hoare boasted of his speech to the League Assembly in September 1935: 'I was the first public man, so far as I know, outside Italy who admitted the Italian case for expansion and economic development'.[16] A key to internationalist evaluations lies in their economic assumptions, notably that Italy was a 'have-not' power driven by a quest for autarky. In fact, Mussolini wanted to revenge the humiliation of defeat by Ethiopia at Adwa/Adowa in 1896, and to demonstrate Italian military competence to Germany. His misgivings about Germany, aroused in 1934 by an attempted coup in Vienna by Austrian Nazis, led Italy to dispatch troops to the Brenner Pass and reach agreements with France in the first half of 1935. A military convention with France directed against Germany enabled Italy to focus on adding to its Eritrean and Somali colonies.[17] But British internationalists also sought an explanation in the economic dislocation caused by the war and perpetuated by Britain's protectionist policies.

To liberals, protectionism strangled world trade. The Liberal ministers Samuel and Sinclair had resigned in September 1932 after resisting import duties and imperial preference (arranged with the rest of the Empire in Ottawa), and complaining that the protectionist regime would sabotage a forthcoming World Economic Conference.[18] Bizarre claims about the impact on Italy included the assertion that 'the road to Ottawa has led to Adowa'.[19] But the initiator of protectionism, the United States, did not attend the Conference, President Roosevelt stating that US interests came first. Subdued in their criticism of the United States, liberal internationalists seem to have swallowed denigration of Europe as the prime source of the world's evils. Bias also characterised liberal analyses of the depression, few commenting on the collapse of Wall Street margin trading or structural weaknesses in the US economy. The League's economic director, Sir Arthur Salter, argued that the crash had been impelled by undercurrents of political tension in Europe and US fears of another European war. [20] Most commentators stressed the war's bequest of reparations, debts and economic dislocation. The war provided a shorthand explanation for economic collapse. Lionel Robbins, the neoliberal economist at the LSE, contended that it had stimulated inflation and government interference.[21]

More specifically, the economic clauses of the Treaty of Versailles also served to explain 'have-not' aggression. Hardly had the ink dried on the Treaty before Norman Angell compiled a list of 'indispensable revisions'. They included the transfer of all colonial possessions to the League and their redistribution as mandates, to include German participation.[22] Liberal internationalists had long been aware that the mandate system devised by Smuts and Cecil worked to Britain's advantage. Yet in his critique of Versailles, Keynes (*The Economic Consequences of the Peace*, 1919) had refrained from weakening his case by citing Germany's meagre colonial trade. Hitler made little use of the issue before 1937, and then primarily as diplomatic leverage. By contrast, Italy's only 'legal' claim to colonial territory fell under Article 13 of the secret Treaty of London (1915). Nevertheless, *The Times* (23 September 1935) pursued the argument: 'the inequality between the "Haves" and "Have Nots" which affects other countries besides Italy – was never regarded with anything but sympathy here'. Although deploring Italy's aggression, the National Peace Council made a similar assessment: '[f]or the greater part of the post-war period an attempt has been made in the name of the Treaty of Versailles to maintain inequalities among neighbouring nations in Europe'.[23]

Paradoxically, cherished articles of classical economics were losing their hold. International debts, for example, became an early casualty of the slump. Germany's inability to pay reparations, recognised at the Lausanne Conference in July 1932, was accepted as inevitable by economic experts and the liberal internationalists.[24] Unlike reparations, inter-allied war debts carried less stigma of injustice. The looming resumption of Britain's payments to the United States on expiry of a moratorium, and despite forgoing German reparations, prompted discontent. There was much praise for the Treasury's reluctance to swell the US 'fund of derelict gold' when an instalment fell due in December 1932.[25] In June 1933 Britain made a final token payment (in silver). Few regretted the breach of financial probity, though it may have strengthened US determination not to spend on European wars (unless for the defence of Finland, which paid in full).

Free trade had also suffered with the crash. Salter had said in 1927 that the reconstruction problem was a question of finding how to get back to the system 'that worked reasonably well before the war'. Five years later, he not only advocated a New Deal approach to recovery but his criticism of protectionist policies had softened.[26] By 1931, Liberal economists, notably Keynes, Hubert Henderson and Josiah Stamp, had opted for a tariff to protect domestic employment, and a substantial wing of the Liberal Party had followed Simon into the protectionist camp. Other Liberals clung to free-trade discourse while advocating 'lower tariffs' rather than 'no tariffs'. Of the eight Samuelite Ministers who resigned in 1932, Lothian drifted back to his old chief, Lloyd George, to promote a New Deal, and Isaac Foot and H.G. White became founders of the Next Five Years Group (see below), seeking discriminatory tariffs. The LNU leadership employed the imagery of free trade but, characteristically, had to avoid turning the issue into yet another fratricidal struggle.[27] A trend towards state intervention to remedy unemployment, was marked by the establishment of liberal groups with no revolutionary intent: Political and Economic Planning (1931), the Next Five Years Group (1933–35) and the Council of Action sponsored by Lloyd George (1935). On international trade, the authors of *The Next Five Years* (Salter, Macmillan, Allen, Geoffrey Crowther and the ubiquitous Arnold-Forster) advocated a low-tariff club, with reciprocal concessions.[28] Its economic manifesto, signed by both J.A. Hobson of the Independent Labour Party and clothing mogul Sir Montague Burton, also embraced principles on national planning for domestic recovery.

The contradiction between continuing faith in the global open door (with its implications for economic appeasement) and emergency resort to protectionism also troubled supporters of 'welfarism'. Welfarists envisaged 'world planning' on the lines of a socialist welfare state. Of the four prominent welfarists – Hobson, Cole, Laski and Brailsford – only Hobson made common cause with the Next Five Years Group. Operating through the Labour Party and the New Fabian Research Bureau, the four conformed to Fabian and guild socialist gradualism, but gave these traditions an international dimension. Hobson, for example, advocated a World Economic Council, with delegates from all sides of industry and Cole spoke of governments needing to represent the pluralistic 'communal point of view' as the precondition of economic internationalism. Brailsford, the most prolific propagandist, looked forward to a federal parliament within the League, to control the global economy. But he based his early hopes for reformism on the promotion of low tariffs and open door policies, and on the gradual undercutting of state sovereignty by agencies such as the International Labour Office.[29] He anticipated loyalty to the system because workers could expect social benefits, including the ten-hour day (a measure recommended by the ILO but unratified by the National Government). Intergovernmental reform might also pressurise reactionary governments into making concessions to the working classes. To the extent that welfarists advocated a kind of Cobdenite free-trade cosmopolitanism, they were indistinguishable from the Edwardian Radicals who had opposed imperialism. In Hobson, indeed, welfarism had a veteran critic of the nineteenth-century scramble for raw materials. But welfarists embraced a second strand that predisposed them to take note of the grievances of 'have-not' powers – a belief in scientific administration of global resources. They shadowed the technocratic world-state ideal of H.G. Wells, for whom the essentials of economics were 'problems in applied physics and chemistry'.[30] Like Wells, the welfarists envisaged an organic transformation of international life to preclude 'have-not' grievances from arising. They advocated more fundamental reforms than did the low-tariff policy pursued by the bulk of the Labour Party. Wells had previously suggested in *The World of William Clissold* (1926) that all classes in society would be served by technocrats and 'cosmopolitan capitalists', who would undertake the collective purchase of raw materials. But by 1934 and completion of his autobiography, this had given way to belief in a socialist world-state.

Socialist internationalism, a third strand in welfarism, increasingly overshadowed the elements of Cobdenism and technocracy. Class animosity was a nuisance to Wells, who refuted the contention that capitalism led inevitably to war, but it featured strongly in welfarist writings, especially after the 1931 political crisis. Anxious that Labour should maintain a clear perception of socialist objectives, and impelled by a sense of betrayal, some welfarists flirted with the notion of class war. Harold Laski, for instance, joined the Socialist League and fully expected blood to flow in the streets. It was a reaction which extended to international policy. Brailsford condemned the League's reformism and its ineffectual handling of the war in China. In a trenchant attack on liberal internationalism, Laski argued that 'Socialists would do better to trust to Lenin than to Sir Norman Angell as a guide to international realities'. But Laski momentarily rejected a world socialist state and, following Stalin (or Hobson) rather than Lenin (or Trotsky), urged intense development of the home market, less production for foreign trade and concentration on increasing standards of living at home. The answer to imperialism would be socialist autarky in one country.[31]

Mussolini's venture and the menace of fascism abroad forced welfarists into reconsidering economic internationalism. The New Fabian Research Bureau, a body influenced since its inception in 1931 by welfarism, divided into several schools. C.R. Buxton, for example, remained more or less faithful to the ideal of the global open door and continued to emphasise justice for the 'have-nots' through economic appeasement. By contrast, G.D.H. Cole and Laski (involved since 1933 in alleviating the plight of German academic refugees) deserted liberal internationalism for an Anglo-Soviet alliance. Leonard Woolf and the young Hugh Gaitskell also opposed economic concessions but favoured a democratic front against fascism. Brailsford wavered; a leading critic of Versailles and the League, he advocated League members drawing not only their security from Geneva 'but the daily bread of their economic life'. The first step, however, was to direct collective security against fascism by establishing a vanguard of socialist states inside the League.[32]

Others on the left, notably Dalton, Attlee and Woolf, reached a similar conclusion about the need to reform collective security, but rejected the original economic foundations of welfarism. Woolf explained that neither the USSR nor any other nation had the slightest intention of accepting an internationalised world economy, and ridiculed the notion that only economic factors led to wars.[33] Labour Party officials were content to mention League supervision of international trade and finance in the vaguest of terms.[34] Moreover, Ernest Bevin had already conjured up a nationalist policy for the 1930 TUC – closer development of Empire trade. Congress rejected it, and Labour's ACIQ pointed out that the Dominions would never agree to remain unindustrialised in a quasi-mercantilist system.[35] But confronted by the urgent problem of distress at home, the labour movement's adherence to economic internationalism crumbled to the extent that by 1933 free trade had been abandoned.

Although the rhetoric of liberal and socialist internationalism remained a potent force in political debate, recovery proposals usually involved a degree of economic nationalism. Conservatives had plumped for tariffs and imperial preference; the Next Five Years Group outlined reciprocal preferences; Keynes advocated a tariff to safeguard employment; Laski mooted a focus on the home market. And although Italy reminded internationalists that 'have-not' demands required immediate consideration, the nature of the Italian regime and its threat to peace meant that the prospect of economic appeasement contradicted the ethical dimension of liberal internationalism. Once Italian troops began moving en masse through Suez (from the spring of 1935), liberal internationalists re-examined their condemnation of autarky and Versailles. *The Economist* (24 August 1935) abandoned all sympathy for Italy's economic plight, and indulged in *schadenfreude* over the drain on Italy's gold reserves and its balance of payments crisis. But rationalisations to explain why the 'have-not' notion should be qualified, if not discounted, only gained ground between the end of June and the end of August. During this period, Italy rejected various peace initiatives – including an exchange of territory and an Anglo-French proposal for collective 'assistance' to help Ethiopia make social and economic advances. Italy merely intensified war preparations. It then became rare for leaders of mainstream opinion not to stipulate that concessions to

Italy must be acceptable to Ethiopia, to the League, and to the dictates of liberal morality. This last qualification provided the unifying factor in liberal internationalist responses to the crisis. 'After all', wrote Murray, 'there is such a thing as honour, there are such things as clean hands, and they count for a good deal in international affairs'.[36]

Only a few presentiments of this ethical posture had emerged in parliamentary debates on territorial exchange. A deal, worked out by the Foreign Office and presented to Mussolini by Eden in June, had offered Italy the barren Ogaden plain and promised to cede Ethiopia a corridor to Zeila/Zaila port in British Somaliland. Defending the plan on 11 July, the new Foreign Secretary, Hoare, said that Britain recognised Italy's economic requirements: 'We admit the need for Italian expansion.' Attlee quickly exploited the imperialist connivance, which, he said, undermined the League's idealism. The government also came under fire from Churchill, who condemned secession of British protected territory and subjects 'in order to get round some diplomatic difficulty, or in order to assuage the disputes of foreign countries'. To liberal internationalists, however, the crisis was not 'some diplomatic difficulty' but a war against international order. This concern, and the compensation for Ethiopia in the deal, explains the lack of Liberal outrage and the backing that Attlee might reasonably have expected. Mander and Lloyd George thought that the offer had been worthwhile. With some justification, Eden and Hoare complained that had Italy agreed to the price offered, there would have been widespread rejoicing.[37] The LNU acknowledged as much, and deplored Labour's criticism of Eden.[38] In spite of the legacy of the Peace Ballot, Italy's threats were met at this stage not by demands for the application of collective security but by faith in a colonial deal.[39]

Liberal internationalist opinion hardened when Mussolini refused to trade and mobilised two more divisions in July. Thus Vyvyan Adams, a Tory stalwart of the League, rebuked an Italian expatriate with the comment that Ethiopia had offered Italy 'enormous economic concessions'.[40] Support for League principles began to take on the attributes of a moral crusade, and Hoare informed Ambassador Drummond in Rome that there were signs of Britain 'being swept with the kind of movement that Gladstone started over the Bulgarian atrocities'.[41] The leftist Archbishop of York, William Temple, reflected this mood in a letter to *The Times* (20 August 1935): 'To fail now in loyalty to the League because that loyalty might have grave consequences would be sheer wickedness involving indelible disgrace'. Typical of converts to this campaign, Herbert Stanley Jevons, retired professor of economics, had defended the Zeila exchange as more acceptable than the casualties of a war.[42] By August he had become secretary of the new Abyssinia Association.

Moral outrage brought public demands for a government declaration in support of the Covenant. This played upon a favourite theme of the interwar years: the idea that Britain's indecision in 1914 had encouraged German aggression and that 'clarity in advance' would discourage future law breakers. So far, Britain had made no perceptible impact on war preparations, and an arms embargo imposed on both sides on 25 July had discriminated against unindustrialised Ethiopia. Liberal internationalists demanded more, including a firm statement to deter Italy.[43] The foreign secretary complained of his leader's inadequate response and noted 'the makings of a first-class crisis which the Government will lose heavily if we appear to be repudiating the Covenant'.[44] Fellow Conservatives had no doubt that Britain needed to make a gesture of League support. Austen Chamberlain believed that some economic sanctions were inevitable, predicting that '[i]f we edged out of collective action of this kind, a great wave of opinion would sweep the Government out of power'. Churchill now concurred, seeing the League as a powerful deterrent against Germany and argued that Britain and France should even contemplate going to war.[45] William Ormsby-Gore MP, former undersecretary for the Colonies and delegate to the League Mandates Commission, traversed the gamut of reasons for British leadership:

> Quite apart from the crash of the League of Nations I am convinced that sooner or later we shall have leave to meet the Italian challenge to our prestige, power & interests by force or go under in Africa & the Mediterranean . . . I am convinced we must stand up to this New Latin military bully, who despises us as rotten with pacifism . . . The co-existence of the British Empire and militarist dictatorships on the make are irreconcilable and . . . with public opinion in this country remarkably stirred against Italy any running away by the Government will result in the scorn we deserve . . . Because we try to stand up for international right, order, justice, Treaties and our Imperial interests, we are daily insulted by this dago dictator.[46]

Hoare's speech at the Geneva Assembly of 11 September, declaring that Britain stood by the League 'for the collective maintenance of the Covenant in its entirety, and particularly for steady and collective resistance to all acts of unprovoked aggression', was widely praised. *Headway* (October 1935) called it a turning point, and Murray referred to it as 'magnificent'.[47] Hoare also referred to economic deprivation and the need for improved access to raw materials. The NLF Executive Council greeted the speech as a recognition that trade barriers should be removed, migration freed and monopolies of colonial resources ended.[48] But this remained a distant objective, not the key to a bargain with Italy.

The cabinet failed to make this distinction and attempted to convert the 'have-not' theory into a policy of the moment. After Mussolini started the war on 3 October, *The Economist*, which had earlier mentioned 'pooling' the Empire's raw materials, now (26 October 1935) warned against encouraging the aggressor's appetite. Liberal internationalists ruled out territorial transfer as unreasonable, partly because colonial possessions (as opposed to the open door) were overvalued, and partly because it would be immoral to deliver native populations to a new suzerain like so many head of cattle.[49] Lansbury and C.R. Buxton gained support in the National Peace Council, for a world conference to consider resource grievances, but at the Labour Party Conference, delegates demanded 'pooled' resources – not redistribution. As Dalton noted, this policy reflected the socialist predisposition to stress the economic causes of war;[50] it did not in practice amount to a belief in *Danegeld*. The majority suspected government intentions. Indeed, Hoare aroused disquiet in the Commons on 22 October by his emphasis on 'peace by negotiation', and when the press reported on peace initiatives in Paris, Labour's leadership made a damning analogy: 'It does not seem to us conducive to respect for law and order that the policeman should be bargaining with the burglar while he is still inside the house he has entered to rob and murder'.[51] Labour repeatedly warned of the government's hypocrisy. The Hoare–Laval plan was not, therefore, an entirely unexpected outrage.

But before the plan emerged, the government played its cards well enough in the 1935 General Election campaign to disarm liberal internationalist criticism. Tories were divided about sanctions. The longer war dragged on (and it was widely expected to last a year or so), the more vulnerable to criticism the government would become. The government made qualified statements on collective security in its manifesto and campaigned on its stand in Geneva. The right-wing press hardly mentioned collective security at all, and concentrated on domestic politics; *The Times* (25 October 1935) repeated government platitudes. On the left, the *New Statesman* (9 November 1935) observed that since Simon's removal, it was 'much more difficult to establish the charge that Sir Samuel Hoare is also betraying the League'. In his election post-mortem, Laski not only mentioned Hoare's impressive performance at the League Assembly, but 'the strongly pro-League' appeal of Eden 'among non-party voters of a progressive outlook in foreign affairs'.[52] Liberal internationalism had trespassed effectively across political divides.

The relative calm was shattered by the deal concluded between Hoare and the French prime minister and Foreign Secretary Pierre Laval on 8 December. Although Hoare had merely applied 'have-not' theory by offering Italy more territory and economic influence Ethiopia, liberal internationalists reacted furiously. The only good thing to come out of the plan, commented *Headway* (January 1936), was the Gladstonian indignation which it produced. Duff Cooper later recalled: 'During my experience of politics I have never witnessed so devastating a wave of public opinion'.[53] Hoare's PPS reported deep and widespread unease in the party.[54] By applying economic appeasement *after* Italy had defied international law, the foreign secretary had betrayed the social movement. It would poison relations between liberal internationalists and most Conservatives for the rest of the decade.

Ethiopia rapidly grew into a *cause célèbre* for the liberal conscience. Subscribers to the 'have-not' concept were naturally indignant at the Cabinet's cynical, perverted application of their views. And whilst holding fast to the ultimate ideals of freer trade, collectivised resources, or a socialist commonwealth, their enthusiasm for Italy's case as a deprived power all but vanished. In *The Great Illusion, 1933* (an updated version of his 1909 classic), Angell had pointed out that during the Depression, the problem was not in obtaining raw materials but in getting rid of them. After the Hoare–Laval plan, adherents to this critique included historians and economists who demolished Mussolini's economic arguments, blaming excessive military expenditure for Italy's poverty, rather than non-possession of colonies. Ethiopia had survived until now partly because it was devoid of any obvious resources, and Italian migration to existing African colonies was negligible.[55]

Liberal internationalists now concluded that mere talk of territorial revision was 'disturbing, mischievous, and dangerous', that it provided opportunities for blackmail and that economic adjustments were out of the question without the strengthening of collective security by other means.[56] This was not anti-appeasement, but anti-imperialism. Germany's case was stronger because of the acknowledged blight of Versailles, and Germany was not aping nineteenth-century overseas expansion. Certainly, the LNU, the Labour and Liberal parties, a proportion of the Conservative Party, and the New Commonwealth Society discounted the argument favoured by Churchill, Vansittart and others (as well as Laval) that Germany should be subdued by forming an anti-German front with Italy and France, rather than by a demonstration of the League's power.

Economic sanctions

To some extent, the 'have-not' argument had detracted from the problem of upholding the League's authority. For instance, at the Labour Party Conference in October, Dalton had devoted the first half of his speech to the need for a world economic conference. But the notion that economic measures alone could halt Italian aggression dominated the liberal internationalist approach to the dispute. Even before the Italian military campaign got underway, Keynes had urged ratification of a League loan of £10 million to Ethiopia and lifting the arms embargo to enable Emperor Haile Selassie to purchase weapons. He anticipated that economic measures would prolong Italy's financial and military agony and avoid League force.[57] Keynes thus lent authority to the belief in the potency of economic power and underestimated the political and military factors operating in Italy's favour. Depression had encouraged belief in the efficacy of such measures, but part of the appeal can be attributed to the idea that 'we should object to...putting force in the forefront. Britain's great strength is economic and financial. It is the sort of pressure that we should contemplate'.[58] And when Cecil, Lothian, Walter Citrine, Josiah Wedgwood and Vyvyan Adams went further by supporting a Suez Canal blockade to cut Italian communications, they called upon a traditional British naval role, though apart from suggesting an 'accidental sinking', it was unclear how the use of force would be arranged.[59]

In the first instance, however, liberal internationalists expected that a ban on trade with Italy would work. The New Commonwealth relied on vigorous economic sanctions to avoid war. It specifically rejected mobilising an improvised IPF after the outbreak of war: 'in view of the fact that the supreme value of an international policing system obviously lies in its deterrent effect'.[60] As in the Peace Ballot campaign, Cecil played down the possibility that fulfilment of Britain's obligations to the League would lead to war, arguing that sanctions should be 'as little likely to provide actual fighting with the Italians as can be managed'.[61] This studied evasion meant that the LNU's stance differed little from that of ministers keen to exclude sanctions that might lead to military involvement. Conservative politicians employed an unimpeachable argument for limited economic pressure: action had to be truly collective. Hence, France and the non-League United States provided insurance against excessive bravado. Fleet movements in September were purely defensive. From the private statements of Londonderry, Hoare and the two Chamberlains it is clear that they supported sanctions, with an eye to public opinion in the run up to the election.[62]

Liberal internationalist thinking was characterised by a vague, cautious and uncertain vision of sanctions, perhaps understandable in view of their novelty. The National Council of Labour fostered the belief that 'even weak economic and financial sanctions will gnaw at the feeble constitution of Fascist Italy like a cancerous growth'.[63] An erudite, circumspect study, *International Sanctions*, begun early in 1933, held in abeyance during the crisis, and finally published in 1938 symbolised the LNU's ambivalence. But internationalists were also trapped in a paradox. They detected Mussolini's insensitivity to liberal reasoning. He had not been persuaded by the mere threat of economic measures, and he was unlikely to yield without a struggle when the League eventually imposed them. But the sanctionists resisted the logic that some kind of military victory over Italy would be necessary. Arnold Toynbee judged that 'the newfangled institution of "economic sanctions" had commended itself as a substitute which was both comfortable and ingenious, and thus doubly attractive, for the old-fashioned institution of war'.[64] Sanctionists had to think again when economic sanctions (from which oil was excluded) galvanised Mussolini into a speedy resolution of the war and replaced Gen. De Bono, his commander in East Africa, with the more vigorous Gen Badoglio. Now, internationalists agitated for the inclusion of oil in the trade ban to bring Italy's military to a halt, though as a new LNU paper *Abyssinia* (8 January 1936) admitted, US oil producers would have to cooperate. This lobbying extended beyond the LNU and the Liberal–Labour wing of mainstream opinion – the *Daily Telegraph* (2 December 1935), for example, urged other League members to agree to an oil sanction. Eventually, at a cabinet meeting in February, the government bowed to the pressure and backed collective action on oil. Common ground on economic sanctions gave liberal internationalism a semblance of unity which resisted fairly successfully the challenge of extreme right and left-wing critics.

Anti-sanctionists were weak or divided. Italophiles mentioned above were not numerous. Only the BUF functioned with a degree of coherence, but the Blackshirts soon abandoned their 'peace crusade' when funds ran low and the tide of anti-Italian opinion proved strong. A more mainstream group, a hundred Tory backbenchers led by Amery, petitioned Baldwin on 15 October to extract assurances that the government would discount forceful sanctions, but they failed to rouse him.[65] Churchill provided little guidance. He operated in a political limbo. Privately, he told Hoare that Britain could declare her willingness to go to war if necessary, while relying on France to prevent the League imposing risky sanctions. Simultaneously, he publicly criticised the Amery objectors on the grounds that the League had now passed 'from shadow into substance'.[66] Right-wing anti-sanctionists formed a Conservative Imperial Policy Group in 1934, with representation in the House of Lords. But reactionaries were wracked by ambiguity because of Italy's potential threat to Egypt and other interests in the Eastern Mediterranean. They were willing to pay any price to avoid sanctions – except parts of the Empire. The crucial issue was whether Italy would be a rival or an accomplice in imperialism. Croft enthused about Italy's civilising mission but not about its imperial claims. With Duncan Sandys, he insisted that the government must not regard British mandates as negotiable in the face of German or Italian pressure.[67] To other antisanctionists, the Hoare–Laval proposals had been acceptable, involving a miniscule territorial cession to Ethiopia, yet promising to end sanctions. This line had been followed by the *Mail*, *Express* and *Post*, and Hoare claimed to have many letters of support on his resignation.[68] However, in April 1936, Baldwin gave the party a lengthy pep-talk on the value of collective security to the Empire, and throughout the crisis Tory diehards on the Executive passed no resolution on sanctions or possible peace terms.[69]

It may be true that 'pacifists' and 'diehards' were at one against sanctions during the crisis. But beyond the occasional complimentary references no common effort to oppose sanctions emerged. Not only were the differences on other issues such as rearmament too great, the peace groups also equivocated. The crisis exposed divergence in the National Peace Council, its Congress in the summer of 1935 unable to agree on sanctions. Consequently, the NPC emphasised economic justice for Italy and toyed with the contradictory idea of maintaining Ethiopia's independence as a virtual League mandate. As a pressure group the NPC 'had to face one of the most perplexing periods of its existence'.[70] Ethicists had a difficult time. The pacifist philosopher C.E.M. Joad, for example, argued the case for unilateral disarmament but also advocated 'controlled force' by the League as a 'second best'.[71] By contrast, Bertrand Russell took power into account, noting that the League was too weak: 'If the League were strong enough I should favour sanctions, because the effect would suffice, or the war would be short and small. This whole question is quantitative'.[72] Joad's wavering and Russell's power politics reflected the extent to which pacifists were hard-pressed to sustain pure negativism of the type that offered Ethiopians sympathy and suggested they lay down their arms, or hoped that 'by sheer fluke' the world would scrape by.[73] Members of peace groups were torn between their duty to oppose collective security as a formula for war and their desire to give practical effect to their moral outrage. The Ethiopian crisis tested the individual conscience. The wartime conscientious objector Max Plowman observed 'that among the sponsors of the PPU there was no more real agreement than among the first people one might happen upon in Piccadilly'.[74]

The Marxists divided over doctrine, and in the ILP it crippled policy-making. At one level, the issue was simple – no support for the government or League on sanctions. As Brockway argued: 'It would be better for the working class to fail in the policy of the class struggle rather than to identify itself with Capitalist Governments in an Imperialist war.'[75] But how to distinguish between government sanctions and mass action by the workers? A workers' ban on handling goods for Italy, initially favoured by the ILP, was later overturned by an 'Inner Executive' comprising Maxton, McGovern, Campbell Stephen and John Aplin (with Brockway opposing). Conflict between two obnoxious dictatorships dictated neutrality and a focus on fighting imperialism at home. Incredibly, Maxton's election manifesto made no reference to the war at all. When the Party Conference met in April 1936, the ILP's governing body was censored by 70 votes to 57 for its policy on working-class sanctions, and one section defected to the Communist Party in support of League action. For the rump of the party, Brockway engineered a compromise: the Conference vote was simply ignored and Maxton retracted a resignation threat.[76] The various strands of ideology lacked punch. Brockway's faith in working-class sanctions was wishful thinking, and Maxton's belief that British imperialism was more deadly than foreign fascism lacked credibility. The Socialist League had similar disputes. Cripps opposed the sanctions of an imperialist League; Cole and Trevelyan supported the notion of military sanctions, provided France and the USSR participated; Laski hoped that a League of Nations success would deter Germany and urged cooperation with the Communist Party. Nothing but confusion emerged from a series of Socialist League Conferences throughout the country.[77] Critics pointed out that working-class action had even less chance of restraining Italy than did League sanctions; Mussolini did not need cooperative workers in other countries. Worse, the Socialist League was vulnerable to the jibe that it was an accessory to fascist aggression. Despite their factionalism, the anti-sanctionists of both left and right exercised an influence on mainstream internationalist opinion. Controversy at the 1935 Labour Party Conference led sanctionists to pay a great deal of attention to rebutting the arguments of Cripps and Lansbury. Bevin launched a celebrated diatribe against Lansbury, one of many denunciations. For example, a *New Statesman* pamphlet by Konni Zilliacus dealt at length with sanctions-resistance, arguing that '[t]he practical result of the Socialist League's proposals would be to put the Labour Party on the side of Mussolini and international anarchy, against the Soviet Union and the collective system'.[78]

Nevertheless, critics of liberal internationalism could play on raw nerves by asserting that sanctions could lead to war with Italy. Furthermore, liberal internationalists had not thought out a calculus of League action: would sanctions merely steel Mussolini's resolve; would Ethiopia collapse before sanctions had time to bite; to what extent could Britain rely on French and US cooperation? These unknowns made the internationalists less secure against criticism than might be supposed from their assured discourse about economic sanctions. In the Labour Party, they faced an additional problem, backing the League without appearing to support the government. As noted in the previous chapter, a keen distrust of capitalist foreign policy permeated the Labour movement after the 1931 domestic 'betrayal' and the Manchurian crisis. Although a catastrophic discourse of capitalism had waned since 1933, Conservative pressure for rearmament did nothing to lower the left's guard. The government spoke the language of the League, but it disguised 'the Tory policy of the strong right arm'.[79] A promise by Labour's Executive to keep the government under surveillance unravelled with the Hoare–Laval plan, providing Marxists with more evidence of the futility of an alliance with capitalism.

Organisations not only contended with the detractions of anti-sanctionists but also the effects of 'competition', for the Ethiopian crisis generated its own pressure groups and brought additional prestige to the Communist Party. The communists quibbled less about means than ends and offered to cooperate with the Labour Party in the 1935 General Election. Now that the USSR had entered the League, social democracy and capitalist imperialism could be employed to undermine fascism. As John Strachey put it, 'Only fools go into battle pledged never to use the divisions within their enemies' ranks'.[80] Indeed, the CPGB made the best of the crisis by supporting working-class sanctions as well. Between July and 1935 and 1937, party membership increased from 7,700 to 12,500.[81] Much of the increase occurred during the Spanish Civil War, when the CPGB organised opposition to Franco's rebellion.

But, despite the Labour Party's continued refusal to confer respectability on the CPGB, it seems that the communists laid the basis for their broader acceptance during the Ethiopian crisis.

Head of the sectarian groups was Sylvia Pankhurst's Abyssinia Association, with 500 members paying the high subscription of 10 shillings (£28 in 2012). The membership included: Sir George Paish (chair), Snowden, Adams, Angell, Noel Baker, Margery Perham (reader in Colonial Administration at Oxford) and Eleanor Rathbone. The association acted as sanctions pressure group, Ethiopian propaganda office and war charity – it ran jumble sales to raise money for gas masks, which would have been useless against the mustard gas used on the Ethiopians. Like the other groups – Friends of Abyssinia, British Red Cross for Abyssinia, Dr Martin's Defence Loan – the association attracted support. Although practical aid for Ethiopia could only be limited, sending medical supplies ensured that Sylvia Pankhurst would acquire national heroine status in Ethiopia.[82] With a suffragette's dynamism, she took the circulation of her paper, *New Times & Ethiopia News*, to 40,000 and carried her anti-appeasement message beyond Popular Front circles. On the question of sanctions, however, the association was hardly more radical than the LNU.

Splinter groups and anti-sanctionists apart, liberal internationalists expected the worst. Lothian anticipated a national upheaval and advised Lloyd George not to declare his attitude to the crisis until splits in the other parties gave him a chance to bid for power.[83] Commitment to economic sanctions gave internationalists a degree of unity. E.H. Carr explained its collapse as the product of a discrepancy between the man in the street's attachment to the spirit of the Covenant and the intellectual's belief in the letter of its text. But he overlooked the 'perilous confusion of mind' affecting intellectuals themselves in their imaginative quest for peace.[84] The very process of defining collective security, of reappraising the function of sanctions, whether deterrent or punitive, fostered dissent. Membership of the LNU split between boycotters and blockaders, unilateralists and collectivists. The closer Italy came to victory, the more stridently Cecil and the sanctionists believed that the Italian economy teetered on the brink of collapse. But Murray had an awkward time persuading the General Council in December to agree on cutting Italy's communications with Africa, though he made it seem ingenuously simple: '[a] gun-boat from practically every Member of the League that has got one would suffice'. In the ensuing acrimony delegates voted against it and also against a unilateral ban on oil.[85] When asked whether he was prepared for war against Italy, Cecil replied with customary obtuseness: 'I am not prepared to make war on Mussolini, but if, as a consequence of carrying out our obligations under the Covenant, Mussolini makes war on me, then I shall be prepared to resist'.[86] He had no real idea how the League would assemble gunboats, how other states could be persuaded to participate, or whether Italy would construe blockade as a *casus belli*. Sanctionists had relied too readily on collective security as deterrence.

After Badoglio entered Addis Ababa on 5 May 1936, consensus began disintegrating. The National Council of Labour, the Council of Action, the National Liberal Federation and the LNU continued to call for the vindication of collective security. A packed Albert Hall heard Cecil, Attlee, Lytton and Sir Archibald Sinclair argue for the extension of League sanctions. Conservatives, led by Churchill and the Chamberlains, supported by *The Times* (8 June 1936), the *Telegraph* (15 June 1936) and the anti-League press, were worried that the burden of escalation would fall almost exclusively on the Royal Navy and urged the government to recognise failure and bring the fleet home.[87] In May–June bitter debates in the Commons saw no quarter given but the government had a comfortable 384 to 170 majority in favour of recommending an end of sanctions. Outside Parliament, the international lawyer Sir John Fischer Williams argued that Article 16 of the Covenant had no punitive function.[88] Murray privately admitted a loss of faith but hoped vaguely that intensifying sanctions could still be used to bargain with Mussolini, without carrying the stigma of retribution.[89]

A keen sense of betrayal, on the grounds that collective security had not been properly applied, pervaded a noisy LNU Council Meeting in June. Delegates demanded Austen Chamberlain's removal from the Executive and heckled Sir Paul Latham MP, who supported him. Already weakened by the expense of the Peace Ballot and the IPF wrangle, the LNU never fully recovered from Italy's imperialism. Lytton, Murray and Cecil appealed for £10,000 'to tide over the present crisis'; the secretary, Garnett, announced that the LNU was gravely embarrassed; and a drastic curtailment of activities followed. Murray explained to David Davies that the LNU's finances were 'strained to the utmost' and proposed merging with the New Commonwealth: 'I want to embrace you with one arm and Austen with the other'! But Davies' belief in international military force was confirmed by the crisis, and Chamberlain and other Tories left the LNU in droves. Paid-up membership fell by about 80,000 during 1935 and 1936.[90]

Conclusion

Although the crisis demonstrated that League measures against a European state amounted to little more than an expression of moral disapproval which neither helped nor hindered Italy's 'civilising mission', liberal internationalists had opened a debate on imperialism and international economic leverage. Indeed, the slump had reinforced socialist and liberal concerns for economic justice. Although many welfarists adopted economic nationalism as a solution to domestic troubles, a distributive approach to international security was also seized upon, and liberal internationalists clearly drove formation of the UN's Economic and Social Council and the Bretton Woods system in the 1940s. For interwar liberal internationalists, however, distributive justice also had racial and imperialistic content. Economic justice could be applied to advanced, white-controlled, capitalism, and 'have-not theory' reflected this. Ambivalence about imperialism could be reduced to: British Empire and mandates inherently noble; Italian imperialism and mandates justifiable only if negotiated internationally. These strains of liberal superiority persisted in the later twentieth century in the form of liberal peace, but the interwar debates exposed the hypocrisy of colonialism, and a reaction against 'have-not' theory set in after Italy's conquest. In wartime, the British Empire proved both indefensible and essential for Britain's survival as a European state. Trappings of global power lingered in UK imaginations long after the war, but there would be no stopping the determination of UN members to hasten decolonisation, and liberal internationalism had prepared domestic and international opinion for the disintegration of overt military/administrative control of non-white peoples. The UN's Trusteeship Council established international involvement in 11 colonial dependencies as integral to its role in decolonisation processes. Moreover, an element of international supervision in the form of the peacekeeping would occur – overwhelmingly in former imperial spaces.

Economic revision and sanctions, complementary aspects of collective security, also nurtured ambiguities and contradictions. Mitigation of Italy's economic situation had to be a long-term objective. In the immediate situation, the League's authority had to be upheld, and Mussolini's intransigence merited sanctions that would worsen Italy's economy. Thus, contradictions between economic liberalisation and punishment were resolved in favour of liberal moral discipline in the international order; there could be no rewards for aggression. However, in the absence of machinery to implement leverage, internationalists relied on boycotts to ensure peace. In a roundabout way, Lothian hit upon the only contemporary option that would have brought Italy to heel – an immediate British naval action in the Mediterranean. Of course, this would have denied the essence of peace through collective security on two counts: no peace and no collectivism. Besides, the proponents of League action encountered state power politics and underestimated the flat refusal of French leaders to divert attention from German nationalism. Lothian could only make his assertion by minimising a German threat which, in protecting naval strength, the British Staff Chiefs took seriously. Clearly, liberal internationalists overestimated economic leverage in the Italian case. 'Smart sanctions', such as targeting the finances and travel options of political leaders could be devised fifty years later, and internationalists contemplated international machinery, anticipating UN Security Council authorisations and sanctions committees.[91] They remain an instrument of the powerful, though also complex and uncertain in their impacts on conflict prevention and crisis management, usually augmenting corruption in the affected societies.

For interwar liberal internationalism, the crisis strained its position in framing the British mindset because, in contrast to the conflict in Asia, the African war had been proclaimed as a last test for its definition of peace. Fresh from its triumph with the Peace Ballot, the LNU should have been poised to manage internationalism in civil society. Instead, Italy's refusal to submit split liberal internationalists in their attempts to define the fundamentals of collective security and induced a retreat from reliance on the architecture of international organisation. Universalism had already been dented in the early 1920s by US, German and Soviet exclusion; after 1936, the internationalist movement retreated into less ambitious, more partial and statist collectivism. As demonstrated in the next chapter, demands for League reform, regional pacts, popular fronts and grand alliances grew significantly.

8
Revisionism: Rearmament and Peaceful Change

Liberal internationalists were not as doctrinaire about collective security as one might suppose from their reluctance to admit the inadequacies of economic sanctions against Italy. Core liberal internationalism may have had a Gladstonian moral tone, but it was far from dogmatic. Its leaders had always defined peace liberally, and had adjusted their framing of ideas about internationalism according to domestic and international circumstances. This chapter demonstrates the fluidity of liberal internationalists responses to German grievances. The first section shows that opposition to revision of Versailles grew in the context of Germany's attitude to the World Disarmament Conference. The second section examines the rise of a peaceful change consensus from 1933 when Germany sought negotiated settlements. The third section shows how the issue of rearmament was bedevilled by the government's inability to clarify its threat perception and the belief of many liberal internationalists that rearmament would foster an arms race. The alternative, peaceful change, is discussed in the fourth section as an alternative to rearmament and a means of enticing Germany back in the League. The fifth section considers the way that revisionism began melting away in 1936 as it became clear that Germany would not adhere to regulation, and beginnings of a broad front in support of containment emerged.

Leading internationalists did not abandon their normative approach or cease to discuss imaginative ideas. Debates about these issues highlight both the fluidity of campaigning for peace and the continuing influence of idealistic internationalism. However, on arms control, internationalists were heavily influenced by fractious domestic politics. In both the LNU and the Labour Party, an abiding suspicion of the National Government's foreign policy meant that Cecil, Dalton and Bevin encountered huge difficulties in 1936 when attempting to convince followers of the merits of rearmament. And in justifying rearmament, its proponents did little to clarify security perceptions. In their concern to avoid rearmament, many internationalists believed that Germany would be induced to sign an arms convention if Versailles was unravelled. A 'revision consensus' ruled liberal internationalism between 1934 and 1938, and as Neville Thompson has pointed out, 'anti-appeasers' were few in number and ill-organised.[1] Nevertheless, in deconstructing the ethics of revision, it is notable that the internationalists reacted angrily to Germany's departure from the League and queried revisionism after the 1936 Rhineland crisis. 'Peaceful change', as revision was often called, denoted various designs: revision of the Peace Treaties on grounds of natural justice; attempts to induce Germany to return to the League; expedient acquiescence in Germany's transgressions; and open-ended negotiations addressing Germany's grievances or at encouraging Germany to turn to the east. For example, radical revisionists such as Lothian, Lloyd George and Noel Buxton aimed to meet Germany's 'needs' as a matter of restoring international justice, whereas Cecil and Murray regarded revision as a lever for establishing international control over the German regime's behaviour. For much of liberal internationalist opinion a normative approach meant conformity to international law as the vital collateral for revising Versailles.

Anti-revisionism

The roots of revisionism lay in the admonitions of the immediate postwar years. Versailles remained an undercurrent as demands for treaty revision arose intermittently throughout the 1920s on specific issues such as reparation payments. A greater sense of urgency informed discussions as the Disarmament Conference got under way. Liberal internationalists were acutely aware that the outcome of the negotiations depended on the extent to which Germany gained sovereign equality. Arms control became the touchstone of revision. On the eve of the conference, Willoughby Dickinson, veteran exponent of liberal internationalism, voiced the sentiments of many when he defied the government to refuse the demands of the defeated powers for equality.[2] His point gained force as the negotiations failed to progress. But it was no longer simply a question of moral obligation. The growth of nazism gave German claims a keener edge, and the foremost authority on disarmament, Noel Baker, concluded that Hitler's demands were 'irresistible'; it was no longer practical politics to keep Germany down.[3]

Commentators also redefined their attitudes to revision in the light of Nazi consolidation and supplemented discussion of war guilt, reparations and colonial adjustment with reference to 'equality of status', Germany's 'inferiority complex' and its 'psychological needs'. The scope and discourse of concerns narrowed and hardened. Perhaps one of the last occasions on which Wilson's Fourteen Points featured in a political resolution was at the Annual Meeting of the UDC in 1929, when members reiterated the complaint that the Versailles system was inconsistent with Wilson's vision.[4] Concern about the Fourteen Points faded with the UDC itself. Far more attention was given to Article 19 of the Covenant, which ran: 'The Assembly may from time to time advise the reconsideration by Members of the League of treaties which have become inapplicable and the consideration of international conditions whose continuance might endanger the peace of the world'. Gilbert Murray, for example, argued that revision of the treaties was irrelevant; by 1933 there was little left to revise and those who believed in treaty revision to satisfy Germany were doomed to disappointment. On the other hand, a method of recognising the changes in international circumstances, without recourse to war, would be 'of vast permanent importance'.[5]

Whereas Murray lost his enthusiasm for Article 19 when Germany failed to return to the League, others broadened debate beyond the proscriptions of Versailles. In *Germany under the Treaty* (1933), an interpreter of German thought and society, W.H. Dawson, advocated sweeping changes to the territorial status quo, arguing that Britain and Germany should establish a concert of 'the Northern people' of Europe and America and undertake an unbiased investigation of Germany's claims – without the interference of France. He anticipated, among other possibilities, the return of the Polish Corridor to Germany. Dawson went much further than most liberal internationalists in promoting peaceful change, but his anticipation of grievances exemplified the renewed interest in revision prompted by the imminent collapse of the Disarmament Conference.

However, in the period 1931 to 1933, there was no overwhelming public pressure for territorial revision, and many observers expressed serious reservations about granting any concessions to Germany. As argued in Chapter 6, the Austro-German *zollverein* bid in 1931 had already caused concern and German nationalism had aroused some sympathy for the Tardieu security scheme of 1932. Initial reluctance to contemplate revision influenced the reception given Mussolini's proposal for a Four Power Pact in March 1933. The Pact entrusted Britain, France, Italy and Germany with maintaining European peace by ensuring *gleichberechtigung* ('equal status') for Germany in stages, conducting treaty revision within the League framework. Whereas *The Times* (24 March 1933) welcomed the attempt to make Article 19 'a reality', the LNU and other groups opposed it. MacDonald had expected as much in his negotiations in Rome, telling Mussolini that

> [a] large section of opinion in England held that a good many injustices must be undone, but was somewhat apprehensive as to the after effects of undoing them; for instance, the grant of equality to Germany might mean rearmament, and if that were so England [*sic*] would have to consider whether she would not, much against her will, increase her navy and air force.[6]

MacDonald may well have used the democratic card to remind Mussolini that Britain, like France, had to safeguard its military security, but liberal internationalists generally favoured allied disarmament to the German level rather than permitting Germany to breach the treaties. Diverse advocates such as Cecil, Murray, Grey, Dalton, Salter, Lloyd George, Lansbury and Cripps, argued that German rearmament would unlock the door for other states.[7]

A further argument against revisionism emerged in a Commons debate in April 1933 when three Jewish MPs, H. Samuel and B. Janner (National Liberal) and H. Nathan (Liberal), condemned Nazi barbarity with a vigour rarely heard in subsequent debates on Germany. From their disparate ideologies, Attlee, Churchill, Austen Chamberlain and Eleanor Rathbone nevertheless agreed that Article 19 should be ignored. Scarcely any MP objected to Austen Chamberlain's remark: '[w]hat is this new spirit of German nationalism? The worst of the all-Prussian Imperialism, with an added savagery...Are you going to discuss revision with a Government like this?'[8] Liberal and Labour adherents became revision deniers – on account of the persecution of German Jews and academics. On a visit to Berlin in April 1933, Dalton understood the state of terror among the intelligentsia, and this alerted him to the dangers of a rearmed Germany.[9] Suppression of the German trade unions deeply impressed trade union leaders, including Bevin and Citrine, who had far closer links with German unionists than with the Spanish, for example. In the summer of 1933, Bevin and Citrine persuaded the Joint Council of Labour to boycott German goods, and their views predominated in the *Daily Herald* and in the Joint Council's own publication, *Labour*, one of the earliest and most stringent sources of anti-nazism.

The LNU Executive couched its opposition to revision as avoiding capitulation to German nationalism. As a *Headway* report explained:

> Eventually, of course, there must be a treaty revision by pacific means, using Article 19 of the Covenant. But to grant consideration of the ways and means of rendering that particular Article effective when narrow nationalism is in the ascendant in the country that most desires it is but courting disaster. Germany, unfortunately, has recently made a habit of taking all and in return giving nothing if possible.[10]

Endorsing concern about extremism in Germany, organisations such as the Academic Freedom League organised at the London School of Economics by Beveridge in 1933 and the Council for German Jewry of March 1936, secured practical help for refugees.

By June, the Four Power Pact proposals had been watered-down to such an extent that when Britain signed, it was hardly noticed. But opinion continued to harden against Germany when it withdrew from the Disarmament Conference and the League in October 1933. Germany's refusal to consider equality of rights by stages meant that MacDonald had little difficulty in convincing Parliament where the onus for the breakdown lay.[11] In Parliament, none of the opposition MPs, apart from Lloyd George, levelled any substantial criticism against the government. Lansbury ruled out revision that would place more people under dictatorship. A prominent collective security advocate, Geoffrey Mander, agreed with Austen Chamberlain that the government had worked hard and honestly to get an agreement but the Germans were nursing a grievance to provide an army. Economic sanctions and a blockade would be appropriate if it were proved that Germany had rearmed.[12] Editorials in the *Morning Post* culminated on 13 October with the comment: 'An iron ring of her own devising is the only thing that can prevent a defiant and rearmed Germany from becoming a disturber of the peace'.[13] A leader in the *Manchester Guardian* (16 October 1933) set the tone of liberal internationalist dismay: 'This is the moment when the Nazi Government has chosen to destroy the whole agreement at Geneva, to secede from the League of Nations, and to complete the moral isolation which the triumph of the Nazi system has gradually brought on Germany'. On the left, the *New Statesman* excluded any hopes of territorial revision and ridiculed the idea that Sir John Simon's defence of the Anglo-French standpoint had driven Germany out of the Conference.[14] Expressing the post-Conference view of many internationalists, *Labour* argued that the Treaty of Versailles 'bore at least the promise of international cooperation in the effort to create the conditions of permanent peace and progressive disarmament'.[15] In sum, there was no such thing as an appeasement consensus in Hitler's first year as chancellor. Germany's claims to equality had been widely acknowledged, but Hitler had antagonised British opinion to such an extent that anti-revisionism trespassed across party lines.

Revision consensus

Why then, after 1933, did leading liberal internationalists almost without exception turn to a policy of negotiating revisions? Liberal internationalists seem to have believed that German nationalism answered domestic problems and that Hitler would become 'internationally responsible' once firmly in power. Austen Chamberlain, for example, remarked that 'the bigger he is and the more dominating the more chance there seems to me of his gradually becoming more reasonable'.[16] When Nazis gained a hefty majority in the Reichstag in November 1933 and withdrawal from Geneva was confirmed by a referendum in which 95 per cent of the votes cast were in favour, German foreign policy appeared more reasonable. In January 1934, Germany concluded a Non-Aggression Pact with Poland, and throughout the spring held out hopes of an Air Pact, reinforcing the thesis that power bred responsibility.

But to fully explain the move to a peaceful change consensus, it is necessary to consider the liberal governmentality crisis. For a heterogeneous movement, controversy over conscientious objection, socialist war resistance and an IPF were taxing. But the notion of peaceful change commanded wider support, partly because two of the groups which challenged the status quo for different reasons – the peace movement and the IPF advocates – had ideological commitments to the process. The New Commonwealth Society subscribed to the idea of an 'equity tribunal' as an institutional solution to the problem of arbitration in non-justiciable disputes. A tribunal appealed as potential machinery for operating Article 19 of the Covenant, and for airing grievances rather than judging specific disputes about rights. Without a tribunal, German grievances would persist and disturb neighbouring states.[17] By contrast, because pacifists claimed that collective security endangered peace, they had no real alternative to revisionism for dealing with Germany. *Peace* (November 1933) warned its readers 'not to be blind to the fact that Nazism leads to war', but added that 'the inescapable fact is that we must win Germany's loyal collaboration as a partner, sooner or later'. The alternatives seemed too grim to contemplate.

The LNU leaders could accommodate pressure for peaceful change more easily than demands for an IPF or conscientious objection. Cecil and Murray, though privately sceptical about the value of revision, endorsed an LNU deputation to meet Eden on the issue in August 1935. Led by the IPF advocate Allen, the deputation told Eden confronting Germany and other states with a definite invitation to join in negotiating an all-round settlement. The only provisos mentioned were that a settlement should be arranged on the basis of equal status and that no grievances should be withheld from the agenda.[18] This policy carried weight in the LNU – though it ran contrary to the anti-revision stance favoured by Cecil. The leadership would have found it difficult to openly criticise the principles of justice and equity which formed the ethical basis of revisionism. And the internal harmony associated with discussion of peaceful change helped to reduce the tensions created by passion over other issues. In particular, the government's revival of an air defence programme in 1934 signalled the start of a new controversy over rearmament.

Rearmament

The tough stance towards Germany adopted by Mander and other liberal internationalists gave way to support for almost any European security arrangement that promised to rehabilitate Germany and avoid an arms race. According to Lloyd George, consideration of Germany's grievances was the clear alternative to a policy of rearmament.[19] Government supporters also elevated the settlement of German claims; an agreement with Germany would minimise the risk of war and avoid the need to prepare an expeditionary force.

Furthermore, the rearmament controversy reveals the extent to which perception of the German threat had blurred. Liberal internationalists complained that British defence measures were aimless. In March 1934, when Attlee announced his party's decision to vote against completion of a 1923 air expansion programme, he focused on the government's lack of purpose. The Air Minister, Philip Sassoon, could only remark that the modest increase in the estimates took account of prevailing international uncertainty.[20] Labour's case gained support from the strategist Liddell Hart. Commenting on the Defence White Paper of 1936 he wrote: 'We appear to be building up forces without clarifying our minds as to what they are for'. It was a pertinent remark, taken up by others against a background of evasive and contradictory official explanations.[21]

Government spokesmen and the conservative press stressed that in the absence of a disarmament treaty and with other powers rearming rapidly, Britain had to repair military deficiencies in order to catch up.[22] Baldwin argued this in Parliament in July 1934 to justify the creation of 41 air squadrons over five years. While pointing out the dangers of a militant nationalist spirit in Europe, and Britain's strategic interest in the Rhine frontier, he also spoke about arms expenditure in other countries as though British rearmament was guided by the international environment rather than a specific threat. This naturally failed to satisfy the opposition. Attlee countered that Britain could not arm against some vague air danger, without assessing where it would come from, and Samuel argued that the Liberals would vote with Labour explicitly on the grounds that the government had made no case for any German threat.[23]

The government's explanations were regarded as a confession that principles of arms competition guided its actions. Prompted by Churchill's claims about German rearmament in November, Baldwin offered a more explicit statement on a possible German menace. But in general, the ministers appeared reluctant to comment publicly on any discernible threats, and justified rearmament as a response to a deteriorating international environment. This, paradoxically, contributed to the waning of former antagonism towards Germany; rearmament seemed aimless. This hedging probably reflected serious divisions among officials about whether to strike a deal with Japan (at the risk of offending the United States) in order to concentrate on Germany. Under the influence of Fisher, Vansittart and Neville Chamberlain, the creation of an air deterrent against Germany became an important item in defence expenditure. Chamberlain noted in his diary: 'we shall be more likely to deter Germany...if we have an air force which, in case of need, could bomb the Ruhr from Belgium'.[24] Baldwin told Crozier of the *Manchester Guardian* that Germany had prompted the defence increase.[25] Clearly, however, in presenting rearmament to the country, the government avoided declarations that smacked of a 'nationalistic' response.

Baldwin used a second validation for rearmament – the need to fulfil collective security obligations. Conservatives repeated the argument for the 1935 and 1936 Defence White Papers. Austen Chamberlain, for example, incorporated it into a parliamentary resolution in March 1935.[26] The 1936 Defence White Paper referred to 'playing our part in the enforcement by common action of international obligations', and Chamberlain employed it to put pressure on the LNU.[27] As discussed below, this campaign had an important, though perhaps isolated, success by converting Cecil to a rearmament policy in March 1936, but the great bulk of liberal internationalist opinion remained highly sceptical, given what they regarded as the government's abysmal record in Geneva.

Rearmament critics also forgot their earlier tirades against Hitler and fostered the idea that Britain had 'paralysed and finally destroyed the Conference'.[28] Concessionists such as Lothian and T. P. Conwell-Evans claimed that Britain and France had driven Germany out; the three-to four-year preliminaries (during which an international inspectorate could have been established) was nothing less than an extension of the military clauses of Versailles. It became a stock-in-trade accusation of anti-rearmers and Germanophiles.[29] Pro-German internationalists tried to paint the Nazi regime in a favourable light, whereas disarmers were concerned primarily to slot the government's rearmament into a betrayal thesis. Left-wing critics rebutted the collective security motive for arms expansion as 'the most insolent of sophistry'. [30]

Indeed, the government was hardly consistent. In November 1934, Baldwin had told Scottish Tories that a collective system was 'hardly worth considering' without the United States, Japan and Germany.[31] Neville Chamberlain stressed national safety through air deterrence at a meeting of his constituents in March 1936,[32] yet cited the League as an argument against nationalist critics who cavilled at the financial limits on rearmament. The discrepancy between posture and policy is illustrated by a run-of-the-mill dilemma faced by Hoare shortly after his elevation in June 1936 to the post of First Lord. Hoare asked his speech writer to prepare a vindication for rearmament, because he had no wish to say that collective security was unworkable: 'such an admission will make it much more difficult to retain the support of the centre to our policy of rearmament'. His secretary produced the formula that rearmament was necessary for Britain to maintain her loyalty to the League in view of the unfair burden imposed on the Royal Navy in the Ethiopian crisis.[33] But whatever reason rearmers gave, they could not hope to satisfy the critics. If they emphasised the German and Japanese threats to national and imperial interests, they were censured for succumbing to nationalism – the grounds for the LNU's condemnations in 1935 and 1936.[34] If they claimed to be strengthening collective security, Herbert Morrison and Arthur Greenwood on the Joint Council of Labour, for example, could retort that such a pledge would not be accepted as genuine by the labour movement.[35]

Anti-rearmers claimed that no great armaments were required for collective purposes. Even when acknowledging the inadequacy of economic sanctions, liberal internationalists argued that small military contributions from several states would suffice to repel aggression.

They made two assumptions: that a collective security system would act as a kind of shield between a German airforce and its targets; and that Germany was not so much a direct threat to Britain as a menace to the international system. But national and imperial defence could not be equated to international security, and contingency planning for collective security could not be precise. In their annual review of 1933, the Chiefs of Staff avoided the implications of Article 16 and had no plans for contributing to a collective force.[36] Moreover, the government belied its supposed faith in collective security by increasing expenditure on a national air deterrent for home security not for operation in conjunction with French, or indeed British, land forces.[37] The public discourses on defence and collective security seemed to bear little relationship to immediate defence problems. Reference to collective security had become an empty signifier. The left, for example, distinguished between a limited commitment through pooling national forces, and what the *Daily Herald* (7 March 1935) described as the government's deliberate opening up of an arms race. This meant that left-wing internationalist could not countenance rearmament specifically against Germany. Attlee criticised the 1935 Defence White Paper for 'picking out' Germany, because in his view the German problem could only be dealt with by the whole world and not on the basis of national armaments.[38] Many internationalists thus denied a Germany threat, except to the collective system, and they preferred the generality of Covenant obligations to specific commitments. As Cecil observed during the 1936 Rhineland crisis, 'My experience in this country is that Locarno is far more unpopular than the larger obligations of the Covenant'.[39]

Many on the right, by contrast, had a definite perception of a potential German threat. 'The issue we have to face at no distant date in Europe', said Lord Lloyd in an address at Chatham House, 'is the issue of Germany armed to the teeth, whose sole god is might, and who is imbued with one single idea, the expansion of the German Reich'.[40] Lord Rothermere, subsequently an ardent Germanophile, initiated a campaign for 5,000 aircraft and an Anglo-French alliance a month after the collapse of the Disarmament Conference. He grossly exaggerated Germany's air strength and, in 1935, established the National League of Airmen and financed the production costs of a proto-type aircraft – the *Britain First*.[41] With his views on the inevitability of war and the perils of retribution for weakness, he reflected the nationalist's dismissal of collective security. The Imperial Policy Group believed that Germany would be tempted by Britain's military weaknesses; the fate of Ethiopia, said Churchill, had shown what could happen to an unarmed state.[42]

A dispute broke out between Tory nationalists and internationalists, the latter represented by Neville Chamberlain, who wanted to avoid tax increases, damage to trade and industry, and what *The Economist* (2 May 1936) referred to as the problem of harnessing both a housing and a rearmament boom. But at the 1935 Conservative Party conference, Lloyd, Churchill and the Duchess of Atholl renewed the attack and called for the reorganisation of industry to facilitate conversion for defence purposes, an accelerated programme for the RAF and a reconstructed fleet. The Duchess accepted the need for higher taxation and postponement of domestic reforms, and Sir Patrick Hannon advocated a defence loan. This horrified Chamberlain, who argued that the League still had a role to play and should be given every chance to solve the Ethiopian crisis before being abandoned.[43]

In sum, between 1931 and the end of 1933, there were signs that German rearmament had alerted a wide cross-section of liberal internationalism to the need for vigilance and even to the possible use of coercive measures. But by frequently presenting rearmament under the aegis of international security, or catching up after years of unilateralism, the government revealed no apparent strategic aim. After years of agitation, liberal internationalists resisted ditching the tenet that armaments would lead to war, long after all possibility of an arms convention had vanished. The rearmers attempted to overcome this by appealing less to national safety than to the requirements of collective security, but an immense obstacle stood in the way of any general acceptance of such a view. Rearmers almost all identified with the National Government, which by its performances in the Manchurian and Ethiopian crises, and by its hostility to the Peace Ballot, had forfeited, in the view of its opponents, any claim to be supporting the League. Angell could justifiably claim that the strongest backers of rearmament were also those most bitterly opposed to the Covenant.[44]

Revision revived

The absence of controversy over revision of Germany's international status was a stark contrast to the divisive impact of the government's rearmament proposals. Obviously, the two, rearmament and revision, were not incompatible; reactionaries such as Londonderry adopted a soft line towards Germany but pursued rearmament as well. But to liberal internationalists, British rearmament threatened to set off an arms race, invalidating the formal procedures whereby consideration of German claims would be a *quid pro quo* for its re-entry into the League and its adherence to an arms control convention. Support for revision and opposition to rearmament were complementary aspects of a policy that aimed at arms control and rehabilitation. Various proposals on air forces, navies and the demilitarised Rhineland were to be widely greeted as holding out promises of 'fresh starts'.

In disaggregating the gamut of views on German grievances, some regarded their removal as just or ideologically sound, while others regarded revision as a necessary but limited expedient for making normative gains internationally. It cannot be said that Cecil, Samuel, Mander, Cripps, Dalton and Austen Chamberlain had any truck with the fascistic sympathies of Lothian, Londonderry or Rothermere. The liberal internationalists wanted Germany back in the League so that its actions could be ordered, whereas pragmatists were more anxious to free Germany from restrictions so that its energies might be diverted. Austen Chamberlain, for example, though not averse to orderly revision was antagonised by Hitler's maverick approach to diplomacy and asked whether it was time 'to ask the German Government to tell us frankly all that she claims, so that we may know and tell her how far we are prepared to go, either now or at a later time'.[45] Others, including Cecil and Liberals led by Samuel, were plainly anxious to pin Germany down to some sort of agreement that would lead to a disarmament convention or that would at least avoid the need for 'excessive' rearmament. Cecil opposed the rearmament plans in 1935 but accepted them in 1936 as an 'interim' measure, a 'breathing space' so that efforts to secure a more 'permanent pacification' could be made.[46] Clearly, too, the Labour movement linked arms control and peaceful revision. At a meeting on 22 May 1935, the Parliamentary Party decided to oppose the defence estimates, against the advice of Citrine, Bevin and Dalton, not only out of distrust of the government, but because Hitler had held out the prospect of an air pact. The following March, a caucus of Labour MPs agreed to oppose the 1936 White Paper. Reflecting the majority view, a National Council of Labour pamphlet, *Labour and the Defence of Peace* (1936), explained that ideally an IPF should be substituted for rearmament, but that in the meantime: 'A sincere effort must be made to discover a basis of negotiations with Hitler'.[47]

During the months preceding the 1935 Saar plebiscite, Labour had shown little inclination to put its IPF commitment to the test. Indeed, Lansbury had secured from Simon an assurance that British troops would not be sent to the Saar, an attitude endorsed by the *Daily Herald* (6 November 1934). The government itself was unenthusiastic about policing the Saar, partly for practical reasons and partly because non-intervention seemed safer. But pressure from Eden and Neville Chamberlain (who saw it as an opportunity to put his own IPF proposal into operation), brought about a reversal in December. Internationalists exploited the success of the policing, though, as Liddell Hart noted, 'the results were singularly unproductive of data that might serve for a memorandum or throw light on the concrete problems of a permanent International Force'.[48] More significantly, the harmonious resolution of the Saar problem was greeted with relief, as evidence of Germany's willingness to accept regulated revision. According to *Headway* (January 1935), the episode had contributed to the widespread spirit of optimism engendered by negotiations for European security pacts.

A Western Air Pact proposed by Britain and France in February 1935 received a warm welcome by liberal internationalists because it offered Germany equality of rights in armaments, in return for re-entry into the League and completion of an Eastern Locarno with the Soviet Union, Poland and Czechoslovakia. The French would receive a British guarantee against aggression, with the promise of immediate air assistance. The approval of liberal internationalists affords a marked contrast to earlier Anglo-French initiatives, such as the naval compromise of 1928. While the *New Statesman* (23 February 1935) urged Germany's return to Geneva and the Eastern Locarno as preconditions for equality of military status, liberal internationalists generally emphasised the value of a 'sane and sensible' extension to collective security and the prospect of a step towards disarmament.[49]

The same recommendations applied to the Anglo-German Naval Agreement of 18 June 1935, which fixed the German naval tonnage at 35 per cent of the British, and granted the principle of parity in submarines. Despite the agreement breaching the Versailles Treaty and its affront to France, internationalists argued that this sort of limited control held out the promise of more regulation. As *The Economist* (22 June 1935) suggested, the agreement appeared to confirm Hitler's essentially moderate designs. While the Cambridge University branch of the LNU expressed outrage at the undermining of Geneva principles, Cecil defended the agreement as a measure of arms control and *Headway* asserted that the provisions seemed 'to await incorporation in a general arms agreement'.[50] Labour equivocated. The *Daily Herald* (14 June 1935) noted that the measure broke away from the 'rearmament spiral', but later argued to the contrary. Labour's National Executive objected to the policy of bilateralism which seemed to imply that the government was allying with the 'wrong side' ideologically. But Ponsonby, the Leader of the Opposition in the Lords, summarised the party's stance when he criticised the diplomatic procedure but said that the agreement could not have been refused. Moreover, at least one realist in the party felt the opportunity worth grasping. Dalton repeatedly argued that Hitler be taken at his word, that his offer of air parity be 'snapped up'. He also approved of bilateral naval negotiations: 'We should have no illusions about Hitler or his regime. But we must negotiate with the Germany which now exists, and with its present ruler'. Impressed by revelations about German air rearmament, Dalton sought reconciliation to enable Britain to maintain air parity. This was quite consistent with his pressure for rearmament behind the scenes, but it puts rather a different complexion on the anti-appeasement image portrayed in his autobiography. True, Dalton opposed talk of frontier revisions, but compared to Aneurin Bevan (who objected to any dealings with nazism whatsoever) or Seymour Cocks (who advocated the encirclement of Germany until it collapsed from within), Dalton, like Eden, did little more than 'make faces' at the dictators.[51] By contrast, stringent comments on the Naval Agreement came from the *Morning Post*, Churchill in the Commons and Lloyd in the Lords, conveying the view that the measures would act as a 'soporific' and put the Royal Navy with its global responsibilities and obsolete ships at a disadvantage.[52] But clearly, the demand for negotiation with Germany on a basis of equal status and reconciliation had been overwhelming.

Liberal internationalists approached the next open transgression, the German Army Law of 16 March 1935, in the same fashion, as an opportunity to reconcile Germany and the League. While *Headway* (April 1935) deplored Hitler's unilateral breaching of Versailles, and deprecated the move to conscription as a 'psychological lurch' towards war, it advised readers to 'keep calm'; the main task was to ensure Germany's return to the League. Cecil wrote to Baldwin on behalf of the LNU Executive in similar terms, complaining that unilateral action undermined peaceful relations, but suggesting that an offer be extended to Germany and other powers to join in an arms convention.[53] Much of the press followed suit and the *Army Quarterly* (July 1935), hardly a fanatical supporter of the League and disarmament, hoped that the government would act swiftly to get Germany back in the League and participating in disarmament negotiations. Marxists, also, counselled non-intervention. The *New Leader* (22 March 1935) summed up ILP policy as follows: 'British workers must not allow their hatred of Fascism and Hitler to lead them to support policies making for war against Germany...It is the first duty of the British workers to overthrow the Capitalist class in this country'. Only German workers could stifle Nazi warmongering.

To liberal internationalists, the Stresa Conference declaration of April 1935 by Italy, Britain and France, prompted by German rearmament and conscription, was an exploratory exercise for establishing orderly relations with Germany. It declared the willingness of Britain, France and Italy to uphold Austrian independence and oppose 'by all practicable means, any unilateral repudiation of treaties'. Naturally, Cecil complained that Stresa perpetuated 'pact diplomacy' and undermined the League's authority. All the same, he hoped that when the League Council considered Germany's breach of Versailles it would be more constructive than offering mere condemnation.[54] In addition, the League Council adopted a Stresa-inspired proposal for an investigation of the sanctions that might be applied in cases of future transgression, leading the *New Statesman* (20 April 1935) to remark that policymakers were committed 'to a rather more positive affirmation of support for the system of collective security than they have hitherto been willing to give'. But it was mainly a spirit of reconciliation, and the intention to reach agreement with Germany on air forces and security in Eastern Europe, that found favour with liberal internationalists and the LNU.[55] By his offer of May to enter discussions for an air agreement, and to cooperate in a collective system which recognised the need for treaty revision and 'regulated evolution', Hitler further encouraged the liberal internationalist movement to welcome what the *New Commonwealth* (June 1935), described as a 'fresh start'.

It was an objective censured only by the Communist Party on the one hand, and backers of the *Morning Post*'s prescription for encirclement on the other. The *Post* observed that Stresa held out the prospect that Britain, France and Italy would unite to check Germany:

Ever since Germany left the League of Nations British policy has been obsessed with the *idée fixe* of trying to bring her back. It is a policy of sitting on Germany's doorstep, asking the price of her return and endeavouring to effect a composition which the others are prepared to pay. Naturally Germany is flattered by our attentions. The longer we sit the higher goes the price...let the rest of us leave her to her own devices, and organise that [collective security] system on our own without her. Let us make it so strong that to challenge it would expose Germany to the certainly of another defeat such as she suffered last time.[56]

The Stresa communiqué was general enough, however, to please most shades of British opinion.

Any possibility of the ex-allies combining against Germany when Hitler remilitarised the Rhineland was, of course, scotched by the Ethiopian crisis. One of the Locarno guarantors could hardly be invited to condemn Germany's action while itself conducting a war in contravention of the Covenant. Liberal internationalists agreed overwhelmingly that France had forfeited the right to demand collective action against Germany for not cooperating over sanctions against Italy. On the eve of Germany's reoccupation of the Rhineland, Cecil suggested to Eden that France be told that what was sauce for the Abyssinian goose would be sauce for the French gander.[57] And while most internationalists dismissed Germany's legal case against the Franco-Soviet Pact, first mooted at the end of 1934, the agreement had not been popular in Britain. The *Daily Herald* (24 November 1934) had referred to it as a counsel of blackest despair, likely to lead to a resurrection of the pre-war alliance system.

After the Rhineland crisis, the distinctions between the extremist Lothian (Allen) school and the Cecil/Murray school on the issue of peaceful change grew sharper, but all sections of opinion greeted remilitarisation of the zone with a call for non-intervention. At an emergency meeting of the LNU Executive, the Dean of Chichester remarked that ordinary men almost breathed a sigh of relief when German troops entered the zone.[58] 'Ordinary men' also discriminated between the German and Italian transgressions. *Headway* (April 1936) noted: 'Germany has not made war; no life has been lost because of her action'. Few internationalists would have quarrelled with the rationalisation for non-intervention produced by *The Economist* (21 and 28 March 1936) – to the effect that the reoccupation had been a symbolic act rather than a 'flagrant breach' of Locarno.

Now that Germany had achieved near equality in military status, all shades of opinion hoped for a new settlement. Virtual unanimity existed in Parliament on this point, in contrast to the disquiet caused by proposed staff talks between France and Britain – a reminder of pre-war militarism.[59] Speakers agreed on the desirability of accepting Hitler's olive branch in March 1936, indicating Germany's willingness to sign non-aggression pacts and return to the League (in the expectation that the Covenant would be freed from the Versailles connections and that the question of colonial rights would be clarified). Even the *Morning Post* (9 and 10 March) temporarily deviated from customary hostility towards Germany: 'Let us take them [Hitler's peace offers] at their face value as concrete and definite proposals for a permanent peace, knowing that the rest of Europe had to live with Germany and must make the best of her methods and her manners'. About two-thirds of the letters in the correspondence columns supported this policy in the week after the reoccupation. By 20 March, the *Post* had reverted to its 'stand by France' appeals, but the hedging had reflected ambiguity in much of nationalist opinion. Naturally, Nazi sympathisers looked forward to revision. After the Night of the Long Knives, the *Daily Mail* lauded Hitler as 'a man of action'; Rothermere saw Germany as a powerful ally against communism, especially as France would be unreliable after the Popular Front victories of 1936. Londonderry (former Minister for Air) intrigued against Eden's policies, appalled at what he considered a complete lack of appreciation of 'the Communist danger' on the part of the Foreign Office.[60] Others, including Lloyd George, Arnold Wilson (Tory backbencher), Corder Catchpool (Quaker) and T.P. Conwell-Evans (academic), blazed a trail for Neville Chamberlain's later visits to Hitler – as did British Legion leaders with the help of Catchpool and the encouragement of Edward VIII.[61] These appeasement influences on the policymaking elite, and new pressure groups such as the Anglo-German Fellowship (which published the *Anglo-German Review*) have been extensively examined in the appeasement literature.[62]

Internationalists overwhelmingly endorsed the view that attempts should be made to secure Germany's rehabilitation. Some went beyond the *idée fixe* of getting Germany back into the League and proposed a broad examination of Germany's grievances without reciprocity. In *The Times* (9 March 1936), Dawson and R. Barrington-Ward even expressed gratitude to Hitler for providing an opportunity to press forward with peaceful change. Germany had far stronger claims than Italy to be treated as a 'have-not' power. Germany would absorb Danzig, Memel and Austria; achieve economic ascendancy in the Danube basin; and perhaps receive a colonial mandate. There were various impulses to make peace, future regulation and norm-building being the most significant. Christian convictions were plainly important for Allen and Lansbury, and the Liberal Lothian.

Pacifist groups presented an almost united front in favour of a grievance conference to consider territorial changes. Speakers at the National Peace Congress in Leeds (26–29 June 1936) made a concerted attack on the Versailles system, swamping the pro-encirclement views of Lord Marley.[63] In the Labour movement, C.R. Buxton and George Catlin, two members of the ACIQ, outlined a powerful case for opening up the Danube basin to German capital and enterprise. Brailsford refused to condone the capitalist Versailles arrangement and announced that he would pledge no worker's blood to defend the eastern tier states. Inevitably, the foreign policy resolution at the 1936 Labour Party Conference included a reference to the need for application of Article 19 of the Covenant.[64] The LNU Council passed a similar resolution in June, with Allen, Megan Lloyd George and Maxwell Garnett urging colonial mandates and frontier adjustment in eastern Europe to Germany's benefit.[65]

Anti-revision restored

However, many close to the ruling elite rebelled against open-ended revisionism. In Chatham House, only nine out of the 24 members who spoke during three meetings on the Rhineland crisis supported an apologia by Lothian for Germany. Others, including Cecil, Angell, Boothby, Spears, Eleanor Rathbone and A.V. Alexander, concurred with the view that concessions should be limited.[66] The private comments of Dalton, Murray and Angell show a similar irresolution regarding German unilateralism,[67] but they grew increasingly sceptical of Hitler's professed intentions and began to work for rearmament to ensure that the League, with or without Germany, would uphold the rule of law.

Moreover, Bevin, Citrine and Dalton played a significant role in left-wing politics in moulding anti-revisionist and pro-rearmament opinion. At an international meeting of trade union and labour leaders in March 1936, Bevin and Dalton joined in the condemnation of German reoccupation, regarding it as a war preparation and urging that national armaments be 'regulated' by a plan for contributions to collective security. But they were unable to overcome the Labour Party's hostility towards the government's security policies. Dalton and a dozen other Labour MPs (including the New Commonwealth president, Barnes) abstained from voting against the defence estimates in July. By then, however, the Spanish Civil War had supplanted the German problem in the labour movement's deliberations. Spain dominated the Edinburgh Conference, at which the Party Executive presented a resolution containing the words: 'the armed strength of the countries loyal to the League of Nations must be conditioned by the armed strength of the potential aggressors'. Brushing aside the 'safety-net' of collective security, Dalton warned that the rearmament of Germany could mean a direct attack on Britain. The resolution was passed, but both he and Bevin despaired at the party's disregard of Germany, especially as many of the opponents of rearmament also clamoured for military aid to Spain.[68] Indeed, while the Civil War dealt a blow to socialist war resistance, the left suspected the government's foreign policy more than ever, persisting in the discourse of international ideological struggle, rather than national rearmament.

Not until July 1937 did Labour formally abstain rather than vote against the defence estimates.

A more effective anti-revision and pro-rearmament campaign was waged in the LNU. As might be expected, Austen Chamberlain produced a powerful indictment of Germany for breaching Locarno, telling the LNU Executive that the fleet should be brought back from the Mediterranean and negotiations refused until German troops had withdrawn from the Rhineland.[69] Cecil concurred and called for the League to be strengthened and prepare for war, and in the House of Lords he indulged in the 'heresy' of defending the government's provision for military staff talks with France. By November 1936, Cecil was convinced that Germany was using grievances to justify an arms policy: 'What is the use of Berlin assuring us that they mean peace', he wrote, 'when Germany never loses an opportunity of arrogance and Anti-international action'.[70] Cecil was driven to a tougher stand, perhaps, not so much by the nature of nazism but by concern about Hitler's continual snubbing of the League's goal of regularised conduct in international affairs. It had become plain to the LNU leadership that Germany was only offering to rejoin the League as a lever for concessions and had no intention of abiding by international law, and so colonial concessions would make no difference.[71]

Cecil and Angell had already taken steps to forge closer links with French internationalists in the *Reassemblement Universel Pour la Paix* (the International Peace Campaign, IPC) which had originated at a peace conference in Brussels in August 1935. In a circular to members of the LNU Executive in February 1936, Cecil explained that the League of Nations societies abroad were extremely weak and that the international situation made it necessary for the LNU to participate in a kind of League popular front to uphold treaty obligations and strengthen collective security.[72] In October, the Executive decided to affiliate with the IPC. It was opposed by the two secretaries, Garnett and Eppstein, by Harold Nicolson and by the remaining Conservatives in the LNU, on the grounds that the IPC received communist support.[73] Indeed, affiliation brought the British Section (Cecil, Angell, Lady Hall and Dame Livingstone) into close contact with French radicals, the communist, Marcel Cachin and other anti-fascists. The departure marked a further shift away from the LNU's traditional role as a non-party, social movement towards a sectarian, anti-appeasement and (though it supported non-intervention in Spain) increasingly anti-fascist organisation. The shift caused apprehension and great controversy.[74] But it marked the extent to which LNU leaders had lost faith in attempts to win Germany's allegiance to international authority. With the governmental discourse shifting the LNU could hardly resist reframing the strategy of liberal moderation between revolutionary and pacifist extremes.

The LNU also reconsidered its policy on rearmament. *Headway* (December 1936) echoed the Executive's reasoning: 'There can be no doubt that attempts to uphold international law have not benefited from the comparative decline of British strength in arms which has existed in recent years...Those arms will never be used for a purpose inconsistent with the Covenant of the League or the Pact of Paris'. But suspicion of government motives prevailed at the LNU Council meeting in December, and the Council opposed defence expenditure until such time as the government had clarified its purposes. The leadership laboured to reverse this policy and, despite the debilitating split in the movement, in June 1937 a majority of the Council agreed to rearmament for collective security purposes.[75] Discord continued, but the amendment to policy in the space of a year (after 18 years of disarmament campaigning) signified a remarkable switch. Cecil reported that he had 'combated a rather strong movement amongst supporters of the League of Nations Union – particularly the young ones – to declare against the re-armament policy of the Government; and I have assured them that they may rely on the armaments being used for League purposes and nothing else'.[76]

Although converts to rearmament continued to regard national defence as subservient to the requirements of collective security, it did not mean that they continued to lack a clear perception of the regime in Germany. On the contrary, liberal internationalists had always tended to have a Eurocentric view of international affairs, more so than some policymakers such as Hankey and the Chiefs of Staff who kept an eye on southeast Asia. LNU members had little confidence that the League could operate effectively outside Europe, especially after the Manchurian débâcle. Moreover, belief in collective action as an alternative to rearmament had been undermined, not only by the failure of economic sanctions against Italy, but also by exaggerated reports of German air power. The German Government insisted that it could not accept arms control unless it included Soviet air power. It became increasingly obvious to liberal internationalists after the Rhineland crisis that the Nazi Party had not moderated in office, that German nationalism diverged from normative standards of international behaviour and that the main object of peaceful change – to get Germany to abide by international regulation – had failed. In addition, liberal internationalists who continued to cling to League security did so in the hope and belief that the League would become a kind of grand alliance against the fascist dictatorships.

The anti-appeasers failed to make progress on a wide political front. Before 1936 some of them had been at loggerheads. Churchill exuded a reactionary, militaristic spirit and had attacked the gullibility of League supporters in *Headway* (January 1933). And, of course, many nationalist anti-appeasers, such as Croft, put great store by national defence and none at all by the Covenant. Although Churchill and Cecil drew closer in October 1936,[77] the difficulties of trespass across party lines grew. When Citrine shared a platform with Churchill, Bevin questioned his party loyalty. The most that could be achieved on an inter-party basis was the elite dining club, Focus, initiated in the summer of 1935, an 'Arms and the Covenant' rally in the Albert Hall on 3 December 1936 and a letter in *The Times* (1 January 1937) signed by Cecil, Dalton, Mander, Attlee and the Duchess of Atholl.[78] The legacy of bitterness between the left and right wings of liberal internationalism over rearmament and foreign policy, and the debilitating effect of the League's impotence, counted against the formation of a broader anti-German movement. Even limited cooperation was jeopardised. Churchill became immersed in the abdication crisis, and the Spanish Civil War fostered deep divisions in internationalist opinion. The Left Book Club became the main vehicle for anti-nazism, launched in March 1936 and catering for people who sought a stronger ideological commitment against fascism than that offered by the Labour Party or the LNU.

Conclusion

For the liberal internationalist movement, 'peaceful change' had been an alternative to rearmament. However, Hitler increasingly antagonised not only left-wing ideologues and nationalists, but liberals who upheld an ideal of ethical international conduct. Certainly, the claims of anti-appeasers have been exaggerated; they equivocated. Few internationalists would have favoured military action to defend Versailles until after the Munich agreement. Perhaps fewer still would have agreed with Douglas Jerrold, who championed revision because he believed justice was more likely to be on the side of the disrupters than the defenders of the status quo.[79] If, as Thorne and others have suggested, appeasement was symptomatic of a crisis in the Gladstonian high-minded liberal conscience, so too was much of the opposition to appeasement.[80] But bearing in mind the distinction between Lothian's belief in unsolicited territorial concession, and Cecil's conditional support for limited revision in Germany's status, it is arguable that liberal consciences were influenced in more than one direction. By 1937, the prospect of Germany fulfilling Cecil's conditions by returning to Geneva had all but vanished. And while rank-and-file members of the LNU continued to advocate peaceful change, their leaders ruled out revision until collective security had been firmly established. They postponed dealing with grievance indefinitely. By taking unilateral action, Hitler robbed France and Britain of bargaining points. There would soon be nothing left to barter for German conformity to international norms.

The military occupation of the Rhineland abrogated a treaty that Germany had voluntarily signed: Locarno was no diktat. Greeted with relief by some, with reluctant acquiescence and foreboding by others, the Rhineland occupation marked a parting of the ways in the movement for peace through collective security. Revisionists lost patience with 'League legalism', regarding it as sterile, outmoded and inappropriate for coping with the new forces in Europe. Other leading internationalists accepted that Germany could not be driven out of the Rhineland, but increasingly equated collective security with a potential alliance of rearmed, 'democratic' states against future German predation. From their different viewpoints, both streams considered rewriting the rules of international security that had remained virtually unchanged, though often ignored by states, since the League Covenant was adopted in 1919.

9
Conclusion: Retrenchment, Reform and Colonisation

By 1938 the heyday of liberal internationalism was apparently over. A resurgence of moral indignation in 1939 played a major part in the liberal internationalist's belief that the attack on Poland required a British declaration of war, but the League machinery which had once inspired confidence had broken down. As a result, the social movement clamoured for Covenant reforms, for alternative security arrangements or for none at all. Even the LNU leaders conceded the desirability of some reform to the system, though the usual defence was to point out that a workable system had been betrayed by governments. Yet to some extent, the demands for reform signified that other chickens were coming home to roost. Furthermore, Cecil had not been burdened with undue modesty about the League's potential for securing peace – in spite of the fact that the disarmament negotiations and the crises in Asia and Africa had already exposed its limitations and the continued pursuit of national interests. Following so quickly after the Peace Ballot, discontent was aimed as much at the LNU as at the British and other governments.

This concluding chapter surveys the reassessment that occurred in the liberal internationalist domains, focusing first on the geographical and ideological concepts of reconstruction. Second, it indicates the consideration given to reform of the League Covenant. Third, it indicates liberal internationalism's subjugation to the pre-Great War solution to interstate competition, an alliance for war. Finally, the chapter appraises the social movement as producer of innovation in identifying peace with a liberal governmental framework.

Geographical and ideological reconstitution

Of course, the antecedents of the reform controversy were as old as the League itself, and the broad outline of dispute between those who wished to see collective security strengthened and those who wanted it narrowly defined had been evident, in the 1920s and debates over Locarno. Further, as noted in Chapter 3, a demand for the total elimination of Article 16 had gained currency among the Round Table group after the completion of the Kellogg–Briand Pact. These detractions made little impression, however, while the movement's attention remained firmly fixed on disarmament. To the contrary, a Labour government had signed various 'paper guarantees', such as the Optional Clause, with the aim of strengthening the international system and improving the prospects for a disarmament treaty. Far more powerful opposition to the League, especially from socialist and pacifist war resisters, had developed after the Manchurian crisis and Germany's departure from the Disarmament Conference. On the right, too, some observers had welcomed Mussolini's demands at the end of 1933 for League reform and, like the *Morning Post* (24 November 1933), had argued that there would have to be a new, less-ambitious League. On the other side, liberal internationalists had usually challenged any proposal which even remotely threatened to undermine the Covenant. In the *News Chronicle* (21 December 1933), Cecil castigated 'reformers' for setting out to wreck the League. Only once had he deviated – at the International Federation of the League of Nations Societies meeting in 1934 when he aired a Tardieu-type security arrangement of geographical liabilities.[1] Left-wing internationalists had occasionally gone further and advocated reorganisation, not according to geographical distinctions, but on the basis of ideological compatibility, anticipating that the League would have to shrink into a group of progressive and socialist states prepared to work against fascism.[2] In the early months of the Ethiopian crisis, however, talk of reform and reorganisation abated – only to become more difficult for liberal internationalists to address the following year.

Core liberal internationalism encountered resistances in civil society, notably from the Peace Pledge Union (PPU). After a lull in its activities, the PPU held mass meetings in London, Glasgow and Birmingham in November 1936; increased its membership to 10,000 by the end of the year; and enlarged its network of local groups from 183 in October 1936 to more than 500 by March 1937.[3] Resistance to the League's security provisions intensified, not with the aim of withdrawal from the League, but of reforming the Covenant. As Aldous Huxley put it, 'Morality and common sense are at one in demanding that Article XVI should be omitted from the covenant and that the League should concentrate on active cooperative work for removing the causes of war'.[4] Others were less circumspect and the PPU's campaign incited a great deal of bitterness among Covenant supporters. At an LNU Council meeting in December 1936, several delegates made strident declarations against the PPU for following a policy that would allegedly encourage aggressive states to make war. A censure motion was narrowly avoided after an intervention by Cecil, anxious not to lose any remaining 'pacifist' adherents.[5]

At the other end of the political spectrum, imperialists proved less troublesome than pacifists because there had been little previous cooperation with them on issues such as arms control. Reactionary isolationists and nationalists in the Palmerstonian tradition had never given generous backing to a League policy, and the more the Soviet Union showed an interest in it, the less they approved. It came as no great challenge to the LNU when, like Douglas Jerrold, they wrote off the 'bolshevik' League entirely or, like the Earl of Mansfield, called for its emasculation.[6] However, others imperialists (Churchill, Boothby, Spears and the editor of the *Morning Post*, for example) had perceived an identity of interest between the Empire's survival and a strong League against Germany. Though few in number, they drew closer in outlook to the LNU, whereas the pacifist Dick Sheppard and his followers moved further away.

Nor did the Round Table present a united front against the League: there was a rough correspondence between attitudes to the League and anxiety to accommodate Germany. Lothian and Curtis agitated for removing Article 16 from the Covenant because the League hindered Germany's justifiable expansion. Smuts reversed his 1934 standpoint and advocated strengthening the League operationally, regarding it as valuable for the very purpose of hindering Germany.[7] Much depended on an individual's assessment of German policy and level of prejudice against France and/or bolshevism. Lothian was certainly an irritant to League supporters, partly because he had access to *The Times* and the governing elite (including Simon, Hoare and Chamberlain) to promote liberal imperialist views. But he developed no consistent position on collective security. He diverged from his colleagues in advocating League force against Italy, and he could never quite decide whether he preferred restoration of the nineteenth-century balance of power system, with the Empire and United States lurking in the wings, or a pattern of regional pacts, with Britain contributing to Asian, Mediterranean and a 'new' Locarno group.[8]

Nevertheless, the notion that collective security obligations should be parcelled up into regions represented a major reform issue that liberal internationalists had to consider afresh. It made geographical sense, and it was an acknowledgement that Britain could not hope to police the Empire with limited resources. The regional concept was tenaciously backed by the cabinet, the vast majority of Conservatives, and the Tory press. It had become a hallmark of Neville Chamberlain's approach to European affairs since March 1934. The Ethiopian and Rhineland crises confirmed him in the belief that Britain should concentrate on shoring up the security of Western Europe with an air pact or a new Locarno. Part of Chamberlain's 'midsummer of madness' speech in June 1936, critical of continuing sanctions against Italy, had been devoted to the advocacy of a fundamental reconstruction of the League.[9] Typical of the support for his campaign against universalism were observations in the *Army Quarterly* calling for a drastic curtailment of the League's scope and the limitation of Britain's obligations to the defence of frontiers in Western Europe and vital sea communications.[10] Eden also equated national interests with collective security in a speech in November 1936: 'nations cannot be expected to incur automatic military obligations save for areas where their vital interests are concerned'.[11] He qualified this in December, speaking of Britain's quest for peace being world-wide. But there can be little doubt that regional security had strong support on the right wing of liberal internationalism. For Austen Chamberlain, the League's 'incompetence' had left the government with no viable alternative.[12]

Although Neville Chamberlain imagined he had brought 'a fresh air of reality into the idea of collective security',[13] conservatives in general hardly adjusted policy to circumstances. The regional approach still diverged from the integrated condition of the international system. Since the 1920s, the veneer of reconciliation which Briand, Stresemann and Austen Chamberlain had achieved in Europe had been stripped off. Outside Europe, Japan and Italy had already signalled the re-emergence of imperialist aggression. Conservatives failed to acknowledge that, however small the regional groupings, members' interests were as likely to conflict as to agree. Neville Chamberlain's quest for pacts with Germany and Italy were fanciful because they presupposed non-existent degrees of mutual interest, a delusion that many liberal internationalists ceased to entertain. Nor did the regional approach take adequate account of the fact that, although Britain could contribute to security in Europe, it was not feasible to prescribe a geographical range for future collective action. In a devastating examination of Chamberlain's IPF proposal, the Chiefs of Staff indicated that it would be impossible to prevent a war from expanding beyond the bounds set by politicians. There would be no card-index of international incidents to which a regional system might conform. As the Great War had shown, Germany's strategic position in Europe was not conducive to a policy of avoiding intervention in remote incidents.

Yet, the 1930s debate on the reconstruction of collective security hinged less on the question of universalism or regionalism than on whether collective security should have geographical or ideological glue. Resisters had no hesitation in intensifying the call for a united socialist front against fascism. In view of the fact that this usually meant turning the League into an anti-fascist instrument, and bringing a socialist government to power in Britain first, the underlying principles of the concept had limited attraction for liberal internationalists. All the same, the notion of security based on ideological interest had the advantage of being directed against those states causing the League most trouble; it was to be a 'democratic variant' of the Marxist theme which, from another direction, core internationalists in the LNU eventually adopted.

Curiously, the question of Labour's tactical approach to the reconstruction of security did not lead to hard and fast divisions. The party's official standpoint, contained in the Executive's report to the 1937 conference, 'International Policy and Defence', called for a strong League policy and expressed scepticism about reconstruction of the organisation.[14] Behind the scenes, liberal internationalists and Socialist League members lobbied for a radical departure in Labour policy. Not all were as innovative as Herbert Morrison, who advocated a new Geneva Protocol and a consultative international parliament based on proportional representation.[15] C. Delisle Burns, for example, had a clear view that the old, liberal assumptions of 'civilised' relations between governments had been broken, and therefore even a reformed League would be useless.[16] Leonard Woolf believed that the party would have to go for an alliance with France and the Soviet Union. Together with Ivor Thomas, he provoked a resignation threat from Noel Baker by forwarding to the National Executive a paper outlining his belief that continuing to rely on the League for security was 'to ignore irrefutable facts'.[17] A shift likewise occurred in the policies of the dissenting left. Some continued to detect what Brailsford referred to as class war among nations, so that abandoning the League and overthrowing the government remained the preconditions for preserving peace.[18] But with G.D.H. Cole, Brailsford also urged Labour to coordinate its activities with Liberals, the LNU and left-wing Tories, as well as with the communists and the ILP. A united front in the deteriorating international situation supplanted political strife at home. Moreover, the Socialist League admitted the need for an old-fashioned alliance between Britain, France and the USSR. It implied a policy of encirclement in cooperation with the 'old enemy' France (redeemed by Blum's Popular Front government).[19] For veteran champions of the UDC such as Brailsford, it symbolised a revolutionary departure in strategy, and contributed to bridging the policy gap between dissenters and the main body of the Labour Party. Ironically, too, the Communist Party may actually have had a moderating effect. Soviet membership in 1934 made the League more acceptable to left-wing opinion, and the CPGB leader, Harry Pollitt, acknowledged that not all capitalist governments were striving for war. In accordance with Stalin's policy, the CPGB regarded the strengthening of the League of Nations as a prime objective in the struggle against fascism.[20]

But it was the demise of the League itself which did most to minimise differences on the question of reconstructing collective security. However much the communists or liberal internationalists continued to pay it homage, the League had virtually become unimportant and Labour's policy adjustments reflected this. 'Day by day', commented a member of the New Fabian Research Bureau, 'our old Geneva vocabulary means less and less'. The answer to the deterioration in European stability was a 'democratic front'.[21] Whether this emerged from within a League framework or not was secondary. What divided the labour movement was the domestic itinerary of Cripps and his followers. The Socialist League's Unity Campaign of 1936–37 involved negotiations with the CPGB and this became an issue of party loyalty that provoked a swift reaction from the hypersensitive Labour Party Executive. By the end of March 1937, the Socialist League had been disaffiliated and its members threatened with expulsion. The bitterness over domestic tactics masked the trend common to most sections of the left, national security on the basis of ideological and strategic interests. Eventually, in September 1938, during the Czech crisis, the National Council of Labour formally announced that a security bloc based on France, Britain and the Soviet Union would best serve the cause of peace.

Covenant reform

The general agitation for 'reform and reconstruction' naturally stimulated debate in the LNU, which took up the League Assembly's call for states to suggest ways of improving security. But the movement was extremely cautious about advocating change. A campaign in the late 1930s to stem the flow of criticism acknowledged the need for 'marginal' improvements, but stressed that discontent 'should be more justly directed against certain Governments than against the Covenant, which they have failed to implement'. Internationally, there was also an initial reluctance 'to divide the democratic sheep from the Fascist goats' for security purposes.[22] Moreover, when the core liberal internationalists did

advocate policy adjustments, they could not admit that basic principles of liberal internationalism had failed. They usually bridged the
gap between League principles and practice by contending that the
breakdown of international norms was reversible in the long run.
Paradoxically, the liberal idealism led to a revulsion against accommodating the Axis Powers, and to a reappraisal of collective security that
served Allied interests well after the Second World War.

Some reform proposals were of little consequence. Among the suggested Covenant amendments, four attracted particular attention. One
concerned Article 19. Sir Arthur Salter proposed that any state refusing
to comply with a League recommendation for peaceful change would
forfeit the right to protection in any resulting war. An LNU committee
investigating Covenant amendment proposals made no comment on
this, but suggested the establishment of commissions of inquiry to look
into the facts of any claims made under the Article.[23] It is difficult to
imagine, though, how even an amended Article 19 could have provided
the necessary vehicle for peaceful change. Any issues brought before
the Assembly under its terms would have been subjected to slow and
uncertain treatment. If a proposal eventually gained the Assembly's
acceptance (with the required unanimous vote), there would be no procedure for implementing the decision. The process would have relied
on the power of global opinion. To have backed an economic or territorial change by force against an objecting state would have been contrary to the spirit of peaceful change. Moreover, any tampering with
frontiers would have activated Article 10, by which states undertook to
'respect and preserve' one another's territorial integrity. The reformers
might well have reflected on historical record to see that changes in
sovereignty without the threat of force had been comparatively few –
such as the dissolution of the union of Norway and Sweden in 1905.
The dissolution of the USSR at the end of the Cold War and the division of Czechoslovakia in 1993 broke relatively new ground – without
UN intervention – but in the 1930s the international lawyer, Sir John
Fischer Williams, concluded that Article 19 could not be operated without a threat to peace.[24]

A less-controversial idea was to separate the Covenant and the peace
treaties. The LNU Council meeting of June 1937 agreed on it a year
before the League Assembly did so. It accorded with the widespread
desire to remove a complication that had always antagonised Germany,
but without signifying a conscious attempt by liberal internationalists
to appease Hitler's regime. It was a side-issue bound up with Covenant
reform and not expected to have a marked effect on international

relations or to mitigate Germany's resentment.[25] The Versailles treaties had ceased to regulate European security, anyway.

The third and fourth proposals were linked and attempted to render Article 16 more efficient. To begin with, LNU leaders believed that the unanimity rule for League Council decisions had caused interminable delays during crises, thus precluding early intervention for conflict resolution. A switch to majority verdicts would speed up the process.[26] As to Article 16 itself, LNU leaders proposed an amendment to bind states to 'special military obligations', and suggested a pre-organised system of sanctions.[27] But like the other proposals, the strengthening of Article 16 relied on the willingness of member states to fulfil their obligations. Altering the legal provisions of collective security had become an academic exercise in the late 1930s, and provided no adequate answer to the criticisms being voiced by commentators such as E.H. Carr (who argued that only a direct threat would 'arouse the warlike passions of the British people') or Delisle Burns (who denied the existence of a normative framework, and goodwill, to make the League work).[28] Nevertheless, some of the innovations, such as abandonment of unanimity and strengthening the Council's executive power, foreshadowed the institutional arrangements of the UN and its dominance by the victorious states.

Collective security for peace as an alliance for war

A more grounded adaptation by the LNU was the trend, parallel to but not specifically influenced by that in the labour movement, towards advocacy of a like-minded power bloc directed against the dictatorships. There could be no place for aggressors in the League; Italy and Japan had pariah status – as did Germany after Munich. While admitting that Britain could hardly send an army into central Europe, the LNU rejected Chamberlain's regionalism.[29] The LNU could not condone a policy aimed at replacing the League rather than supplementing it. To single out defence of the Empire and the Rhine would only encourage war in eastern Europe and 'smash the Covenant altogether', as proved to be the case. Further, by limiting its commitments, Britain might forgo the opportunity to help suppress a dangerous situation outside its sphere of interest which, if allowed to spread, might ultimately involve Britain in a major war. Finally, the potential 'allies' of a victim were not restricted to any one region.[30]

Norman Angell's solution to the deteriorating situation was typical of that favoured by many liberal internationalists – the dictators should be given the opportunity to cooperate in maintaining peace, but failing this, a 'Grand Defensive Alliance' should be formed with Britain, France and the Soviet Union at its core.[31] By 1938, liberal internationalists, including Sir Alfred Zimmern, Montague Burton Professor of International Relations at Oxford and LNU Executive member, argued that the time had arrived. In common with others, Zimmern had always preferred to think of the League as a kind of Cooperative Society, exercising authority through the will of the peoples of the member states, rather than as an embryonic superstate with a solid code of law. The outcry over the Hoare–Laval Pact had demonstrated the successful operation of this will.[32] But Mussolini and Hitler had raised the problem of states which seemed less interested in promoting international welfare than in territorial and resource gains. Obviously, the League could not command the loyalty of all countries. Zimmern, therefore, proposed a club of 'welfare' states from which the 'military' states would be excluded. According to Zimmern, it was 'only in the free, constitutional, and democratic states that the co-operative nature of man is fully utilised in service to his fellows and to the community, and that there has thus been provided a moral basis for the extension of the duty of man to his neighbours which the practice of collective security demands'. By contrast: '[w]hat reaches Geneva from Rome, Berlin or Tokyo is bound to be tainted with lawlessness'.[33] Zimmern discounted the notion of world citizenship, but also derided economic nationalism.[34]

His infusions were a response to the change in international circumstances and liberal internationalist disenchantment with Geneva. But reformism and restructuring could not repair liberal internationalism's prestige. The LNU was too closely associated with the League in its original, Wilsonian form, and by 1938 the Geneva institution was on its last legs. Already, the smaller European states (including the Scandinavians) had declared their lack of confidence in the Covenant, and in October 1936 Belgium had reverted to neutrality. The United States remained as far removed from European security issues as ever, and of the Dominions, only New Zealand (the weakest, most isolated and most tied by sentiment to Britain) professed much concern for the League. Neville Chamberlain seemed to be stating the obvious when he announced in the Commons in February 1938 that the League had passed away.

However, during the Spanish Civil War, many liberal internationalists saw merit in the popular front resistance policies of Bevan, Cole and Cripps. The tribulations which this caused the Labour Party have been discussed above, but the LNU experienced similar woes. Murray even rebuked the LNU's Youth Committee for sending a representative to Spain without consultation. The Executive stood aloof from the great ideological struggle of the decade. 'I am afraid', wrote Murray, 'it is impossible for the L.N.U. to do anything useful: anything like mediation seems impossible and ... in the present state of Europe I do not see how the League could act'.[35] The most that the LNU Executive would consider was a League investigation into the extent of foreign involvement.[36] The Spanish *cause célèbre* of the dissenting UDC tradition left many liberal internationalists subdued, in contrast to their agitations during the Ethiopian crisis. Moreover, the Spanish conflict weakened links in the social movement for peace coalition, making it more difficult for Cecil to maintain the LNU's colonisation of British opinion. The health of liberal internationalism thus faltered at a time of increasing international tension. Liberal internationalists responded to the pressure for retrenchment and reform by adapting their discourses and policies with an evolution that owed more to contemplating a 'League' based on states with common strategic and ideological interests than to any proposals for amending the Covenant. The imperialist, reactionary Churchill could warm to this:

> The old policy was an effort to establish the rule of law in Europe and build up through the League of Nations, or by regional pacts under the League of Nations, effective deterrents against the aggressor. That is the policy which we have followed. Is the new policy – I hope we shall hear more about it – to come to terms with the totalitarian Powers in the hope that by great and far-reaching acts of submission... peace may be preserved?[37]

But the LNU continued to lose members and experience financial difficulties. It moved into overt opposition to the government, sympathising with Eden, who resigned in February 1938 in part because Chamberlain was conducting foreign policy independently and in part because he was expected to appease Italy.[38]

Nevertheless, the ethics of liberal internationalism survived both the decline of the LNU and the collapse of the League. The Munich crisis in September 1938 had a cathartic effect, not simply for the huge relief from threat of war that the agreement promised to bring. Liberal internationalism had betrayed itself, wholly complicit in smashing the very international norms that it pledged to uphold (as well as undermining the French agreements in Eastern Europe and causing Stalin to conclude that Germany and the west would turn against the Soviet Union). Public rejoicing quickly reverted to unease after the Munich crisis, for example, that the 'public conscience' had been pricked by the bargain with Hitler.[39] Some 30 Tory MPs abstained from voting on the Munich settlement, concerned as much about the strategic implications of giving up Czech defences and weakening encirclement as about the ethical implications. After Munich, revulsion against Germany's brutality and Chamberlain's foreign policy gathered pace. At the LNU Council of December 1938, delegates formally approved a 'grand alliance' policy. The Labour Party continued to fret about capitalism and war, but was never completely won over to the Cripps line of dissent. Henderson and MacDonald had laid foundations of liberal internationalism, which under the influence of Dalton, Woolf, Arnold-Forster, Noel Baker, Bevin and Citrine continued to serve as the guiding principle of the party's approach to international relations.

In the last months of peace, collective security was no longer regarded as an abstract, arbitrary system, but as a political–military instrument directed against tyranny and competing imperialisms. And, whether or not one agrees that Germany represented an inevitable threat to Britain or agrees with liberal concepts of peace, liberal internationalists certainly believed in the threats to a normative system of international conduct. They responded soberly, perhaps not even hopefully, but in the belief that they possessed superior, rational, knowledge and moral right.

Conclusion

The Liberal Party's disintegration had been accompanied by the spread of 'liberal' ideas throughout British politics, thanks in significant measure to the colonisation of British opinion by liberal internationalism. To parody Herbert Butterfield's comment about the aristocratic influence in British history: 'when the Liberals were sent to the laundry, the dye ran out into the rest of the washing'.[40] Organisations such as the UDC, Socialist League, PPU, New Commonwealth and Round Table often resisted their pure faith in a League of victors prepared either to avoid war through the deterrent effect of global opinion or to risk war by imposing sanctions. Eventually, it was not easy to distinguish between the nationalist demand for an alliance against nazism and liberal internationalist support for collective security. The LNU's semi-attachment to realism, statism and imperialism gave way to more or less full attachment in 1939. But the governmentalities of liberal internationalism had been so effective in interwar politics that the new war could be presented ideologically as integral to the struggle for liberal internationalist concepts. 'The war', said Gilbert Murray, 'is an ordinary war of self-defence in the sense that we have been fighting to save ourselves from conquest by Germany; but it is an ideological war in the sense that we and other normal law-abiding nations like us, have discovered that we cannot live with nations which think as the Germans do'.[41]

The ideal of peace through regulated international conduct, rules, norms, sanctions and intergovernmental institutions had permeated civil society through innovation, education, vibrant activism at home and abroad, tactical manipulation, transgressions of political space, adaptation to international events, fluid personal attachments and close linkage with the ruling class, participation in government, epistemic communities of military and legal experts and the popular press. Essentially a bourgeois phenomenon for the protection of national interests and values in an international framework of stability through collective security international regulation and justice, it kept transactions between government and civil society steady. Its liberal influence on the 'mentalities' of British opinion through peace education gives some support to a Gramscian concept of civil society. Its place in British 'governance' as a social movement dependent upon, and contributing to, the tolerance of government priorities and dispositions suggests a Foucauldian relevance for assessing this social movement. It is not clear, however, whether or how a continuing crisis of liberal internationalism is resolvable.

In 1939, the LNU was supposed to have arranged celebrations for the twenty-first year of its existence. Instead, the leaders planned to remove Head Office out of London so that the organisation could continue through the forthcoming war.[42] Celebrating Cecil's birthday in September 1944, Churchill remarked, perhaps with tongue in cheek: 'It must be a satisfaction to you to see that the great causes of international peace and justice for which you have so faithfully pleaded are now being vindicated by the sword'.[43] Some of the leaders were prominent in the formation towards the end of the war of a United Nations Association to replace the LNU: Cecil, Noel Baker, Smuts and Lytton among them. But some of the vibrancy of the old LNU had gone. Allen, Austen Chamberlain and Davies were dead and the other nineteenth-century liberals were ageing. In 1945, Cecil was 81, Murray 79, Angell 71 and Lytton almost 70. The UN Association, led by the 35-year old Air Vice-Marshal Donald Bennett DSO, continued to attract liberal internationalists.

Paradoxically, the UN subverted national sovereignty to a greater extent, in theory, than the League had done. It required a militarised collective security primed by the most powerful states. It provided a new political space for the replacement of territorial imperialism, with the emergence of financial and corporate imperialism in competition with state socialist imperialism. It also presided over an even more draconian victor's peace than its predecessor. Germany and Austria, were territorially reduced, pillaged and (temporarily) disarmed, and divided to a degree that the allies of 1918 might have envied. German Europe would, however, eventually draw on interwar domestic resources of economic knowledge deriving from the Austrian school of the late nineteenth century and the interwar Freiburg school, to capture the state for neoliberalism.[44] Much further into the future, varieties of neoliberal internationalism would help determine the roles of global trade and international financial institutions, and the political economy of UN peacebuilding. Concepts and policies deriving from the liberal internationalist condition implemented by self-inscribed liberal states continue to prove stimulating and controversial, generating new critique and resistant social movements.

Appendix I: Group Memberships

A Statistics

It is advisable to treat the statistical membership claims with caution, since the definition of 'member' can vary, membership lists were not necessarily up to date, and there was, perhaps, a natural inclination for the pressure groups to inflate the extent of their support. The figures given here are thus only approximate. The figures are obviously not indicative of the strength of commitment to a group.

League of Nations Union[1]	Nominal membership	Subscribed membership
16 Jan. 1926	514,789	– (2,813 branches)
31 Dec. 1926	587,224	279,990
1 Jan. 1928	665,011	–
1 Jan. 1929	747,945	–
1 Jan. 1930	822,903	–
1 Jan. 1931	889,500	–
19 Nov. 1931	933,060	410,000
31 Dec. 1932	994,121	388,255
25 Nov. 1933	1,011,603	377,824
31 Dec. 1934	–	396,000
– – 1937	–	315,000

Abyssinia Association[2]		
1936	500	

British Legion[3]		
1926	155,660	
1934	343,000	
1936	483,760	

British Union of Fascists[4]		
1934	15,000	(5,000 Activists)

Communist Party[5]		
1926	10,730	
1930	1,376	
1931	2,500	
1935	7,700	
1937	12,500	

Council of Action[6]
1937   10,624

Fellowship of Reconciliation[7]
1926   7,584

Independent Labour Party[8]
1931   21,000
1935   4,400

Labour Party[9]
1933   2,000,000   (371,607 individual members)

New Commonwealth Society[10]
Jan. 1934   1,400
Sept. 1934   1,826
Feb. 1936   1,772
Sept. 1936   1,911
Sept. 1937   2,153

New Fabian Research Bureau[11]
1936   400

No More War Movement[12]
1926   3,000
1933   3,000
1936   3,500

Peace Pledge Union[13]
1936   100,000
1939   130,000

Socialist League[14]
1933   2,000
1935   3,000

Union of Democratic Control[15]
1926   2,000

Womens International League for Peace and Freedom[16]
1926   3,500
1936   3,000

B   Officers

Officers are given for five of the pressure groups most clearly concerned with foreign affairs and collective security.

League of Nations Union[17]

Officers and Committees in 1931

Joint Presidents:
Rt Hon. the Viscount Grey of Falloden, KG
Rt Hon. the Viscount Cecil, KC

Hon. Presidents:
Rt Hon. Stanley Baldwin, MP
Rt Hon. J.R. Clynes
Rt Hon. D. Lloyd George, OM, MP

Chairman of Executive Committee:
Professor Gilbert Murray, LLD, DLitt., FBA

Vice-Presidents:
The Marchioness of Aberdeen and Temair
Field Marshal Rt Hon. the Viscount Allenby, GCMG, GCB
The Viscountess Astor, MP
The Duchess of Atholl, MP
Rt Hon. the Lord Baden-Powell, GCMG, GCVO, CB
Col. Sir Gilbert Barling, Bt, CB, CBE
Rt Hon. G.N. Barnes, CH
Dame Henrietta Barnett, DBE
Admiral of the Fleet Rt Hon. the Earl Beatty, OM, GCB
Rt Hon. Miss Margaret Bondfield, LLD
Rt Hon. Sir Robert Borden, GCMG
Chair of the British Legion
Rt Hon. S.M. Bruce, CH, MC
The Viscountess Bryce
His Grace the Archbishop of Canterbury
Rt Hon J.G. Coates, MC
W.T. Cosgrave, LLD
Annie Viscountess Cowdray
Rt Hon. the Lord Craigmyle, KC

Mrs Creighton
Rt Hon. T.A. Crerar
Most Hon. the Marquess of Crewe, KG, GCVO
Dame Rachel Crowdy, DBE, RRC
Rt Hon. the Lord Cullen, KBE
David Davies
Rt Hon. the Earl of Derby, KG, GCB
His Grace the Duke of Devonshire, KG, GCMG
Rt Hon. the Lord Dickinson, KBE
Rt Hon. H.A.L. Fisher
Rt Hon. Sir G.E. Foster, KCMG
The President of the Free Church Council
Rev. R.C. Gillie, DCL
The Viscountess Gladstone
Mrs Ogilvie Gordon, DSc, PhD
Gen. Sir H. De La Poer Gough, GCMG
Sir Arthur Haworth, Bt
Very Rev. J.H. Hertz, PhD
General the Hon. J.B.M. Hertzog, LLD
Rt Hon. the Earl of Home
Rt Hon. the Lord Irwin, GCSI, GCIE
Rt Hon. Sir W.F. Lloyd, KCMG
The Marchioness of Londonderry, DBE
Sir Henry Lunn, MD, JP
Dame Edith Lyttelton, DBE
Rt Hon. W.L. MacKenzie King, CMG
Rt Hon. Sir Donald Maclean, KBE, MP
Rt Hon. the Lord Marshall, KCVO
Professor Gilbert Murray, LLD, DLitt., FBA
H.H. the Maharaja Jamsaheb of Nawanagar
Rt Hon. the Lord Parmoor, KCVO, KC
Most Hon. the Marquess of Reading, GCB
Miss Maude Royden, CH, DD

Most Hon. the Marquess of Salisbury, KG, GCVO
Rt Hon. Sir Herbert L. Samuel, GCB, GBE, MP
Rt Hon. Srinivase Sastri
Rt Hon. the Earl of Selborne, KG, GCMG
Rt Hon. Tom Shaw, CBE
Rt Hon. the Lord Shuttleworth, LLD,
Rt Hon. Sir John Simon, GCSI, KCVO, MP
Lt.-Gen. the Rt Hon. J.C. Smuts, KC
Sir Hugh Shaw Stewart, CB
Mrs Swanick, CH
Sir William Vincent, GCIE, KCSI
Rt Hon. Lord Wakefield of Hythe, CBE
A. Whitehead
Rt Hon. J.H. Whitley
His Grace the Archbishop of York

Executive Committee, as on 31 December 1931
Chairman: Professor Gilbert Murray, LLD, DLitt.
Vice-Chairman: Major the Rt Hon. J.W. Hills, MP
Vice-Admiral J.D. Allen, CB
Sir Norman Angell
P.J. Noel Baker
C. Delisle Burns, MA, DLitt.
Major Anthony Buxton, DSO
L.J. Cadbury
Colonel David Carnegie, CBE, FRS
Miss K.D. Courtney
The Viscount Cranbourne, MP
Lt.-Col. G.R. Crosfield, CBE, DSO, TD
David Davies
R.J. Davies, MP
Rt Hon. the Lord Dickinson, KBE
Vice-Admiral S.R. Drury-Lowe, CMG
Mrs E. Dugdale
H.H. Elvin
The Viscountess Gladstone
Hon. Mrs Ralph Glyn
Captain L.H. Green, MA
Miss E.M. Guinness
Lady Hall

J.H. Harris
Sir Percy Harris, MP
Sir Arthur Haworth, Bt
Lt.-Gen. Sir Hugh Jeudwine, KCB, KBE
Rt Hon. the Lord Rhayader
Morgan Jones, MP
Lt.-Com. the Hon. J.M. Kenworthy
C.W. Kimmins, Dsc
Lady Layton
Rt Hon. the Earl of Lytton, GCSI, GCIE
G. Le M. Mander, MP
Sir Walter Napier, DCL
The Lady Parmoor
Rt Hon. Lord Eustace Percy, MP
Sir John Power, Bt, MP
Rt Hon. the Lord Queenborough, GBE
Mrs Walter Runciman
W.J. Salmon
John Sherborne
Rennie Smith, Bsc
H.S. Syrett, CBE, LLB
Sir Ben Turner, CBE
H.D. Watson, CIE, CBE
Hon. Mrs Wilson-Fox, CBE
Herbert Worsley
L.M. Wynch, CIE, CBE
Professor A.E. Zimmern

Treasurer: Rt Hon. the Lord Queenborough, GBE
Secretary: J.C. Maxwell Garnett, CBE, ScD
Trustees: David Davies; Rt Hon. Reginald McKenna

National Peace Council[18]

Executive 1936
Dr E.W. Barnes (President)
Harrison Barrow (Chairman)
Dame Elizabeth Cadbury (Treasurer)
Gerald Bailey (Secretary)
Vera Brittain
Mrs Corbett-Ashby
Archdeacon F.L. Donaldson
G.P. Gooch

Gerald Heard
Dr J.H. Hertz
Dr Hewlett Johnson
A.D. Lindsay
P.J. Noel Baker
Dr F.W. Norwood
Lady Parmoor
Hon. Alexandrina Peckover
Lord Ponsonby
Dr A. Maud Royden
Canon H.L. Sheppard
Sir Ben Turner

New Commonwealth British Section[19]

1934
Presidents: Rt Hon. Lord Gladstone;
Hon. G.N. Barnes (International
Section)
Chairman: Rt Hon. Lord Davies

Vice-Presidents:
The Rt Hon. Lord Allen of Hurtwood
Mr S. Vyvyan Adams, MP
Major C.R. Attlee, MP
Sir Norman Angell
Mrs Corbett Ashby
The Rt Hon. G.N. Barnes
Professor P.J. Noel Baker
Colonel John Buchan, MP
Sir Anton Bertrum
Sir Charles Barrie, KBE, MP
Sir T. Comyns Berkeley
Sir John Field Beale, KBE
The Rt Rev. the Lord Bishop of Bangor
The Rt Hon. Ralph Beaumont, MP
Mr J. Davies Bryan
Dame Henrietta Barnett
Sir Montague Burton
The Rt Hon. Viscount Cecil
Major-General Sir B.E. Wyndham
Childs, KCMG, CB, KBE
Vice-Admiral Gordon Campbell, VC,
MP
Sir John Cadman, GCMG
Mr A. Duff Cooper, MP
Mr Laurence Currie, MA
Mr Laurence J. Cadbury, OBE, MA
The Rt Hon. Lord Clwyd

Sir Julien Cahn
Lt.-Col. G.R. Crosfield, CBE, DSO
Mr F. Dudley Docker, CB, JP
Mr O. Picton Davies
Mr Daniel Daniel
Vice-Admiral S.R. Drury-Lowe, CMG
The Rt Hon. Viscount Esher
Dr C.A. Edwards, Principal,
University College, Swansea
Mr Cyril F. Entwistle, MP
Dr Kenneth Fisher, Headmaster,
Oundle School
Sir Edward Grigg, KCMG, MP
Sir Philip Gibbs, KBE
The Rt Rev. the Bishop of Guildford
Dr L. Haden Guest
Mr J.L. Garvin
Sir Richard Gregory, Bt., LLD
Lady Gladstone of Hawarden
Mr A.G. Gardiner
Maj.-Gen. the Rt Hon. Lord
Hutchinson of Montrose, KCMG
The Rt Hon. Lord Horder, KCVO, MD,
FRCP
The Rt Hon. Sir Robert Horne, GBE,
MA, LLD
Dr J.H. Hertz, Chief Rabbi
Mr Frederick Hyde
Professor H.J. Hetherington, MA, LLD, JP
Mrs May Hamilton
The Rt Hon. Thomas Johnston
Sir Evan D. Jones, Bt
Sir Henry Stuart-Jones, MA
The Rev. J.D. Jones, CH, MA, DD
The Rev. Canon Maurice Jones, DD
Sir Thomas Artemus Jones, KC
Sir Oliver Lodge, FRS, Dsc
Lady Dorothea Layton
Sir Henry Lunn
Maj.-Gen. the Rt Hon. Lord
Mottistone, CB, CMG
Maj.-Gen. Sir Frederick Maurice,
KCMG, CB
The Rt Hon. Lord Merthyr
Lt.-Gen. Sir George Macdonogh, GBE,
KCB
The Rt Rev. Norman Maclean, DD
Lt.-Col. J.T.C. Moore-Brabazon,
MC, MP

Mr Geoffrey Le M. Mander, MP
Principal John Murray, MA
(University College of South West
England, Exeter)
The Rt Hon. Lord Moynihan, KCMG
Sir Harry McGowan, KBE
Mr D.M. Mason, MP
The Hon. Lord Mackenzie, LLD
Mr Beverley Nichols
Sir Christopher Needham
Sir Charles Petrie, Bt
The Rt Hon. Sir Frederick Pollock,
Bt., KC
Sir Felix Pole
The Rt Hon. Lord Rutherford, OM,
Dsc
Col. R.M. Raynsford, DSO
Principal J.F. Rees, University
College, Cardiff
James A. de Rothschild, MP
The Viscountess Rhondda
Sir Arthur Salter
Mr J.T. Shepherd, MBE, MA, Litt.D
The Viscountess Snowden, JP
Sir Josiah Stamp, GBE
Brig.-Gen. E.L. Spears, C.b, MP
Mr Wickham Steed
Mr Herbert Sidebottom
Dr R. Franklin Sibly, LLD (Vice-
Chancellor, Reading University)
Maj.-Gen. Sir Ernest Swinton, KBE
The Rt Hon. Lord Snell
The Rt Rev. the Lord Bishop of St.
Davids
Professor H.V. Temperley, OBE, MA
Col. Norman Thwaites, CBE, MVO
The Rt Rev. Lauchlan Maclean Watt,
MA, DD
The Rt Hon. Josiah Wedgwood, MP
Sir Richard Winfrey, JP
Mr J.C. Wilmot, MP
Professor W.H. Young, DSc, FRS

Peace Pledge Union[20]

Leaders: Rev. H.R.L. Sheppard; Brig.-
Gen. F.P. Crozier
Sponsors: Aldous Huxley
            George Lansbury
            Vera Brittain

Rose Macaulay
Capt. Philip Mumford
Lord Ponsonby
Siegfried Sassoon
Donald O. Soper
Bertrand Russell
Ellen Wilkinson
Canon C.E. Raven

Union of Democratic Control[21]

Executive Committee, 1926–27:
George Aitken
Mrs Barton
F. Seymour Cocks
Professor C. Raymond Beazley
Hamilton Fyfe
J.A. Hobson
H.J. Laski
H.B. Lees Smith, MP
Arthur Ponsonby, MP
F.J. Shaw
Mrs H.M. Swanwick (editor, *Foreign
Affairs*)
Rt Hon. C.P. Trevelyan, MP (Hon.
Treasurer)
Miss E.G. Webb (Secretary)

General Council, 1926–27
Major Leigh Aman
Norman Angell
The Hon. Lady Barlow
Rev. James Barr, MP
Harrison Barrow
S. Bettman
Francis Birrell
H.N. Brailsford
J. Bromley, MP
C. Delisle Burns
Rev. Harold Buxton
Lady Courtney
Gilbert Dale
Robert Dell
Miss M.E. Durham
A.E. Everett
W. Arnold-Forster
W.T. Goode
Duncan Graham, MP
Capt. Grenfell, RN
Edward Grubb

C.A. Hooper
J.H. Hudson, MP
E.E. Hunter
Rev. R.V. Holt, BA
Mrs Huth Jackson
Thomas Johnston, MP
Joseph King
J.W. Kneeshaw
Rt Hon. William Graham, MP
F.W. Pethick Lawrence, MP
Alexander MacLaren
Neil MacLean, MP
W.H. Martin, C.A.
Mrs E.D. Morel
Miss S.E. Morel
Robert Murray
G.H. Oliver, MP
R.L. Outhwaite
Sir George Paish
Miss Payne

F.E. Pollard
M. Phillips Price
Hon. Bertrand Russell
Hugh Spender
Joseph Sturge
Mrs F. Strickland
Douglas Tatlock
David C. Thompson
Mrs C.P. Trevelyan
R.C. Trevelyan
Ben Turner
Mrs E.F. Wallis
Rev. Walter Walsh, DD
Lord De La Warr
J.H. Whitehouse
Dr Ethel Williams
Miss I. Cooper Willis
Alexander Wishart
Leonard Woolf

Appendix II: Circulation Figures

British Legion Journal (monthly)[1]	
1934	103,455
1935	112,860
Headway (monthly)[2]	
1933	94,500
Labour Monthly[3]	
1935	5,000
1936	6,500
Naval Review (quarterly)[4]	
1934	approx. 1,000 (reading membership)
New Commonwealth (monthly)[5]	
1934	6,000
New Statesman (weekly)[6]	
1933	14,000
1934	18,000
New Times and Ethiopia News (weekly)[7]	
1936	40,000

Notes

1 Introduction: Liberal Internationalism, a Social Movement for Peace

1. Viscount Milner, *Questions of the Hour*, London: Nelson, 2nd edn, 1925, pp. 211–14.
2. Richard Overy, *The Morbid Age*, London: Penguin, 2010, p. 264.
3. Cited in, *Headway*, March 1927, p. 42.
4. E.g., Michael W. Doyle, *Ways of War and Peace*, New York: W.W. Norton, 1997; Bruce Russett and John O'Neal, *Triangulating Peace: Democracy, Interdependence, and International Organizations*, New York: W.W. Norton, 2000. See, Cecelia Lynch, *Interpreting Interwar Peace Movements in World Politics*, Ithaca, NY: Cornell University Press, 1999; Andrew Williams, *Liberalism and War: The Victors and the Vanquished*, London: Routledge, 2006; David Cortright, *Peace: A History of Movements and Ideas*, New York: Cambridge University Press, 2008.
5. Ceadel uses 'pacificism' to identify a 'middle-way' between militarism and absolutist war resisters/pacifists; Martin Ceadel, *Pacifism in Britain, 1914–1945: The Defining of a Faith*, Oxford: Oxford University Press, 1980, p. 61; *Semi-detached Idealists: The British Peace Movement and International Relations, 1854–1945*, Oxford: Oxford University Press, 2000; *Living the Great Illusion: Sir Norman Angell, 1872–1967*, Oxford: Oxford University Press, 2009. Peter Wilson, *The International Theory of Leonard Woolf: A Study in Twentieth Century Idealism*, Basingstoke: Palgrave Macmillan, 2003.
6. E.g., R.B.J. Walker, 'Social Movements/World Politics', *Millennium: Journal of International Studies*, Vol. 23, No. 3, 1994, pp. 669–700; Marco Giugni, Doug McAdam and Charles Tilly (eds), *How Social Movements Matter*, Minneapolis, MN: University of Minnesota Press, 1999; Marco Giugni, *Social Protest and Policy Change: Ecology, Antinuclear, and Peace Movements in Comparative Perspective*, Lanham, MD: Rowman & Littlefield, 2004; Robert D. Benford and David A. Snow, 'Framing Processes and Social Movements: An Overview and Assessment', *Annual Review of Sociology*, Vol. 26, 2000, pp. 611–39; Richard Price, 'Transnational Civil Society and Advocacy in World Politics', *World Politics*, Vol. 55, No. 4, 2003, 579–606.
7. Beate Jahn, 'Liberal Internationalism: From Ideology to Empirical Theory – and Back Again', *International Theory*, Vol. 1, No. 3, 2009, pp. 409–38; Roger Mac Ginty, 'The Liberal Peace at Home and Abroad', *British Journal of Politics and International Relations*, Vol. 11, No. 4, 2009, pp. 690–708; Oliver P. Richmond and Henry C. Carey, *Mitigating Conflict: NGOs in Peace Processes,*London: Cass, 2003; Oliver P. Richmond, *A Post-Liberal Peace*, Abingdon: Routledge, 2011.
8. Adam Ferguson, *An Essay on the History of Civil Society* (1767), is discussed in Foucault, *The Birth of Biopolitics*, pp. 296–307.
9. Antonio Gramsci, *The Prison Notebooks*, London: Lawrence & Wishart, [orig. 1949] 1971, pp. 210–76.

10. Robert D. Putnam, Robert Leonardi and Raffaella Y. Nanetti, *Making Democracy Work. Civic Traditions in Modern Italy*, Princeton, NJ: Princeton University Press, 1993.
11. See *inter alia*, Richard Price, 'Review Article: Transnational Civil Society and Advocacy in World Politics', *World Politics*, Vol. 55, No. 4, 2003, pp. 579–606; Richard Higgott, Geoffrey Underhill and Andreas Bieler, *Non-State Actors and Authority in the Global System*, Abingdon: Routledge, 2000; Sanjeev Khagram, James V. Riker and Kathryn Sikkink (eds), *Restructuring World Politics: Transnational Social Movements, Networks, and Norms*, Minneapolis: University of Minnesota Press, 2002.
12. E.g., Margaret Keck and Kathryn Sikkink, *Activists beyond Borders: Advocacy Networks in International Politics*, Ithaca, NY: Cornell University Press, 1988; Mary Kaldor, *Global Civil Society: An Answer to War?* London: Polity, 2003; Martin Shaw, 'Civil Society', in George Fink (ed.), *Stress of War, Conflict and Disaster*, San Diego, CA: Academic Press, 2010, pp. 200–8.
13. James C. Scott, *Domination and the Arts of Resistance: Hidden Transcripts*, New Haven, CT: Yale University Press, 1990.
14. Homi K. Bhabha, *The Location of Culture*, London: Routledge, 1994; Ilan Kapoor, *The Postcolonial Politics of Development*, Abingdon: Routledge, 2008; Oliver P. Richmond and Audra Mitchell (eds), *Hybrid Forms of Peace: Everyday Agency and Post-Liberalism*, Basingstoke: Palgrave Macmillan, 2011.
15. Jean-François Bayart, *Global Subjects: A Political Critique of Globalization*, London: Polity, [orig. 2004] 2007, p. 60. For Michael Hardt and Toni Negri, NGOs are the 'mendicant orders of Empire', *Empire*, Cambridge, MA: Harvard University Press, 2000, p. 36.
16. François Debrix, *Re-Envisioning Peacekeeping: The United Nations and the Mobilization of Ideology*, Minneapolis, MN: University of Minnesota Press, 1999.
17. Nicholas J. Wheeler, *Saving Strangers: Humanitarian Intervention in International Society*, Oxford, Oxford University Press, 2000.
18. Robert W. Cox, 'Civil Society at the Turn of the Millennium: Prospects for an Alternative World Order', *Review of International Studies*, Vol. 25, No. 1, 1999, p. 5.
19. Charles Jones, *Global Justice: Defending Cosmopolitanism*, Oxford: Oxford University Press, 1999.
20. R.B.J. Walker, 'Social Movements/World Politics', *Millennium: Journal of International Studies*, Vol. 23, No. 3, 1994, pp. 669–700 (pp. 683–5).
21. Alejandro Colás, *International Civil Society*, Cambridge: Polity, 2002. On governmentality see Michel Foucault, *The Birth of Biopolitics: Lectures at the Collège de France, 1978–1979*, Basingstoke: Palgrave Macmillan, [orig. 2004] 2010, pp. 68–9; Foucault, *The Government of Self and Others: Lectures at the Collège de France 1982–1983*, New York: Picador, 2011; Graham Burchell, Colin Gordon and Peter Miller (eds), *The Foucault Effect: Studies in Governmentality*, Chicago, IL: University of Chicago Press, 1991.
22. See *inter alia*, Gayatri C. Spivak, 'Can the Subaltern Speak?' in Cary Nelson and Lawrence Grossberg (eds), *Marxism and the Interpretation of Culture*, Chicago: University of Illinois Press, 1988; Michel Foucault, *Society Must be Defended: Lectures at the Collège de France, 1975–1976*, New York: Picador, [orig. 1997] 2003, pp. 54–5.

2 Governance: Ideological and Political Trespass

1. *Headway*, September 1928, supplement, p. i.
2. Lord Cecil, *The Moral Basis of the League of Nations*, London: Lindsey Press, 1923, p. 12.
3. Ernest Gellner, *Nations and Nationalism*, Ithaca, NY: Cornell University Press, 1983; Robert Kaplan, *Balkan Ghosts, A Journey Through History*, New York: Picador, 2005.
4. Murray to Cecil, 13 July 1931, Cecil Papers, Add. 51132.
5. Foucault, *The Birth of Biopolitics*, p. 297.
6. *LNU Yearbook*, 1934, p. 37; LNU, Minutes, 18th Annual Meeting, 15–18 June 1937, p. 3. Paid-up membership reached 410,000 in 1931, declining to 315,000 in 1937 – LNU, Minutes, 19th Annual Meeting, 15–17 June 1938, p. 29; *LNU Yearbook*, 1933, p. 53; National Peace Council, *Peace Year Book*, 1932, p. 157.
7. Michael Howard, *War and the Liberal Conscience*, Oxford: Oxford University Press, 1989, ch. 1.
8. See Martin Ceadel, *Semi-detached Idealists: The British Peace Movement and International Relations, 1854–1945*, Oxford: Oxford University Press, 2000.
9. E.H. Carr, *The Twenty Years' Crisis 1919–1939: An Introduction to the Study of International Relations*, London: Macmillan, 2nd edn, 1946, p. 27.
10. See Martin David Dubin, 'Toward the Concept of Collective Security: The Bryce Group's "Proposals for the Avoidance of War"', 1914–1917', *International Organization*, Vol. 24, No. 2, 1970, pp. 288–318; Keith G. Robbins, 'Lord Bryce and the First World War', *Historical Journal*, Vol. 10, No. 2, 1967, pp. 255–77. On proposals in Britain generally, and the divisions between the League of Nations Society and the League of Free Nations Association, see H.R. Winkler, *The League of Nations Movement in Great Britain, 1914–1919*, New Brunswick, NJ: Rutgers, 1952.
11. The classic depiction of terminal decline by George Dangerfield, a British emigrant to the United States is *The Strange Death of Liberal England*, New York: Smith & Haas, 1935, which if nothing else gave rise to a persistence of 'Strange Death' and 'Strange Survival' titles. For the debate see: Paul Adelman, *The Decline of the Liberal Party, 1910–31*, London: Longmans, 1981; Geoffrey R. Searle, *The Liberal Party: Triumph and Disintegration, 1986–1929*, Basingstoke: Palgrave/Macmillan, rev. edn, 2000; Carolyn W. White, '*The Strange Death of Liberal England* in its Time', *Albion: A Quarterly Journal Concerned with British Studies*, Vol. 17, No. 4, 1985, pp. 425–47.
12. Copy of Cecil to Davidson, 30 December 1927, AC Papers, 55/57.
13. *Manchester Guardian*, 25 June 1927, p. 14.
14. A.J. Toynbee, 'The Unity of Gilbert Murray's Life and Work', in Gilbert Murray and Friends (Jean Smith and Arnold Toynbee eds), *Gilbert Murray: An Unfinished Autobiography*, London: Allen & Unwin, 1960, p. 212; Francis West, *Gilbert Murray, A Life*, Beckenham: Croom Helm, 1984; Peter Wilson, 'Gilbert Murray and International Relations: Hellenism, Liberalism and International Intellectual Cooperation as a Path to Peace', *Review of International Studies*, Vol. 37, No. 2, 2010, pp. 881–909; 'Retrieving Cosmos: Gilbert Murray's Thought on International Relations', in Christopher Stray (ed.), *Gilbert Murray Reassessed: Hellenism, Theatre, and International Politics*, Oxford: Oxford University Press, 2007, pp. 239–60.

15. Trevor Wilson (ed.), *The Political Diaries of C.P. Scott, 1911–1928*, London: Collins, 1970, p. 399. However, for Grey, the League was always second best to an Anglo-French alliance.

16. Dorothy Paget had married Gladstone's fourth son, Herbert, a political organiser for Asquith who died in 1930. Henry Gladstone (W.E.'s third son) was a president of the New Commonwealth Society (an offshoot of the LNU) from 1932 to 1935.

17. This and other letters, in LNU, *The Tragedy of Abyssinia* (June 1936), pp. 36ff. See, Richard T. Shannon, *Gladstone and the Bulgarian Agitation 1876*, London: Nelson, 1963.

18. 'Conservative, pious adherent of the High Church, Lord Cecil is a remarkable mix of traditionalism and idealism about the future, which each Englishman has at root beneath party divides' [author's translation]. Paul Vaucher and Paul Henri Siriex, *L'Opinion Britannique: La Société des Nations et la guerre Italo-Ethiopienne*, Centre d'Études de Politique Étrangère, Paris, 1936, p. 34. For Cecil's admiration of Grey, see Cecil, *A Great Experiment*, London: Jonathan Cape, 1941, p. 32.

19. See Maurice Cowling, *The Impact of Labour 1920–1924: The Beginning of Modern British Politics*, Cambridge: Cambridge University Press, 1971, pp. 60ff.

20. Max Beer, *The League on Trial: A Journey to Geneva*, London: Allen & Unwin, 1933, p. 378.

21. Cecil, 'The Party System and Peace', in *The Way of Peace: Essays and Addresses*, London: Philip Allan, 1928, pp. 15ff.

22. *Manchester Guardian*, 30 August 1927, p. 8.

23. Foucault, *The Birth of Biopolitics*, p. 297.

24. The 1926 membership figures for associated bodies: Arbitrate First Bureau (3,254); No More War Movement (3,000); International Peace Society (5,000); Fellowship of Reconciliation (7,584); Women's International League (3,500); UDC (2,000); and smaller groups. NCPW, *Peace Year Book*, 1927, pp. 50ff. The activities of the 1920s peace groups has been described as a 'series of gestures'. A.C.F. Beales, *The History of Peace*, London: Bell, 1931, p. 326.

25. Curtis, Memo for Discussion by Round Table at Blickling Hall, 7 October 1932, Lothian Papers, GD 40, 17/268.

26. Ibid., Curtis to Lothian, 19 July 1936, Lothian Papers, GD 40, 17/319; Dove to Brand, 14 March 1925, in R.H. Brand (ed.), *The Letters of John Dove*, London: Macmillan, 1938, p. 204.

27. Cecil, copy of Memo on League Policy, 26 May 1936, to Eden and Halifax, Cecil Papers, Add. 51083.

28. Austen Chamberlain (AC) to F.S. Oliver, 3 August 1933 and to Lord Tyrrell, 13 February 1933, AC Papers, 40/5/84 & 12. However, Chamberlain later wrote to Murray: 'I think I could always with perfect satisfaction follow a lead from E. Grey or take an oar in his boat'. AC to Murray, 28 August 1933, Murray Papers. Grey's concept of the League was not necessarily that of the rank and file in the LNU.

29. AC to Cranborne, 12 May 1932 and Simon to AC [?] May 1932, AC Papers, 39/5/34 & 35.

30. AC to Cecil, 18 July 1934, Cecil Papers, Add. 51079

31. AC to Murray, 19 November 1934, AC Papers, 40/6/55.

32. AC to Cecil, 16 December 1935, Cecil Papers, Add. 51079.
33. AC to Lord Tyrrell, 13 February 1933, AC Papers, 40/5/12.
34. George Bernard Shaw, *Geneva: A Fancied Page of History in Three Acts*, London: Constable, 1938, p. 64.
35. Balfour to Hankey, 22 December 1928. Balfour Papers, Add 49705. Austen Chamberlain even wrote: 'We must work wherever possible with and through the League', in 'Great Britain as a European Power', *Journ. RIIA.*, Vol. 9, No. 2, 1930, pp. 180–88 (at 185–88).
36. J.R. Seeley, *The Expansion of England*, London: Macmillan, 1883.
37. Cited in, *Liberal Magazine*, Vol. 39, No. 454, 1931, p. 328.
38. Shaw, 'As I See It', *George Bernard Shaw 1856–1950: Some of his Broadcasts* (2 November 1937), BBC Radio Enterprises Recording, REB, 32M.
39. Maj.-Gen. Sir W.D. Bird, 'The Renunciation of War', *Army Quarterly*, Vol. 17, No. 1, 1928, pp. 100–103 (p. 102). See also, the statement by Maj. W.G. Carlton Hall that Europe had been kept peaceful for half a century after 1815 through fear of the consequences of war, in H. Wickham Steed, 'Armament and Disarmament Since 1918', *RUSI Journ.*, Vol. 76, November 1931, pp. 824–42 (p. 837). At least one spokesman for the services drew inspiration from the 1929 Field Service Regulations: 'The aim of providing Security must be to ensure liberty of action, to be prepared to meet and defeat the enemy's counterstrokes, to conserve strength and to maintain essential interests. Rear-Admiral W.A. Egerton, 'Practical Security', *RUSI Journ.*, Vol. 76, February 1931, pp. 27–36 (p. 30).
40. Lord Hankey, 'The study of Disarmament' (compiled 1925), in *Diplomacy by Conference: Studies in Public Affairs 1920–1946*, London: Ernest Benn, 1946, p. 119. Hankey's biographer also notes that the Cabinet Secretary feared disarmament would affect the nation's virility. Stephen Roskill, *Hankey: Man of Secrets*, 3 Vols, London: Collin, 1972, II, p. 413.
41. Neal Wood, *Communism and British Intellectuals*, London: Gollancz, 1959, p. 23.
42. 192 *H.C. Deb.*, 5s., 2774ff. (11 March 1926).
43. *Labour Party Annual Report*, 11–15 October 1926, p. 256
44. Hugh Dalton, *Towards the Peace of Nations: A Study in International Politics*, London: Routledge, 1928, pp. 154–56, 211.
45. *War and Socialism*, Labour Party, London, October 1932, p. 11.
46. See, K.E. Miller, *Socialism and Foreign Policy: Theory and Practice in Britain to 1931*, The Hague: Martinus Nijhoff, 1967, p. 143.
47. Cecil, *The Moral Basis*, p. 22.
48. Thorne, 'Viscount Cecil', p. 824.
49. Note, 12 September 1935, Liddell Hart Papers, Reflections (1935).

3 Education: Democratic Accountability and Paper Guarantees

1. Purportedly sent by Grigori Zinoviev, chair of the Comintern, to the Communist Party of Great Britain (CPGB), it was subsequently exposed as a forgery, probably concocted by White Russians in Latvia in league with the British intelligence services which provided it to friends in the Conservative

Party. It was used in the 1924 General Election to back up accusations that Labour was soft on communism and to scupper a trade deal with the USSR. Gill Bennett, '"An Extraordinary and Mysterious Business": The Zinoviev Letter of 1924', Historians LRD No. 14, Foreign and Commonwealth Office, London, January 1999.

2. T.P. Conwell-Evans, *Foreign Policy from a Back Bench, 1904–1918: A Study Based on the Papers of Lord Noel-Buxton*, Oxford: Oxford University Press, 1932, pp. 46–7.

3. Cited in *Headway*, January 1932, p. 11.

4. G.P. Gooch and H. Temperley (eds), *British Documents on the Origins of the War: 1898–1914*, 11 vols, London: HMSO, 1926–1938. See H.R. Winkler, *British Labour Seeks a Foreign Policy, 1900–1940*, Piscataway, NJ: Transaction, 2004, pp. 55–6; *Paths Not Taken: British Labour and International Policy in the 1920s*, Chapel Hill, NC: University of North Carolina Press, 1994.

5. Morel had spearheaded a pre-war campaign against slavery and Belgian atrocities in the Congo; after it, he wrote an inflammatory and racist UDC pamphlet on black allied soldiers stationed in the Rhineland, *Horror on the Rhine* (1920).

6. Elspeth Y. O'Riordan, *Britain and the Ruhr Crisis*, Basingstoke: Palgrave, 2001.

7. *Headway*, September 1926, p. 164; letters by J.L. Morison, *The Times*, 8 July 1927, p. 15, and C.S. Cobb, Chairman of the Navy League, 5 July 1927, p. 17.

8. Jonathan Wright, 'Locarno: A Democratic Peace?' *Review of International Studies*, Vol. 36, No. 2, 2010, pp. 391–411; Gaynor Johnson (ed.), *Locarno Revisited: European Diplomacy 1920–1929*, London: Cass, 2004.

9. Cecil and Lord Percy had been the only cabinet members to back Chamberlain's proposal for an agreement with France. Douglas Johnson, 'Austen Chamberlain and the Locarno Agreements', *Univ. Birmingham Historical Journ.*, Vol. 8, No. 1, 1962, pp. 62–81 (pp. 73, 75); Murray to Major Jack Hills, 17 September 1926, Murray Papers.

10. Murray to AC, 10 February 1926 & 11 February 1926, AC Papers, 53/495 & 24/8/42.

11. L.R. Lumley to AC, 25 February 1926, AC Papers, 24/8/39; *The Times*, 23 February 1926, p. 18.

12. *Daily Telegraph*, 2 March 1926, p. 10; *The Times*, 23 February 1926, p. 17.

13. *Foreign Affairs*, March 1926, p. 255; April 1926, pp. 286, 289–90; *Daily Express*, 25 February 1926, p. 8.

14. *The Times*, 23 February 1926, p. 13; 24 February 1926, p. 16; David Carlton, 'Great Britain and the League Council Crisis of 1926', *Historical Journ.*, Vol. 9, No. 2, 1968, pp. 354–64 (pp. 355–56).

15. *Daily Mail*, 13 March 1926, p. 8; 17 March 1926, p. 8; Sir Alfred Mond (Conservative, Camarthen), 192 *H.C. Deb.*, 5a., 1685–90 (4 March 1926).

16. Letter from Conservative MPs, *The Times*, 26 February 1926, p. 15; *The Times*, 27 February 1926, p. 12. It wasn't all they had in common. Macmillan married the Marquess's sister and Boothby later had an affair with her, among others.

17. 192 *H.C. Deb.*, 5a., 1655ff. (4 March 1926).

18. 193 *H.C. Deb.*, 5s., 1057ff. (23 March 1926).

19. Cecil to Baldwin, 21 March 1926, Cecil Papers, Add. 51080.

20. *Headway*, June 1926, p. 111. LNU Executive resolution, *Headway*, April 1926, p. 62; *Report of Proceedings of 43rd Annual Meeting*, NLF, 15–18 June 1926, pp. 13, 48–9.
21. George Bernard Shaw, *The League of Nations*, London: Fabian Society, 1929, p. 10.
22. Cecil to AC, 11 February 1926, AC Papers, 53/98; Grey letters, in *The Times*, 18 February 1926, p. 15; 26 February 1926, pp. 12, 14.
23. Tyrrell to AC, 11 March 1926, AC Papers, 53/553.
24. RIIA., *International Sanctions*, London, 1938, pp. 138–9; Sir Rennell Rodd, in *British Legion Journ.*, Vol. 11, No. 11, pp. 395, 398; Sir Arthur Willert, *Aspects of British Foreign Policy*, New Haven, CT: Yale University Press, 1928, pp. 55–64; Harold Nicholson, 'Modern Diplomacy and British Public Opinion', *Journ. R.I.I.A.*, Vol. 14, No. 5, 1935, pp. 599–618 (p. 612).
25. Baldwin's Cabinet of 1925 contained 9 aristocrats, 12 middle-class and 1 working-class members, almost identical with Asquith's Cabinet of 1914. The Labour Cabinets of 1924 and 1929 were exceptional in their complements of working-class members. W.L. Guttsman, *The British Political Elite*, London: MacGibbon & Kee, 1963, p. 178. For an analysis of the 'oligocratic élite', see D.C. Watt, 'The Nature of the Foreign-Policy-Making Elite in Britain', in *Personalities and Policies*, London: Longmans, 1965.
26. Commenting on Chamberlain's illness in 1928, Cecil indicated the foreign secretary's particular value to the LNU: 'Please take care of yourself for I regard you as the chief bulwark against the tendencies of a certain section of Conservative opinion'. Cecil to AC, 11 August 1928, AC Papers, 38/3/35.
27. Cecil to Halifax, 7 June 1927, Cecil Papers, Add. 51084.
28. Cecil to Baldwin, 6 January 1926, Cecil Papers, Add. 51080; Cecil to Baldwin, 6 April 1927, ibid.
29. Cecil to Salisbury, 31 July 1927, Cecil Papers, Add. 51086; Cecil to Murray, 14 September 1927, Murray Papers; correspondence between Cecil and Chamberlain, 8, 10, 14 & 16 August 1927, Cecil Papers, Add. 51079. See, Carlton, 'Great Britain and the Coolidge Naval Disarmament Conference of 1927', *Political Science Quarterly*, Vol. 83, No. 4, 1968, pp. 573–98.
30. Cecil to Salisbury, 2 September 1927, Cecil Papers, Add. 51086; Tyrrell to AC, 17 September 1927, AC Papers, 54/481.
31. Diary entries 3 & 5 December 1929, Diary 13, Dalton Papers. Recalling the original snub, MacDonald wrote a vicious letter to Murray, 12 July 1933, Murray Papers. Snowden's opinion of the LNU was also far from complimentary. Carlton, *MacDonald versus Henderson; The Foreign Policy of the Second Labour Government*, London: Macmillan, 1970, p. 19.
32. Cecil to Simon, 30 November 1931, 9 January 1932, Cecil Papers, Add. 51082; to Cadogan 20 October 1931, Add. 51089 and to Noel Baker, 21 July 1932, Add. 51107. He refused to attend the 1934 League Assembly on account of anti-disarmament statements by Lord Londonderry and Bolton Eyres-Monsell MP, First Lord of the Admiralty. Cecil to Simon, 30 June 1934, Cecil Papers, Add. 51082.
33. Murray to Shaw, 13 August 1938, Shaw Papers, Add. 50542.
34. Andrew Webster, '"Absolutely Irresponsible Amateurs": The Temporary Mixed Commission on Armaments, 1921–1924', *Australian Journ. of Politics & History*, Vol. 54, No. 3, 2008, pp. 373–88; Carlton, 'Disarmament with Guarantees: Lord Cecil, 1922–1927', *Disarmament and Arms Control*, Vol. 3, No. 2, 1965, pp. 143–64.

35. *New Leader*, 6 January 1928, p. 4. See also, *Westminster Gazette*, 22 October 1927, p. 6; Grey, in *Liberal Magazine*, Vol. 35, No. 407, 1927, p. 510.
36. Drury-Lowe to Murray, 9 August 1927 and Arnold-Forster to Murray, 20 August 1927, Murray Papers.
37. Mowat to Murray, 2 September 1927 and Parmoor to Murray, 22 September 1927, Murray Papers.
38. Cecil to Murray, 10 September 1928, Murray Papers; Murray to Samuel (6), 5 October 1927, Samuel Papers, A/70.
39. J.R.M. MacDonald, *Protocol or Pact*, Labour Party, [1927?], pp. 5–6; *Daily Herald*, 14 September 1927, p. 1.
40. Cecil, *The Way of Peace*, London: Philip Allan, 1928, p. 200; Parmoor to Murray, 22 September 1927, Murray Papers.
41. *Westminster Gazette*, 29 July 1927, p. 2.
42. *Westminster Gazette*, 15 September 1927, p. 6. See also, *Daily Chronicle*, 12 September 1927, p. 6; *Report of Proceedings of 42nd Annual Meeting*, NLF, 13–16 May 1925. On the discontent Liberal reluctance aroused in the LNU: Murray to Samuel (4), 12 September 1927, Samuel Papers, A/70; letters in *Manchester Guardian*, 14 September 1927, pp. 9, 10.
43. *Headway*, July 1920, Supplement, p. ii.
44. Copy of Cecil to Davidson, 30 December 1927, AC Papers, 55/57; Murray to AC, 6 January 1928, AC Papers 55/384; AC to Murray, 11 January 1928, AC Papers, 55/385; *Daily News & Westminster Gazette*, 19 April 1928, p. 7; Cecil–Cushendun correspondence, *The Times*, 16 & 17 April 1928. Murray later thought Cushendun did rather well at Geneva, to which Maj. Hills added: 'He is really, in spite of his fire-eating, a bit of a pacifist at heart'. Murray to Hills and reply, 19 September 1928, Murray Papers.
45. Grey to Samuel (5), 17 September 1927, Samuel Papers, A/70; Lloyd George to Murray, 3 September 1927, Murray Papers. Lloyd George was often angling for a Lib–Lab Coalition with himself in place of MacDonald. Hobhouse to Samuel (9), 9 October 1927, Samuel Papers, A/70.
46. Speech, *Manchester Guardian*, 8 November 1927, p. 6; Liberal Council Executive Minutes, 19 October 1927, Liberal Party Archives.
47. *Daily News & Westminster Gazette*, 19 April 1928, p. 6.
48. Memo of conversation between Cecil and Grey, 13 July 1929, Cecil Papers, Add. 51073.
49. P.J. Noel Baker, *The Geneva Protocol*, London: King & Son, 1925, p. 118.
50. *Headway*, March 1928, p. 52.
51. LNU, *The Optional Clause*, 1931, p. 11; *Headway*, September 1928, p. 165; LNU, *The Alternative to War: Arbitration*, 1927.
52. *Manchester Guardian*, 20 October 1927, p. 4; 22 October 1927, p. 12.
53. *Headway*, August 1928, p. 150. MacDonald, too, had indicated the special position of Empire relations when promoting the Protocol, *Daily Herald*, 14 September 1927, p. 1.
54. Henderson convinced a Cabinet sub-Committee that a Monroe doctrine would not do and to name Egypt specifically 'would be to advertise the fact that our legal status in Egypt was untenable'. Cecil complained that Australia was starting to hold a *liberum veto* in foreign policy. Diary entries, 19 February, 10 June, 1, 8 July, 19 August 1929, Diary 10, Dalton Papers; Minutes, 29 July 1929; Dalton Papers, File 4; Cecil to Henderson 23 July 1929, Cecil Papers,

Add. 51081. Also, Hugh Dalton, *Call Back Yesterday, 1887*–1931, London: Muller, 1953, pp. 237–9; Carlton, *MacDonald versus Henderson*, pp. 75–8.

55. Balfour to AC, 10 May 1929, Balfour Papers, Add. 49736; 234 *H.C. Deb.*, 5s., 668 (27 January 1930); *The Times*, 20 September 1929, p. 15; *Daily Telegraph*, 20 September 1929, p. 8.

56. 249 *H.C. Deb.*, 5s., 839 (9 March 1931); *Morning Post*, 10 March 1931, p. 10; *Daily Herald*, 9 March 1931, p. 8.

57. Cecil to Grey, 19 March 1929, Cecil Papers, Add. 51073; Cecil to MacDonald, 21 June 1929, Cecil Papers, Add. 51081.

58. Carlton, 'The Anglo-French Compromise on Arms Limitation, 1928', *Journ. British Studies*, Vol. 8, No. 2, 1969, pp. 141–62.

59. Hankey to Balfour, 16 May 1928, Balfour Papers, Add. 49705; *New Leader*, 13 January 1928, p. 3.

60. Cecil, *The Way of Peace*, pp. 11–12; Grey to Murray, 3 March 1928, Murray Papers.

61. *Manchester Guardian*, 20 July 1928, p. 10.

62. LNU, *Minutes*, 9th Annual Meeting, 20–22 June 1928, pp. 26–27. Chamberlain agreed: 'it originated as a move to quiet the conscience of that not inconsiderable section of American opinion which is strongly pacifist in a good sense and [feels] that the United States had failed to "stand for" peace'. AC to Howard, 6 January 1929, AC Papers, 55/277.

63. Murray to Cecil, 29 February & 1 March 1928, Cecil Papers, Add. 51132.

64. Murray to Webster, 29 May 1928, Murray Papers.

65. Drury-Lowe to Murray, 26 May 1928, Murray Papers.

66. Noel Buxton to Cecil, 27 July 1928 & Cecil to Noel Buxton, 1 August 1928, Cecil Papers, Add. 51140.

67. Grey to Murray, 25 July 1928, Murray Papers.

68. *Headway*, March 1929, Supplement, p. i.

69. *Daily News & Westminster Gazette*, 17 April 1928, p. 6; 9 July 1028, p. 8; 20 July 1928, p. 8.

70. *Daily News & Westminster Gazette*, 27 August 1928, p. 6; *Manchester Guardian*, 27 August 1928, p. 8.

71. Lord Grey, *A Great Opportunity*, LNU, London, 1928, pp. 6–7; LNU, *Minutes* 9th Annual Meeting of the General Council, 20–22 June 1928, p. 29.

72. Amendments to the Covenant, drafted by Kerr and Noel Baker, 25 February 1929, Lothian Papers, GD 40, 17/117; Kerr to Cecil, 8 March 1929, ibid., GD 17/239; Kerr to Levinson, 19 February 1929, ibid., GD 40, 17/242.

73. LNU Statement on the Pact of Paris, 12 March 1929; Minutes of LNU Executive Committee, 14 March 1929, Lothian Papers, GD 40, 17/118.

74. Kerr to Cecil, 14 June 1929; Cecil to Kerr, 17 June 1929; Kerr to Murray, 25 June 1929, Lothian Papers, GD 40, 17/119.

75. LNU Memo on Naval Disarmament by Drury-Lowe, 17 February 1930, Lothian Papers, GD 40, 17/91.

76. Note by C. Delisle Burns on the London Naval Conference, 19 February 1930, Lothian Papers, GD 40, 17/91.

77. Lothian to Garvin, 3 April 1930 & 9 May 1930, Lothian Papers, GD 40, 17/248.

78. Cecil to Arnold-Forster, 3 March 1930, Cecil Papers, Add. 51140; Cecil to Noel Baker, 27 February 1930, ibid., Add. 51007. See also, Cecil's letter in

The Times, 25 February 1930, p. 15; Copy of Salter to Sir Eric Drummond, 20 December 1929, Cecil Papers, Add. 51111; Copy of Memo, 'The United States and the League', by Salter, enclosed with Drummond to Cecil, 3 January 1930, ibid., Add. 51112; Eppstein to Kerr, 8 May 1929, Lothian Papers, GD 40, 17/119. Chamberlain agreed with Cecil: '[t]he more I see the United States constitution at work ... the more I am led to wonder whether any of us ought to wish that the United States should join the League'. AC to Howard, 13 April 1926, AC Papers, 53/368.
79. Dalton, p. 253.

4 Disarmament: White Robes of Peace or Jackboots and Spurs?

1. Lieutenant-General Sir A.A. Montgomery-Massingberd, 'The Role of the Army in Imperial Defence', *Army Quarterly*, Vol. 15, No. 2 , 1928, pp. 235–58 (pp. 247–50). This did not preclude support of disarmament on economic grounds. Lord Cushendun, 'Disarmament', *Journ. RIIA*, Vol. 7, No. 2, 1928, pp. 77–93 (pp. 79–84).
2. Michael Howard, *The Continental Commitment*, London: Temple Smith, 1972, pp. 90–1; Lord Ismay, *The Memoirs of General the Lord Ismay*, London: Heinemann, 1960, pp. 60–2.
3. See, S.W. Roskill, *Naval Policy Between the Wars*, I, *The Period of Anglo-American Antagonism 1919–1929*, London: Collins, 1968, pp. 452, 464, 537.
4. G.R. Crosby, *Disarmament and Peace in British Politics 1914–19*, Cambridge, MA: Harvard University Press, 1957, pp. 67, 69, 126, 132; Cecil to Drummond, 27 January 1926, Cecil Papers, Add. 51111.
5. P.J. Noel Baker, *Disarmament*, London: Hogarth Press, 2nd edn, 1927, p. 37.
6. *Army Quarterly*, Vol. 26, No. 1, April 1928, p. 8.
7. Brig.-Gen. H. Clifton Brown (Conservative, Newbury): 'I am glad to see that, at least, the Indian Army are retaining the lance ... It is a far more useful weapon than the sword'. 214 *H.C. Deb.*, 5s., 1288 (8 March 1928).
8. Captain Guest (Bristol N.) 192 *H.C. Deb.*, 5s., 2676 (11 March 1926).
9. 214 *H.C. Deb.*, 5s., 2148 (15 March 1928). The Admiralty succumbed to Treasury pressure in 1927 partly because it had no clear idea of what ships to build. Roskill, *Naval Policy*, I, p. 556; Sir Peter Gretton, *Former Naval Person*, London: Cassell, 1968, pp. 243ff.; Robert Rhodes James, *Churchill: A Study in Failure 1900–1939*, London: Weidenfeld & Nicolson, 1970, pp. 16–68.
10. Lt-Comdr J.M. Kenworthy, 'Disarmament: The Freedom of the Seas', *19th Century*, Vol. 111, 1932, pp. 35–48 (p. 41). He crossed from Liberal to Labour when Lloyd George became Liberal leader.
11. Morgan Jones MP (Labour, Caerphilly), 203 *H.C. Deb*, 5s., 960 (7 March 1927).
12. *Liberal Magazine*, Vol. 39, No. 452, May 1931, p. 233. See also, the Liberal manifesto drawing attention to the tax burden of defence, *Manchester Guardian*, 19 October 1927, p. 11; 22 October 1927, p. 12.
13. Sir Josiah Stamp, *Studies in Current Problems in Finance and Government*, London: P.S. King, 1924, pp. 96–7. A.L. Bowley, *Some Economic Consequences of the Great War*, London: Thornton Butterworth, 1930, p. 88; Francis W. Hirst, *The Consequences of the War to Great Britain*, London: Oxford University Press, 1934.

14. A.C. Pigou, *Industrial Fluctuations*, London: Macmillan, 1927, pp. 305ff.; John Maynard Keynes, *The General Theory of Employment, Interest and Money*, London: Macmillan, 1936, p. 130. Keynes supported disarmament on ethical grounds, but by the summer of 1936 he had squared his economic and ethical positions and. in a series of articles in the *New Statesman*, argued that the international situation pointed to rearmament. R.F. Harrod, *The Life of John Maynard Keynes*, London: Macmillan, 1972, pp. 564–65.
15. *Manchester Guardian*, 26 February 1932, p. 8.
16. Major W.G. Carlton Hall, 'British Re-Armament', *Journ. RUSI*, Vol. 79, August 1934, pp. 595–99 (p. 596); Resolution of Metropolitan Division, National Union of Conservatives and Unionist Associations, Minutes of Executive Committee, 18 March 1930.
17. *TUC Report*, 3–8 September 1928, p. 69.
18. Sir Edward Grey, *Twenty-five Years*, 2 Vols, London: Hodder & Stoughton, 1925, I, pp. 91–2.
19. Noel Baker, *Disarmament*, p. 18; Hugh Dalton, *Towards the Peace of Nations: A Study in International Politics*, London: Routledge, 1928, p. 141; Arthur Henderson, *Consolidating World Peace*, Oxford: Clarendon, 1931, pp. 10–12.
20. 191 *H.C. Deb.*, 5s., 34 (2 February 1926).
21. 192 *H.C. Deb*, 5s., 768ff. (25 February 1026).
22. See Carlton, 'Great Britain and the Coolidge Naval Disarmament Conference of 1927', *Political Science Quarterly*, Vol. 83, No. 4, 1968, pp. 573–98; Lord Chatfield, *It Might Happen Again*, London: Heinemann, 1947, p. 43.
23. National Union of Conservative and Unionist Associations, Minutes of Annual Conference, 6–7 October 1927, p. 42; *The Times*, 28 July 1927, p. 13 and Navy League letter, 5 July 1927, p. 17.
24. Grey, in *Liberal Magazine*, Vol. 35, No. 407, 1927, p. 510; McKenna to Murray, 10 June 1927, Murray Papers.
25. *Headway*, June 1927, p. 105; Carlton, 'Great Britain and the Coolidge Naval Conference', p. 581.
26. AC to Cecil, 8 August 1927, Cecil Papers, Add. 51079.
27. Cecil (Memorandum on Naval Disarmament) to MacDonald, 17 December 1929, Cecil Papers, Add. 51081.
28. Noel Baker, *Disarmament and the Coolidge Conference*, London: Hogarth, 1927, pp. 30–40, 199; ACIQ Memorandum No. 351 (November 1926).
29. *Liberal Magazine*, Vol. 35, No. 409, 1927, p. 590. Liberal pamphlets included: *The Foreign Policy in the Liberal Party* [ca. 1928]; C.J.L. Brock, *Peace and Disarmament* (1928); Sir Herbert Samuel, *Peace and Free Trade* (1928). The LNU published: *Towards Disarmament* (1927); *What is Meant by Disarmament?* (3rd edn, 1931). Noel Baker published: *Disarmament and the Coolidge Conference*, London: L&V Woolf, 1927. For the LNU's Ocean Locarno policy, see *Headway*, August 1927, p. 145 & Supplement, p. ii.
30. *NLF Conference Report*, 11–12 October 1928, pp. 18–23.
31. 210 *H.C. Deb.*, 5s., 2089ff. (24 November 1927).
32. *Labour Party Annual Report*, 1–5 October 1928, p. 188.
33. *Manchester Guardian*, 1 December 1927, p. 10, 2 December 1927, p. 17.
34. Ibid., 3 December 1927, p. 16.
35. National Executive Committee Minutes, National Joint Council, 8 December 1927, Labour Party archives. The ACIQ submitted that the Soviet proposals

accorded with party policy and that they should not be completely dismissed in the quest for drastic and progressive reductions. ACIQ Minutes, 4 April 1928. For Lansbury's comment, see, *Labour Party Annual Report*, 1–5 October 1928, p. 155.

36. *NCPW Annual Report*, 1926–27; *Peace Year Book*, 1927, pp. 59–60.
37. *Manchester Guardian*, 2 December 1927, p. 17; 3 December 1927, p. 15. The UDC also suggested that the Russian offer was genuine, *Foreign Affairs*, January 1928, p. 195.
38. *Foreign Affairs*, March 1931, p. 483. See also, Arthur Ponsonby, 'Disarmament by Example', *Journ R.I.I.A.*, Vol. 7, No. 4, 1928, pp. 225–40.
39. *Workers' Life*, 9 December 1927, pp. 2–3; 16 December 1927, p. 2.
40. David Carlton, 'The Anglo-French Compromise on Arms Limitation, 1928', *Journ. British Studies*, Vol. 8, No. 2, 1969, pp. 141–62.
41. D. Lloyd George, *We Must Work for Peace*, London: Liberal Publication Dept., 1928, p. 7.
42. *The Observer*, 23 September 1928, p. 16. UDC and ILP reactions are in *Foreign Affairs*, September 1928, p. 39; December 1928, p. 51; *New Leader*, 14 September 1928, p. 6.
43. *Labour Party Annual Report*, 1–5 October 1928, p. 183. Also, *Daily News & Westminster Gazette*, 6 October 1928, p. 6; 27 September 1928, p. 8.
44. Murray to Hills, 2 October 1928, Murray Papers.
45. *The Times*, 23 October 1928, p. 17; *Army Quarterly*, 17, No. 2, 1929, pp. 232–3. J.H. Morgan, one-time adviser to the president of the Control Commission in Berlin, castigated Lloyd George and others who would limit the size of the French army, which provided a necessary deterrent to German war preparations. Germany could command the services of 840,000 newly trained reserves, military expenditure was being concealed in civil estimates and was twice that of Britain. Letter, in *The Times*, 15 November 1928, p. 12. By 1928 the CID was considering a Chief of Imperial General Staff Memo of 13 December 1927 which estimated Germany's military manpower at 2 million instead of the 100,000 permitted by the Treaty of Versailles. See, Correlli Barnett, *The Collapse of British Power*, London, 1972, p. 324.
46. *Daily News & Westminster Gazette*, 4 October 1928, p. 6.
47. *Liberal Magazine*, Vol. 39, No. 451, 1931, p. 159; Geoffrey Mander, in Vol. 38, No. 447, 1930, p. 522.
48. *The Times*, 24 January 1930, p. 15; *Daily Telegraph*, 3 September 1929, p. 10.
49. Carolyn J. Kitching, *Britain and the Problem of International Disarmament, 1919–1934*, Abingdon: Routledge, 1999.
50. ACIQ Memorandum No. 406 (December 1929).
51. Brailsford, *Olives of an Endless Age, Being a Study of this Distracted World and Its Need of Unity*, New York: Harper, 1928, p. 386; Kenworthy, 'Disarmament', pp. 42–3; *Daily Herald*, 29 April 1929, p. 1; 4 March 1929, p. 4. On the Belligerent Rights Sub-Committee of the CID (1928–29), see Roskill, *Hankey*, II, pp. 451–5; *Naval Policy*, I, p. 550.
52. Letter, *The Times*, 16 October 1929, p. 10; Cecil and W. Arnold-Forster, 'The Freedom of the Seas', *Journ. RIIA.*, Vol. 8, No. 2, 1929, pp. 89–117.
53. Grey, 'Freedom of the Seas', *Foreign Affairs* [New York], Vol. 8, No. 3, 1930, pp. 325–35 (p. 327).
54. Cecil to Noel Baker, 27 January 1930 and to Halifax, 10 January 1930, Cecil Papers, Add. 51107 & 51084; NCPW, *Peace Year Book*, 1931, p. 47; *Liberal Magazine*, Vol. 38, No. 439, 1930, p. 189.

55. Sir Herbert Richmond, 'Immediate Problems of Naval Reduction', *Foreign Affairs* [New York], Vol. 9, No. 3, 1931, pp. 371–88; Diary entry 22 January 1930, Diary 13, Dalton Papers. See also, Robin Higham, *The Military Intellectuals in Britain: 1918–1939*, New Brunswick, NJ: Rutgers University Press, 1960, pp. 33–4.

56. Diary entries 18 & 30 December 1929, 10 & 20 January 1930, Diary 13, Dalton Papers; Lord Chatfield, *It Might Happen Again*, London: Heinemann, 1947, p. 60.

57. E.g., *The Times*, 3 July 1930, p. 15; *Daily Telegraph*, 23 April 1930, p. 10; *Daily Mail*, 7 April 1930, p.8.

58. *Naval Review*, Vol. 18, No. 3, August 1930, p. 561. Most navalists were concerned about a sudden cascade of expenditure in 1936 after the naval holiday. Alexander to MacDonald, 18 September 1929, Alexander Papers, 5/2/6.

59. *Headway*, May 1930, p. 86. Cecil to Hankey, 28 October 1933, Cecil Papers, Add. 51088; Dalton, 'British Foreign Policy 1929–31', *Political Quarterly*, Vol. 11, No. 4, 1931, pp. 484–505.

60. *Labour Party Annual Report*, 6–10 October 1930, pp. 238–40; *Foreign Affairs*, July 1929, p. 151; *New Leader*, 25 April 1930, p. 1.

61. Rt. Hon. J. Ramsay MacDonald, 'The London Naval Conference 1930', *Journ. R.I.I.A.*, Vol. 9, No. 4, 1930, pp. 429–51.

62. *Daily Telegraph*, 16 May 1930, p. 14; 238 *H.C. Deb.*, 5s., 2096ff. (15 May 1930).

63. *Daily Telegraph*, 10 March 1930, p. 10; *Daily Herald*, 28 December 1928, p. 4. Interestingly, the *Manchester Guardian's* jolt towards isolationism occurred after Edward Scott succeeded his father C.P. Scott as proprietor. The son rivalled Beaverbrook in his condemnation of French policy and rejected outright military obligations under the Covenant when the definition of aggression might hinge on a technicality. The case for a free hand in collective security had never been more clearly enunciated, and it earned a rebuke from Angell, in *Manchester Guardian*, 12 April 1930, p. 9.

64. Carlton, *MacDonald versus Henderson; The Foreign Policy of the Second Labour Government*, London: Macmillan, 1970, p. 129; Diary entries, 3–9, 12, 20–21 March; 5, 7, 13 April 1930, Diary 13, Dalton Papers.

65. Noel Baker, *Disarmament*, pp. 67, 129. Both Noel Baker and Cecil saw little prospect of France renouncing conscription.

66. *Headway*, November 1927, p. 211.

67. Ibid., February 1926, p. 31; June 1927, p. 111.

68. ACIQ Memorandum No. 416 (February 1931), by Arnold-Forster.

69. *Daily Herald*, 11 December 1930, p. 3; Noel Baker, in *Manchester Guardian*, 24 January 1931, p. 14; *Headway*, January 1931, pp. 7, 10.

70. *News Chronicle*, 21 May 1931, p. 6; 21 May 1931, p. 6; *The Times*, 26 March 1931, p. 15.

71. *The Times*, 30 June 1931, p. 15; 254 *H.C. Deb.*, 5s., 907ff. On the Three-Party Sub-Committee, see Viscount Templewood, *Nine Troubled Years*, London: Collins, 1954, pp. 117–19; Roskill, *Hankey*, II, p. 539.

72. Cecil to Angell, 16 January 1931, Cecil Papers, Add. 51140. See, Carlton, *MacDonald versus Henderson*, p. 72.

73. Lothian to Lloyd George, 15 May 1931, Lothian Papers, GD 40, 17/257.

74. Liddell Hart to Murray, 21 July 1932, Murray Papers, B.H. Liddell Hart, *The Memoirs of Captain Liddell Hart*, 2 Vols, London: Cassell, 1965, I, pp. 183–9. See also, Liddell Hart's report from Geneva, *Daily Telegraph*, 1 February 1932, p. 16.

75. *Liberal Magazine*, Vol. 40, No. 464, 1932, p. 238.
76. Jeudwine to Murray, 21 April 1932, Murray Papers. J.F.C. Fuller, strategist of mechanised warfare, was another critic, 'Aggression and Aggressive Weapons', *Army Ordnance*, Vol. 14, No. 79, 1933, pp. 7–11.
77. Following a 15 per cent cut in teachers' salaries a group of intellectuals (including Edmund Blunden, G.D.H. Cole, G.P. Gooch, Aldous Huxley, C.M. Joad, Bertrand Russell, H.G. Wells, and Osbert Sitwell) supported a 25 per cent cut in defence expenditure: 'There is no sane individual who would not prefer economy on tanks to economy in the salaries of those who are responsible for the upbringing of the next generation of British men and women, and in the preservation of our national health', *Headway*, October 1931, p. 200.
78. *Labour Party Annual Report*, 5–8 October 1931, pp. 184–7.

5   Innovation: Arming the League with Air Power

1. George Barnes, a former Labour Party leader and member of Lloyd George's War Cabinet, had chaired the League to Abolish War advocating an IPF.
2. *An International Police Force*, London, 1934.
3. *New Commonwealth*, July 1935, p. 371; New Fabian Research Bureau, *Labour's Foreign Policy*, NFRB, London, 1934, p. 19.
4. E.g., W.B. Thomas, *An International Police Force*, London: Allenson, 1936.
5. Published by the LNU as *The Problem of the Air*, London, 1935.
6. Published by the RIIA as *International Sanctions*, London, 1938.
7. 'Note on Research into "The Problem of the Creation and Use of an International Force in the light of History and present technical conditions"', [ca. 1932], Liddell Hart Papers, Disarmament Files.
8. Brig.-Gen. P.R.C. Groves, in *Manchester Guardian*, 18 August 1928, p. 11; Sir Allan Cobham, in *Daily Herald*, 13 August 1927, p. 1. Experts based projections on the effects of the German daylight raids over Britain in 1917 and 1918. In 1924, the Air Staff estimated that there would be 50 casualties per ton of bombs, rising to 72 from information on the Spanish Civil War. The actual figure in the Second World War was 15–20 per ton. In part, too, the predictions had been useful to air chiefs agitating for an independent air force in their disputes with the Admiralty. F.C. Iklé, *The Social Impact of Bomb Destruction*, Norman, OK: Oklahoma University Press, 1958, p. 17.
9. Robin Higham, *The Military Intellectuals in Britain: 1918–1939*, New Brunswick, NJ: Rutgers University Press, 1966, p. 78. Basil Liddell Hart regarded a knock-out blow as unattainable and with Thomas Inskip, Minister for Coordination of Defence in 1936, advocated strong defences against air raids.
10. *Westminster Gazette*, 27 July 1927, p. 6. A similar conclusion was reached about the 1928 exercises; Cdr. Sir C.D. Burney, *The World, the Air and the Future*, London: Knopf, 1929, p. 74.
11. Less cerebral than H.G. Wells (*The War in the Air*, 1908), L.E.O. Charlton, a former air attaché to the embassy in Washington, wrote pot-boilers predicting the mutual destruction of states with air power (e.g., *War From the Air; Past, Present, Future*), London: Nelson, 1935.
12. E.g., Lord Arnold, 89 *H.L. Deb*, 5s., 112 (8 November 1933); Bertrand Russell, *Which Way to Peace?* London: Jonathan Cape, 1936, ch. 2.

13. Dr Vernon Davies (Conservative, Royton, Lancs.), 214 *H.C. Deb.*, 5s., 1630 (12 March 1928). See, P.R.C. Groves, 'The Influence of Aviation on International Affairs', *Journ. RIIA*, Vol. 8, No. 4, 1929, pp. 289–317 (p. 298); Groves and Adm. Mark Kerr, in *Westminster Gazette*, 29 July 1927, pp. 1–2; A.E. Blake, 'The Future of Air Warfare', *Fortnightly Review*, No. 127, January 1930, pp. 29–40 (p. 36).
14. Margaret Cole (ed.), *Beatrice Webb's Diaries 1924–1932*, London: Longmans, 1956, pp. 221–2.
15. *Manchester Guardian*, 16 August 1928, p. 8.
16. Rennie Smith (Labour Penistone) 214 *H.C. Deb.*, 5s., 1635 (12 March 1928).
17. C.D. Burney, *The World, the Air and the Future*, London: Knopf, 1929, pp. 62, 65. Also, Squadron-Leader C.G. Burge, in *British Legion Journal*, Vol. 9, No. 7, 1930, p. 186.
18. Rennie Smith (Labour, Penistone), 214 *H.C. Deb.*, 5s., 1635 (12 March 1928); Capt. A.S. Cunningham-Reid (Conservative, Warrington), 192 *H.C. Deb.*, 5s., 859 (25 February 1926); H.B. Lees-Smith (Labour, Keighley), 203 *H.C. Deb.*, 5s., 1412–13 (10 March 1927).
19. J.M. Spaight, *Pseudo-security*, London: Longmans, 1928, p. 58. Also, Air Commodore J.A. Chamier, 'Air Bombing and Air Disarmament, Part II', *Army Quarterly*, Vol. 27, No. 2, 1934, pp. 284–8.
20. 192 *H.C. Deb.*, 5s., 1963 (8 March 1926). Also, Hugh Dalton, *Towards the Peace of Nations: A Study in International Politics*, London: Routledge, 1928, p. 291; ACIQ Memorandum No. 36A (June 1927); *Labour Party Annual Report*, 30 September–4 October 1929, p. 216.
21. Lord Robert Cecil, *The Way of Peace*, London: Philip Allen, 1928, p. 208.
22. *Foreign Affairs*, December 1927, p. 190.
23. *Foreign Affairs*, April 1928, p. 317. However, by fourteen votes to eight, it was decided not to restrict membership of the UDC to anti-sanctionists.
24. H. Swanwick and W. Arnold-Forster, *Sanctions of the League of Nations Covenant: A Debate*, London: UDC, 1928.
25. *Nation and Athenaeum*, 10 September 1927, pp. 738, 742; *Westminster Gazette*, 1 November 1927, p. 6.
26. *Headway*, March 1931, p. 54.
27. ACIQ Memorandum No. 410A (June 1930). See Peter Wilson, *The International Theory of Leonard Woolf*, Basingstoke: Palgrave Macmillan, 2003.
28. *Manchester Guardian*, 25 March 1931, p. 10.
29. H.N. Brailsford, *Property or Peace?*, London: Gollancz, 1936, p. 140; *New Leader*, 23 May 1930, p. 1.
30. Russell to Murray, 8 March 1931, Murray Papers.
31. H.G. Wells, in 'The ABC of World Peace', *After Democracy: Addresses and Papers on the Present World Situation*, London: Watts, 1932, p. 157.
32. Cecil to Arthur Henderson, 1 June, to MacDonald, 18 August 1930, Cecil papers, Add. 51081.
33. See, *Headway*, July 1930, p. 133.
34. Michael Astor, *Tribal Feeling*, London: John Murray, 1964, p. 144.
35. See Lothian to Lloyd George, 9 April 1930, Lothian Papers, GD 40, 17/250.
36. 270 *H.C. Deb.*, 5s., 632–6 (10 November 1932).
37. *DBFP*, 2s., III, Nos 247–48.
38. The Cabinet agreed, on 20 September 1933 (CAB 23/77) that Britain could not bind to undertake any action at all if German violated Locarno. A memo by MacDonald argued that Britain could not give a world-wide guarantee

to take common action in support of a disarmament convention, could not guarantee any particular country, and would only go as far as the United States with economic sanctions to uphold a disarmament convention. Cabinet Committee on the Disarmament Conference, DC (m) (32) 98, CAB 27/506 (6 April 1934).

39. Cecil to Murray, 29 November 1930, Cecil Papers, Add. 51132.
40. S.W. Roskill, *Hankey: Man of Secrets*, London: Collins, 1972, II, p. 539.
41. See, *DBFP*, 2s., IV, No. 92. The government did not concede German equality in principle until after Germany withdrew from the conference in the autumn of 1932, and then on the obscure condition of the establishment of security for all states.
42. Cecil to K.D. Courtney, 26 September 1932, Cecil Papers, Add. 51141; resolutions on the Conference by the LNU's Reading Branch and London Regional Federation: 27 July 1932, Murray Papers; Murray to Samuel (57), 16 July 1932, Samuel Papers, A/155 (viii); Cecil to Simon, 25 May, 24 June 1932, Cecil Papers, Add. 51082.
43. Zimmern, in *Headway*, April 1932, p. 68; Carter, in *Manchester Guardian*, 11 June 1932, p. 15. Horsfall Carter became secretary of the New Commonwealth.
44. Liddell Hart to Murray, 10 July 1932, Murray Papers. Ironically, Austen Chamberlain opposed Londonderry on 'police bombing' (AC to Londonderry, 26 June 1933, AC Papers, 40/5/42) but Murray thought tanks and bombers might be retained for imperial frontiers (Murray to Liddell Hart, 6 September 1932, Liddell Hart Papers, Disarmament Files). On the Hoover proposals, see Maj.-Gen. A.C. Temperley, *The Whispering Gallery of Europe*, London: Collins, 1938, pp. 208–11.
45. Noel Baker to Liddell Hart, 30 March 1933, Liddell Hart Papers, *Confidential Report, Disarmament Files*. Arnold-Forster also reported that the Draft Convention deserved general support, Memorandum No. 3, 29 April 1933, Cripps Papers, File 531.
46. Liddell Hart to Davies, 22 December 1932, Liddell hart Papers, Notes for History (1932).
47. Davies to Murray, 20 May 1932; Murray to Davies, 23 May 1932, Murray Papers.
48. Murray to Clifford Allen, 18 February 1933, Murray Papers.
49. LNU, *Minutes*, 14th Annual Meeting, 20–22 June 1933, p. 25. Murray complained about defections and told Cecil: 'You and I walk on rather a narrow ledge, supporting an International Air Force for the sake of getting disarmament. But ... even among the faithful there is a minority that feels strongly against the use of force', Murray to Cecil, 3 October 1933, Cecil Papers, Add. 51132.
50. LNU, *Minutes*, General Council Meeting, 7–8 December 1932, p. 30.
51. *Peace*, July–August 1934, p. 20.
52. Allen, in *The Times*, 8 February 1933, p. 8; *Peace*, May 1934, p. 6.
53. *Manchester Guardian*, 5 February 1932, p. 16.
54. H.N. Brailsford, 'A Socialist Foreign Policy', in C. Addison and others (eds), *Problems of a Socialist Government*, London: Gollancz, 1933, pp. 252–86. (p. 253); *Property or Peace?* p. 286. Labour's ACIQ had argued (Memorandum No. 429A, December 1932) that the Party could not object in principle to French plans for an extension of collective security, but Woolf later

observed a considerable drift to pacifism and isolation in the Party, ACIQ Memorandum No. 431A (March 1933).

55. *Morning Post*, 15 November 1932, p. 10. Paul-Boncour, the socialist Prime Minister who subsequently signed the UN Charter for France offered three concentric circles of differing levels of security obligation. As a member of the second circle, Britain would have to cooperate in applying Article 16 of the Covenant, but would not have to join a Mutual Assistance Pact reserved for states in the centre circle. It ran into the sand when Italy refused to join the inner élite.

56. National Union of Conservative and Unionist Associations, Minutes of Annual Conference, 5–6 October 1933, p. 24; Minutes of Executive Committee, 10 May and 8 November 1933.

57. Memo by Grigg, 'The British Empire, the League of Nations and the Rhodes Ideal', 28 September 1932, Lothian Papers, GD. 40, 17/268; Lothian to Grigg, 26 April 1933, Lothian Papers, GD 40, 17/269.

58. 284 *H.C. Deb.*, 5s., 445ff. (13 December 1933). The motion was withdrawn after assurances by Eden (Undersecretary to the Foreign Office) that the government was investigating the control of civil aviation in conjunction with its policy on the abolition of most kinds of bombing.

59. *New Commonwealth*, March 1936, pp. 504–5.

60. Davies to Murray, 23 November 1932, Murray Papers; *New Commonwealth*, November 1932, p. 3.

61. Lord Davies, *Suicide or Sanity?* London: Williams & Norgate, 1932, p. 15; *The Problem of the Twentieth Century*, London: Benn, 1930, p. 633; *New Commonwealth*, November 1932, p. 1.

62. *New Commonwealth*, October 1932, p. 1.

63. Davies, *Problem of the Twentieth Century*, p. 12.

64. Ibid., pp. 456–65. A Commonwealth member would not have to send troops against another, a state with internal troubles would not have to comply, and geographical position in relation to the crisis would be taken into account, ibid., pp. 390–3.

65. Ibid., p. 387.

66. Ibid., p. 533.

67. *New Commonwealth Annual Reports*, 1932–33, pp. 13, 41ff.; 1933–34, p. 26; *New Commonwealth*, June 1934, p. 135.

68. Murray to Courtney, 17 November 1934, Murray Papers. Davies (in, *Force*, pp. 206–7) contrived to blame the LNU for the plight of the League of Nations by chasing the shadow of disarmament.

69. E.g., LNU, *Minutes*, meetings of June 1934 (pp. 49ff.); June 1936 (p. 69); December 1937 (p. 8); June 1938 (pp. 51–3). On Chamberlain in the controversy see, AC to Cecil, 3 April 1933, Cecil to AC, 10 April 1933, Cecil Papers, Add. 51079; AC to Cranborne, 12 May 1932, AC Papers, 39/5/34.

70. *New Commonwealth*, December 1936, pp. 39–40.

6 Resistance: Pacifism and the Power of Defiance

1. Bertrand Russell, *Which Way to Peace?* London: Jonathan Cape, 1936, p. 151.

2. See Reginald Bassett, *Democracy and Foreign Policy: A Case History, The Sino-Japanese Dispute, 1931–1933*, London: Longmans, 1952; Christopher Thorne,

The Limits of Foreign Policy. The West, the League and the Far Eastern Crisis of 1931–1933, London: Hamish Hamilton, 1972.

3. Martin Ceadel's work on pacifism is the standard disaggregation of its varieties. His use of 'pacificism' roughly corresponds to liberal internationalism in this book. *Pacifism in Britain, 1914–1945: The Defining of a Faith*, Oxford: Oxford University Press, 1980.

4. Cecil to Murray, 13 November 1931, Murray Papers; Cecil to Simon, 16 November 1931, Cecil Papers, Add. 51082. Also, Thorne, 'Viscount Cecil, the Government and the Far Eastern Crisis of 1931', *Historical Journ.*, Vol. 14, No. 4, 1971, pp. 805–26.

5. Murray to Cecil, 25 November 1931, Cecil Papers, Add. 51132; Cecil to Sir Walford Selby, 20 February 1932, Cecil Papers, Add. 51090.

6. National Peace Council, (NPC), *Annual Report, 1931–1932*, p. 8; Dorothy Woodman to Cripps, 16 November 1932, Cripps Papers, File 588. Also, *Liberal Magazine*, Vol. 40, No. 464, May 1932, p. 238; *News Chronicle*, 11 November 1931, p. 8; 1 February 1932, p. 8; *Manchester Guardian*, 30 January 1932, p. 10. Labour's Joint Council, 23 February 1932, recognised that Article 16 of the Covenant should be employed if Japan persisted. *Labour Party Annual Report*, 3–7 October 1932, p. 68.

7. *Labour Party Annual Report*, p. 68; Attlee, 270 *H.C. Deb.*, 5s., 526 (10 November 1932).

8. *Headway*, March 1932, p. 51.

9. Copy of Lytton to Lady Balfour, 23 May 1932, Cecil Papers, Add. 51129; *Headway*, August 1932, p. 153; LNU, *Minutes*, General Council Meeting, 7–8 December 1932, p. 29. After 24 February 1932, when the League Assembly had accepted that Japan had violated Chinese territory, the LNU stressed the prohibition of loans and war material, and diplomatic sanctions. LNU, *Manchuria* (London, 1933), p. 4; LNU, *Minutes*, General Council Meeting, 14–15 December 1933, pp. 21–2.

10. *Manchester Guardian*, 13 February 1932, p. 6; Helena Swanwick, *Manchester Guardian*, 3 March 1932, p. 16.

11. LNU, *Minutes*, Emergency General Council Meeting, 27 February 1932; *Headway*, March 1932, p. 50.

12. Letters, in *Manchester Guardian*, 26 February 1932, p. 18; 12 March 1932, p. 4.

13. *The Observer*, 10 January 1932, p. 12; *Daily Express*, 3 November 1931, p. 10; *Morning Post*, 9 November 1931, p. 10; *Daily Mail*, 4 November 1931, p. 12; L. Amery (Conservative, Sparkbrook), 275 *H.C. Deb.*, 5s., 81 (27 February 1932); Churchill, in *The Times*, 18 February 1933, p. 6.

14. *The Times*, 18 February 1933, p. 6. Austen Chamberlain also defended the League's European role, though unlike Churchill's, his faith in Japan waned. See, AC to Garnett, 17 May 1933, AC Papers, 40/5/67; 275 *H.C. Deb.*, 5s., 67–70 (27 February 1933). For pro-Japanese, Eurocentric views see, *Army Quarterly*, Vol. 26, No. 1, April 1933, pp. 4–5; *Morning Post*, 3 February 1932, p. 10.

15. Thorne, 'The Quest for Arms Embargoes: Failure in 1933', *Journ. Contemp. Hist.*, Vol. 5, No. 4, 1970, pp. 129–49.

16. Copy of Murray to Hills, 31 March 1933, Cecil Papers, Add. 51132; Murray to Cecil, 7 March 1933, Cecil Papers, Add. 51132; *Headway*, March 1932, p. 51; LNU, *London Bulletin*, No. 59, June 1933; Norman Angell, *The Defence of Empire*, London: Hamish Hamilton, 1937, pp. 115–16; Noel Baker, 'Note

on the Breakdown of the Collective System over the Manchurian Dispute', 26 February 1935, Lothian Papers, GD 40, 17/108.

17. J.A. Spender, *Between Two Wars*, London: Cassell, 1943, p. 27.

18. *New Leader*, 19 February 1932, p. 1.

19. W.J. Chamberlain, *Fighting for Peace: The Story of the War Resistance Movement*, London: NMWM, 1929, pp. 126; Gertrude Bussey and Margaret Tims, *Women's International League for Peace and Freedom 1915–1965*, London: Allen & Unwin, 1965.

20. Many new societies were offshoots of religious bodies: the Baptist Pacifist Fellowship (founded 1932); the Methodist Peace Fellowship (1933); PAX (Catholic, 1936); the Anglican Pacifist Fellowship (1937).

21. Forster was a glutton for 'punishment by committee'. He was involved in the UDC, NPC, LNU, Labour's ACIQ, New Fabian Research Bureau, Next Five Years Group, and Lloyd George's Council of Action. He seems to have had no time to associate with the New Commonwealth. Simon described him as 'conceited busybody', Simon to AC, 28 February 1933, AC Papers. 40/5/18.

22. See, Louis Bisceglia, 'The Politics of a Peace Prize', *Journ. Contemp. Hist.*, Vol. 7, Nos 3–4, 1972, pp. 263–73.

23. Brig.-Gen. F.P Crozier, *A Brass Hat in No Man's Land*, London: Jonathan Cape, 1930, pp. 82–3, 111, 155.

24. Aldous Huxley (ed.), *An Encyclopaedia of Pacifism*, London: Chatto & Windus, 1937, p. 112. Some wartime absolutists recanted, Allen even promoting an IPF, arguing that the pacifist might save his own soul but see mankind destroyed. Brockway, his old NCF colleague, believed in force in certain circumstances and was to defend communism in Spain. Lord Allen, *Effective Pacifism*, London: LNU, 1934, p. 21; A. Fenner Brockway, *Inside the Left*, London: Allen & Unwin, 1942, pp. 338–40.

25. Liddell Hart to Glasgow, 14 May 1934, Liddell Hart Papers, 'Notes for History'. Also comment by Steel-Maitland, who felt that the 'violence' of pacifists made them suspect to the Conservative Party, in V.K. Krishna Menon (ed.), *Young Oxford and War*, London: Selwyn & Blount, 1934, p. 210.

26. H.R.L. Sheppard, *We Say 'No'*, London: PPU, 1935, p. 5; A.A. Milne, *Peace with Honour*, London: Methusen, 1934, p. 198.

27. *Peace*, July 1933, p. 15.

28. Huxley, *What Are You Going to Do About It?* London: PPU, 1936, pp. 135–7.

29. Russell, *Which Way to Peace?* pp. 135–37.

30. PPU, *Is Pacifism Scientific or Sentimental?* 1932, p. 10.

31. John Strachey, *The British Anti-War Movement*, London: BAWM, 1933, pp. 6–7; *New Statesmen*, 11 March 1933, pp. 283–4; *Manchester Guardian*, 9 June 1932, p. 12; *Peace*, June 1933, p. 9.

32. Ponsonby to Lansbury, 22 October 1933, Lansbury Papers, Vol. 13; Raymond Postgate, *The Life of George Lansbury*, London: Longmans, 1951, p. 287.

33. Ben Pimlott, 'The Socialist League: Intellectuals and the Labour Left in the 1930s', *Journ. Contemp. Hist.*, Vol. 6, No. 3, 1971, pp. 12–38.

34. L. Anderson Fenn, *Problems of the Socialist Transition*, London: Gollancz, 1934, p. 24.

35. *Labour Party Annual Report*, 2–6 October 1933, p. 186.

36. Pethick-Lawrence, *Fate Has Been Kind*, London: Hutchinson, 1943, p. 186.

37. ACIQ Memorandum No. 433A (April 1933); Leonard Woolf, 'Labour's Foreign Policy', *Political Quarterly*, Vol. 4, No. 4, 1933, pp. 504–24.
38. 292 *H.C. Deb.*, 5s., 2340–4 (30 July 1934).
39. *Labour Party Annual Report*, 2–6 October 1933, p. 190.
40. Letter in, *New Statesman*, 23 September 1933, p. 841. Other signatories included Allen, Woolf, Noel Baker, Mander and Joad.
41. The Conservative Central Office understood pacifism to have been the major issue in the East Fulham by-election of October 1933, but the Labour candidate, John Wilmot, followed Dalton on foreign policy. See, Robert Rhodes James, *Memoirs of a Conservative: J.C.C. Davidson's Memoirs and Papers, 1910–1937*, London: Weidenfeld & Nicholson., 1969, pp. 397–8; Richard Heller, 'East Fulham Revisited', *Journ. Contemp. Hist.*, Vol. 6, No. 3, 1971, pp. 172–96.
42. Alan Bullock, *The Life and Times of Ernest Bevin*, 2 Vols, London: Heinemann, 1960, I, pp. 546–7; TUC *Annual Report*, 3–7 September 1934, pp. 320ff.
43. Labour Party, *Annual Report*, 1–5 October 1934, Appendix II, pp. 242–5.
44. Ibid., p. 176. For the policy approved by the Socialist League's Conference in May 1934, see Fenn, pp. 193–220. To complaints that communists were making all the running against fascism, the Labour Executive responded by banning communist front organisations and publishing *The Communist Solar System* (1933). Also, TUC *Annual Report*, 4–8 September 1933, Appendix C; Labour Party, *Annual Report*, 2–6 October 1933, Appendix IX.
45. Hugh Dalton, *The Fateful Years*, London: Muller, 1957, p. 55.
46. S. Davis, 'The British Labour Party and British Foreign Policy, 1933–1939', PhD thesis, University of London, 1950, p. 378.
47. Original emphasis. Brockway, *Socialism over 60 year the Life of Jowett of Bradford, 1864–1944*, London: Allen & Unwin, 1946, p. 331; *New Leader*, 11 November 1932, p. 6.
48. Disaffiliation from the Labour Party and internal schisms caused the ILP's membership to fall from 21,000 in 1931 to 4,400 in 1935. Stephen Hornby, *Left Wing Pressure Groups in the British Labour Movement, 1930–1940*, Liverpool: University of Liverpool Press, 1966.
49. *Labour Monthly*, March 1935, p. 133.
50. Ibid., August 1934, pp. 465–66.
51. *Daily Worker*, 17 September 1934, p. 1.
52. *Labour Monthly*, January 1935, p. 17.
53. *Daily Telegraph*, 18 November 1933, p. 11; *Daily Mail*, 21 July 1934, p. 8.
54. Memorandum of the London Round Table Group, Blickling, 29 May 1933, Lothian Papers, GD 40, 17/276; National Union of Conservative and Unionist Associations, Resolution of Edmonton Association, Minutes of Executive Committee, 14 November 1934; *Daily Express*, 22 December 1933, p. 8. Vansittart contemplated the recruitment of liberal internationalism against Germany and enquired how far the LNU had fallen under the sway of pacifists. Murray to Cecil, 5 December 1933, Cecil Papers, Add. 51132. For the wrangle between the anti-German and anti-Japanese opinion, see D.C. Watt, *Personalities and Policies*, London: Longmans, 1965; Michael Howard, *The Continental Commitment*, London: Temple Smith, 1972, pp. 85–9.
55. Gen. J.C. Smuts, 'The Present International Outlook', *Journ. R.I.I.A.*, Vol. 14, No. 1, 1935, pp. 3–19 (p. 6).
56. LNU, *Minutes*, 14th Annual Meeting, 20–22 June 1933, p. 47.

57. Jonathan Griffin, letter, *New Statesman*, 25 February 1933, p. 219; R.B. McCallum, *Public Opinion and the Last Peace*, London: Oxford University Press, 1944, pp. 177–80; Martin Ceadel, 'The "King and Country" Debate, 1933: Student Politics, Pacifism and the Dictators', *Hist. Journ.*, Vol. 22, No. 2, 1979, pp. 397–422.
58. Interview with Frank Hardie, London, 27 February 1974.
59. Michael Foot, in Menon (ed.), pp. 19–24.
60. Ibid., pp. 24, 43–47.
61. *Peace*, August 1933, p. 11.
62. Cecil to Noel Baker, 16 November 1932, Cecil Papers, Add. 51107.
63. NPC, *Peace Year Book*, 1934, p. 7.
64. LNU, *Minutes*, 19th Annual Meeting, 15–17 June 1938, p. 29; *Headway*, October 1932, Supplement, p. I; *LNU Yearbooks*, 1933, p. 18; 1934, p. 5; LNU *London Bulletin*, No. 60, July–August 1933.
65. Memo, A.J.C. Freshwater, John Eppstein, D.A. Mills and Alan Thomas to Murray [ca. 20 March 1934], Murray Papers.
66. *News Chronicle*, 21 December 1933, p. 6. Lytton argued that the complexity of the situation in Asia justified the prolonged efforts. *The Lytton Report – And After*, London: LNU, 1933.
67. Murray to AC, 21 June 1934, Dugdale to AC, 9 November 1934, AC Papers, 40/6/45, 47.
68. LNU, *Minutes*, 15th Annual Meeting, 26–29 June 1934, p. 29. The Glasgow and Dundee branches, for example, initially considered the ballot impractical. G.F. Barbour to Murray, 1 September 1934, Murray Papers.
69. National Declaration Committee, 'Yellow Leaflet' (1935); *War or Peace? The Workers' Guide to the National Declaration* (1935). Cecil emphasised that economic sanctions would rarely be invoked, but would work. *Daily Herald*, 6 November 1934, p. 10.
70. Percy to Murray, 19 November 1934, Murray Papers; Chamberlain, letter *The Times*, 12 November 1934, p. 15; *The Times*, 19 November 1934, p. 14; *Morning Post*, 4 July 1935, p. 10; National Union of Conservative and Unionist Associations, Minutes of Executive Committee, 9 May 1934.
71. Cecil to Baldwin, 26b November 1934, Cecil Papers, Add. 51080; Murray letter, *The Times*, 28 November 1934, p. 10.
72. Dalton, p. 111: *Daily Herald*, 13 November 1934, p. 10; *The Times*, 28 November 1934, p. 15.
73. Sheppard, p. 149; Adelaide Livingstone, *The Peace Ballot: The Official History*, London: Gollancz, 1935.
74. Jean-Félix Charvet, *L'Influence Britannique dans la S.D.N.*, Paris: Rodstein, 1938, p. 157.
75. *Daily Herald*, 6 November 1934, p. 10.
76. Cecil's concluding statements, in Livingstone, p. 64.
77. Noel Baker to Cecil, 3 January 1938; Cecil's reply, 6 January 1938, Cecil Papers, Add. 51107.
78. *Morning Post*, 15 May 1934, p. 8; Next Five Years Group, *The Next Five Years, an Essay in Political Agreement*, London: Macmillan, 1935, pp. 312–14.
79. Next Five Years Group, p. 281. Thomas C. Kennedy 'The Next Five Years Group and the Failure of the Politics of Agreement in Britain', *Canadian Journ. Hist.*, Vol. 9, No. 1, 1974, pp. 45–68.
80. *New Commonwealth*, December 1936, p. 33.

7 Imperialism: Economic Security and Sanctions

1. Evelyn Waugh, *Waugh in Abyssinia*, London: Longmans, 1936, p. 49.
2. Gilbert Murray, *The Cult of Violence*, London: Lovat Dickinson, 1934, p. 8.
3. R.B. McCallum, *Public Opinion and the Last Peace*, London: Oxford University Press, 1944, p. 15; R.J.B. Bosworth, 'The British Press, the Conservatives, and Mussolini, 1920–34', *Journ. Contemp. Hist.*, Vol. 5, No. 2, 1970, pp. 163–82 (p. 182).
4. 98 *H.L. Deb.*, 5s., 1127 (22 October 1935); 99 *H.L. Deb.*, 5s., 97 (5 December 1935). Viscount Wolmer agreed that victory for Africans would be a disaster for the Empire, 305 *H.C. Deb.*, 5s., 76 (22 October 1935).
5. Money to Lloyd George, 14 September 1935; ca. May 1936, Lloyd George Papers, G/14/23, 36; letter, *New Stateman*, 21 September 1935, p. 371.
6. Maj-Gen. J.F.C. Fuller, *The First of the League Wars; Its Lessons and Omens*, London: Eyre & Spottiswoode 1936, p. 12; Mosley, in *Blackshirt*, 4 October 1935, p. 2; *Fascist Quarterly*, Vol. 2, No. 3, 1936, pp. 377–95; Joyce, in *Fascist Quarterly*, Vol. 1, No. 4, 1935, p. 429; Michael Pugh, 'Peace with Italy: BUF Reactions to the Abyssinian War 1935–1936', *Wiener Library Bull.*, Vol. 27, No. 32, 1974, pp. 11–18.
7. Waugh, pp. 25, 27, 49. Cardinal Hinsley, cited in Arnold J. Toynbee, *Survey of International Affairs 1935*, 2 Vols, London: Oxford University Press, 1936, II, pp. 103–4.
8. Sir John Marriott, 'England and Italy', *Fortnightly Rev.*, August 1935, pp. 194–202; Sir Charles Petrie, *Mussolini*, London: Holme Press, 1931.
9. Lord Lugard, 'The Basis of the Claim for Colonies', *Journ. RIIA*, Vol. 15, No. 1, 1936, pp. 3–25.
10. Hoare to Baldwin, 29 December 1935, Baldwin Papers, *Foreign Affairs*, Series B, Vol. 123, 1935/3; 'Extracts from Political Notes', Templewood Papers, Box VIII, File 1.
11. A government interdepartmental commission reported in June that the only British interest that might be affected by Italy's venture concerned the headwaters of the Nile. The report was photographed in the British Embassy in Rome by the Italian spy network. Viscount Templewood, *Nine Troubled Years*, London: Collins, 1954, pp. 156–7.
12. *Morning Post*, 24 March 1936, p. 12.
13. 305 *H.C. Deb.*, 5s., 194–5 (23 October 1935); L.S. Amery, *My Political Life*, III, *The Unforgiving Years, 1929–1940*, London: Hutchinson, 1955, p. 427.
14. C.F. Adam, *Life of Lord Lloyd*, London: Macmillan, 1948, pp. 268–9; Lord A.B. Cunningham of Hyndhope, *A Sailor's Odyssey*, London: Hutchinson, 1951, pp. 173–6; Arthur Marder, 'The Royal Navy and the Ethiopian Crisis of 1935–36', *American Historical Rev.*, Vol. 75, No. 5, 1970, pp. 1327–56; Lord Chatfield, *It Might Happen Again*, London: Heinemann, 1947, pp. 87–90.
15. NPC, *Peace Year Book*, 1936, p. 16. Also, Lothian in *Round Table*, Vol. 25, No. 100, 1935, p. 667.
16. 305 *H.C. Deb.*, 5s., 31 (22 October 1935).
17. George W. Baer, *The Coming of the Italian-Ethiopian War*, Cambridge, MA: Harvard University Press, 1967, pp. 18–43, 60–1; Aaron L. Goldman 'Sir Robert Vansittart's Search for Italian Co-operation against Hitler 1933–36', *Journ. Contemp. Hist.*, Vol. 9, No. 3, 1974, pp. 93–130 (pp. 109–110);

D.C. Watt, 'The Secret Laval–Mussolini Agreement of 1935 on Ethiopia', *The Middle East Journal*, Vol. 15, 1961, pp. 69–78.

18. Samuel to Wigram for the King, (48), 16 September 1932, Samuel Papers, A/89; Ramsay Muir, in *Liberal Magazine*, Vol. 40, No. 469, 1932, p. 492.

19. Maj. Nathan (Labour, Bethnal Green), 305 *H.C. Deb.*, 5s., 125 (22 October 1935), Sir Herbert Samuel (Nat. Lib., Darwen), 55–6, Issac Foot (Nat. Lib., Bodmin), 171.

20. Sir Arthur Salter, *Political Aspects of the World Depression*, Oxford: Clarendon, 1932, p. 16. Lionel Robbins blamed European financiers for persuading the US Treasury to lower interest rates in 1927, releasing a flood of speculation. *The Great Depression*, London: Macmillan, 1934, p. 53.

21. Robbins, pp. 3, 193–94. Also, Lloyd George, *The Truth about Reparations and War Debts*, London, Heinemann, 1932, p. 4.

22. Norman Angell, *The Peace Treaty and the Economic Chaos of Europe*, London: Swarthmore, 1919, p. 97.

23. *Peace*, November 1935, p. 122.

24. Keynes, letter *New Statesman*, 16 January 1932, pp. 57–8; Salter, *Recovery; The Second Effort*, London: Bell, rev. edn, 1933, p. xxviii; John W. Wheeler-Bennett, *The Wreck of Reparations, Being the Political Background of the Lausanne Agreement 1932*, London: Allen & Unwin, 1933.

25. *Morning Post*, 13 December 1932, p. 10; *Daily Express*, 15 December 1932, p. 8.

26. Salter, *The Economic Consequences of the League*, London: Europa, 1927, p. 1; *Recovery*, pp. 175ff.; *The World's Economic Crisis and the Way of Escape*, London: Allen & Unwin, 1932, p. 26.

27. Murray to MacDonald, 7 October 1930, and to Bartlett, 18 August 1930, Murray Papers. On the retreat from free trade, see Robert Skidelsky, *Politicians and the Slump: The Labour Government of 1929–1931*, London: Penguin, 1970 edn, pp. 255–9.

28. Next Five Year Group, *The Next Five Years, an Essay in Political Agreement*, London: Macmillan, 1935, p. 142; Arthur Marwick, *Clifford Allen: The Open Conspirator*, Edinburgh: Oliver & Boyd, 1964, pp. 131–2. Lloyd George claimed the Council of Action had 10,624 members, 58 branches (1936), and a fund of £400,000. 'Analysis of membership, 24 July 1937, Lloyd George Papers, C/A Organisation and Policy File, Box 159.

29. H.N. Brailsford, *Olives of an Endless Age*, New York: Harper, 1928, pp. 326, 405–406; J.A. Hobson, *From Capitalism to Socialism*, London: Hogarth, 1932, pp. 50–1; *New Statesman*, 18 April 1931, pp. 274–5; G.D.H. Cole and Margaret Cole, *The Intelligent Man's Review of Europe To-Day*, London: Gollancz, 1933, p. 780; H.J. Laski, *Problems of Peace*, London: Allen & Unwin, 1932, pp. 188–209 (pp. 194–5).

30. H.G. Wells, *The World of William Clissold*, 2 vols, London: Modern Library, 1933 edn, II, pp. 368ff.; *After Democracy: Addresses and Papers on the Present World Situation*, London: Watts, 1932, pp. 101–16; *The Open Conspiracy and Other Writings*, London: Modern Library, 1933 edn, II, pp. 643–827. For criticism of Wells, see Hobson, *Wealth and Life: A Study in Values*, London: Macmillan, 1929, p. 402.

31. Laski, 'The Economic Foundations of Peace', in Leonard Woolf (ed.), *The Intelligent Man's Way to Prevent War*, London: Gollancz, 1933, pp. 505, 514, 524, 539–41; *Labour*, Vol. 3, No. 2, 1935, pp. 36–7; Brailsford, *Property or Peace?* London: Gollancz, 1936 edn, p. 142.

32. Brailsford, *Towards a New League*, London: New Statesman, 1936, pp. 61–4; NFRB, *Labour's Foreign Policy* (1934), p. 11; Hugh Gaitskell, *NFRB, Quarterly Journ.*, No. 1, 1936, pp. 31–7.
33. Woolf, *The League and Abyssinia*, London: Hogarth, 1936, pp. 32–4.
34. E.g., *Labour Bull.*, Vol. 5, No. 5, 1929, pp. 32–4.
35. ACIQ Memorandum No. 413A (July 1930).
36. *Peace*, December 1935, p. 139.
37. Speeches in 304 *H.C. Deb.*, 5s., 517–630 (11 July 1935). Eden remained convinced of Italy's weakness and regretted 'the lost opportunity afforded by Abyssinia of not pulling ... [Mussolini] up'. John Harvey (ed.), *The Diplomatic Diaries of Oliver Harvey, 1937–1940*, London: Collins, 1970, p. 28.
38. Cecil to Eden, 11 July 1935, Cecil Papers, Add. 51083. Ironically, Eden had drafted the statement sent by the Conservative Party to the LNU objecting to the Peace Ballot questions. LNU Correspondence, Baldwin Papers, Foreign Affairs, Series B, Vol. 133.
39. James C. Robertson, 'The Origins of British Opposition to Mussolini over Ethiopia', *Journal of British Studies*, Vol. 9, No. 1, 1969, pp. 122–42 (p. 139).
40. Adams to Signor Vespucci, 27 August 1935, Adams Papers, File 6.
41. Hoare to Drummond, 27 July 1935, Templewood Papers, Box VIII, File 3.
42. Letter, *Morning Post*, 9 July 1935, p. 17.
43. *Headway*, September 1935, p. 162.
44. Hoare to Neville Chamberlain, 18 August 1935, Templewood Papers, Box VIII, File 1.
45. Conversations with Austen Chamberlain and Churchill, 20, 21 August 1935, Templewood Papers, Box VIII, File 1.
46. Ormsby-Gore to Baldwin, 8 September 1935, Baldwin Papers, Foreign Affairs, Series B, Vol. 123, 1935/3.
47. Murray to Cecil, 12 September 1935, Murray Papers.
48. *Liberal Magazine*, Vol. 43, No. 505, 1935, p. 491. Similarly, a resolution of the LNU General Council in early December called for 'a new organisation of the resources of the world' to erase the fundamental causes of war. LNU, *Minutes*, General Council Meeting, 4–5 December 1935, pp. 31–3.
49. E.g., Layton's Draft Memorandum on Peace, for the Councils of Action, September 1935, Lothian Papers, GD 40, 17/113, p. 9.
50. Lansbury, in *The Times*, 19 August 1935, p. 11; Buxton, in *Headway*, November 1935, p. 209; Labour Party, *Annual Report*, 30 September–October 1935, pp. 153–4. A similar resolution had been passed by the TUC a few weeks earlier.
51. *Labour*, Vol. 3, No. 33, 1935, p. 51.
52. Laski, 'The General Election 1935', *Political Quarterly*, Vol. 7, No. 1, 1936, pp. 1–15 (p. 3).
53. Duff Cooper, *Old Men Forget*, London: Dutton, 1954, edn, p. 192.
54. Patrick to Hoare, 12 December 1935, Templewood Papers, Box VIII, File 1; Cosmo Lang to Baldwin, 13 December 1935, Baldwin Papers, Foreign Affairs, Series B, Vol. 123, 1935/3; Robert Rhodes James, *Chips: The Diaries of Sir Henry Channon*, London: Weidenfeld and Nicholson, 1967, p. 48; Vyvyan Adams, in *New Commonwealth*, January 1936, p. 465. Cecil denounced the author of the plan, Vansittart: 'if I get the chance I will press for his transference to some distant Embassy'. Cecil to Murray, 16 December 1935, Cecil Papers, Add. 51132. For public reactions to the Hoare–Laval plan, see Toynbee, pp. 67–70; LNU, *The Tragedy of Abyssinia* (1936), pp. 36ff.

55. H.D. Dickinson, in *Headway*, February 1936; Elizabeth Monroe, 'Abyssinia as a Colonial Asset', *Fortnightly Rev.*, November 1935, pp. 541–9; Angell, *This Have and Have-Not Business: Political Fantasy and Economic Fact*, London: Hamish Hamilton, 1936, pp. 109–20.

56. See, e.g., Prof. R.B. Mowat, 'The Mischief of Revisionism', *Fortnightly Rev.*, February 1936, pp. 160–9 (p. 164); Lionel Birch, *The Demand for Colonies*, London: LNU, 1936, p. 44; Hugh Gaitskell, in NFRB, *Quarterly Journ.*, No. 10 (June 1936), p. 4; ACIQ, 'The Demand for Colonial Territories and Equality of Economic Opportunity', 159/460B (July 1936); *New Commonwealth*, November 1935, p. 429.

57. *New Statesman*, 28 September 1935, p. 401.

58. Murray to Cecil, 9 March 1934, Cecil to Lytton, 29 March 1935, Cecil Papers Add. 51132.

59. Citrine, *TUC Annual Report*, 2–6 September 1935, p. 348, Adams to Hoare, 4 October 1935, Adams Papers, File 6; J.C. Wedgewood (Ind., Newcastle-under-Lyme), 305 *H.C. Deb*, 5s., 231 (23 October 1935); Lothian to Smuts, 16 August 1935, & to Hoare, 18 October 1935, Lothian Papers, GD 40, 17/301, 5; Lothian, 'Europe, The League and Abyssinia', *Round Table*, Vol. 25, No. 100, 1935, pp. 660–72.

60. *New Commonwealth*, November 1935, p. 439; December 1935, p. 445.

61. *Headway*, August 1935, p. 144, Cecil to Cranbourne, 3 October 1935, Cecil Papers, Add. 51087.

62. Hoare to Runciman, 22 November 1935, Londonderry to Hoare, 23 October 1935, Templewood Papers, Box VIII, File 3; Amery, p. 174.

63. *Labour*, December 1935, p. 74.

64. Toynbee, p. 449.

65. Amery, p. 175; James, p. 59.

66. 305 *H.C. Deb.*, 5s., 367 (24 October 1935); Conversation with Churchill, 21 August 1935, Templewood Papers, Box VIII, File 1.

67. Lord Henry Page Croft, *My Life of Strife*, London: Hutchinson, 1948, p. 261; 305 *H.C. Deb.*, 5s., 410 (24 October 1935); National Union of Conservative and Unionist Associations, Minutes of Annual Conference, 1–2 October 1936, pp. 26–7.

68. Hoare to Neville Chamberlain, 27 December 1935 and to Lady Maude, Templewood Papers, Box VIII, Files 1, 5a & b. Support came from Amery, Malcolm Muggeridge, Waldorf Astor and Rex Leeper of the Foreign Office News Dept.

69. National Union of Conservative and Unionist Associations, Minutes of Executive Committee, 8 April 1936. King George V and the Prince of Wales were anti-sanctionists. Wigram to Hoare, 13 October 1935, Templewood Papers, Box VIII, File 4; Conversation between Liddell Hart and Geoffrey Dawson, 7 February 1936, Liddell Hart Papers, Notes for History; Edward Duke of Windsor, *A King's Story*, London: Cassell, 1957, pp. 277, 296–7.

70. *Peace*, June, 1936, p. 34; also, January 1936, p. 163; NPC *Peace Year Book*, 1936, p. 75.

71. *New Statesman*, 9 November 1935, pp. 665–6.

72. Russell to Kingsley Martin, 7 August 1935, cited in Martin, *Editor: A Second Volume of Autobiography 1931–45*, London: Hutchinson, 1968, p. 194.

73. Clive Bell, letter *New Statesman*, 28 September 1935, p. 405; Alfred Salter, in Labour Party, *Annual Report*, 20 September–4 October 1935, p. 167.

74. Cited in Martin, p. 200.

75. Letter, *New Statesman*, 14 September 1935, pp. 338–9.

76. *New Leader*, 13 September 1935, p. 1; 17 April 1936, p. 4; A. Fenner Brockway, *Inside the Left*, London: Allen & Unwin, 1942, pp. 325–8. The No More War Movement took the same anti-imperialist line as did the ILP. Reginald A. Reynolds, in *New Statesman*, 28 September 1935, p. 406.

77. J.T. Murphy to Cripps, 18 September 1935; Trevelyan to Cripps, 15 September 1935, Cripps Papers, Files 540, 590. Laski, in *Labour Monthly*, March 1936, pp. 131–2; S.R. Cripps, *Fight Now against War*, London: Socialist League, 1935. Cripps changed his view and urged the formation of a nucleus of League states sympathetic to socialist ideals of economic justice. *The Struggle for Peace*, London: Gollancz, 1936, pp. 131–2.

78. 'Vigilantes' (pseud.), *Abyssinia: The Essential Facts in the Dispute and an Answer to the Question – 'Ought We to Support Sanctions?'* London: New Statesman, 1935, pp. 38–9.

79. *Labour*, November 1935, p. 60.

80. Letter in *New Statesmen*, 28 September 1935, pp. 405–6. Also, *Labour Monthly*, February 1936, p. 73; Emile Burns, *Abyssinia and Italy*, London: Gollancz, 1935, p. 187.

81. Henry Pelling, *The British Communist Party: A Historical Profile*, London: A & C Black, 1958, p. 192.

82. *New Times and Ethiopia News*, No. 2, 16 May 1936, p. 4; David Mitchell, *The Fighting Pankhursts; A Study in Tenacity*, London: Jonathan Cape, 1967, pp. 250–5. Benefactors included Viscount Wakefield who donated a Red Cross plane, Lothian who gave £300, and the Duke of Westminster who guaranteed £2,000 to a medical aid fund. The Red Cross Unit reported attending 2,500 civilian mustard gas casualties on the northern front between 1 and 18 March 1936. Copy of Surrett to Wakefield, 25 October 1935, Murray Papers; Lugard to Lothian, letters between 30 July and 4 November 1935; Lothian Papers, GD 40, 17/297. *New Times and Ethiopia News*, No. 2, 16 May 1936, p. 1.

83. Lothian to Lloyd George, 10 September 1935, Lothian Papers , GD 40, 17/113 and 17/319.

84. E.H. Carr, 'Public Opinion as a Safeguard of Peace', *Journ. RIIA*, Vol. 15, No. 6, 1936, pp. 846–62; Woolf, 'Meditation on Abyssinia', *Political Quarterly*, Vol. 7, No. 1, 1936, pp. 16–32 (p. 22).

85. LNU, *Minutes*, General Council Meeting, 4–5 December 1935, pp. 53–9; Cecil to Eden, 14 November 1935, Cecil Papers, Add. 51083.

86. LNU, *Minutes*, 17th Annual Meeting, 19–23 June 1936, pp. 3–24; *Headway*, July 1936, p. 129.

87. Toynbee, pp. 455–69; Churchill to Cecil, 18 April 1936, Cecil Papers, Add. 51073l; Andrew Holt, '"No More Hoares to Paris": British Foreign Policymaking and the Abyssinian Crisis, 1935', *Rev. of Int. Studs*, Vol. 37, No. 3, 2011, pp. 1382–401.

88. Letter in *The Times*, 4 June 1936, p. 13; 'Sanctions under the Covenant', *British Year Book of International Law*, Vol. 17, 1936, pp. 130–49 (pp. 132–3).

89. Murray to Courtney, 19 May 1936; to Wakehurst, 20 June 1936, Murray Papers; Murray to AC 24 June 1936, AC Papers, 41/3/51.

90. *LNU Yearbook*, 1936, pp. 22–3; Murray to Davies, 11 May 1936, Murray Papers; *Headway*, February 1935, p. 23; June 1936, p. 120; July 1936, p. 140; LNU, *Minutes*, 19th Annual Meeting, 15–17 June 1938, p. 29. Conservative

resignations included Lord Queenborough (Treasurer), Lord Home (Chairman of the Scottish National Council), Edward Grigg, the Duchess of Atholl and Austen Chamberlain. *Morning Post*, 30 April 1936, p. 13; *Daily Mail*, 12 June 1936, p. 14; G.F. Barbour to Murray, 17 October 1936, Murray Papers; Correspondence between AC and Murray, 5 May–23 June 1936, AC Papers, 41/3/46–50.

91. *New Commonwealth*, December 1935; Lloyd George annotation, Gerothwohl Memo of Policy Suggestions, n.d. [1936] Lloyd George Papers, Box 159.

8 Revisionism: Rearmament and Peaceful Change

1. Neville Thompson, *The Anti-Appeasers, Conservative Opposition to Appeasement in the 1930s*, Oxford: Clarendon, 1971. The terms 'revision' and 'peaceful change' are used here to mean reappraisal of the Versailles status quo with Germany's situation in mind. They have been qualified in the text where appropriate. The word 'appeasement' is used in the specific sense to denote the policy of granting Germany concessions to satisfy an appetite, following Keith Middlemas, *Diplomacy of Illusion: The British Government and Germany 1937–39*, London: Weidenfeld & Nicholson, 1972, p. 8 (note).
2. Rt. Hon. Lord Dickinson, 'Dis-arm or Re-arm?' *19th Century*, Vol. 111, February 1932, pp. 129–39 (p. 134).
3. P.J. Noel Baker, 'Disarmament', *Journ. RIIA*, Vol. 13, No. 1, 1934, pp. 3–26 (p. 6). Also, *Manchester Guardian*, 6 June 1931, p. 12. Arnold-Forster argued that Hitlerism should be robbed of any justifiable pretext to rearm: 'Arbitration, Security, Disarmament', in Leonard Woolf (ed.) *The Intelligent Man's Way to Prevent War*, London: Gollancz, 1933, pp. 314–455 (p. 455). On the attitudes to the rise of nazism, see Brigitte Granzow, *A Mirror of Nazism: British Opinion and the Emergence of Hitler 1929–1933*, London: Gollancz, 1964; Martin Gilbert and Richard Gott, *The Appeasers*, London: Weidenfeld & Nicholson, 1967, pp. 3–24.
4. *Foreign Affairs*, April 1929, p. 115.
5. Gilbert Murray, 'Revision of the Peace Treaties', in Woolf (ed.), pp. 67–153 (pp. 67–9); C.A.W. Manning (ed.), *Peaceful Change. An International Problem*, London: Macmillan, 1937; Murray to Swanwick, 22 December 1934, Murray Papers.
6. Conversation between Sir John Simon, J.R.M. MacDonald and Mussolini, 19 March 1933 in *DBFP*, 2s., V, No. 44 (Enclosure No. 5).
7. Letter in *The Times*, 12 October 1932, p. 8; *New Statesman*, 18 March 1933, p. 313.
8. 276 *H.C. Deb.*, 5s., 2759, (13 April) 1933.
9. Hugh Dalton, *The Fateful Years, 1931–1945,* London: Muller, 1957, pp. 37–41.
10. *Headway*, May 1933, p. 91, Supplement, p. ii.
11. MacDonald's speech, in *Daily Telegraph*, 10 November 1933, p. 13; Austen Chamberlain, 285 *H.C. Deb.*, 5s., 1036 (6 February 1934); E.L. Spears (Conservative, Carlisle), ibid., 1026.
12. 281 *H.C. Deb.*, 5s., 126–8 (7 November 1933). Lansbury, ibid., 68–77. Six days later, Labour divided the House on a resolution calling for bold disarmament measures. Liberals abstained, but within the month deserted the government benches in protest at economic and disarmament policies.

13. *Morning Post*, 10 October 1933, p. 10. In general, however, the right-wing press refrained from excessive criticism of Germany, e.g., *Daily Telegraph* (17 October 1933). By contrast, Vansittart aired the suggestion of an occupation of Germany under League auspices: Memo on the present and Future Position in Europe, CAB 24/243, CP 212 (33), 28 August 1933, National Archives.

14. *New Statesman*, 14 October 1933, pp. 436–7; 21 October 1933, p. 469.

15. *Labour*, Vol. 1, No. 3, November 1933, p. 50; see also, D. Graham Hutton 'British Foreign Policy and the Peace of Europe', *19th Century*, Vol. 113, April 1933, pp. 396–406.

16. AC to Rumbold, 13 November 1933, AC Papers, 40/5/127. *New Statesman* (18 March 1933) had hoped that Hitler would be able to control the zeal of his followers. Also, Vernon Bartlett, *Nazi Germany Explained*, London: Gollancz, 1933.

17. *New Commonwealth*, May 1936, p. 530.

18. Allen, Notes on an LNU Deputation to Eden, 21 August 1935, Cecil Papers, Add. 51083.

19. 295 *H.C. Deb.*, 5s., 918 (28 November 1934). See generally, Anthony Lentin, *Lloyd George and the Lost Peace: From Versailles to Hitler, 1919–1940*, Basingstoke: Palgrave Macmillan, 2001.

20. 286 *H.C. Deb.*, 5s., 2027ff. (8 March 1934). The only speakers in this debate to give explicit warnings about German expansionism were Wedgwood, Guest and Churchill.

21. Notes on Defence Debate, 9 March 1936; Memorandum, 21 July 1936, Liddell Hart Papers, Notes for History; Arnold-Forster, in *Labour*, Vol. III, No. 7 (March 1936), p. 2155; Lord Allen, 'The Hour of Decision, II, A New Plan for Collective Security', *Fortnightly Rev.*, July 1936, pp. 11–19 (p. 15). A.V. Alexander, 310 *H.C. Deb.*, 5s., 80–2 (16 March 1936).

22. E.g., *The Times* leaders: 11 March 1935, p. 13; 7 March 1936, p. 14.

23. 292 *H.C. Deb.*, 5s., 2325ff. (30 July 1934). Winding up the debate Simon indicated that he could give no accurate figures for German rearmament. The division on a motion regretting the Government's decision to rearm was defeated by 60 votes to 404. The Conservative, Adams, voted with Labour.

24. Cited in Keith Feiling, *The Life of Neville Chamberlain*, London: Macmillan, 1970, p. 253. The major defence review was prompted by the Asian crisis (the ten-year rule was abandoned in March 1932 and given additional impetus by the developments in Germany). Neville Chamberlain made drastic cuts in the 1934 estimates – which had the effect of giving greater weight to air rearmament. Like Chamberlain, Fisher and Vansittart were more concerned than Hankey to build aircraft against Germany than battleships against Japan. On rearmament, see Keith Middlemas and John Barnes, *Baldwin: A Biography*, London: Weidenfeld & Nicholson, 1969, pp. 730–41, 754–8: Stephen Roskill, *Hankey: Man of Secrets*, London: Collins, 1974, III, pp. 87–117; D.C. Watt, *Personalities and Policies*, London: Longmans, 1965, pp. 85–107; *Too Serious a Business; European Armed Forces and the Approach to the Second World War*, London: Norton 1975, pp. 95–103.

25. Crozier's interview notes, 12 June 1934, in A.J.P. Taylor (ed.), *Off the Record: Political Interviews 1933–1943*, London: Hutchinson, 1973, p. 26.

26. 299 *H.C. Deb.*, 5s., 67ff. (11 March 1935).

27. Chamberlain's address to the LNU's Rugby branch, *The Times*, 7 March 1936, p. 14.

28. *Labour,* November 1935, p. 62.
29. Letter to Lothian and Conwell-Evans, 18 March 1935, Lothian Papers, GD 40, 17/202; 'Vigilantes' (Zilliacus), *Inquest on Peace,* London: Gollancz, 1935, p. 17; H.N. Brailsford, 'Class War among the Nations', *New Republic,* Vol. 87, August 1936, pp. 41–3 (p. 41). Philip Gibbs, *Across the Frontiers,* London: Michael Joseph, 1938, p. 143.
30. *Daily Herald,* 20 July 1934, p. 10. See also, Stafford Cripps, 292 *H.C. Deb.,* 5s., 2427 (30 July 1934).
31. *The Times,* 24 November 1934, p. 7.
32. Ibid., 7 March 1936, p. 14.
33. Memo, Hoare to P.S., 17 June 1936, & reply, 20 June 1936, Templewood Papers, Box IX, File 5.
34. LNU, *Minutes,* General Council Meeting, 4–5 December 1935, p. 72; *Headway,* March 1936, p. 42; *The Times,* 6 March 1936, p. 8; LNU, *Minutes,* 17th Annual Meeting, 19–23 June 1936, p. 67. Conservatives still in the LNU complained that the LNU could not resist defence measures whilst assailing the government for not taking action against Italy and Japan. Sir Roger Keyes to Cecil, 20 January 1936, Cecil Papers, Add. 51136.
35. National Executive Council Minutes, Meeting of the PLP, NEC and TUC Council, 4 March 1936, Labour Party Archives; Dalton, *Fateful Years,* p. 90.
36. Chiefs of Staff Sub-Committee of the CID, Annual Review, 1933, CAB 22/244. CP 264(33), 12 October 1933, National Archives. As Chatfield subsequently insisted: 'Collective security inflicted on the Chiefs of Staff impossible responsibilities', *It Might Happen Again,* London: Heinemann, 1947, p. 87. Also, LNU, *The League and the Crisis: Making Collective Defence Effective,* September 1936, p. 25.
37. The 1936 White Paper reflected Neville Chamberlain's concern to avoid the financial and psychological objections to a large military commitment. General Dill (Director-General of Military Operations and Intelligence) complained of British unpreparedness for a continental war; the service ministers, he revealed, gave no strategic guidance, and had no policy to substitute for rapprochements with Germany. Cited in Donald McLachlan, *In the Chair; Barrington-Ward of 'The Times' 1927–1948,* London: Weidenfeld & Nicholson, 1971, p. 125. Liddell Hart thought land forces would be unable to reach the Continent in time to affect the course of a battle and believed the French would be satisfied with a token force. Conversation with Halifax, 22 January 1936, Liddell Hart Papers, 'Notes for History'; Liddell Hart to Temperley, 23 November 1936, ibid., In 1936 W.G. Carlton Hall, and Lt.-Col. Coulthred Thompson were in a minority in proposing a large expansion of the Regular and Territorial forces. Thompson letter, *The Times,* 9 March 1936, p. 10; W.G. Carlton Hall, 'British Re-armament', *Journ. RUSI,* Vol. 79, August 1934, pp. 595–9.
38. 299 *H.C. Deb.,* 5s., 40 (11 March 1935).
39. 100 *H.L. Deb.,* 5s., 535 (8 April 1936).
40. Lord Lloyd, 'The Need for the Rearmament of Great Britain: Its Justification and Scope', *Journ. R.I.I.A.,* Vol. 15, No. 1, pp. 57–79 (p. 69).
41. *Daily Mail,* 28 November 1933, p. 12; 30 November 1933, p. 10; Lord Rothermere, *Warnings and Predictions,* London: Eyre & Spottiswoode, 1939, pp. 14ff. The *Mail* (25 March 1935) announced that Germany already possessed 10,000 planes, based on Hitler's verbal statement to Rothermere

given as a favour. Rothermere to Croft, 8 May 1935, Croft Papers, RO/8, File 1/17. This was utter nonsense; as Roskill points our (Hankey, III, p. 668), there were probably only a tenth that number.

42. Speech at Camberwell, 1 November 1935, in *Daily Telegraph*, 2 November 1935, p. 14.

43. National Union of Conservative and Unionist Associations, Minutes of Annual Conference, 4–5 October 1934, pp. 24–6; 3–4 October 1935, pp. 26–30.

44. Norman Angell, in *Labour*, Vol. 3, No. 9, 1936, p. 208.

45. 285 *H.C. Deb.*, 5s., 1043 (6 February 1934). Churchill stipulated that Britain could only agree to revision of Versailles from a position of military strength. *Daily Mail*, 9 July 1934, p. 10.

46. Cecil, 100 *H.L. Deb.*, 5s., 152 (19 March 1936); Samuel (Nat. Lib., Darwen) 299 *H.C. Deb.*, 5s., 65 (11 March 1935); Mander (Nat. Lib., Wolverhampton E.), ibid., 132.

47. Dalton, pp. 63–4, 90.

48. Liddell Hart to Davies, 28 March 1935, Liddell Hart Papers, Correspondence Files. Internationals claimed vindication: *New Commonwealth*, Vol. 3, No. 5, February 1935, p. 265; LNU, *The League Succeeds*, Leaflet No. 1 (London, 1935). For government policy during the crisis, see, C.J. Hill, 'Great Britain and the Saar Plebiscite of 13 January 1935', *Journ. Contemp. Hist.*, Vol. 9, No. 2, April 1974, pp. 121–42.

49. See, e.g., *Daily Herald*, 4 February 1935, p. 10; Arnold-Forster, in *Peace*, March 1935, pp. 8–9. Noel Baker argued that the pact should be accepted on condition that Germany returned to the League; ACIQ Memorandum No. 454B (March 1935); Lothian to Ribbentrop, 7 March 1935, Lothian Papers, GD 40, 17/202; LNU, *The Problem of the Air*, London, 1935, pp. 15–16. The pact was killed by Hankey and the Service Chiefs. See, Roskill, *Hankey*, III, pp. 155–64.

50. *Headway*, July 1935, p. 122; LNU, *Minutes*, General Council Meeting 4–5 December 1935, p. 61.

51. For Labour's objections to the Naval Agreement, see: Attlee, 304 *H.C. Deb.*, 5s., 534ff. (11 July 1935); Labour Party, *Annual Report*, 30 September–4 October 1935, pp. 4–6; ACIQ Memorandum No. 458A (July 1935), by Arnold-Forster. Also, Ponsonby, 97 *H.L. Deb.*, 5s., 898 (26 June 1935); For Dalton, 'The Present International Situation', *Political Quarterly*, Vol. 6, No. 3, 1935, pp. 323–32 (pp. 327–31); 'England and Europe', *Contemp. Rev.*, No. 148, August 1935, pp. 129–35 (pp. 133–34). Contrast with, Seymour Cocks (Labour, Broxtowe), 304 *H.C. Deb.*, 5s., 584 (11 July 1935); Aneurin Bevan (Labour, Ebbw Vale), 295 *H.C. Deb.*, 5s., 939 (28 November 1934).

52. *Morning Post*, 6 July 1935, p. 10; Lloyd, 97 *H.L. Deb.*, 5s., 843–50 (26 June 1935); Churchill, 304 *H.C. Deb.*, 5s., 544–5 (11 July 1935).

53. Cecil to Baldwin, 2 May 1935, Baldwin Papers, Foreign Affairs, Series B. Vol. 123 1935/2.

54. Cecil to Baldwin, 29 March 1935, Cecil Papers, Add. 51080.

55. E.g., *Headway*, May 1935, p. 82; *The Times*, 13 April 1935, p. 15.

56. *Morning Post*, 9 April 1935, p. 12. Austen Chamberlain, in *The Times*, 11 April 1935, p. 15.

57. Cecil to Eden, 6 March 1936, Cecil Papers, Add. 51083; Sir Charles E. Hobhouse, 'International Disorder', *Contemp. Rev.*, Vol. 149, May 1936, pp. 513–21 (p. 514); *The Economist*, 11 April 1936, p. 67.

58. N.A. Rose (ed.), *Baffy: The Diaries of Blanche Dugdale, 1936–1947*, London: Valentine Mitchell, 1973, p. 8.
59. In the Commons, both Churchill and Neville Chamberlain remarked on the consensus. Dalton distinguished between the Italian and German transgressions, called for a friendly gesture to Germany and opposed staff conversations with the French. 310 *H.C. Deb.*, 5s., 1435ff. (26 March 1936).
60. Londonderry to Croft, 3 July 1936, Croft Papers, LO/3/1–3. File 1/15; Marques of Londonderry, *Ourselves and Germany*, London: Robert Hale, 1938, p. 21.
61. *British Legion Journ.*, Vol. 15, No. 2, 1935. Until the end of 1936, little policy difference existed between the Foreign Office and Cabinet Ministers, when disillusion set in among the advisers and the Eden wing of the cabinet. Vansittart, for example, lost faith in colonial concessions. W.N. Medlicott, *Britain and Germany, the Search for Agreement 1930–37*, London: Athlone, 1969, pp. 27–8, 31.
62. Members of the Anglo-German Fellowship included Lord Mount Temple (President), the Lords Mottistone, Redesdale, Londonderry, Lothian, Stamp and Arnold, several Tory MPs including Sir Thomas Moore, Douglas Jerrold (editor of the right-wing Catholic *English Review*), and Sir Barry Domville, one-time Director of British Naval Intelligence. Its predecessor, the Anglo-German Association, was dissolved in the spring of 1935 because much of its liberal internationalist membership (which included Lord Reading, Cecil, Sir Archibald Sinclair and H.A.L. Fisher) opposed nazism. An Anglo-German Relations Committee included Allen, Noel-Buxton, C.R. Buxton , Bartlett, T.P. Conwell-Evans and the Quaker, H.G. Alexander. Alexander to Lothian, 6 June 1935, Lothian Papers, GD 40, 17/202; Arthur Marwick, *Clifford Allen: The Open Conspirator*, Edinburgh: Oliver & Boyd, 1964, pp. 159ff. For the Fellowship, see, Simon Haxey, *Tory M.P.*, London: Gollancz, 1939, pp. 194–238; 'Gracchus', *'Your' M.P.*, London, 1944, pp. 42–50. Keith Robbins, *Munich 1938*, London: Cassell, 1968, pp. 102ff.
63. *Peace*, July–August 1936, pp. 58–9. See also, Aldous Huxley, *What Are You Going to Do About It? The Case for Constructive Peace*, London: Chatto & Windus, 1936, pp. 24–7. Gerald Bailey (Secretary of the Peace Council) favoured the fullest use of the 'constructive proposals' in Hitler's peace offer, to Lothian, 12 March 1936, Lothian Papers, GD 40, 17/311/.
64. Labour Party, *Annual Report*, 5–9 October 1936, pp. 181ff.; Charles Roden Buxton, *The Alternative to War*, London: Allen & Unwin, 1936, p. 18; ACIQ Memorandum No. 463A, by Buxton, 11/13 March 1936; Catlin to Lothian, n.d., GD 40, 17/326; H.N. Brailsford, in NFRB, *Quarterly Journ.*, Autumn 1936, p. 35.
65. LNU, *Minutes*, 17th Annual Meeting, 19–23 June 1036, p. 47; Allen, in *Headway*, December 1936, pp. 230–1; Megan Lloyd George, in *Headway*, April 1936, p. 70; Maxwell Garnett, 'War Need Not Come', *Contemp. Rev.*, No. 149, April 1936, pp. 400–8.
66. RIIA, *Germany and the Rhineland*, London, 1936.
67. Cecil, in *Daily Herald*, 6 March 1935, p. 4; 15 April 1935, p. 10. Murray indicated that he was not averse to the transfer of an African colony on certain conditions. Murray to Cecil, 24 July 1936, Cecil Papers, Add. 51132. Dalton had hopes for disarmament discussions and a conference on colonies and markets, Diary 16, Dalton Papers. Angell and Liddell Hart were also irresolute during the Rhineland crisis. Angell Memo on Collective Security,

14 July 1936, Cecil Papers, Add. 51147; Notes on the Reoccupation of the Rhineland, 7 March 1936, Liddell Hart Papers, Notes for History. Noel Baker was a member of the Anglo-German Group, but after the Rhineland crisis he transferred to the anti-nazi organisation Focus.

68. Labour Party Annual Report, 5–9 October 1936, pp. 182–204; Dalton, *Fateful Years*, pp. 63–4; Diary Entry, 27 July 1936, Diary 16, Dalton Papers; Alan Bullock, *The Life and Times of Ernest Bevin*, London: Heinemann, 1960, I, pp. 582–93; Citrine was approached by Baldwin in September 1935 seeking trade union support for rearmament. Lord Citrine, *Men and Work: The Autobiography of Lord Citrine*, London: Hutchinson, 1964, pp. 353–4.

69. Rose (ed.), p. 8; AC to Murray, 11 March 1936, AC Papers, 41/3/24; *Headway*, April 1936, p. 72.

70. Cecil to Murray, 17 November 1936, Murray Papers; *The Crisis*, No. 16, 25 March 1936, p. 1; 100 *H.L. Deb*, 5s., 533 (8 April 1936). Cecil refused to sign a public declaration urging colonial appeasement. Noel Buxton to Cecil, 20 September 1937, Cecil Papers, Add. 51140.

71. Noel Baker, in *Headway*, April 1936, pp. 68–9. LNU, *The Reform and Development of the League of Nations*, July 1936, p. 18.

72. Cecil to Noel Baker, 28 February 1936, Cecil Papers, Add. 51108; Cecil to Murray, 30 July 1936, ibid., Add. 51132.

73. Memo on the LNU and IPC, 17 November 1936, ibid., Add. 51147; Copy of Noel Baker to Cecil, 1 January 1938, ibid., Add. 51108; LNU, *Minutes*, General Council Meeting, 15–16 December 1936, pp. 53–7. The National Peace Council gave support to the IPC on condition it did not become anti-fascist. *Peace*, September 1936, p. 90.

74. See, Ernest Bramsted, 'Apostles of Collective Security: The L.N.U. and Its Functions', *Australian Journ. Pol. & Hist.*, 13, No. 3, 1967, pp. 347–64 (pp. 360ff.). Neville Chamberlain to Cecil, 24 June 1937, Cecil Papers, Add. 51087.

75. LNU, *Minutes*, General Council Meeting, 15–17 December 1936, pp. 29–32; LNU, *Agenda (Appendix 6) and Minutes*, 18th Annual Meeting, 15–18 June 1937, pp. 40ff.; Donald S. Birn, 'The League of Nations Union and Collective Security', *Journ. Contemp. Hist.*, Vol. 9, No. 3 1974, pp. 131–59 (pp. 140–42).

76. Cecil to Halifax, 26 May 1937, Cecil Papers, Add. 51044.

77. Churchill to Cecil, 21 October 1936, Cecil Papers, Add. 51073.

78. Liberal internationalists figured prominently in the Focus group, including Cecil , Davies Angell, Murray, Eleanor Rathbone, Noel Baker, Salter and Austen Chamberlain. Eugen Spier, *Focus; A Footnote to the History of the Thirties*, London: Wolff, 1963.

79. Douglas Jerrold, *They That Take the Sword: The Future of the League of Nations*, London: Lane, 1936, p. 176; 'The League and the Future: A Commentary', *19th Century*, Vol. 118, December 1935, pp. 657–74 (p. 669); 'What Is Collective Security?', *English Rev.*, September 1935, pp. 261–69.

80. Christopher Thorne, *The Approach of War, 1938–1939*, London: Macmillan, 1973 edn., p. 22.

9 Conclusion: Retrenchment, Reform and Colonisation

1. Enclosure, Garnett to Lothian, 9 July 1934, Lothian Papers, GD 40, 17/283.
2. NFRB, *Labour's Foreign Policy* (July 1934), pp 15–16; *New Statesman*, 30 November 1935, p. 801.

3. See, David C. Lukowitz, 'British Pacifists and Appeasement: The Peace Pledge Union', *Journ. Contemp. Hist.*, Vol. 9, No. 1, 1974, pp. 115–27 (pp. 117–18).

4. Aldous Huxley (ed.), *An Encyclopaedia of Pacifism*, London: Chatto & Windus, 1937, p. 113.

5. LNU, *Minutes*, Meeting of General Council, 15–17 December 1936, pp. 24–29.

6. 99 *H.L. Deb.*, 5s, 960ff. (11 March 1936); W. G. Carlton Hall, letter in *Morning Post*, 24 December 1935, p. 7; Douglas Jerrold, *They That Take the Sword: The Future of the League of Nations*, London: John Lane, 1936.

7. Curtis to Lothian, 19 July 1936; Smuts to Lothian, 22 June 1936, Lothian Papers, GD 40, 17/319, 323; Smuts to Murray 29 September 1936, Murray Papers.

8. Lord Lothian, 'World Crisis', *Round Table*, Vol. 26, No, 103, 1936, pp. 449–59; Lothian to Eden, 3 June 1936, Lothian Papers, GD 40, 17/445.

9. Andrew Stedman, *Alternatives to Appeasement: Neville Chamberlain and Hitler's Germany*, London: I.B. Tauris, 2011, p. 104.

10. *Army Quarterly*, Vol. 32, No. 2, 1936, pp. 193–95; *The Times*, 30 June 1936, p. 17.

11. *The Times*, 21 November 1936, p.14.

12. AC to Murray, 25 June 1936, AC Papers, 41/3/53.

13. Chamberlain to Lothian, 10 June 1936, Lothian Papers, GD 40, 17/445.

14. *Labour Party Annual Report*, 4–8 October 1937, pp. 3–4. *Labour* (August 1936) expressed alarm at talk about reform of the League.

15. Herbert Morrison, 'A New Start with the League of Nations', 21 August 1936, Labour Party Archives, Documents on the European situation from 1935.

16. C. Delisle Burns, in *Spectator*, 29 May 1936, p. 981.

17. ACIQ Memoranda Nos. 468A (29 July 1936); 473A (December 1936) and Noel Baker, Memorandum No. 480 (May 1937); Leonard Woolf, 'The Ideal of the League Remains', *Political Quarterly*, Vol. 7, No. 2, 1936 pp. 330–45; 'The Resurrection of the League', ibid., Vol. 8, No. 2, 1937, pp. 337–52 (pp. 344–50).

18. H.N. Brailsford, 'Class War Among the Nations', *New Republic*, 87 (19 August 1936), pp 41–43; *Towards a New League*, London: New Statesman, 1936; G.D.H. Cole, *The People's Front*, London: Gollancz, 1937, p. 6.

19. Brailsford to Cripps, 31 July 1936, Cripps Papers, File 591; Cole, 'A British People's Front: Why and How?', *Political Quarterly*, Vol. 7, No. 4, 1936, pp. 490–98. Cripps advocated a 'democratic' bloc to resist fascist aggression, *World Rev. of Revs.*, Vol. 1, No. 5, 1936, p. 16.

20. *Labour Monthly*, May 1936, p. 304; August 1936, p. 469.

21. R.W.B. Clarke, in NFRB, *Quarterly Journ.*, No. 13, Spring 1937, pp. 4–6.

22. LNU, *The League and the Crisis: Making Collective Defence Effective* (September 1936), pp. 14–16. Other LNU pamphlets in the campaign were: *Collective Resistance to Aggression* (1936); *Collective Security or helping each other in defence* (1937); *More Members and More Money* (June 1937).

23. Sir Arthur Salter, 'The Future of the League: Immediate Policy', *Spectator*, 12 June 1936, pp. 1071–72; 'Reform of the League', *Political Quarterly*, Vol. 7, No. 4, 1936, pp. 472–73; LNU, *The Reform and Development of the League of Nations* (July 1936), p. 15. The New Fabian Research Bureau also found inadequacies in Article 19 and suggested qualified majorities in voting on recommendations under its terms: *Revision of Treaties and Changes in International Law* (1934), p. 18.

24. Sir John Fischer Williams, *Some Aspects of the Covenant of the League of Nations*, London: Oxford University Press, 1934, pp. 179–82. See also, similar comments by: G.M. Gathorne-Hardy, 'Territorial Revision and Article

19 of the League Covenant', *Journ. RIIA*, Vol. 14, No. 6, 1935, pp. 818–36; A.J. Toynbee, 'The Lessons of History', in Charles A.W. Manning (ed.), *Peaceful Change. An International Problem*, London: Chatto & Windus, 1937), pp. 29–38.

25. LNU, *Reform and Development*, p. 7; LNU, *Minutes*, 18th Annual Meeting, 15–18 June 1937, p. 52.

26. John Eppstein, in *Headway*, June 1936, p. 112; Cecil to Halifax 30 July 1936, Cecil Papers, Add. 51084.

27. LNU, *Minutes*, Meeting of General Council, 15–17 December 1936, p. 20 (Maj. C.F. Entwhistle); Murray to Cecil, 11 August 1936, Murray Papers; Cecil to Halifax, 30 July 1936 Cecil Papers, Add. 51084.

28. E.H. Carr, 'Public Opinion as a Safeguard of Peace', *Journ R.I.IA*. Vol. 15 No. 6, 1936, pp. 846–62 (p. 861); Burns (n. 16 above).

29. Cecil to Halifax, 30 July 1936, Cecil Papers, Add. 51084; LNU, *Minutes*, 17th Annual Meeting, 19–23 June 1936, p. 43.

30. Cecil to Halifax (n. 29 above); LNU, *Minutes*, Meeting of General Council, 15–17 December 1936, pp. 18–19; LNU, *The League and the Crisis: Making Collective Defence Effective* (September 1936), p. 20.

31. Norman Angell, *The Defence of Empire*, London: Hamish Hamilton, 1937, p. 211; Earl of Lytton, 'The Future of the League: Basic Principles', *Spectator*, 22 May 1936, p. 923.

32. Sir Alfred Zimmern, *The League of Nations and the Rule of Law, 1918–35*, London: Macmillan, 1936, pp. 277–84, 460; 'The Testing of the League', *Foreign Affairs* (New York), Vol. 14, No. 3, 1936, pp. 385–86.

33. Zimmern, 'The Problem of Collective Security', in Quincy Wright (ed.), *Neutrality and Collective Security* Chicago: Chicago University Press, 1936, pp. 23, 66; 'The Future of the League: A Like-Minded Society', *Spectator*, 15 May 1936, pp. 872–73.

34. Zimmern, in Wright (ed.), pp. 49, 70.

35. Murray to G.R. Gauntlet, 21 August 1936; to Angell, 22 August 1936, Murray Papers.

36. LNU, *Minutes*, General Council Meeting, 15–17 December 1936, p. 45; 18th Annual Meeting, 15–18 June 1937, pp. 31, 34.

37. *H.C. Deb.*, 5s (2 February 1938).

38. Eden to Chamberlain, 20 February 1938, CAB 23/92f252. Eden was also more interested in arranging a partnership with the United States to protect Britain's Asian interests.

39. Keith Robbins, *Munich 1938*, London: Cassell, 1968, p. 345; Roger Eatwell, 'Munich Public Opinion, and Popular Front', *Journ. Contemp. Hist.*, Vol. 6, No. 4, 1971, pp. 122–39.

40. Cited in A.P. Thornton, *The Habit of Authority: Paternalism in British History*, London: Allen & Unwin, 1966, p. 17.

41. Gilbert Murray, *From the League to U.N.*, London: Oxford University Press, 1948, pp. 144–45. See also, Murray's essay, 'Hard Instinct: For Good and Evil', in W.G. S. Adams (ed.), *The Deeper Causes of the War and its Issues*, London: Allen & Unwin, 1940, pp. 28–55.

42. Minutes of LNU Executive Committee, 27 July 1939, Liddell Hart Papers, Disarmament Files.

43. Viscount Cecil, *All the Way*, London: Hodder & Stoughton, 1949, p. 234.

44. Michel Foucault, *The Birth of Biopolitics: Lectures at the Collège de France, 1978–1979* [orig. 2004], Basingstoke: Palgrave Macmillan edn, 2010, p. 131.

Appendix I: Group Memberships

1. *Headway*, the February editions of 1926–1931, 1935; December 1931; *LNU Yearbook*, 1933 & 1934; LNU, *Minutes*, 19th Annual Meeting, 15–17 June 1938, p. 29.
2. *New Times & Ethiopia News*, No. 2, 16 May 1936, p. 4.
3. Graham Wootton, *The Official History of the British Legion*, London: Macdonald, 1956, p. 305.
4. Colin Cross, *The Fascists in Britain*, London: Barrie & Rockliff, 1961, p. 131.
5. Neal Wood, *Communism and British Intellectuals*, London: Gollancz, 1959, p. 23; R.E. Dowse, *Left in the Centre: The Independent Labour Party, 1893–1940*, London: Longmans, 1966, p. 194; Henry Pelling, *The British Communist Party*, London: A & C Black, 1958, p. 192.
6. 'Analysis of membership, 24 July 1937', Lloyd George Papers, C/A Organisation and Policy File, Box 159.
7. NCPW, *Peace Year Book*, 1927, pp. 50ff.
8. S. Hornby, *Left Wing Pressure Groups in the British Labour Movement*, 1930–1940, University of Liverpool, 1966, p. 70.
9. Bjarne Braatoy, *Labour and War*, London: Allen & Unwin, 1934, p. 125.
10. *New Commonwealth*, February 1934, p. 63; March 1936, p. 505; *New Commonwealth Annual Reports*, 1933–34; 1935–36; 1936–37.
11. NFRB, *Quarterly Journal*, No. 11, Autumn 1936, p. 2.
12. NCPW, *Peace Year Book*, 1927, pp. 50ff.; Cmd. 5292, *Royal Commission on the Private Manufacture of and Trading in Arms (1935–36): Report*, October 1936, pp. 80ff.
13. NPC, *Peace Year Book*, 1937, p. 101; David C. Lukowitz, 'British Pacifists and Appeasement: The Peace Pledge Union', *Journal of Contemporary History*, 6, No. 3, 1971, pp. 12–38 (pp. 27, 35).
14. Ben Pimlott, 'The Socialist League: Intellectuals and the Labour Left in the 1930s', *Journal of Contemporary History*, 6, No. 3, 1971, pp. 12–38 (pp. 27, 35).
15. NCPW, *Peace Year Book*, 1927, pp. 50ff.
16. Ibid., Cmd. 5292.
17. LNU, *Annual Report*, 1931, pp. 84–6.
18. NPC, *Peace Year Book*, 1937, p. 130.
19. *New Commonwealth*, June 1934, p. 135.
20. NPC, *Peace Year Book*, 1937, pp. 91, 101.
21. *Foreign Affairs*, April 1926, p. 308.

Appendix II: Circulation Figures

1. *British Legion Journal*, Vol. 15, No. 9, March 1936, p. 359.
2. *LNU Yearbook*, 1933, p. 53.
3. *Labour Monthly*, March 1935, p. 133; Henry Pelling, *The British Communist Party*, London: A & C Black, 1958, p. 84.
4. Membership lists in issues of *Naval Review*.
5. *New Commonwealth Annual Report*, 1933–34, p. 17.
6. Edward Hyams, *The New Statesman*, London: Longmans, 1963, p. 184.
7. David Mitchell, *The Fighting Pankhursts*, London: Jonathan Cape, 1967, p. 255.

Bibliography

A   Archives

(a)   Private Papers

Adams, Vyvyan: London School of Economic and Political Science.
Alexander of Hillsborough: Churchill College, Cambridge.
Baldwin: Cambridge University Library.
Balfour: British Library.
Cecil of Chelwood: British Library.
Chamberlain (Sir Austen): University of Birmingham Library.
Cripps: Nuffield College, Oxford.
Dalton: London School of Economic and Political Science.
Liddell Hart: King's College London.
Lloyd George: Beaverbrook Library.
Lothian: Scottish Record Office.
Murray: Bodleian Library, Oxford.
Samuel: House of Lords Record Office.
Templewood: Cambridge University Library.

(b)   Reports and Minutes

Geneva Institute of International Relations: *Problems of Peace*, 1927–1936.

Labour Party:

Annual Reports, 1926–1937.

League of Nations Union:

Minutes, of Annual Meetings of the General Council, 1928–1938.
Minutes, of Meetings of the General Council in London, 1932–1938.
Minutes, of an Emergency Meeting of the General Council, 27 February 1932.
Annual Reports, of the Executive Committee to the General Council, 1929–1931.
Reports, of the Executive Committee of the London Regional Federation, 1928–
   1936.
The League of Nations Yearbook, 1933–1938.
Armaments: Their Reduction and Limitation, Report of an LNU Committee,
   October 1926.
Crisis in the Far East, Resolution adopted by the Executive Committee, 11
   February 1932.
The Private Manufacture of Arms, Report of a Special Committee of the LNU, July
   1933.
*Proposals for the Abolition of National (Military and Naval) Air Forces and for the
   Creation of an International Air Force*, approved and adopted by the Executive
   Committee of the LNU, 1 November 1934.

Final Agenda, of the meeting of the General Council, 13–15 December 1934.

Preliminary Programme, of a Conference on Aviation as an International Problem, February 1935.

The Problem of the Air, Report of a Conference on Aviation as an International Problem, 3–4 April 1935.

The Reform and Development of the League of Nations, Report by the Executive Committee, July 1936.

Minerals and War, Report on Mineral Sanctions (suggested by Sir Thomas Holland), by an LNU Committee, November 1935.

Statement of Policy, Approved by the General Council, December 1938.

Liberal Party: National Liberal Club.

National Peace Council (National Council for the Prevention of War): *Annual Reports*, 1925–1933.

Peace Year Book, 1927–1937.

National Union of Conservative and Unionist Associations: Central Office.

New Commonwealth Society: *Annual Reports*, 1932–1936.

New Fabian Research Bureau: *Revision of Treaties and Changes in International Law*, Report of the International Section of the Bureau (Chairman, Mr Leonard Woolf), 1934.

Trades Union Congress: *Annual Reports*, 1926–1937.

B Official Papers

Cabinet Papers, Public Record Office

Command Papers:

Statement Relating to Defence, Cmd. 4827, March 1935.

Statement Relating to Defence, Cmd. 5107, March 1936.

Report of the Royal Commission on the Private Manufacture of and Trading in Arms (1935–36), Cmd. 5292, October 1936.

Documents on British Foreign Policy, edited by E.L. Woodward, Rohan Butler and J.P.T. Bury.

1st series 1919–1928.

2nd series 1929–1938.

Hansard:

House of Commons Debates, 5th series.

House of Lords Debates, 5th series.

C Press and Periodicals

Daily Chronicle

Daily Express

Daily Herald

Daily News

Daily News & Westminster Gazette

Daily Mail

Daily Telegraph

Daily Worker

Manchester Guardian

Morning Post

News Chronicle

The Observer

The Times

Westminster Gazette

Periodicals

Abyssinia (LNU)
Action (BUF)
Army Quarterly
Blackshirt (BUF)
British Legion Journal
British Union Quarterly (BUF)
Clarion
Contemporary Review
The Crisis (LNU)
The Economist
Enforcing Peace (LNU)
Fabian News
Fascist Quarterly (BUF)
Foreign Affairs (New York)
Foreign Affairs (UDC)
Fortnightly Review
Headway (LNU)
Journal Royal Institute of International Affairs
Journal Royal United Service Institution
Labour
Labour Bulletin
Labour Monthly (CPGB)
Liberal Magazine
London Bulletin (London Regional Fed., LNU)
Nation & Athenaeum
Naval Review
New Commonwealth
New Leader (ILP)
New Statesman & Nation
New Times & Ethiopia News (Abyssinia Association)
Nineteenth Century & After
Peace (National Peace Council)
Political Quarterly
Quarterly Journal New Fabian Research Bureau
Round Table
Socialist Review (ILP)
Speakers Notes (LNU)
The Week
Workers Life
Workers Weekly
World Review of Reviews

D   Pamphlets

British Anti-War Movement: *The British Anti-War Movement*, by John Strachey, May 1932.

British–Italian League:

The British–Italian Bulletin, 27 December 1935.

Abyssinia, Italy, and the League of Nations, 1936.
British Union of Fascists: *Fascism for the Million*, April 1936.
Cambridge University Anti-War Committee: *British Armaments and World Peace*, Cambridge, 1936.
Communist Party of Great Britain: *The Army – Weapon for Victory*, n.d. [1941?].

Council of Action for Peace and Reconstruction:

A Call to Action, 1935.
Peace and Reconstruction, 1935.
Dante Alighieri Society: *Italian Civilization in Ethiopia*, by Mario Pigli, 1936.

Fabian Society and New Fabian Research Bureau:

Labour's Foreign Policy, by H.M. Swanwick, 1929.
The League of Nations, by George Bernard Shaw, 1929.
Labour's Foreign Policy, July 1934.
The Prevention of War or Labour and the League of Nations by H.R.G. Greaves, 1934.
Labour & War Resistance, by 'Covenanter', 1936.

Labour Party:

Protocol or Pact, by J.R.M. MacDonald, n.d. [1926?].
Arbitrate! Arbitrate! Arbitrate!, 1927.
Labour and the Nation, 1928.
Arbitration: Tory Record and Labour Policy, 1929.
Labour's Appeal to the Nation, 1929.
Disarm! Disarm! Disarm!, n.d. [1931?].
War and Socialism, October 1932.
The Communist Solar System, 1933.
Labour's Foreign Policy, by Arthur Henderson, 1933.
For Socialism and Peace, 1934.
Hawkers of Death: The Private Manufacture & Trade in Arms, by P.J. Noel Baker, January 1934.
Labour's Peace Policy: Arbitration, Security, Disarmament, by Arthur Henderson, 1934.
Nazis, Nazism, Nazidom, 1934.
The Case Against the 'National' Government, 1935.
Labour and Sanctions, by Herbert Morrison, 1935.
The Betrayal of Collective Security, by Clement Attlee, 1936.
The Demand for Colonial Territories and Equality of Economic Opportunity, 1936.
Labour and the Defence of Peace, 1936.
Labour and the Crisis in Foreign Policy, 1938.
Labour and Defence: The Truth, 1938.

League of Nations Union:

Public Opinion, by N. Angell, August 1926.
The Alternative to War: Arbitration, December 1927.
Towards Disarmament, December 1927.

A Great Opportunity, by Lord Grey, 1928.

The Optional Clause, 1931.

What is Meant by Disarmament? by G.A. Innes, 1931.

The Disarmament Conference and the League of Nations, by Rt Hon. Lord Dickinson, KBE, 1932.

International Police Force, by James R. Ashton, Leeds, 1932.

A Call to the Churches, 1933.

The Lytton Report – And After, by Rt Hon. the Earl of Lytton, March 1933.

Manchuria, 1933.

Canvassers' Answers: To objections concerning the League of Nations, by Sir Norman Angell, 1934.

Effective Pacifism, by Lord Allen, 1934.

A New Plan for Europe, 1935.

The Abyssinian Dispute, by Freda White, October 1935.

The Christian Church and the League of Nations, April 1935.

How to Defend World Peace, 1935.

The League Succeeds, 2 leaflets, 1935.

Collective Resistance to Aggression, 1936.

The Demand for Colonies, by Lionel Birch, 1936.

The League and the Crisis: Making Collective Defence Effective, September 1936.

The Tragedy of Abyssinia … A Selection of Some Recent Expressions of Feeling and Opinion by British Men and Women etc., foreward by E. Rathbone, June 1936.

Collective Security or Helping Each Other in defence, 1937.

The Four Points of the International Peace Campaign, 1937.

More Members and More Money, June 1937.

The Alternative to War or Why Fight About it? 1938.

Liberal Party:

We Must Work for Peace, by D. Lloyd George, 1928.

Peace and Disarmament, by C.J.L. Brock, August 1928.

Peace and Free Trade, by Sir Herbert Samuel, December 1928.

The Foreign Policy of the Liberal Party, n.d. [1929?].

National Declaration Committee:

Peace Ballot Leaflets, 1935.

War or Peace? The Workers' Guide to the National Declaration, 1935.

National Peace Council (National Council for the Prevention of War):

Sanctions of the League of Nations Covenant: A Debate, by H.M. Swanwick & W. Arnold-Forster, n.d. [1928?].

Ourselves and Disarmament, 1931.

'Abhor That Which Is Evil', by Rt Rev. E.W. Barnes, 1934.

New Commonwealth Society:

The Aims and Objects of the New Commonwealth, 1932.

Aviation for World Service, 1933.

An International Police Force, by C.R. Attlee, 1934.

New Statesman and Nation:

Abyssinia: The Essential Facts in the Dispute and an Answer to the Question – 'Ought We to Support Sanctions?' by 'Vigilantes', September 1935.
No More War Movement: *An Open Letter to Every Patriot*, 1932.

Peace Pledge Union:

What Are You Going to Do About It? The Case for Constructive Peace, by Aldous Huxley (1936).
Is Pacifism Scientific or Sentimental, n.d. [1937?].

Royal Institute of International Affairs:

Abyssinia and Italy, September 1935.

Socialist League:

The Break with Imperialism, by J.F. Horrabin, n.d. [1933?].
The Labour Party and the Constitution, by J.J. Laski, n.d. [1933].
Fight Now against War, by S.R. Cripps, 1935.
'National' Fascism in Britain, by S.R. Cripps, 1935.

Union of Democratic Control:

The Secret International: Armaments Firms at Work, by Dorothy Woodman, 1932.
Patriotism Ltd. An Exposure of the War Machine, by Dorothy Woodman, September 1933.

Women's International League for Peace and Freedom:
New Wars for Old, by H.M. Swanwick, 1934.

Others

Allen, Lord, *Peace in Our Time*, 1936.
Cecil, Lord, *The Moral Basis of the League of Nations*, 1923.
Cecil, Lord, *International Arbitration*, Oxford, 1928.
D'Abernon, Lord, *Foreign Policy*, 1930.
Henderson, Arthur, *Consolidating World Peace*, Oxford, 1928.
Lothian, The Marquis of, *Pacifism is Not Enough; Nor Patriotism Either*, Oxford, 1935.
Murray, Gilbert, *The Cult of Violence*, 1934.
Salter, Sir Arthur, *Political Aspects of the World Depression*, Oxford, 1932.
H.R.L. Sheppard, *We Say 'No'*, London: PPU, 1935.
Wintringham, T.H., *Air Raid Warning! Why the Royal Air Force is to be doubled*, 1934.
Woolf, Leonard, *The League and Abyssinia*, 1936.

E   Books and Articles

Adam, C.F., *Life of Lord Lloyd*, London: Macmillan, 1948.
Adelman, Paul, *The Decline of the Liberal Party, 1910–31*, London: Longmans, 1981.

Allen, Lord Clifford, 'The Hour of Decision, II, A New Plan for Collective Security', *Fortnightly Review*, July 1936, pp. 11–19.

Amery, L.S., *My Political Life*, III, *The Unforgiving Years, 1929–1940*, London: Hutchinson, 1955.

Angell, Norman, *The Defence of Empire*, London: Hamish Hamilton, 1937.

Angell, Norman, *The Peace Treaty and the Economic Chaos of Europe*, London: Swarthmore, 1919.

Angell, Norman, *This Have and Have-Not Business: Political Fantasy and Economic Fact*, London: Hamish Hamilton, 1936.

Arnold-Forster, W., 'Arbitration, Security, Disarmament', in Leonard Woolf (ed.), *The Intelligent Man's Way to Prevent War*, London: Gollancz, 1933, pp. 314–455.

Astor, Michael, *Tribal Feeling*, London: John Murray, 1964.

Baer, George W., *The Coming of the Italian-Ethiopian War*, Cambridge, MA: Harvard University Press, 1967.

Barnett, Correlli, *The Collapse of British Power*, London: Eyre Methuen, 1972.

Bartlett, Vernon, *Nazi Germany Explained*, London: Gollancz, 1933.

Bassett, Reginald, *Democracy and Foreign Policy: A Case History, The Sino-Japanese Dispute, 1931–1933*, London: Longmans, 1952.

Bayart, Jean-François, *Global Subjects: A Political Critique of Globalization*, London: Polity, [orig. 2004] 2007.

Beales, A.C.F., *The History of Peace*, London: Bell, 1931.

Beer, Max, *The League on Trial: A Journey to Geneva*, London: Allen & Unwin, 1933.

Benford, Robert D. and David A. Snow, 'Framing Processes and Social Movements: An Overview and Assessment', *Annual Review of Sociology*, Vol. 26, 2000, pp. 611–39.

Bennett, Gill, '"An Extraordinary and Mysterious Business": The Zinoviev Letter of 1924', Historians LRD No. 14, Foreign and Commonwealth Office, London, January 1999.

Bhabha, Homi K., *The Location of Culture*, London: Routledge, 1994.

Bird, Maj.-Gen. Sir W.D., 'The Renunciation of War', *Army Quarterly*, Vol. 17, No. 1, 1928, pp. 100–3.

Birn, Donald S., 'The League of Nations Union and Collective Security', *Journal of Contemporary History*, Vol. 9, No. 3, 1974, pp. 131–59.

Bisceglia, Louis, 'The Politics of a Peace Prize', *Journal of Contemporary History*, Vol. 7, Nos 3–4, 1972, pp. 263–73.

Blake, A.E., 'The Future of Air Warfare', *Fortnightly Review*, No. 127, January 1930, pp. 29–40.

Bosworth, R.J.B., 'The British Press, the Conservatives, and Mussolini, 1920–34', *Journal of Contemporary History*, Vol. 5, No. 2, 1970, pp. 163–82.

Bowley, A.L., *Some Economic Consequences of the Great War*, London: Thornton Butterworth, 1930.

Braatoy, Bjarne, *Labour and War*, London: Allen & Unwin, 1934.

Brailsford, H.N., *Olives of an Endless Age, Being a Study of this Distracted World and Its Need of Unity*, New York: Harper, 1928.

Brailsford, H.N., 'A Socialist Foreign Policy', in C. Addison (and others), *Problems of a Socialist Government*, London: Gollancz, 1933, pp. 252–86.

Brailsford, H.N., *Towards a New League*, London: New Statesman, 1936.

Brailsford, H.N., *Property or Peace?* London: Gollancz, 1936.

Brailsford, H.N., 'Class War among the Nations', *New Republic*, Vol. 87, August 1936, pp. 41–3.

Bramsted, Ernest, 'Apostles of Collective Security: The L.N.U. and Its Functions', *Australian Journal of Politics and History*, Vol. 13, No. 3, 1967, pp. 347–64.

Brand, R.H. (ed.), *The Letters of John Dove*, London: Macmillan, 1938.

Brock, C.J.L., *Peace and Disarmament*, Liberal Party pamphlet, 1928.

Brockway, A. Fenner, *Inside the Left*, London: Allen & Unwin, 1942.

Brockway, A. Fenner, *Socialism over 60 Years: The Life of Jowett of Bradford, 1864–1944*, London: Allen & Unwin, 1946.

Bullock, Alan, *The Life and Times of Ernest Bevin*, 2 Vols, London: Heinemann, 1960, I.

Burchell, Graham, Colin Gordon and Peter Miller (eds), *The Foucault Effect: Studies in Governmentality*, Chicago, IL: University of Chicago Press, 1991.

Burge, Squadron-Leader C.G., *British Legion Journal*, Vol. 9, No. 7, 1930, p. 186.

Burney, Cdr. Sir C.D., *The World, the Air and the Future*, London: Knopf, 1929.

Burns, Emile, *Abyssinia and Italy*, London: Gollancz, 1935.

Bussey, Gertrude and Margaret Tims, *Women's International League for Peace and Freedom 1915–1965*, London: Allen & Unwin, 1965.

Buxton, Charles Roden, *The Alternative to War*, London: Allen & Unwin, 1936.

Carlton, David, 'Disarmament with Guarantees: Lord Cecil, 1922–1927', *Disarmament and Arms Control*, Vol. 3, No. 2, 1965, pp. 143–64.

Carlton, David, 'Great Britain and the Coolidge Naval Disarmament Conference of 1927', *Political Science Quarterly*, Vol. 83, No. 4, 1968, pp. 573–98.

Carlton, David, 'Great Britain and the League Council Crisis of 1926', *Historical Journal*, Vol. 9, No. 2, 1968, pp. 354–64.

Carlton, David, 'The Anglo-French Compromise on Arms Limitation, 1928', *Journal of British Studies*, Vol. 8, No. 2, 1969, pp. 141–62.

Carlton, David, *MacDonald versus Henderson: The Foreign Policy of the Second Labour Government*, London: Macmillan, 1970.

Carlton Hall, Major W.G., 'British Re-Armament', *Journ. R.U.S.I.*, Vol. 79, August 1934, pp. 595–9.

Carr, E.H., 'Public Opinion as a Safeguard of Peace', *Journ. R.I.I.A.*, Vol. 15, No. 6, 1936, pp. 846–62.

Carr, E.H., *The Twenty Years' Crisis 1919–1939: An Introduction to the Study of International Relations*, London: Macmillan, 2nd edn, 1946.

Ceadel, Martin, 'The "King and Country" Debate, 1933: Student Politics, Pacifism and the Dictators', *Historical Journal*, Vol. 22, No. 2, 1979, pp. 397–422.

Ceadel, Martin, *Pacifism in Britain, 1914–1945: The Defining of a Faith*, Oxford: Oxford University Press, 1980.

Ceadel, Martin, *Semi-detached Idealists: The British Peace Movement and International Relations, 1854–1945*, Oxford: Oxford University Press, 2000.

Ceadel, Martin, *Living the Great Illusion: Sir Norman Angell, 1872–1967*, Oxford: Oxford University Press, 2009.

Cecil, Robert, *The Moral Basis of the League of Nations*, London: Lindsey Press, 1923.

Cecil, Robert, *The Way of Peace*, London: Philip Allan, 1928.

Cecil, Robert, 'The Party System and Peace', in *The Way of Peace: Essays and Addresses*, London: Philip Allan, 1928, pp. 15ff.

Cecil, Robert, *A Great Experiment*, London: Jonathan Cape, 1941.

Cecil, Robert, *All the Way*, London: Hodder & Stoughton, 1949.

Cecil, Robert and W. Arnold-Forster, 'The Freedom of the Seas', *Journ. RIIA*, Vol. 8, No. 2, 1929, pp. 89–117.

Chamberlain, Austen, 'Great Britain as a European Power', *Journ. RIIA*, Vol. 9, No. 2, 1930, pp. 180–8.

Chamberlain, W.J., *Fighting for Peace: The Story of the War Resistance Movement*, London: NMWM, 1929.

Chamier, Air Commodore J.A., 'Air Bombing and Air Disarmament, Part II', *Army Quarterly*, Vol. 27, No. 2, 1934, pp. 284–8.

Colás, Alexandro, *International Civil Society*, Cambridge: Polity, 2002.

Charlton, L.E.O., *War from the Air: Past, Present, Future*, London: Nelson, 1935.

Charvet, Jean-Félix, *L'Influence Britannique dans la S.D.N.*, Paris: Rodstein, 1938.

Chatfield, Lord, *It Might Happen Again*, London: Heinemann, 1947.

Citrine, Lord, *Men and Work: The Autobiography of Lord Citrine*, London: Hutchinson, 1964.

Cole, G.D.H., 'A British People's Front: Why and How?', *Political Quarterly*, Vol. 7, No. 4, 1936, pp. 490–98.

Cole, G.D.H., *The People's Front*, London: Gollancz, 1937.

Cole, G.D.H. and Margaret Cole, *The Intelligent Man's Review of Europe To-Day*, London: Gollancz, 1933.

Cole, Margaret (ed.), *Beatrice Webb's Diaries 1924–1932*, London: Longmans, 1956.

Conwell-Evans, T.P., *Foreign Policy from a Back Bench, 1904–1918: A Study Based on the Papers of Lord Noel-Buxton*, Oxford: Oxford University Press, 1932.

Cooper, Duff, *Old Men Forget*, London: Dutton, 1954.

Cortright, David, *Peace: A History of Movements and Ideas*, New York: Cambridge University Press, 2008.

Cowes, P.R.C., 'The Influence of Aviation on International Affairs', *Journ. RIIA*, Vol. 8, No. 4, 1929, pp. 289–317.

Cowling, Maurice, *The Impact of Labour 1920–1924: The Beginning of Modern British Politics*, Cambridge: Cambridge University Press, 1971.

Cox, Robert W., 'Civil Society at the Turn of the Millennium: Prospects for an Alternative World Order', *Review of International Studies*, Vol. 25, No. 1, 1999, p. 5.

Cripps, S.R., *Fight Now against War*, London: Socialist League, 1935.

Cripps, S.R., *The Struggle for Peace*, London: Gollancz, 1936.

Cripps, S.R., *World Review of Reviews*, Vol. 1, No. 5, 1936.

Croft, Lord Henry Page, *My Life of Strife*, London: Hutchinson, 1948.

Crosby, G.R., *Disarmament and Peace in British Politics 1914–19*, Cambridge, MA: Harvard University Press, 1957.

Cross, Colin, *The Fascists in Britain*, London: Barrie 7 Rockliff, 1961.

Crozier, Brig.-Gen. F.P, *A Brass Hat in No Man's Land*, London: Jonathan Cape, 1930.

Cunninghan of Hyndhope, Lord A.B., *A Sailor's Odyssey*, London: Hutchinson, 1951.

Cushendun, Lord, 'Disarmament', *Journ. RIIA*, Vol. 7, No. 2, 1928, pp. 77–93.

Dalton, Hugh, *Towards the Peace of Nations: A Study in International Politics*, London: Routledge, 1928.

Dalton, Hugh, 'British Foreign Policy 1929–31', *Political Quarterly*, Vol. 11, No. 4, 1931, pp. 484–505.

Dalton, Hugh, *Call Back Yesterday, 1887–1931*, London: Muller, 1953.

Dalton, Hugh, *The Fateful Years, 1931–1945*, London: Muller, 1957.

Dangerfield, George, *The Strange Death of Liberal England*, New York: Harrison Smith & Robert Haas, 1935.

Davies, Lord David, *The Problem of the Twentieth Century*, London: Benn, 1930.

Davies, Lord David, *Suicide or Sanity?*, London: Williams & Norgate, 1932.

Davis, S., 'The British Labour Party and British Foreign Policy, 1933–1939', PhD thesis, University of London, 1950.

Debrix, François, *Re-Envisioning Peacekeeping: The United Nations and the Mobilization of Ideology*, Minneapolis, MN: University of Minnesota Press, 1999.

Dickinson, G.W., 'Dis-arm or Re-arm?'*19th Century*, Vol. 111, February 1932, pp. 129–39.

Dowse, R.E., *Left in the Centre: The Independent Labour Party*, 1893–1940, London: Longmans, 1966.

Doyle, Michael W., *Ways of War and Peace*, New York: W.W. Norton, 1997.

Dubin, Martin David, 'Toward the Concept of Collective Security: The Bryce Group's "Proposals for the Avoidance of War"', 1914–1917', *International Organization*, Vol. 24, No. 2, 1970, pp. 288–318.

Eatwell, Roger, 'Munich Public Opinion, and Popular Front', *Journal of Contemporary History*, Vol. 6, No. 4, 1971, pp. 122–39.

Egerton, Rear-Admiral W.A., 'Practical Security', *RUSI Journ.*, Vol. 76, February 1931, pp. 27–36.

Feiling, Keith, *The Life of Neville Chamberlain*, London: Macmillan, 1970.

Fenn, L. Anderson (ed.), *Problems of the Socialist Transition*, London: Gollancz, 1934.

Foucault, Michel, *Society Must be Defended: Lectures at the Collège de France, 1975–1976*, New York: Picador edn, [orig. 1997] 2003.

Foucault, Michel, *The Birth of Biopolitics: Lectures at the Collège de France, 1978–1979*, Basingstoke: Palgrave/Macmillan edn, [orig. 2004] 2010.

Foucault, Michel, *The Government of Self and Others: Lectures at the Collège de France 1982–1983*, New York: Picador, 2011.

Fuller, Maj.-Gen. J.F.C., 'Aggression and Aggressive Weapons', *Army Ordnance*, Vol. 14, No. 79, 1933, pp. 7–11.

Fuller, Maj.-Gen. J.F.C., *The First of the League Wars: Its Lessons and Omens*, London: Eyre & Spottiswoode, 1936.

Gannon, Franklin Reid, *The British Press and Germany, 1936–39*, Oxford: Clarendon, 1971.

Garnett, Maxwell, 'War Need Not Come', *Contemporary Review*, No. 149, April 1936, pp. 400–8.

Gathorne-Hardy, G.M., 'Territorial Revision and Article 19 of the League Covenant', *Journ. RIIA*, Vol. 14, No. 6, 1935, pp. 818–36.

Gellner, Ernest, *Nations and Nationalism*, Ithaca, NY: Cornell University Press, 1983.

Gibbs, Philip, *Across the Frontiers*, London: Michael Joseph, 1938.

Gilbert, Martin and Richard Gott, *The Appeasers*, London: Weidenfeld & Nicholson, 1967.

Giugni, Marco, *Social Protest and Policy Change: Ecology, Antinuclear, and Peace Movements in Comparative Perspective*, Lanham, MD: Rowman & Littlefield, 2004.

Giugni, Marco, Doug McAdam and Charles Tilly (eds), *How Social Movements Matter*, Minneapolis, MN: University of Minnesota Press, 1999.

Goldman, Aaron L., 'Sir Robert Vansittart's Search for Italian Co-operation against Hitler 1933–36', *Journal of Contemporary History*, Vol. 9, No. 3, 1974, pp. 93–130.

Gooch, G.P. and H. Temperley (eds), *British Documents on the Origins of the War: 1898–1914*, 11 Vols, London: HMSO, 1926–1938.

Gramsci, Antonio, *The Prison Notebooks*, London: Lawrence & Wishart, [orig. 1949] 1971.

Granzow, Brigitte, *A Mirror of Nazism: British Opinion and the Emergence of Hitler 1929–1933*, London: Gollancz, 1964.

Gretton, Sir Peter, *Former Naval Person*, London: Cassell, 1968.

Grey, Sir Edward, *Twenty-five Years*, 2 Vols, London: Hodder & Stoughton, 1925.

Grey, Sir Edward, 'Freedom of the Seas', *Foreign Affairs* (New York), Vol. 8, No. 3, 1930, pp. 325–35.

Guttsman, W.L., *The British Political Elite*, London: MacGibbon & Kee, 1963.

Hankey, Lord, 'The Study of Disarmament' (compiled 1925), in *Diplomacy by Conference: Studies in Public Affairs 1920–1946*, London: Ernest Benn, 1946.

Hardt, Michael and Toni Negri, *Empire*, Cambridge, MA: Harvard University Press, 2000.

Harrod, R.F., *The Life of John Maynard Keynes* London: Macmillan, 1972.

Harvey, John (ed.), *The Diplomatic Diaries of Oliver Harvey, 1937–1940*, London: Collins, 1970.

Haxey, Simon, *Tory M.P.*, London: Gollancz, 1939.

Heller, Richard, 'East Fulham Revisited', *Journal of Contemporary History*, Vol. 6, No. 3, 1971, pp. 172–96.

Henderson, Arthur, *Consolidating World Peace*, Oxford: Clarendon, 1931.

Higgott, Richard, Geoffrey Underhill and Andreas Bieler, *Non-State Actors and Authority in the Global System*, Abingdon: Routledge, 2000.

Higham, Robin, *The Military Intellectuals in Britain: 1918–1939*, New Brunswick, NJ: Rutgers University Press, 1966.

Hill, C.J., 'Great Britain and the Saar Plebiscite of 13 January 1935', *Journal of Contemporary History*, Vol. 9, No. 2, April 1974, pp. 121–42.

Hirst, Francis W., *The Consequences of the War to Great Britain*, London: Oxford University Press, 1934.

Hobhouse, Sir Charles E., 'International Disorder', *Contemporary Review*, Vol. 149, May 1936, pp. 513–21.

Hobson, J.A. *Wealth and Life: A Study in Values*, London: Macmillan, 1929.

Hobson, J.A., *From Capitalism to Socialism*, London: Hogarth, 1932.

Holt, Andrew, '"No More Hoares to Paris": British Foreign Policymaking and the Abyssinian Crisis, 1935', *Review of International Studies*, Vol. 37, No. 3, 2011, pp. 1382–401.

Hornby, Stephen, *Left Wing Pressure Groups in the British Labour Movement, 1930–1940*, Liverpool: University of Liverpool Press, 1966.

Howard, Michael, *The Continental Commitment*, London: Temple Smith, 1972.

Howard, Michael, *War and the Liberal Conscience*, Oxford: Oxford University Press, 1989.

Hutton, D. Graham, 'British Foreign Policy and the Peace of Europe', *19th Century*, Vol. 113, April 1933, pp. 396–406.

Huxley, Aldous, *What Are You Going to Do About It? The Case for Constructive Peace*, London: Chatto & Windus, 1936.

Huxley, Aldous (ed.), *An Encyclopaedia of Pacifism*, London: Chatto & Windus, 1937.

Hyams, Edward, *The New Statesman*, London: Longmans, 1963.

Iklé, F.C., *The Social Impact of Bomb Destruction*, Norman, OK: Oklahoma University Press, 1958.

Ismay, Lord, *The Memoirs of General the Lord Ismay*, London: Heinemann, 1960.

Jahn, Beate, 'Liberal Internationalism: From Ideology to Empirical Theory – and Back Again', *International Theory*, Vol. 1, No. 3, 2009, pp. 409–38.

James, Robert Rhodes, *Chips: The Diaries of Sir Henry Channon*, London: Weidenfeld & Nicholson, 1967.

James, Robert Rhodes, *Memoirs of a Conservative: J.C.C. Davidson's Memoirs and Papers, 1910–1937*, London: Weidenfeld & Nicholson, 1969.

James, Robert Rhodes, *Churchill: A Study in Failure 1900–1939*, London: Weidenfeld & Nicholson, 1970.

Jerrold, Douglas, 'The League and the Future: A Commentary', *19th Century*, Vol. 118, December 1935, pp. 657–74.

Jerrold, Douglas, 'What Is Collective Security?' *English Review*, September 1935, pp. 261–9.

Jerrold, Douglas, *They That Take the Sword: The Future of the League of Nations*, London: John Lane, 1936.

Johnson, Douglas, 'Austen Chamberlain and the Locarno Agreements', *University of Birmingham Historical Journal*, Vol. 8, No. 1, 1962, pp. 62–81.

Johnson, Gaynor (ed.), *Locarno Revisited: European Diplomacy 1920–1929*, London: Cass, 2004.

Jones, Charles, *Global Justice: Defending Cosmopolitanism*, Oxford: Oxford University Press, 1999.

Kaldor, Mary, *Global Civil Society: An Answer to War?* London: Polity, 2003.

Kaplan, Robert, *Balkan Ghosts: A Journey Through History*, New York: Picador, 2005.

Kapoor, Ilan, *The Postcolonial Politics of Development*, Abingdon: Routledge, 2008.

Keck, Margaret and Kathryn Sikkink, *Activists beyond Borders: Advocacy Networks in International Politics*. Ithaca, NY: Cornell University Press, 1988.

Kennedy, Thomas C., 'The Next Five Years Group and the Failure of the Politics of Agreement in Britain', *Canadian Journal of History*, Vol. 9, No. 1, 1974, pp. 45–68.

Kenworthy, Lieutenant-Commander J.M., 'Disarmament: The Freedom of the Seas', *19th Century*, Vol. 111, 1932, pp. 35–48.

Keynes, John Maynard, *The General Theory of Employment, Interest and Money*, London: Macmillan, 1936.

Khagram, Sanjeev, James V. Riker and Kathryn Sikkink (eds), *Restructuring World Politics: Transnational Social Movements, Networks, and Norms*, Minneapolis, MN: University of Minnesota Press, 2002.

Kitching, Carolyn J., *Britain and the Problem of International Disarmament, 1919–1934*, Abingdon: Routledge, 1999.

Laski, H.J., *Problems of Peace*, London: Allen & Unwin, 1932.

Laski, H.J., 'The Economic Foundations of Peace', in Leonard Woolf (ed.), *The Intelligent Man's Way to Prevent War*, London: Gollancz, 1933.

Laski, H.J., 'The General Election 1935', *Political Quarterly*, Vol. 7, No. 1, 1936, pp. 1–15.

Lentin, Anthony, *Lloyd George and the Lost Peace: From Versailles to Hitler, 1919–1940*, Basingstoke: Palgrave Macmillan, 2001.

Liddell Hart, B.H., *The British Way in Warfare*, London: Faber & Faber, 1932.

Liddell Hart, B.H., *The Memoirs of Captain Liddell Hart*, 2 Vols, London: Cassell, 1965, I.

Livingstone, Adelaide, *The Peace Ballot: The Official History*, London: Gollancz, 1935.

Lloyd George, D., *We Must Work for Peace*, London: Liberal Publication Dept, 1928.

Lloyd George, D., *The Truth About Reparations and War Debts*, London: Heinemann, 1932.

Lloyd, Lord, 'The Need for the Rearmament of Great Britain: Its Justification and Scope', *Journ. RIIA*, Vol. 15, No. 1, pp. 57–79.

Londonderry, Marquess of, *Ourselves and Germany*, London: Robert Hale, 1938.

Lothian, Lord (Philip Kerr), 'World Crisis', *Round Table*, Vol. 26, No. 103, 1936, pp. 449–59.

Lugard, Lord, 'The Basis of the Claim for Colonies', *Journ. RIIA*, Vol. 15, No. 1, 1936, pp. 3–25.

Lukowitz, David C., 'British Pacifists and Appeasement: The Peace Pledge Union', *Journal of Contemporary History*, Vol. 9, No. 1, 1974, pp. 115–27.

Lynch, Cecelia, *Interpreting Interwar Peace Movements in World Politics*, Ithaca, NY: Cornell University Press, 1999.

Mac Ginty, Roger, 'The Liberal Peace at Home and Abroad', *British Journal of Politics and International Relations*, Vol. 11, No. 4, 2009, pp. 690–708.

MacDonald, Rt Hon. J. Ramsay, 'The London Naval Conference 1930', *Journ. R.I.I.A.*, Vol. 9, No. 4, 1930, pp. 429–51.

Manning, C.A.W. (ed.), *Peaceful Change: An International Problem*, London: Macmillan, 1937.

Marder, Arthur, 'The Royal Navy and the Ethiopian Crisis of 1935–36', *American Historical Review*, Vol. 75, No. 5, 1970, pp. 1327–56.

Marriott, Sir John, 'England and Italy', *Fortnightly Review*, August 1935, pp. 194–202.

Martin, *Editor: A Second Volume of Autobiography 1931–45*, London: Hutchinson, 1968.

Marwick, Arthur, *Clifford Allen: The Open Conspirator*, Edinburgh: Oliver & Boyd, 1964.

McCallum, R.B., *Public Opinion and the Last Peace*, London: Oxford University Press, 1944.

McLachlan, Donald, *In the Chair: Barrington-Ward of 'The Times' 1927–1948* , London: Weidenfeld & Nicholson, 1971.

Medlicott, W.N., *Britain and Germany, the Search for Agreement 1930–37*, London: Athlone, 1969.

Menon, V.K. Krishna (ed.), *Young Oxford and War*, London: Selwyn & Blount, 1934.

Middlemas, Keith and John Barnes, *Baldwin: A Biography*, London: Weidenfeld & Nicholson, 1969.

Middlemas, Keith, *Diplomacy of Illusion: The British Government and Germany 1937–39*, London: Weidenfeld & Nicholson, 1972.

Miller, K.E., *Socialism and Foreign Policy: Theory and Practice in Britain to 1931*, The Hague: Martinus Nijhoff, 1967.

Milne, A.A. *Peace with Honour*, London: Methuen, 1934.

Milner, Viscount, *Questions of the Hour*, London: Nelson, 2nd edn, 1925.

Mitchell, David, *The Fighting Pankhursts: A Study in Tenacity*, London: Jonathan Cape, 1967.

Monroe, Elizabeth, 'Abyssinia as a Colonial Asset', *Fortnightly Review*, November 1935, pp. 541–9.

Montgomery-Massingberd, Lieut.-Gen. Sir A.A., 'The Role of the Army in Imperial Defence', *Army Quarterly*, Vol. 15, No. 2, 1928, pp. 235–58.

Mowat, Prof., R.B., 'The Mischief of Revisionism', *Fortnightly Review*, February 1936, pp. 160–9.

Murray, Gilbert, 'Revision of the Peace Treaties', in Leonard Woolf (ed.), *The Intelligent Man's Way to Prevent War*, London: Gollancz, 1933, pp. 67–153.

Murray, Gilbert, *The Cult of Violence*, London: Lovat Dickinson, 1934.

Murray, Gilbert, 'Hard Instinct: For Good and Evil', in W.G.S. Adams (ed.), *The Deeper Causes of the War and Its Issues*, London: Allen & Unwin, 1940, pp. 28–55.

Murray, Gilbert, *From the League to U.N.*, London: Oxford University Press, 1948.

Next Five Years Group, *The Next Five Years, an Essay in Political Agreement*, London: Macmillan, 1935.

Nicholson, Harold, 'Modern Diplomacy and British Public Opinion', *Journ. RIIA*, Vol. 14, No. 5, 1935, pp. 599–618.

Noel Baker, P.J., *The Geneva Protocol*, London: King & Son, 1925.

Noel Baker, P.J., *Disarmament and the Coolidge Conference*, London: Hogarth, 1927.

Noel Baker, P.J., 'Disarmament', *Journ. RIIA*, Vol. 13, No. 1, 1934, pp. 3–26.

O'Riordan, Elspeth Y., *Britain and the Ruhr Crisis*, Basingstoke: Palgrave, 2001.

Overy, Richard, *The Morbid Age*, London: Penguin, 2010.

Pelling, Henry, *The British Communist Party: A Historical Profile*, London: A & C Black, 1958.

Pethick-Lawrence, F.W., *Fate Has Been Kind*, London: Hutchinson, 1943.

Petrie, Sir Charles, *Mussolini*, London: Holme Press, 1931.

Pigou, A.C., *Industrial Fluctuations*, London: Macmillan, 1927.

Pimlott, Ben, 'The Socialist League: Intellectuals and the Labour Left in the 1930s', *Journal of Contemporary History*, Vol. 6, No. 3, 1971, pp. 12–38.

Ponsonby, Arthur, 'Disarmament by Example', *Journ RIIA*, Vol. 7, No. 4, 1928, pp. 225–40.

Postgate, Raymond, *The Life of George Lansbury*, London: Longmans, 1951.

Price, Richard, 'Review Article: Transnational Civil Society and Advocacy in World Politics', *World Politics*, Vol. 55, No. 4, 2003, pp. 579–606.

Pugh, Michael, 'Peace with Italy: BUF Reactions to the Abyssinian War 1935–1936', *Wiener Library Bulletin*, Vol. 27, No. 32, 1974, pp. 11–18.

Putnam, Robert D., Robert Leonardi and Raffaella Y. Nanetti, *Making Democracy Work: Civic Traditions in Modern Italy*, Princeton, NJ: Princeton University Press, 1993.

Richmond, Oliver P., *A Post-Liberal Peace*, Abingdon: Routledge, 2011.

Richmond, Oliver P. and Audra Mitchell (eds), *Hybrid Forms of Peace: Everyday Agency and Post-Liberalism*, Basingstoke: Palgrave/Macmillan, 2011.

Richmond, Oliver P. and Henry C. Carey, *Mitigating Conflict: NGOs in Peace Processes*, London: Cass, 2003.

Richmond, Sir Herbert, 'Immediate Problems of Naval Reduction', *Foreign Affairs* (New York), Vol. 9, No. 3, 1931, pp. 371–88.

Robbins, Keith G., 'Lord Bryce and the First World War', *Historical Journal*, Vol. 10, No. 2, 1967, pp. 255–77.

Robbins, Keith, *Munich 1938*, London: Cassell, 1968.

Robbins, Lionel, *The Great Depression*, London: Macmillan, 1934.

Robertson, James C., 'The Origins of British Opposition to Mussolini over Ethiopia', *Journal of British Studies*, Vol. 9, No. 1, 1969, pp. 122–42.

Rose, N.A. (ed.), *Baffy: The Diaries of Blanche Dugdale, 1936–1947*, London: Valentine Mitchell, 1973.

Roskill, S.W., *Naval Policy between the Wars*, I: *The Period of Anglo-American Antagonism 1919–1929*, London: Collins, 1968.

Roskill, Stephen, *Hankey: Man of Secrets*, 3 Vols, London: Collins, II, 1972; III, 1974.

Rothermere, Lord, *Warnings and Predictions*, London: Eyre & Spottiswoode, 1939.

Royal Institute of International Affairs, *Germany and the Rhineland*, London, 1936.

Royal Institute of International Affairs, *International Sanctions*, London, 1938.

Russell, Bertrand, *Which Way to Peace?* London: Jonathan Cape, 1936.

Russett, Bruce and John O'Neal, *Triangulating Peace: Democracy, Interdependence, and International Organizations*, New York: W.W. Norton, 2000.

Salter, Sir Arthur, *The Economic Consequences of the League*, London: Europa, 1927.

Salter, Sir Arthur, *The World's Economic Crisis and the Way of Escape*, London: Allen & Unwin, 1932.

Salter, Sir Arthur, *Political Aspects of the World*, Oxford: Clarendon, 1932.

Salter, Sir Arthur, *Recovery: The Second Effort*, London: Bell, rev. edn, 1933.

Salter, Sir Arthur, 'Reform of the League', *Political Quarterly*, Vol. 7, No. 4, 1936, pp. 472–3.

Salter, Sir Arthur, 'The Future of the League: Immediate Policy', *Spectator*, 12 June 1936, pp. 1071–2.

Scott, James C., *Domination and the Arts of Resistance: Hidden Transcripts*, New Haven, CT: Yale University Press, 1990.

Searle, Geoffrey R., *The Liberal Party: Triumph and Disintegration, 1986–1929*, Basingstoke: Palgrave/Macmillan, rev. edn, 2000.

Seeley, J.R., *The Expansion of England*, London: Macmillan, 1883.

Shannon, Richard T., *Gladstone and the Bulgarian Agitation 1876*, London: Nelson, 1963.

Shaw, George Bernard, *The League of Nations*, London: Fabian Society, 1929.

Shaw, George Bernard, 'As I See It', *George Bernard Shaw 1856–1950: Some of His Broadcasts* (2 November 1937), BBC Radio Enterprises Recording, REB, 32M.

Shaw, George Bernard, *Geneva: A Fancied Page of History in Three Acts*, London: Constable, 1938.

Shaw, Martin, 'Civil Society', in George Fink (ed.), *Stress of War, Conflict and Disaster*, San Diego, CA: Academic Press, 2010, pp. 200–8.

Skidelsky, Robert, *Politicians and the Slump: The Labour Government of 1929–1931*, London: Penguin, 1970.

Smuts, Gen. J.C., 'The Present International Outlook', *Journ. RIIA*, Vol. 14, No. 1, 1935, pp. 3–19.

Spaight, J.M., *Pseudo-security*, London: Longmans, 1928.

Spender, J.A., *Between Two Wars*, London: Cassell, 1943.

Spier, Eugen, *Focus: A Footnote to the History of the Thirties*, London: Wolff, 1963.

Spivak, Gayatri C., 'Can the Subaltern Speak?' In Cary Nelson and Lawrence Grossberg (eds), *Marxism and the Interpretation of Culture*, Chicago, IL: University of Illinois Press, 1988.

Stamp, Sir Josiah, *Studies in Current Problems in Finance and Government*, London: P.S. King, 1924.

Stedman, Andrew, *Alternatives to Appeasement: Neville Chamberlain and Hitler's Germany*, London: I.B. Tauris, 2011.

Strachey, John, *The British Anti-war Movement*, London: BAWM, 1933.

Swanwick, H. and W. Arnold-Forster, *Sanctions of the League of Nations Covenant: A Debate*, London, n. d. [1928].

Taylor, A.J.P. (ed.), *Off the Record: Political Interviews 1933–1943*, London: Hutchinson, 1973.

Temperley, Maj.-Gen. A.C., *The Whispering Gallery of Europe*, London: Collins, 1938.

Templewood, Viscount, *Nine Troubled Years*, London: Collins, 1954.

Thomas, W.B., *An International Police Force*, London: Allenson, 1936.

Thompson, Neville, *The Anti-Appeasers, Conservative Opposition to Appeasement in the 1930s*, Oxford: Clarendon, 1971.

Thorne, Christopher, 'The Quest for Arms Embargoes: Failure in 1933', *Journal of Contemporary History*, Vol. 5, No. 4, 1970, pp. 129–49.

Thorne, Christopher, 'Viscount Cecil, the Government and the Far Eastern Crisis of 1931', *Historical Journal*, Vol. 14, No. 4, 1971, pp. 805–26.

Thorne, Christopher, *The Limits of Foreign Policy: The West, the League and the Far Eastern Crisis of 1931–1933*, London: Hamish Hamilton, 1972.

Thorne, Christopher, *The Approach of War, 1938–1939*, London: Macmillan, 1973.

Thornton, A.P., *The Habit of Authority: Paternalism in British History*, London: Allen & Unwin, 1966.

Toynbee, Arnold J., *Survey of International Affairs 1935*, 2 Vols, London: Oxford University Press, 1936, II.

Toynbee, A.J., 'The Lessons of History', in Charles A.W. Manning (ed.), *Peaceful Change: An International Problem*, London: Chatto & Windus, 1937, pp. 29–38.

Toynbee, A.J., 'The Unity of Gilbert Murray's Life and Work', in Gilbert Murray and Friends (Jean Smith and Arnold Toynbee eds), *Gilbert Murray: An Unfinished Autobiography*, London, 1960, p. 212.

Vaucher, Paul and Paul Henri Siriex, *L'Opinion Britannique: La Société des Nations et la guerre Italo-Éthiopienne*, Paris: Centre d'Études de Politique Étrangère, 1936.

Vigilantes (pseud.), *Abyssinia: The Essential Facts in the Dispute and an Answer to the Question – "Ought We to Support Sanctions?"* London: New Statesman, 1935.

Vigilantes (Zilliacus), *Inquest on Peace*, London: Gollancz, 1935.

Walker, R.B.J., 'Social Movements/World Politics', *Millennium: Journal of International Studies*, Vol. 23, No. 3, 1994, pp. 669–700.

Watt, Donald Cameron, *Personalities and Policies*, London: Longmans, 1965.

Watt, Donald Cameron, 'The Anglo-German Naval Agreement of 1935: An Interim Judgment', *Journal of Modern History*, Vol. 28, No. 2, June 1956, pp. 155–75.

Watt, Donald Cameron, 'The Secret Laval–Mussolini Agreement of 1935 on Ethiopia', *The Middle East Journal*, Vol. 15, 1961, pp. 69–78.

Watt, Donald Cameron, *Too Serious a Business: European Armed Forces and the Approach to the Second World War*, London, 1975.

Waugh, Evelyn, *Waugh in Abyssinia*, London: Longmans, 1936.

Webster, Andrew, '"Absolutely Irresponsible Amateurs": The Temporary Mixed Commission on Armaments, 1921–1924', *Australian Journal of Politics & History*, Vol. 54, No. 3, 2008, pp. 373–88.

Wells, H.G., 'The ABC of World Peace', *After Democracy: Addresses and Papers on the Present World Situation*, London: Watts, 1932.

Wells, H.G., *After Democracy: Addresses and Papers on the Present World Situation*, London: Watts, 1932.

Wells, H.G., *The Open Conspiracy and Other Writings*, London: Modern Library, 1933, II. Wells, H.G., *The War in the Air*, London: Modern Library, [orig. 1908].

Wells, H.G., *The World of William Clissold*, 2 Vols, London: Modern Library, 1933, II.

West, Francis, *Gilbert Murray: A Life*, Beckenham: Croom Helm, 1984.

Wheeler-Bennett, John W., *The Wreck of Reparations, Being the Political Background of the Lausanne Agreement 1932*, London: Allen & Unwin, 1933.

Wheeler, Nicholas J., *Saving Strangers: Humanitarian Intervention in International Society*, Oxford: Oxford University Press, 2000.

White, Carolyn W., 'The Strange Death of Liberal England in its Time', *Albion: A Quarterly Journal Concerned with British Studies*, Vol. 17, No. 4, 1985, pp. 425–47.

Wickham Steed, H., 'Armament and Disarmament Since 1918', *RUSI Journ.*, Vol. 76, November 1931, pp. 824–42.

Willert, Sir Arthur, *Aspects of British Foreign Policy*, New Haven, CT: Yale University Press, 1928.

Williams, Andrew, *Liberalism and War: The Victors and the Vanquished*, London: Routledge, 2006.

Williams, Sir John Fischer, *Some Aspects of the Covenant of the League of Nations*, London: Oxford University Press, 1934.

Williams, Sir John Fischer, 'Sanctions under the Covenant', *British Year Book of International Law*, Vol. 17, 1936, pp. 130–49.

Wilson, Peter, *The International Theory of Leonard Woolf: A Study in Twentieth Century Idealism*, Basingstoke: Palgrave Macmillan, 2003.

Wilson, Peter, 'Retrieving Cosmos: Gilbert Murray's Thought on International Relations', in Christopher Stray (ed.), *Gilbert Murray Reassessed: Hellenism, Theatre, and International Politics*, Oxford: Oxford University Press, 2007, pp. 239–60.

Wilson, Peter, 'Gilbert Murray and International Relations: Hellenism, Liberalism and International Intellectual Cooperation as a Path to Peace', *Review of International Studies*, Vol. 37, No. 2, 2010, pp. 881–909.

Wilson, Trevor (ed.), *The Political Diaries of C.P. Scott, 1911–1928*, London: Collins, 1970.

Windsor, Edward Duke of, *A King's Story*, London: Cassell, 1957.

Winkler, H.R., *The League of Nations Movement in Great Britain, 1914–1919*, New Brunswick, NJ: Rutgers University Press, 1952.

Winkler, H.R., *Paths Not Taken: British Labour and International Policy in the 1920s*, Chapel Hill, NC: University of North Carolina Press, 1994.

Winkler, H.R., *British Labour Seeks a Foreign Policy, 1900–1940*, Piscataway, NJ: Transaction, 2004.

Wood, Neal, *Communism and British Intellectuals*, London: Gollancz, 1959.

Woolf, Leonard, 'Labour's Foreign Policy', *Political Quarterly*, Vol. 4, No. 4, 1933, pp. 504–24.

Woolf, Leonard, 'Meditation on Abyssinia', *Political Quarterly*, Vol. 7, No. 1, 1936, pp. 16–32.

Woolf, Leonard, 'The Ideal of the League Remains', *Political Quarterly*, Vol. 7, No. 2, 1936, pp. 330–45.

Woolf, Leonard, *The League and Abyssinia*, London: Hogarth, 1936.

Woolf, Leonard, 'The Resurrection of the League', *Political Quarterly*, Vol. 8, No. 2, 1937, pp. 337–52.

Wootton, Graham, *The Official History of the British Legion*, London: Macdonald, 1956.

Wright, Jonathan, 'Locarno: A Democratic Peace?' *Review of International Studies*, Vol. 36, No. 2, 2010, pp. 391–411.

Zimmern, Sir Alfred, 'The Problem of Collective Security', in Quincy Wright (ed.), *Neutrality and Collective Security*, Chicago, IL: Chicago University Press, 1936.

Zimmern, Sir Alfred, 'The Testing of the League', *Foreign Affairs* (New York), Vol. 14, No. 3, 1936, pp. 385–6.

Zimmern, Sir Alfred, *The League of Nations and the Rule of Law, 1918–35*, London: Macmillan, 1936.

Index

Abyssinia Association, 120, 128
  membership, 167
Abyssinian/Ethiopian crisis, 17–18,
  60, 110–30
  arms embargo in, 120
  Germany and, 147
  relief aid in, 128
  see also Italy
Academic Freedom League, 136
ACIQ, *see under* Labour Party
Adams, S. Vyvyan, 15, 87, 119, 123, 128
Admiralty, views on
  arbitration, 38, 39, 51
  disarmament, 32
  Geneva Naval Conference, 53–5
  London Naval Conference, 61
Adowa, Battle of (1896), 114
Afghanistan, 49
aggression, definition of, 38
Air League, 71
Air Ministry, 70–1
air power, 9, 49, 66, 69–86
  air defence, 138
  air estimates, 53
  air manoeuvres, 71
  air pact, 72–3
  bombers and bombing, 78–9, 80
  Britain First (aircraft), 141
  building programme, 72
  fighters, 71
  see also civil aviation; disarmament;
    International Police Force
Air Raid Precautions Department, 71
Alexander, A.V., 62, 149
Allen, Clifford (Lord Allen of
  Hurtwood), 15, 31, 61
  collective force, views on, 63,
    81, 108
  colonies, views on, 138, 149
  Italy, views on, 113, 116
  New Commonwealth Society
    member, 87
Amery, Leo, 2, 32, 83

Italy, views on, 113, 124–5
Peace Ballot, views on, 106
Angell, Norman, 15, 89
  Abyssinian/Ethiopian crisis, views
    on, 122, 128
  alliances, views on, 161–2
  collective security force, views on,
    68, 75
  French security, views on, 150
  'Have-not' theory, views on, 115
  New Commonwealth membership,
    86
  Nobel Peace Prize, 94
  and pacifism, 94
  and rearmament, 142
  and Rhineland crisis, 149
  UDC membership, 19, 27, 75
Anglo-American relations, 53–4, 62
Anglo-French Naval Compromise,
  40, 57–9
Anglo-German Fellowship, 148
Anglo-German Naval Agreement
  (1935), 144
Anglo-German Review, 148
Anglo-Soviet Alliance, 117
anti-appeasement, 137, 152
anti-bolshevism, 112, 148, 156
anti-capitalism, 102, 127
anti-fascism, 101, 112, 127, 152
anti-imperialism, 82, 99, 116–17,
  122, 126
anti-militarism, 32, 57, 82
anti-nazism, 135–6
anti-revisionism, 149–53
anti-semitism, 112
appeasement, 2
  of Germany, 87, 137, 148,
    150, 152
  of Italy, 111–13, 116–18, 122
  of Japan, 92
  see also under Versailles Treaty
arbitration, 13, 26, 34–41, 51
  see also Optional Clause

Armenian massacres by Turkey
    (1894), 17
Arms and the Covenant (1936), 152
arms control, *see* disarmament
arms industry, 52, 93
arms race concerns, 52–3, 142–3
Arnold-Forster, William, 94
    appeasement, views on, 148
    collective security, views on, 74
    disarmament, views on, 34
    international trade, views on, 116
    and Labour Party, 164
    LNU membership, 33, 105
    NCPW membership, 20
    and pacifism, 75, 94
    sanctions, views on, 75, 121
    UDC membership, 19
Asian crisis, *see* Manchurian crisis
Asquith, Lord (Herbert), 16
Astor, Nancy, 77, 112
Atholl, Duchess of, 88, 142
Atlanticism, 45–6, 55, 103–4
Attlee, Clement
    Abyssinian/Ethiopian crisis, views
        on, 119, 129
    Arms and the Covenant
        participant, 152
    collective security, views on, 118
    IPF advocacy, 70, 74, 77, 82, 84
    New Commonwealth Society
        membership, 86
    rearmament, views on, 100, 138–9,
        141
    war resistance, views on, 101
Australia, 38, 39
Austria, 64, 100, 146, 166
    nazism in, 114
autarky, 111, 114, 117, 118

Baldwin, Stanley
    air power, views on, 70, 78, 139–40
    appeasement of Japan, 92
    and Cecil, 33
    collective security, views on,
        125, 139
    in LNU, 15
    and peace movement, 103
    US isolationism, views on, 104
Baldwin Government, 34, 58, 63

Balfour, Lord (Arthur), 22, 39–40
Barnes, G.N., 70, 87, 149
Barrett Brown, A., 94, 108
Barrington-Ward, Robert, 148
battleships, *see* disarmament, naval
Bayart, Jean-François, 6
Beatty, David, 61
Beaverbrook, Lord (Max Aitken), 77,
    103, 107
Beaverbrook press, 38, 65
Belgium, 42, 139, 162
Bennett, Donald, 165
Bernstorff, Johan von, 64
Bevan, Aneurin, 145
Beveridge, William, 51, 136
Bevin, Ernest, views on
    Arms and the Covenant, 152
    international trade, 118
    League of Nations, 101
    nazism, 99–101, 135, 149
    rearmament, 132–3
    sanctions, 127
'Blue Water School', 32
bombing, *see under* air power
Boothby, Robert, 30, 103, 149
Bowley, A.L., 51
Brailsford, H.N.
    global economy, views on, 116
    ILP membership, 91
    Kellogg–Briand Pact, views on, 41
    League's collective security, views
        on, 93, 117, 118
    in UDC and radical dissent, 16, 19,
        74, 82
    united front advocacy, 158–9
    Versailles revision advocacy, 148
Bretton Woods, 130
Briand, Aristide, 29, 76
Britain's Industrial Future, 35
British Anti-War Movement, 94,
    97–8
British Empire, 13, 20–1, 38, 76
    trade preferences in, 118
    see also Dominions; imperialism
British foreign policy, 24
    in Abyssinian/Ethiopian crisis,
        118–25
    accountability of, 27–8, 119, 149,
        163

and collective security, 26, 100, 105, 108, 110, 140
Eurocentrism of, 31–2
and Germany, 135–6, 139, 143, 150, 151
in Manchurian crisis, 90–2
in Munich crisis, 90, 163–4
and Optional Clause, 36, 37–9
British League of Nations Parliamentary Committee, 29
British Legion, 70
British Legion Journal, 177
Hitler, dealings with, 148
membership, 167
British 'New Deal', 115–16
British political establishment, 13–26
trespass in, 11–25, 36, 70, 83–4, 94, 152, 165
British Red Cross for Abyssinia, 128
British Union of Fascists, 112, 124
membership, 167
British–Italian League, 112
Brittain, Vera, 95
Brockway, Fenner, 24, 62, 94, 126
Brüning, Heinrich, 64, 65
Bryce, James, 16
Bryce Group, 16
Buchan, John, 83, 108
'Budapest Programme', 66
BUF, *see* British Union of Fascists
Bulgarian atrocities by Turkey (1876), 17, 110, 119
Bulwer-Lytton, Victor, 15, 90, 129
see also Lytton Commission
Burney, C.D., 73
Burns, C. Delisle, 17, 45, 158, 161
Burns, Émile, 97
Burton, Montague, 116
Butler, R.A. (Rab), 2
Buxton, C.R., 117, 121, 148
Buxton, Noel, 43, 133

Cadbury family, 17
Canada, 38
Cario, Silvio, 112
Carlton, David, 40
Carnegie, David, 17
Carr, E.H., 16, 161
League Covenant, views on, 128

Carter, W. Horsfall, 79
Catchpool, Corder, 148
Catlin, George, 148
Cavendish, Edward, 30
Ceadel, Martin, 4
Cecil, Lord (Robert)
arbitration, views on, 35, 37, 39
disarmament, views on, 50, 53–4, 56, 61, 62, 64, 65, 68, 76, 77–9
and Empire, 21
French and German perceptions of, 18
French security, views on, 79, 147, 150
and Germany, 30–1, 78, 133, 143–5
in government, 31–3, 39
and IPF, 70
and Italy, 123, 128–9
Kellogg–Briand Pact, views on, 41, 43, 45
and Labour, 39, 40
and League reform, 155
as LNU leader, 15–16, 36, 74–5, 81, 87, 129
and Manchuria, 24, 90
New Commonwealth Society member, 70, 86
Oxford Union debate, view on, 104
and Peace Ballot, 105–8
profile of, 7, 18–19
public opinion, reliance on, 27
and rearmament, 139, 143
and Rhineland crisis, 141, 150
resignation from government, 32–3, 36
states in world order, views on, 12
and treaty revision, 133, 138
Chamberlain, Austen
arbitration, views on, 39, 40, 42
and Cecil, 32
and disarmament, 58–9, 65
and French security, 62, 77
German threat, views on, 135, 136, 143
IPF, views on, 81, 87
and Italy, 113, 120, 124, 129
and Japan, 50
League obligations, views on, 37

Chamberlain, Austen – *continued*
  and LNU, 15, 21–2, 31, 81, 87, 129,
    139
  Locarno architect, 29, 103
  'open diplomacy', views on,
    29–30
  and Peace Ballot, 21, 106
  and rearmament, 139
  and regional security, 157
  and Rhineland crisis, 150
Chamberlain, Neville, views on
  air threat, 140
  defence loan, 142
  Germany, 139, 164
  IPF, 22, 70, 83, 144, 157
  Japan, 92
  League's demise, 162
  rearmament, 142
  regional security, 157
  Saar Plebiscite, 144
  sanctions against Italy, 157
Chamberlain, W.J., 94
Chatfield, Lord (Ernle), 113
Chatham House, *see* Royal Institute of
    International Affairs
Chiefs of Staff, 157
China, 39, 90
  see also Manchurian crisis
Chiozza Money, Leo(ne), 112
Christian pacifism, 106–8
Church of England, 3–4, 19
Churchill, Winston
  and Arms and the Covenant, 152
  Cecil's view of, 32
  as Chancellor of the Exchequer, 51
  and Empire, 119
  Eurocentrism of, 92
  German threat, views on, 120,
    139, 163
  and Italy, 125, 129
  Japanese threat, views on, 50
  and League, 88, 120, 125
  and naval power, 53, 58, 62, 129,
    145
  and New Commonwealth Society,
    83, 87–8
  peace and pacifism, views on,
    83, 165
  and rearmament, 23, 141–2

CID, *see* Committee of Imperial
    Defence
Citrine, Walter, 99, 123, 152, 164
  Germany, views on, 135, 149
civil aviation, 73, 78, 84
  see also air power
civil defence, 71
  evacuation, 71
  gas threat, 71–2
civil society, 5–7, 93–4, 104–5, 108–9,
    131, 155, 165
Clynes, J.R., 18
Cobham, Allan, 71
Cocks, Seymour, 145
Colás, Alejandro, 8
Cole, G.D.H., 98, 116, 117, 126, 158
collective security
  arbitration and, 34–5
  Conservatives and, 88, 103, 113,
    121, 125
  disarmament and, 48, 53, 55–6, 58,
    60, 65
  divisions and contradictions in, 88,
    128, 130–1, 155
  against fascism and German threat,
    83, 112, 118, 144, 146, 149–51,
    161–4
  France and, 76–80
  against Italy, 113, 119, 122, 128
  Labour movement and, 99, 100,
    102, 112
  and Manchuria, 90–2
  military force, rearmament, and,
    68, 74, 84, 111, 139–42, 146,
    151
  New Commonwealth Society and,
    83–5
  pacifist opposition to, 89, 92, 95,
    97, 104, 126, 137
  peace as, 2–4, 13, 15, 17, 20–1,
    25–6, 32, 37, 158
  Peace Ballot, LNU and, 105–8, 129
  Socialist League and, 82
  United States and, 45
  and world order, 74
  see also sanctions
Collick, Percy, 97
colonies, *see* 'Have-not theory'
Comintern, 97, 102

Committee of Imperial Defence
(CID), 49–50
Communist Party of Great Britain
(CPGB) and communists
League policy change, 70, 126–8,
159
membership, 23, 167
and Stresa Pact, 146
united front policy, 97–8, 101–4
conflict prevention, 13
conscientious objection, 81, 95–6, 99
Conservative and Unionist Party, 15,
19, 46, 103
and the League, 21–3, 93, 103
Conservatives
and Abyssinian/Ethiopian crisis, 120
air power, views on, 72
arbitration, views on, 34, 39–40
and defence, 53–4
disarmament, views on, 49, 53, 61
French security, views on, 82–3
and international force, 87–8
and International Peace Council,
150
as internationalists, 21, 30, 54, 142
and LNU, 15, 16, 21, 36, 106–7
and Munich, 164
press and, 23, 30, 37, 59
and regional security, 156–7
and sanctions, 123–4
see also Imperial Policy Group
continental commitment, 49, 80, 161
Conwell-Evans, T.P., 140, 148
Cortright, David, 4
cosmopolitanism, 5–8, 116
Council of Action, 129
membership, 168
Council for German Jewry, 136
Cox, Lucy, 57
Cox, Robert, 6
CPGB, *see* Communist Party of Great
Britain
Cranborne, Viscount (Robert) 5th
Marquess of Salisbury, 21
Cripps, Charles, *see* Parmoor
Cripps, Stafford
and Bevin, 98–9, 101
collective security, views on, 91
and Italy, 126–7

and Labour Party, 164
and popular front, 162
rearmament, views on, 135
see also Socialist League
Croft, Henry Page, 112, 125, 152
Crozier, Frank, 91, 95
cruisers, 53–4, 58, 61
parity issue, 56, 62
see also under disarmament
Curtis, Lionel, 20, 83
Curtius, Julius, 64
Cushendun, Lord (Ronald McNeill),
36, 58
Czechoslovakia, 144
defences, 164
post-Cold War division of, 160

Daily Express, 65
Daily Herald, 90
Daily News, 17
Dalton, Hugh
anti-revision views of, 145, 149
and Cecil, 33
collective security, views on, 24,
68, 74
disarmament, views on, 52
and Germany, 135, 145, 149, 164
global economy, views on, 121, 123
Optional Clause, views on, 39
'paper guarantees', views on, 47
and rearmament, 135, 149
and Rhineland crisis, 149
and state security, 98
UDC member, 19
war resistance, views on, 98, 101
Dangerfield, George, 16
Davidson, J.C.C., 36
Davies, David
and French security, 77, 85, 86
IPF advocacy, 80–1, 84–6, 88
LNU member, 17, 80–1
New Commonwealth Society, 70
profile of, 84
published works, 85
The Problem of the Twentieth Century
(1932), 80, 85–6
Dawes Plan, *see under* reparations
Dawson, W.H., 134
and Hitler, 148

defence expenditure, 50–2, 61, 67
  army estimates, 50
  Defence White Paper (1935), 141
  Defence White Paper (1936), 138–9
depression, 114, 123
  and defence expenditure, 50–2
  and protectionism, 114
  nationalism in, 110–11, 114–15,
    118, 130
  see also 'Have-not' theory
deterrence, 9, 72–3, 86, 139
Dickinson, G.L., *see* Lowes
    Dickinson
Dickinson, Lord (Willoughby), 17,
    133
disarmament
  aviation, 78
  campaigns, 79
  disarmament, budgetary, 64, 66
  general, 13, 33, 35, 48–68, 69, 75–6,
    82, 85, 135
  Hoover Moratorium, 65
  Litvinov proposals, 56–7
  naval, 32, 34, 37, 53–5, 57–8, 61–2,
    79
  qualitative and aggressive weapons,
    66–7, 78, 79
  tanks, 66, 68
  unilateral, 24, 48, 57, 98
  see also General Disarmament
    Conference; *and separate treaties*
Dolfuss, Engelbert, 100
Dominions, 21, 38, 39, 40, 149, 162
  see also British Empire
Dove, John, 20, 83
Dr Martin's Defence Loan, 128
Draft Treaty of Mutual Assistance, 34
Drummond, Eric, 91, 119
Drury-Lowe, S.R., 15, 43, 45, 61, 73
Duff Cooper, Alfred, 15, 77, 86, 122
Dugdale, Blanche (Baffy), 15
Dutt, Ranji Palme, 102

Eastern Locarno proposal, 144
The Economist, 51
Eden, Anthony
  and Italy, 119, 163
  and the League, 122
  and mandates, 111
  and regional security, 157
  resignation of, 163
  and the Saar, 144
Edward VIII, 148
Ethiopia, *see* Abyssinian/Ethiopian
    crisis
Europe
  Eurocentrism, 31, 77, 90–2, 103,
    151, 156–7
  security of, 65, 138, 162
  as source of evil, 114
Eyres-Monsell, Bolton, 49

Fabians, *see* New Fabian Research
    Bureau
Federation of League of Nations
    Societies, 84
Fellowship of Reconciliation,
    membership, 168
Ferguson, Adam, 5
First World War, 4, 11, 25, 71, 157
Fisher, Warren, 92, 139
Focus group, 152
Foot, Michael, 104
Foreign Affairs, 19, 27, 75
Foreign Office and foreign policy, 5,
    10, 17, 27, 31, 39
Foucault, Michel, 6–7, 8, 19
  see also governmentality
Four Power Pact (1933), 134–6
France, 15, 28
  and Abyssinian crisis, 114, 124–5
  British perceptions of, 45, 49, 62,
    65, 76–9, 107
  communists in, 97, 150
  security and defence of, 29, 57–9,
    62–3, 64, 69, 78, 81, 83, 88,
    126, 131
  and Stresa, 144–7
Francophiles, 77, 84
Francophobia, 30, 45, 67, 82
Franco-Soviet Treaty of Mutual
    Assistance (1935), 147
free trade, 115–16
  see also depression
Fremantle, Admiral, 62
Friends of Abyssinia, 128
Fuller, J.F.C., 71, 73
  praises Mussolini, 112

Gaitskell, Hugh, 117–18
Garnett, Maxwell, 81, 105, 149
Garvin, J.L., 55, 71, 83, 92
GDC, *see* General Disarmament Conference
General Act, 40
General Disarmament Conference (1932–34), 77–9, 81, 83, 99, 103, 105, 132
  collapse of, 48, 64, 68
  British Draft Convention (1933), 79, 83
  Preparatory Commission, 56, 59, 64
general elections
  1929, 35, 40
  1931, 98
  1935, 121
Geneva Naval Conference (1927), 40, 53–6
Geneva Protocol, 34, 35, 37
Germanophiles, 140
Germanophobia, 30, 87
Germany
  Army Law (1935), 145
  boycott of, 135
  and colonies, 115
  encirclement of, 136
  grievances of, 28–9, 132, 137, 143
  and League, 9, 19, 28–31, 133, 148, 152–3
  military status of, 50, 53, 63. 66, 135
  nationalism and nazism in, 64, 78, 96, 98, 100, 133–5, 137, 145
  non-aggression by, 147
  rearmament of, 65, 136, 151
  refugees from, 136
  territorial concessions to, 148
  threat from, 23, 49, 65, 67, 70, 73, 78, 83, 85, 92–3, 97, 103, 113, 131, 138–9, 146, 151, 153
  withdrawal from Disarmament Conference and League, 136–7
  Versailles treaty revision, 122–3, 145
Gladstone, Henry, 70, 87
Gladstone, William, 17–18
Gladstonianism, 16, 19, 152

GOM, *see* Gladstone, William
Gooch, G.P., 17, 20, 114
governmentality, 5–6, 8, 25, 36, 68, 108, 110, 165
  see also Foucault
Gramsci, Antonio, 5, 8, 15
The Great Illusion (1933 edn), 122
Great War, *see* First World War
Greenwood, Arthur, 140
Gregory, T.E.G., 51–2
Grey, Lord (Edward)
  armaments, views on, 52, 54, 135
  Egypt declaration of, 38
  Kellogg–Briand Pact, views on, 41
  and LNU, 16, 17, 31, 37, 59
  pre-war diplomacy of, 27
  United States, views on, 60
Grigg, Edward, 83, 113
Groves, P.R.C., 71, 73
Gwynne, H.A., 83, 113

Hague Reparations Conference, *see under* reparations
Halifax, Lord (Edward Wood), 15
Hankey, Maurice, 23, 41, 151
Hannon, Patrick, 142
Hardie, Frank, 104
Harris, H. Wilson, 17, 43
Hartington, Lord (Edward Cavendish, Marquess), 15, 30
'Have-not theory', 114–23, 130, 148
Headway, 17, 177
Hellenism, 17
Henderson, Arthur
  disarmament policy of, 62–4, 77, 99–101
  Germany, views on, 64–5, 78
  League policy of, 59, 164
  and LNU, 33
  military force, views on, 68, 74
  Optional Clause, views on, 39
  war resistance, opposes, 24, 98, 100
Hills, Jack, 15, 84, 87
Hinsley, Cardinal, 112
Hirst, F.W., 51–2
Hitler, Adolf, 115, 133, 137
  British view of, 137, 144, 152
  see also Germany

Hoare, Samuel, 53, 65
  appeasement of Italy by, 113–14,
    119, 121, 124
  Geneva Assembly speech of, 120–1
  and rearmament, 140
  resignation of, 125
Hoare–Laval Pact, 111, 121–2, 125
Hobson, J.A., 16, 19, 20, 52, 74,
    116–17
Hogg, Douglas (Viscount Hailsham),
    103–4
Hoover, Herbert, 61, 79
Hoover Administration, 60
House of Commons, 15, 30, 40, 62,
    129, 136
House of Lords, 15
Howard, Michael, 4, 15
Huxley, Aldous, 20, 93, 95, 97, 155
hybrid peace, 6

IAPF, *see* International Air Police
    Force
ideology, 9, 25, 111–12
Ilford Recorder ballot, 106
ILP, *see* Independent Labour Party
imperial defence, 54–5
  policing for, 49, 66, 79
  requirements for, 58
  see also British Empire; imperialism
Imperial Policy Group, 14, 125, 141
imperialism and imperialists, 1, 4,
    20–3, 27, 43–4, 49, 83, 92, 156,
    165–6
  in Abyssinian crisis, 110–31
Independent Labour Party (ILP), 14
  Conference (1936), 126
  and Italy, 126
  and Japan, 93
  membership, 168
  and Nazism, 145
  Revolutionary Policy Committee
    of, 102
  unilateral disarmament, 62
  and United Front, 102
  war resistance of, 23–4, 34, 42, 97,
    98, 126, 145
Inskip, Thomas, 2, 65
International Air Police Force, *see*
    International Police Force

'international anarchy', 52
International Federation of League of
    Nations Societies, 66
International Labour Office, 116
international law, 13, 38
International Peace Campaign (IPC),
    150
International Police Force (IPF), 21,
    22, 24
  campaign for, 69–84, 86, 100,
    123, 137
  Labour support for, 70, 82, 84,
    88, 143
  Neville Chamberlain's proposal for,
    144, 157
  see also Davies; New
    Commonwealth Society; *and
    under* LNU
International Relations, Aberystwyth
    Chair, 3, 85
Irish Free State, 38
isolationism, 14, 38, 83, 99, 108,
    156
Italophiles, 112, 113, 124
Italy, 60, 62
  African war of, 111–30
  as ally, 113
  appeasement of, 119, 122
  Austrian threat to, 113
  blockade of proposed, 129
  and colonies, 115
  economic situation in, 130
  fascism of, 111–12
  as threat, 125
  see also Abyssinian/Ethiopian crisis;
    Hoare–Laval Pact

Japan, 49–50, 53
  aggression of, 89–91
  pro-Japanese opinion, 92
  as threat, 93, 139
  see also Manchurian crisis
Jellicoe, John, 61
Jerrold, Douglas, 152, 156
Jeudwine, Hugh, 67
Jevons, Herbert Stanley, 119–20
Joad, C.E.M., 97, 125–6
Johnson, Hewlett, 20, 95
Joyce, William, 112

Keith, Arthur, 22–3
Kellogg–Briand Pact, 26, 41–6, 74, 75
Kenworthy, J.M., 17, 51, 60
Kerr, Philip (Lord Lothian)
  as Atlanticist, 45–6, 83
  and collective security, 156
  and disarmament, 65
  as German appeaser, 77, 133, 140,
    143, 149, 152, 156
  and Italy, 113, 123, 128
  and LNU, 17, 20, 44–6
  see also Round Table Group
Keynes, J.M., 28, 51, 115, 118, 123
King and Country debate, 103

Labour and the Nation, 40
Labour government(s), 26, 67
  and air power, 49, 72–5, 73
  Cecil in (1929–31), 33, 39
  and collective security, 45, 59, 155
  disarmament policies of, 56, 61, 63,
    65, 72
Labour Monthly, 102, 177
Labour Party, 14
  ACIQ, 60, 64, 76, 118
  Conferences (1933), 99; (1934), 100,
    101; (1935), 121, 123, 127
  democratic front policy, 159, 161
  disarmament policies of, 52, 55–8,
    61–7, 144–5
  economy, views on, 116, 118
  Geneva Protocol, support for, 35–6
  'International Policy and Defence'
    report, 158
  IPF policy, 70, 82, 84, 88, 143
  Italy, views on, 113, 121, 127
  Japan, views on, 90
  Joint Council of, 56, 100–1, 135
  Kellogg–Briand Pact, views on, 42,
    44
  League policies of, 24, 40, 117, 158
  and LNU, 16, 33, 40
  membership, 168
  National Council of, 107, 124, 129,
    159
  National Executive, 99
  Optional Clause, support for, 39
  and pacifism, 100
  Peace Ballot campaign of, 107

rearmament, policy on, 138, 143,
    149–50
  and revision, 148–9
  and Spanish Civil War, 149
  war resistance disputes, 97–102, 164
Lansbury, George
  denunciation of, 127
  disarmament, views on, 23, 56, 82,
    135
  global resources, views on, 121
  pacifist views of, 4, 20, 89, 99, 102
  Saar Plebiscite, views on, 143
  sanctions, views on, 90–1, 101, 113
  treaty revision, views on, 136
Laski, Harold, 74, 91, 98, 105, 116–18,
    122, 126
League of Free Nations Association,
    75, 81
League of Nations, 8–13, 26, 49, 55,
    60, 70, 73, 76, 77, 82, 85–6, 90, 97
  Air Commission of, 78
  as anti-fascist alliance, 151–2, 155,
    158
  Assembly of, 59–60, 77, 160–1
  collapse of, 162
  colonial mandates of, 12–13, 120
  Council of, 29, 31, 64, 146
  'League of Victors/Thieves'
    Kitchen', 16, 19, 24, 74, 102
  'League war', 99, 103
  and Manchuria, 91–2
  and Ruhr occupation, 28
  Sciajola Committee of, 46
  see also General Disarmament
    Conference
League of Nations Covenant, 42, 45,
    74
  Article 10, 160
  Article 16, 44, 75, 78, 79, 91, 129
  Article 19, 134–7, 160
  economic clauses of, 114–15
  revision of, 46, 159–61
League of Nations Society, 16, 75, 81
League of Nations Union (LNU)
  anti-fascism in, 150, 158
  and arbitration, views on, 35–6, 39,
    41, 43–5
  attacks on, 30, 31
  campaigns of, 15, 28, 55, 76, 159

League of Nations Union – *continued*
Conservatives in, 36
Council of, 87, 160–1, 169–71
disarmament, views on, 34, 55, 59, 60–6, 80, 144
disputes and defections in, 21, 128, 129, 131, 165
Executive of, 16, 21, 31, 75
finances of, 15, 17, 129
free trade, views on, 116
French security, views on, 79
Germany, views on, 136, 145, 146, 150–1
grand alliance, views on, 164
and IPF and New Commonwealth Society, 69–70, 76, 80–1, 86–8
Italy, views of, 119
Kellogg–Briand Pact, views on, 45–6
Labour Party, relations with, 16, 33, 40
League reform, views on, 29, 154–5, 160–1
liberal core of, 3, 14, 16–19, 22
Manchurian crisis, views on, 90–1, 105
membership, 15, 17, 92, 105, 107–8, 167
and pacifism, 150, 156
Peace Ballot and National Declaration Committee, 104–9
peaceful change, views on, 138
rearmament, views on, 150–1
regional security, views on, 161
Rhineland crisis, 147
sanctions, views on, 74, 77, 79, 123, 124, 128
and Second World War, 165
as social movement, 1, 4, 7, 9, 12, 13, 15, 19–22, 24–5, 30–3, 36, 46, 84, 109, 129
and Spanish Civil War, 162–3
and Stresa pact, 146
treaty revision, views on, 149
Welsh Council of, 80, 86–7
League to Enforce Peace, 16
Left Book Club, 152
Leverhulme Research Council, 70
liberal imperialism, 44, 83

Liberal Party
Council of, 37
disarmament, views on, 51, 55
and free trade crisis, 115–16
Geneva Protocol, views on, 36, 37
IPF, views on, 70
Kellogg–Briand Pact, views on, 44
and Labour Government, 59
political crisis in, 2, 4, 16, 18, 94
sanctions, views on, 75
Women's Federation of, 37
Young Liberals, 37
'liberal peace', 5, 130
liberal press, 17, 41, 75
liberalism and liberals, 12, 15, 18, 25, 35, 51, 59, 65, 75, 122, 160, 164–6
Liberty and Democratic Leadership Group, 108
Liddell Hart, Basil
disarmament, views on, 66, 79
and IPF, 70, 80
and LNU, 13, 24
pacifists, views on, 95
rearmament, views on, 138
Saar Plebiscite, views on, 144
Little Entente, 38
Lloyd, Lord, views on
German threat, 141
Italian expansion, 113
Naval Agreement with Germany, 145
rearmament, 142
Lloyd George, David, views on
Abyssinian/Ethiopian crisis, 119
arbitration, 37, 50
collective security, 65
disarmament, 65, 135
French militarism, 58
Germany, 112, 133, 136, 138, 148
Locarno, 53
LNU, *see* League of Nations Union
Locarno, Treaty of, 29
criticism of, 37, 43, 103
and Rhineland crisis, 147
spirit of, 32, 40, 44, 53, 55, 59, 67
London Naval Agreement (1930), 49, 61
Londonderry, Lord (Charles Vane-Tempest-Stewart), 15, 124, 142, 148

Lothian, Lord, *see* Kerr, Philip
Lowes Dickinson, Goldsworthy, 17,
    19, 52, 81
Lugard, Lord (Frederick), 113
Lynch, Cecelia, 4
Lytton Commission, 90

Macdonagh, George, 76
MacDonald, Ramsay
  and Disarmament Conference,
    79–80
  French security, views on, 63, 65
  Geneva Protocol, views on, 35
  and German revisionism, 135,
    136
  internationalism of, 164
  and naval agreement with the
    United States, 54–6, 60–2
  Optional Clause, views on, 39
  UDC member, 27, 33
Maclean, Donald, 15, 17, 18
Macmillan, Harold, 30, 103, 116
Manchurian crisis, 77, 82, 85, 89–92,
    105, 108, 110
Mander, Geoffrey, 15, 17, 55, 84, 119,
    136
Marburg, Theodore, 16
maritime law, 37, 39, 40, 49
Marriott, John, 113
Martin, Kingsley, 1
Marxism and Marxists, 5, 14
  and disarmament, 57
  and League, 23–4, 70, 96–7, 102
  and sanctions against Italy,
    126–7
  and war resistance, 89, 94, 108
  see also CPGB; ILP
Maurice, Frederick, 15, 81, 86
Maxton, James, 24, 102, 126
McGovern, John, 113, 126
McKenna, Reginald, 17, 54
military lobby, 50–1
Milne, A.A., 20, 93
Milner, Alfred, 1, 11, 20
moral force, 34, 46, 67, 85, 120
  moral pacifists, 109
  Munich outrage, 154
Morel, E.D., 27, 28, 74
Morrison, Herbert, 140, 158

Mosley, Oswald, 14, 56, 112
Mottistone, Lord, 86, 112
Mowat, R.B., 34
Munich crisis, 159, 163–4
Münzenberg, Willi, 97
Murray, Gilbert
  and Abyssinian/Ethiopian crisis,
    views on, 120–1, 128, 129
  arbitration, views on, 39
  and Conservatives, 21–2, 36
  French security, views of, 59, 81
  Germany, views on, 133
  as Gladstonian, 21
  global economy, views on, 111
  and Hellenism, 17
  hubris of, 12, 28, 33–4, 41, 66, 119
  Kellogg–Briand Pact, views on, 43
  and Labour, 21–2
  as LNU official, 16, 75, 81, 87, 129
  and Peace Ballot, 105
  revision, views on, 133–4, 138
  sanctions, views on, 92, 128
  and Second World War, 164–5
  and Spain, 162
Mussolini, Benito, 18, 112, 114, 121,
    124
  see also Italy

National Council for the Prevention
    of War (NCPW), 44, 56–7, 66
  membership, 20
National Government, 22, 67, 72, 78,
    98, 116, 132
  and League of Nations, 142
  and Manchuria, 90
  and Saar, 143–4
National League of Airmen, 141
National Liberal Federation (NLF), 35,
    37, 55, 129
  and disarmament, 66
  Executive, 121
National Peace Congress (1927), 57
National Peace Council, 66, 94–5,
    108–9, 121, 148
  and sanctions, 125
nationalism and nationalists, 22–3,
    39, 42, 70, 103, 113, 141–2
  and Rhineland crisis, 147–8
  and Stresa, 146

naval power, 50, 53–5, 63, 131
  and belligerent rights, 60
  estimates for, 49
  and Ocean/Mediterranean Pact, 55,
    62, 63, 76
  and prize law, 39
  see also Royal Navy; *and under*
    disarmament
Naval Review, 177
Navy League, 14, 53, 62
nazism, British sympathisers, 148
  see also under Germany
NCPW, *see* National Council for the
  Prevention of War
neoliberalism, 5, 6, 166
New Commonwealth Society, 70,
    83–8, 94, 109, 129
  equity tribunal idea, 86, 137
  and Italy, 113
  membership, 168
  New Commonwealth, 177
  officials, 172–4
  and sanctions, 123
New Fabian Research Bureau, 16, 70,
    116, 117, 159
  membership, 168
New Statesman, 177
New Times & Ethiopia News, 112, 128,
    177
New Zealand, 38, 162
News Chronicle, 65–6
The Next Five Years, 116
Next Five Years Group, 108, 116, 118
Nichols, Beverley, 20, 93
NLF, *see* National Liberal Federation
No Conscription Fellowship, 94
No More War Movement, 14, 57, 91,
    94
  membership, 168
Nobel Peace Prize, 18, 94
Noel Baker, Philip, 94
  Abyssinia Association, member, 128
  arbitration, views on, 38
  collective security, views on, 74
  disarmament, views on, 52, 54–5,
    63, 80
  Germany, views on, 50, 133
  Labour Party, 21–2, 33, 101
  LNU member, 15, 17, 158, 165

NCPW member, 20
New Commonwealth, member, 86
Peace Ballot, views on, 108
non-governmental organisation, *see*
  civil society
Norwood, F.W., 57
NPC, *see* National Peace Council

Ocean/Mediterranean Naval Pact, *see*
  under naval power
'open diplomacy', 3, 15, 17, 19, 27–30,
    31
Optional Clause, 26, 37–8, 63
Ormsby-Gore, William, 120
Ottawa Conference, 114
outlawry of war, *see* Kellogg–Briand
  Pact
Overy, Richard, 2
Oxford University, 104–5

pacifism and pacfists, 46, 56–7, 81–2,
    89–108, 156
  absolute, 20
  and Abyssinian/Ethiopian crisis,
    126
  Christian, 89, 95
  and collective security, 3, 137
  and German revision, 148
  and public opinion, 27
  revisionism of, 137
  socialist, 89
  see also war resistance *and under*
    peace
Paish, George, 52, 128
Pankhurst, Sylvia, 112, 128
'paper guarantees', 26
Parmoor, Lady (Marian), 20
Parmoor, Lord (Charles Cripps), 19,
    34, 81
paternalism, 20
PDC, *see* Preparatory Disarmament
  Commission *under* General
  Disarmament Conference
Peace, 94
Peace Army, 91, 94
Peace Ballot, 21, 103–8, 111, 129
  and Conservatives, 106
  see also under LNU
Peace Brigades International, 91

Peace Conference (1934), 81
Peace Congress (1933), 94, 108
peace crusade, 65–6
peace education, 27–31, 165
Peace Pledge Union (PPU), 20, 94–5,
    107, 109, 126, 155–6
  membership, 96, 155, 168
  officials, 174
Peace Society, 103
Peace Year Book, 94
peaceful change, 137–8, 160
peacekeeping, 69, 76, 130
Permanent Court of International
    Justice, 34, 38–9
Pethick-Lawrence, Frederick, 99
Petrie, Charles, 113
Pigou, A.C., 51
Plowman, Max, 95, 126
Poland, 134, 144
Political and Economic Planning
    group, 116
Pollitt, Harry, 159
Ponsonby, Arthur, 74, 90, 94, 98
'pooled security', *see* collective
    security
popular front, 162
post-colonialism, 5
PPU, *see* Peace Pledge Union
Preparatory Disarmament
    Commission, *see under*
    General Disarmament Conference
public opinion, 1, 72, 162, 163–4
  in Abyssinian/Ethiopian crisis, 110,
    120, 122, 124
  as check on government, 3, 27,
    31–2, 95
  as force for peace, 3, 24, 27, 43, 44,
    46, 69
  and Peace Ballot, 104–7
  and Stresa Pact, 146

Quakers, 43, 81–2
Queenborough, Lord (Almeric
    Paget), 15

Radicalism, 16, 18, 19, 116
RAF, *see* Royal Air Force
Rathbone, Eleanor, 15, 128, 135, 149
reactionaries, 125

realpolitik, 3, 11, 103, 138–42, 164
rearmament, 100, 104, 132–53
  as aimless, 138–41
  in collective security discourse, 141
regional security, 156–7
renunciation of war, 41–3
reparations, 28, 64–5, 115
  Dawes Plan, 28
  Hague Reparations Conference
    (1930), 60, 85
  Lausanne Conference (1932), 115
  Young Plan, 64
resistance, 6, 89–109, 166
revision consensus, 137–8
Rhineland crisis (1936), 133–50, 153
Richmond, Herbert (Admiral), 61, 73
RIIA, *see* Royal Institute of
    International Affairs
Robbins, Lionel, 114
Rothermere, Lord (Harold), 30, 38
  and air power, 141
  and nazism, 148
Round Table group
  Atlanticism of, 44, 55, 77, 103
  and Germany, 156
  Kellogg–Briand Pact, views on, 41
  League Covenant's Article 16, views
    on, 16, 44, 155
  and LNU, 20–1
  split in, 83
  see also Kerr, Philip
Royal Air Force (RAF), 72, 142
  see also air power
Royal Institute of International
    Affairs (RIIA), 3, 31, 62, 80
  and Rhineland crisis, 149
Royal Navy, 54, 140, 145
  and Italian threat, 113
  see also naval power
Royden, Maud, 91, 97
Ruhr occupation, 28
Russell, Bertrand, 74, 76, 89, 94, 96–7
  and sanctions, 125–6

Saar Plebiscite (1935), 107, 143–4
Saklatvala, Shapurji, 97
Salter, Arthur, 80, 114, 115, 116, 135,
    160
Salvemini, Gaetano, 20

Samuel, Herbert, 15, 35, 37, 56, 65, 135, 139
  and Germany, 143
sanctions and sanctionists, 14, 28, 93, 95, 109
  and Japan, 24, 90, 92
  military, 73–84, 95
  non-military, 10, 19, 34, 44, 45, 69, 88, 90–1, 100–1, 110–31
  RIIA study of, 70
  working class, 102, 126–7
  see also Abyssinian/Ethiopian crisis; IPF; League of Nations Covenant, Article XVI
Sassoon, Philip, 138
Sassoon, Siegfried, 95, 108
Scott, James C., 8
Second World War, 2, 96
  and collective security, 160
  and 'victor's peace', 166
secret diplomacy, 33, 58
self-defence, 42–3, 45
Shanghai crisis, 77, 91
Shaw, George Bernard, 22, 23, 31
Sheppard, Dick, 20, 91, 107, 113, 156
Sherriff, R.C., *Journey's End* (1929), 93
Simon, Sir John
  arbitration, views on, 38
  colonial mandates, views on, 111
  and LNU, 15, 21
  and Manchuria, 90, 92
  and protectionism, 115
  and Saar Pelbiscite, 143
Sinclair, Archibald, 129
Singapore base, 50
Sino-Japanese dispute, *see* Manchurian crisis
Smuts, Jan, 20, 104
  and Germany, 156
Snowden, Philip, 51, 128
social movements, 5–7, 165
  see also civil society; *and under* LNU
socialism and socialists, 23–4, 82, 101, 104, 117
Socialist League
  collective security, views on, 82, 100

dissolution of, 159
  and fascism, 126–7
  and French alliance, 158–9
  membership, 98, 168
  sanctions, views on, 126–7
  and united front, 101, 158–9
  and war resistance, 98–9, 101
Society for Socialist Inquiry and Propaganda, 98
Soper, Donald, 96
South Africa, 18, 40
sovereignty
  collective sovereignty, 13, 76, 86
  League as threat to, 22–3, 37–8, 87
Soviet Union
  as alliance prospect, 117, 144, 158–9, 162
  disarmament proposals of, 56–7
  dissolution of, 160
  in League, 70, 102–3, 127, 159
  Red Army, 57
  as threat, 49, 92, 156
  see also CPGB
Spaight, J.M., 73
Spanish Civil War, 69, 102, 127, 162–3
  and war resistance, 149
Spears, E.L., 77, 82, 84, 149
Spender, J.A., 17, 35, 92
Spivak, Gayatri, 8
Stalin, Joseph, 103, 163
Stamp, Josiah, 51, 115
Strachey, John, 96
Strachey, Lytton, 97–8, 127
Stresa Conference (1935), 146
Stresemann, Gustav, 29
Suez Canal, 38, 111, 118
  blockade proposed, 123
Summerskill, Edith, 107
Swanwick, Helena, 19, 20, 75
Sykes, Frederick, 71, 73

Tardieu, André (1932 security plan), 79, 81, 86, 134
Temple, William, 82, 119
Temporary Mixed Commission on Armaments, 27

territorial revision, 121, 134–5, 160
Thomson, Lord (Christopher), 72
Three-Party Disarmament
    Committee, 48, 65, 67, 78
Toynbee, A.J., 17, 124
trade unions, 14, 52, 99, 100
Trades Union Congress (TUC), 99,
    101, 118
Trevelyan, Charles P., 27, 74, 75, 82,
    99, 100, 126
TUC, *see* Trades Union Congress
Turner, Ben, 52
Tyrrell, William, 31, 33

UDC, *see* Union of Democratic
    Control
Union of Democratic Control
    (UDC), 3
  diplomacy, views on, 27–9
  disarmament, views on, 57, 62, 74
  and French security, 57–8
  and Kellogg–Briand Pact, 41, 45
  and League, 19, 29
  membership, 74–5, 168
  officials, 27, 175–6
  and sanctions, 19, 74–5
  Versailles Treaty criticism, 28, 29,
    57, 134
united front against fascism and war,
    97, 101–2, 127
United Nations
  collective security of, 165
  Economic and Social Council, 130
  Military Staff Committee, 76
  Security Council, 2, 59, 86, 130,
    131, 161
  Trusteeship Council, 130
United States
  and economic crisis, 114, 115
  and League foundations, 12, 16
  internationalist views on, 20, 27,
    37, 41, 43–6, 92, 103, 124, 139
  isolationism, 43–4, 46, 85, 92,
    162
  and naval disarmament, 34, 45,
    56–62
  naval power of, 41, 43, 49–54
  UN Association (UK), 165

United States of Europe (USE), 76–7
USSR, *see* Soviet Union

Vansittart, Robert, 31, 92, 139
Versailles, Treaty of
  anti-revision of, 136–7
  critiques of, 27–8, 45, 133
  disarmament in, 50, 53, 63–5
  economic clauses of, 114
  German evasion of, 65
  revision of, 10, 77, 113, 132–53

Walker, Rob (R.B.J.), 7, 11
war resistance, 89–109
  general strike, 99
  literature, 93
  Marxist, 89
  rejection of, 23–4, 103–4
  socialist, 96–103
  War Resisters International, 94
  working class, 97, 101, 126–7
  see also pacifism
Washington Naval Conference/Treaty
    (1921–22), 60, 61
Waugh, Evelyn, and Abyssinia, 110,
    112
Webster, Charles K., 17, 20, 43
welfarism, 111, 116–18, 130, 162
Wellock, Wilfred, 91, 94
Wells, H.G., 3, 16, 71, 76, 117
Williams, John Fischer, 129, 160
Wilson, Peter, 4
Wilson, Woodrow, 16, 134
Women's International League for
    Peace and Freedom (WILPF), 12,
    79
  membership, 168
Women's International Matteotti
    Committee, 112
Wood, Herbert George, 81
Woodman, Dorothy, 97
Woolf, Leonard
  ACIQ member, 76
  and alliance against fascism, 97,
    117–18, 158
  and collective security, 99, 164
  and global economy, 118
  UDC member, 74

World Economic Conference
  (London, 1933), 114, 123
world order, 3, 8, 12, 13, 119, 133,
  155, 159–60, 164
Worthington-Evans, Laming, 32, 50

Young Plan, *see* reparations

Zeila (British Somaliland) exchange
  proposal, 119–20
Zilliacus, Konnie, 127
Zimmern, Alfred, 17, 79, 162
Zinoviev letter, 26
zollverein, Austro-German, 64,
  78, 134